Human Error

James Reason
Department of Psychology
University of Manchester

CAMBRIDGE
UNIVERSITY PRESS

PUBLISHED BY THE PRESS SYNDICATE OF THE UNIVERSITY OF CAMBRIDGE
The Pitt Building, Trumpington Street, Cambridge CB2 1RP, United Kingdom

CAMBRIDGE UNIVERSITY PRESS
The Edinburgh Building, Cambridge CB2 2RU, UK   http: //www.cup.cam.ac.uk
40 West 20th Street, New York, NY 10011-4211, USA   http: //www.cup.org
10 Stamford Road, Oakleigh, Melbourne 3166, Australia

First published 1990
Reprinted 1991, 1994, 1995, 1996, 1997, 1998

Printed in the United States of America

Typeset in Times

A catalogue record for this book is available from the British Library

Library of Congress Cataloguing-in-Publication Data is available

ISBN 0-521-30669-8 hardback
ISBN 0-521-31419-4 paperback

To Jens Rasmussen

Contents

Preface

Human error is a very large subject, quite as extensive as that covered by the term human performance. But these daunting proportions can be reduced in at least two ways. The topic can be treated in a broad but shallow fashion, aiming at a wide though superficial coverage of many well-documented error types. Or, an attempt can be made to carve out a narrow but relatively deep slice, trading comprehensiveness for a chance to get at some of the more general principles of error production. I have tried to achieve the latter.

The book is written with a mixed readership in mind: cognitive psychologists, human factors professionals, safety managers and reliability engineers — and, of course, their students. As far as possible, I have tried to make both the theoretical and the practical aspects of the book accessible to all. In other words, it presumes little in the way of prior specialist knowledge of either kind. Although some familiarity with the way psychologists think, write and handle evidence is clearly an advantage, it is not a necessary qualification for tackling the book. Nor, for that matter, should an unfamiliarity with high-technology systems deter psychologists from reading the last two chapters.

Errors mean different things to different people. For cognitive theorists, they offer important clues to the covert control processes underlying routine human action. To applied practitioners, they remain the main threat to the safe operation of high-risk technologies. Whereas the theoreticians like to collect, cultivate and categorise errors, practitioners are more interested in their elimination and, where this fails, in containing their adverse effects by error-tolerant designs. It is hoped that this book offers something useful to both camps.

The shape of the book

The book is divided into three parts. The first two chapters introduce the basic ideas, methods, research traditions and background studies. They set the scene for the book as a whole.

Chapter 1 discusses the nature of error, makes a preliminary identification of its major categories and considers the various techniques by which it has been investigated.

Chapter 2 outlines the human error studies that have been most influential in shaping the arguments presented later in the book. It distinguishes two traditions of research: the natural science and engineering (or cognitive science) approaches. The former is characterized by its restricted focus upon well-defined, manipulable phenomena and their explanation by 'local' theories whose predictive differences are, potentially at least, resolvable by experimentation. This tradition has provided the basis of much of what we know about the resource limitations of human cognition. The engineering approach, on the other hand, is more concerned with framing working generalisations than with the finer shades of theoretical difference. It synthesises rather than analyses and formulates broadly based theoretical frameworks rather than limited, data-bound models. The more theoretical aspects of the subsequent chapters are very much in this latter tradition.

The middle section of the book, comprising Chapters 3 to 5, presents a view of the basic error mechanisms and especially those processes that give recurrent forms to a wide variety of error types. Whereas *error types* are rooted in the cognitive stages involved in conceiving and then carrying out an action sequence (i.e., planning, storage and execution), *error forms* have their origins in the universal processes that select and retrieve pre-packaged knowledge structures from long-term storage.

Chapter 3 describes a generic error-modelling system (GEMS) which permits the identification of three basic error types: skill-based slips and lapses, rule-based mistakes and knowledge-based mistakes. These three types may be distinguished on the basis of several dimensions: activity, attentional focus, control mode, relative predictability, abundance in relation to opportunity, situational influences, ease of detection and relationship to change. Most of the chapter is taken up with describing the various failure modes evident at the skill-based, rule-based and knowledge-based levels of performance.

Chapter 4 introduces the concept of *cognitive underspecification*. Cognitive operations may be underspecified in a variety of ways, but the consequences are remarkably uniform; the cognitive system tends to 'default' to contextually appropriate, high-frequency responses. Error forms, it is argued, are shaped primarily by two factors: similarity and frequency. These, in turn, originate in the automatic retrieval processes by which knowledge structures are located and their products delivered either to consciousness (thoughts, words, images, etc.) or to the outside world (actions, speech, gestures, etc.). There are two processes involved: *similarity-matching*, by which appropriate knowledge attributes are matched to the current calling conditions on a like-to-like basis; and *frequency-gambling*, by which conflicts between partially matched knowledge structures are resolved in favour of the more frequently employed items. Both of these processes, but especially the latter, come into increasing prominence when cognitive operations are insufficiently specified. Underspecification, though highly variable in its origins, can be rendered down to two functionally equivalent states: insufficient calling conditions to locate a unique knowledge item and incomplete knowledge (i.e., some of the 'facts' associated with a particular knowledge structure — or set of structures — are missing). Both states will increase the natural tendency of the cognitive system to output high-frequency responses and this gives recognisable form to many error types. Evidence drawn from a wide range of cognitive activities is presented in support of these assertions.

Chapter 5 attempts to express these ideas more precisely in both a notional and a computational form. It addresses the question: What kind of information-handling machine could operate correctly for most of the time, but also produce the occasional wrong responses characteristic of human behaviour? The description of the fallible machine is in two parts: first in a notional, non-programmatic form, then in a suite of computer programs that seek to model how human subjects, of varying degrees of ignorance, give answers to general knowledge questions relating to the lives of U.S. presidents. The output of this model is then compared to the responses of human subjects.

The final section of the book focuses upon the *consequences* of human error: error detection, accident contribution and remedial measures.

Chapter 6 reviews the relatively sparse empirical evidence bearing upon the important issues of error detection and error correction. Although error correction mechanisms are little understood, there are grounds for arguing that their effectiveness is inversely related to their position within the cognitive control hierarchy. Low-level (and largely hard-wired) postural correcting mechanisms work extremely well. Attentional processes involved in monitoring the actual execution of action plans are reasonably successful in detecting unintended deviations (i.e., slips and lapses). But even higher-level processes concerned with making these plans are relatively insensitive to actual or potential straying from some adequate path towards the desired goal (mistakes). The relative efficiency of these error-detection mechanisms depends crucially upon the immediacy and the adequacy of feed-back information. The quality of this feed-back is increasingly degraded as one moves up the control levels.

Chapter 7 considers the human contribution to accidents in complex, high-risk technologies. An important distinction is made between *active errors* and *latent errors*. The former, usually associated with the performance of 'front-line' operators (pilots, control room crews, and the like), have an immediate impact upon the system. The latter, most often generated by those at the 'blunt end' of the system (designers, high-level decision makers, construction crews, managers, etc.), may lie dormant for a long time, only making their presence felt when they combine with other 'resident pathogens' and local triggering events to breach the system's defences. Close examination of six case studies – Three Mile Island, Bhopal, *Challenger*, Chernobyl, the *Herald of Free Enterprise* and the King's Cross underground fire – indicate that latent rather than active failures now pose the greatest threat to the safety of high-technology systems. Such a view is amply borne out by more recent disasters such as the Piper Alpha explosion, the shooting down of the Iranian airbus by the U.S.S.

Vincennes, the Clapham Junction and Purley rail crashes and the Hillsborough football stadium catastrophe.

The book ends with a consideration of the various techniques, either in current use or in prospect, to assess and reduce the risks associated with human error. Chapter 8 begins with a critical review of probabilistic risk assessment (PRA) and its associated human reliability assessment (HRA) techniques. It then considers some of the more speculative measures for error reduction: eliminating error affordances, intelligent decision support systems, memory aids, error management and ecological interface design. In conclusion, the chapter traces the shifting preoccupations of reliability specialists: an initial concern with defending against component failures, then an increasing awareness of the damaging potential of active human errors, and now, in the last few years, a growing realisation that the prime causes of accidents are often present within systems long before an accident sequence begins.

The final note is a rather pessimistic one. Engineered safety devices are proof against most single failures, both human and mechanical. As yet, however, there are no guaranteed technological defences against either the insidious build-up of latent failures within the organisational and managerial spheres or their adverse (and often unforeseeable) conjunction with various local triggers. While cognitive psychology can tell us something about an individual's potential for error, it has very little to say about how these individual tendencies interact within complex groupings of people working in high-risk systems. And it is these collective failures that represent the major residual hazard.

Some conspicuous omissions

Although it has featured fairly large in the literature, relatively little special attention has been given in this book to the relationship between errors and stress. This omission was made for two reasons.

First, while there are a small number of 'ecologically valid' studies (Ronan, 1953; Grinker & Spiegel, 1963; Berkun, 1964; Marshall, 1978) indicating that high levels of stress can, and often do, increase the likelihood of error, it is also clear that stress is neither a necessary nor a sufficient condition for the occurrence of cognitive failure.

Recent investigations (Broadbent, Cooper, FitzGerald & Parkes, 1982; Broadbent, Broadbent & Jones, 1986) have suggested that a more interesting question is not so much "Why does stress promote error?" but rather "Why is a relatively marked personal proneness to cognitive failures associated with increased vulnerability to stress?" The second reason for omitting any specific treatment of stress is that this important relationship between error proneness and stress vulnerability has been considered at length elsewhere (Reason, 1988d).

The existence of this recent publication (a chapter in the *Handbook of Life Stress, Cognition and Health*, 1988) also explains why questionnaire studies of error proneness receive only a summary mention in this book (see Chapter 1). There is a further reason for not dealing in any detail with the general issue of individual differences here. Although it is well known that factors such as age and pathology play an important part in error production, there is little compelling evidence to suggest that these individual factors yield unique error types. Rather, they produce an exaggerated liability to the pervasive error forms whose varieties and origins are already treated extensively in Chapters 4 and 5.

A skimmer's guide

Cognitive psychologists with an interest in theory are urged to read the first six chapters. If inclined, they could then go on to skim the remaining two chapters. Much of this material will be unfamiliar to them since little of it has appeared in the conventional cognitive literature.

Those with more practical concerns (and less interest in cognitive psychology) can afford to be more selective without losing too much of the thread. After reading Chapter 1, they could skip to the conclusions of Chapter 2. Chapter 3 contains some human factors material as well as the generic error-modelling system, and is therefore worth rather more than a glance. Practitioners might find much of Chapter 4 rather too academic for their tastes, but they could read the first few pages and the concluding remarks in order to get a sense of the general argument. The first part of Chapter 5 presents a fairly concise summary of the basic theory; whether they read to the end depends on their interest (or faith) in computer modelling. The remaining three chapters, and particularly the last two, were written specifically for those with applied leanings and should not be skipped by them.

Acknowledgements

Jens Rasmussen, to whom this book is dedicated, has had a profound influence on the ideas expressed here, both through his writings and as a result of the many fruitful meetings he has convened (and generously hosted over the years) at the Risoe National Laboratory. His skill-rule-knowledge framework has justifiably become a 'market standard' for the human reliability community the world over. I hope I have done it justice here.

A great debt is owed to Don Norman for his intellectual stimulation, his long-standing encouragement of this work and for his hospitality during my brief spell in La Jolla. We got into the 'error business' at about the same time, but I always seem to find myself trailing several ideas behind him. This is especially apparent after the recent publication of his excellent book, *The Psychology of Everyday Things*, upon which I have preyed extensively here.

Berndt Brehmer, with whom I have spent many pleasant and productive days both in Manchester and in various foreign parts, was kind enough to read and comment upon an early version of the manuscript. It is because of his wise advice that readers are spared a lengthy and self-indulgent chapter covering the history of error from Plato onwards. But I was also considerably heartened by his encouraging remarks on the remainder.

I am greatly indebted to Dietrich Doerner for showing me (along with Berndt Brehmer) that it was possible to study complex and dynamic problem-solving tasks in a rigorous fashion without losing any of their real-world richness and for his kind hospitality on many occasions. These visits not only allowed me to meet many of his distinguished colleagues, they also provided an introduction to the diversity and excitement of the 'new' German psychology. Unfettered by the more sterile aspects of Anglo-American experimentalism and in tune with broader philosophical influences than British Empiricism, they have been making a spirited attack on many of the affective and motivational issues avoided by those who regard human cognition primarily as an information-processing device.

Much is owed to two sets of collaborators. I wish to thank Carlo Cacciabue, Giuseppe Mancini, Ugo Bersini, Francoise Decortis and Michel Masson at the CEC Joint Research Centre, Ispra, where we have been attempting to model the behaviour of nuclear plant operators in emergency conditions, along lines similar to those described in Chapter 5. And special thanks are due to Carlo Cacciabue for instructing me so patiently in the mysteries of nuclear engineering. (And, while on this subject, let me also thank John Harris of the Simon Engineering Laboratories for the same service.) I must also express my great appreciation to Willem Wagenaar, Patrick Hudson and Jop Groeneweg, all of the University of Leiden, who have done much to clarify my thinking about 'resident pathogens' and accident causation during our joint project for Shell Internationale Petroleum Maatschappij.

My sincere thanks are due to John Senders and Ann Crichton-Harris for organising, sponsoring and hosting the First Human Error Conference at Columbia Falls, Maine, in 1980. This gathering, together with Three Mile Island, did much to set the error 'ball' rolling. In addition to his own distinguished contributions to the field, John Senders is also one of the great impresarios of human error. In 1983, together with Neville Moray, he organised a second great error event (sponsored by NATO and the Rockefeller Foundation) at Bellagio on Lake Como. These two meetings have played a great part in giving a sense of identity to human error research and in establishing personal contacts between otherwise scattered (both in geography and across disciplines) members of the reliability community.

I have also benefited a great deal from conversations and correspondence with the following, listed in no particular order: Bernard Baars, Donald and Margaret Broadbent, David Woods, Neville Moray, Alan Swain, Tim Shallice, Ezra Krendel, Duane McCruer, John Wreathall, Ed Dougherty, Joe Fragola, Don Schurman, Alan Baddeley, Tony Sanford, Donald Taylor, Douglas Herrmann, Erik Hollnagel, Bill Rouse, Todd LaPorte, Veronique de Keyser, Jacques Leplat, Maurice de Montmollin, Keith Duncan, Lisanne Bainbridge, Trevor Kletz, Zvi Lanir, Baruch Fischhoff, Beth Loftus, Michael Frese, Antonio Rizzo, Leena Norros, George Apostolakis, Henning Andersen, Ron Westrum, Paul Brown, Abigail Sellen and Barry Turner. A special debt is owed to David Embrey for introducing me to the world of high technology, and for supplying so much excellent incident and event data, and to Deborah Lucas, once my research student and research assistant, now a distinguished 'error person' in her own right.

Closer to home, I must gratefully acknowledge the help and stimulation I have had from my colleagues at the University of Manchester: Sebastian Halliday, Graham Hitch, Tony Manstead, Andrew Mayes and Stephen Stradling; from my research associates: Alan Fish, Janis Williamson, James Baxter and Karen Campbell; from my research students: Philip Marsden, Richard Shotton and Gill Brown; and successive generations of finalists who collected data for me and for their undergraduate projects, especially Victoria Horrocks, Sarah Bailey, Caroline Mackintosh and Karen Feingold.

Still closer to home, I must thank my wife, Rea. It is conventional to express gratitude to spouses for their patience and forbearance. Mine probably did me a far greater service by not indulging writer's tantrums and not allowing me to dodge my share of the household chores; she, after all, had a book of her own to write. More to the point, she gave willingly of her services where they were most needed: as an informed editor and as an eagle-eyed proofreader, for which I am truly thankful.

Finally, I am grateful to the Economic and Social Research Council (or the Social Science Research Council, as it was then more suitably called) for two research grants awarded between 1978 and 1983. The first supported diary and questionnaire studies of everyday errors; the second, a personal research grant, gave me half-time freedom from teaching for two years and allowed me to carry out most of the library research for this book.

James Reason

1 The nature of error

Just over 60 years ago, Spearman (1928) grumbled that "crammed as psychological writings are, and must needs be, with allusions to errors in an incidental manner, they hardly ever arrive at considering these profoundly, or even systematically." Even at the time, Spearman's lament was not altogether justified (see Chapter 2); but if he were around today, he would find still less cause for complaint. The past decade has seen a rapid increase in what might loosely be called 'studies of errors for their own sake'.

The most obvious impetus for this renewed interest has been a growing public concern over the terrible cost of human error: the Tenerife runway collision in 1977, Three Mile Island two years later, the Bhopal methyl isocyanate tragedy in 1984, the *Challenger* and Chernobyl disasters of 1986, the capsize of the *Herald of Free Enterprise*, the King's Cross tube station fire in 1987 and the Piper Alpha oil platform explosion in 1988. There is nothing new about tragic accidents caused by human error; but in the past, the injurious consequences were usually confined to the immediate vicinity of the disaster. Now, the nature and the scale of certain potentially hazardous technologies, especially nuclear power plants, means that human errors can have adverse effects upon whole continents over several generations.

Aside from these world events, from the mid-1970s onwards theoretical and methodological developments within cognitive psychology have also acted to make errors a proper study in their own right. Not only must more effective methods of predicting and reducing dangerous errors emerge from a better understanding of mental processes, it has also become increasingly apparent that such theorising, if it is to provide an adequate picture of cognitive control processes, must explain not only correct performance, but also the more predictable varieties of human fallibility. Far from being rooted in irrational or maladaptive tendencies, these recurrent error forms have their origins in fundamentally useful psychological processes. Ernst Mach (1905) put it well: "Knowledge and error flow from the same mental sources, only success can tell the one from the other."

A central thesis of this book is that the relatively limited number of ways in which errors actually manifest themselves is inextricably bound up with the 'computational primitives' by which stored knowledge structures are selected and retrieved in response to current situational demands. And it is just these

1

processes that confer upon human cognition its most conspicuous advantage over other computational devices: the remarkable ability to simplify complex informational tasks.

1. The cognitive 'balance sheet'

Correct performance and systematic errors are two sides of the same coin. Or, perhaps more aptly, they are two sides of the same cognitive 'balance sheet'. Each entry on the asset side carries a corresponding debit. Thus, automaticity (the delegation of control to low-level specialists) makes slips, or actions-not-as-planned, inevitable. The resource limitations of the conscious 'workspace', while essential for focusing computationally-powerful operators upon particular aspects of the world, contribute to informational overload and data loss. A knowledge base that contains specialised 'theories' rather than isolated facts preserves meaningfulness, but renders us liable to confirmation bias. An extraordinarily rapid retrieval system, capable of locating relevant items within a virtually unlimited knowledge base, leads our interpretations of the present and anticipations of the future to be shaped too much by the matching regularities of the past. Considerations such as these make it clear that a broadly-based analysis of recurrent error forms is essential to achieving a proper understanding of the largely hidden processes that govern human thought and action.

2. Errors take a limited number of forms

On the face of it, the odds against error-free performance seem overwhelmingly high. There is usually only one way of performing a task correctly, or, at best, very few; but each step in a planned sequence of actions or thoughts provides an opportunity to stray along a multitude of unintended or inappropriate pathways. Think of boiling an egg. At what stages and in how many ways can even this relatively simple operation be bungled? The list of possibilities is very long. Thoughts such as these make it appear highly unlikely that we could ever adequately chart the varieties of human error.

Fortunately, the reality is different. Human error is neither as abundant nor as varied as its vast potential might suggest. Not only are errors much rarer than correct actions, they also tend to take a surprisingly limited number of forms, surprising, that is, when set against their possible variety. Moreover, errors appear in very similar guises across a wide range of mental activities. Thus, it is possible to identify comparable error forms in action, speech, perception, recall, recognition, judgement, problem solving, decision making, concept formation and the like. The ubiquity of these recurrent error forms demands the formulation of more global theories of cognitive control than are usually derived from laboratory experiments. Of necessity, these focus upon very restricted aspects of mental function in rather artificial settings.

Far from leading down countless unconnected or divergent pathways, the quest for the more predictable varieties of human error is one that continually draws the searcher inwards to the common theoretical heartland of consciousness, attention, working memory and the vast repository of knowledge structures with which they interact. And it is with these theoretical issues that the first half of this book is primarily concerned.

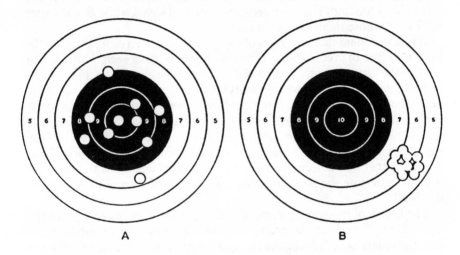

Figure 1.1. Target patterns of ten shots fired by two riflemen. A's pattern exhibits no constant error, but rather large variable errors. B's pattern shows a large constant error, but small variable errors (from Chapanis, 1951).

3. Variable and constant errors

Although it may be possible to accept that errors are neither as numerous nor as varied as they might first appear, the idea of a *predictable* error is a much harder one to swallow. If errors were indeed predictable, we would surely take steps to avoid them. Yet they still occur. So what is a predictable error?

Consider the two targets shown in Figure 1.1 (taken from Chapanis, 1951). Each shows a pattern of ten shots, one fired by rifleman A, the other by rifleman B. A placed his shots around the bull's eye, but the grouping is poor. B's shots fell into a tight cluster, but at some distance from the bull's eye.

These patterns allow us to distinguish between two types of error: *variable* and *constant* errors. A's pattern exhibits no constant error, only a rather large amount of variable error. *B* shows the reverse: a large constant error, but small variable error. In this example, the variability is revealed by the spread of the individual shots, and provides an indication of the rifleman's consistency of shooting. The constant error, on the other hand, is given by the distance between the group average and the centre of the target.

What do these patterns tell us about the relative merits of these two individuals? If we should rely only on their respective scores, then *A* would appear the better shot, achieving a total of 88 to *B*'s 61. But it is obvious from the groupings that this is not the case. A more acceptable view would be that *A* is a rather unsteady shot with accurately aligned sights, while *B* is an expert marksman whose sights are out of true.

It is also evident that the errors of these two marksmen differ considerably in their degree of predictability. Given another ten shots each, with *B* still aiming at the target's centre and his sights still unadjusted, we could say with a high degree of confidence whereabouts his shots would fall; but the variability of *A*'s shooting makes such a confident forecast impossible. The difference is very clear: in *B*'s case, we have a theory that will account for the precise nature of his constant error, namely, that he is an excellent shot with biased sights. But our theory in *A*'s case, that he has accurate sights but a shaky hand, is not one that would permit a precise prediction of where his shots will fall. We can anticipate the poor grouping and have some idea of its spread, but that is all.

The lesson of this simple example is that the accuracy of error prediction depends very largely on the extent to which the factors giving rise to the errors are understood. This requires a theory which relates the three major elements in the production of an error: the nature of the task and its environmental circumstances, the mechanisms governing performance and the nature of the individual. An adequate theory, therefore, is one that enables us to forecast both the *conditions* under which an error will occur, and the particular *form* that it will take.

For most errors, our understanding of the complex interaction between these various causal factors is, and is always likely to be, imperfect and incomplete. Consequently, most error predictions will be probabilistic rather than precise. Thus, they they are liable to take the form: "Given this task to perform under these circumstances, this type of person will probably make errors at around this point, and they are likely to be of this variety," rather than be of the kind: "Person *X* will make this particular error at such-and-such a time in such-and-such a place." Nevertheless, predictions of this latter sort can be made in regard to certain types of error when they are deliberately elicited within a controlled laboratory environment. This is especially true of many perceptual illusions. Not only can we predict them with near certainty (given an intact sensory system), we can also forecast with considerable accuracy how

their experience will vary with different experimental manip
these are exceptions.

The more usual type of prediction is illustrated by the following ~~~ ,
It can be forecast with near certainty that during next January the banks will
return a large number of cheques with this year's date on them. We cannot
necessarily predict the exact number of the misdated cheques (although such
information probably exists for previous years, so the approximate number
could be estimated), nor can we say precisely who will make this error, or on
which day. But we do know that such *strong habit intrusions* are among the
most common of all error forms; that dating a cheque, being a largely routinised activity (at least with respect to the year), is particularly susceptible to
absent-minded deviations of this kind; and that the early part of the year is the
period in which these slips are most likely to happen. Such *qualitative* predictions may seem merely banal, but they are nonetheless powerful. Moreover,
the regular recurrence of this error form is extremely revealing of the covert
processes controlling practised activities.

4. Intentions, actions and consequences

The notions of intention and error are inseparable. Any attempt at defining
human error or classifying its forms must begin with a consideration of the
varieties of intentional behaviour.

One psychologically useful way of distinguishing between the different
kinds of intentional behaviour is on the basis of yes-no answers to three questions regarding a given sequence of actions (Figure 1.2):

Were the actions directed by some prior intention?

Did the actions proceed as planned?

Did they achieve their desired end?

Notice that all of these questions are capable of being answered. In contrast to issues like basic motivation or detailed execution, the nature of the
prior intentions, knowledge of whether or not the subsequent actions devi-
ated from them and an appreciation of their success or failure are potentially
available to consciousness. Indeed, one of the primary functions of consciousness is to alert us to departures of action from intention (Mandler, 1975; 1985)
and, though less immediately, to the likelihood that the planned actions currently underway will not achieve their desired goal.

The notion of intention comprises two elements: (a) an expression of the
end-state to be attained, and (b) an indication of the means by which it is to
be achieved. Both elements may vary widely in their degree of specificity. For
most everyday actions, prior intentions or plans consist of little more than a
series of verbal tags and mental images. With the repetition of an action sequence, fewer and fewer 'intentional tags' come to stand for increasingly larger

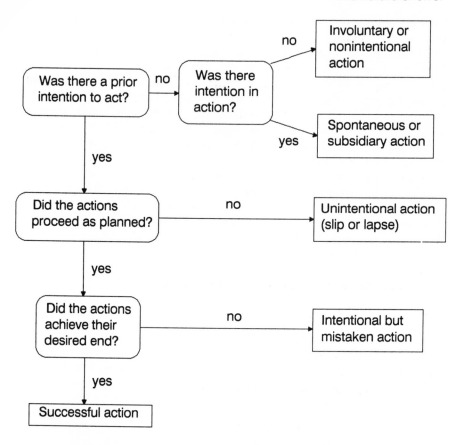

Figure 1.2. Algorithm for distinguishing the varieties of intentional behaviour. The three main categories are non-intentional behaviour, unintentional behaviour (slips and lapses) and intentional but mistaken behaviour.

amounts of detailed movement. The more routine the activity, the fewer the number of low-level control statements required to specify it. In novel activities, however, we are aware of the need to 'talk ourselves through' the actions. Under these circumstances, our activities are guided by the effortful yet computationally-powerful investment of conscious attention.

4.1. Distinguishing prior intention and intentional action

Searle (1980, p. 52) made an important distinction between 'prior intentions' and 'intentions in action': "All intentional actions have intentions in action but not all intentional actions have prior intentions." Actions without prior intentions fall into two broad classes: *intentional* and *nonintentional* actions.

4.1.1. Intentional actions without prior intention

Searle (1980) gives two instances of intentional actions without prior intention: spontaneous and subsidiary actions. Someone might hit another on the spur of the moment without forming any prior intention. In this case, the intention resides only in the action itself, as Searle (1980, p. 52) states "the action and the intention are inseparable." Similarly, in executing well-practised action sequences, only the 'major headings' are likely to be specified in the prior intention (e.g., "I will drive to the office"). We do not, indeed cannot, consciously fill in the 'small print' of each component operation in advance (i.e., opening the car door, sitting down, putting on the seat belt, inserting the ignition key, starting the engine, etc.). For such subsidiary actions, writes Searle (1980, p. 52), "I have an intention, but no prior intentions" (see also Reason & Mycielska, 1982, p. 9).

4.1.2. Non-intentional or involuntary actions

Textbooks of jurisprudence and criminal law are replete with accounts of intentionless behaviour (Hart, 1968; Smith & Hogan, 1973). As Hart (1968, p. 114) put it: "All civilized penal systems make liability to punishment for at any rate serious crime dependent not merely that the person to be punished has done the outward act of the crime, but on his having done it in a certain frame of mind or will." A crime has thus two elements: the *actus rea* and the *mens rea*. To prove a criminal liability, it must be shown not only that the consequences of the criminal act were intended, but also that the act itself was committed voluntarily.

The defence of 'automatism' rests on demonstrating the absence of "a vital link between mind and body" (Smith & Hogan, 1973, p. 35). In such instances, "the movements of the human body seem more like the movements of an inanimate thing than the actions of a person. Someone unconscious in a fit of epilepsy, hits out in a spasm and hurts another; or someone, suddenly stung by a bee, in his agony drops and breaks a plate he is holding" (Hart, 1968, pp. 91-92).

Not only is the issue of volition fundamental to notions of criminal responsibility, it is also crucial to the psychological definition of human error. Thus the term error can *only* be applied to intentional actions. It has no meaning in relation to nonintentional behaviour because error types depend critically upon two kinds of failure: the failure of actions to go as intended (slips and lapses) and the failure of intended actions to achieve their desired consequences (mistakes). To clarify these basic error forms, we need to consider the distinction between intended and unintended actions.

4.2. Distinguishing between intended and unintended actions

Assuming a prior intention and/or an 'intention in action', it is possible to build a psychologically meaningful taxonomy of error and correct performance on the basis of the answers to the second and third questions listed above: Did the actions go as planned? And did the actions achieve their desired consequences? Since our primary concern is with error, we will look first at those cases where actions deviate from intention: unintended actions or actions-not-as-planned.

4.2.1. Unintended actions

Actions that deviate from intention fall into two classes: those that nevertheless achieve their intended goal and those that do not. While just conceivable, the former are highly unlikely. Searle (1980) provides an example of one such 'successful yet unintended action': A man intends to murder someone by shooting at him. He misses, but the shot stampedes a herd of wild pigs, which tramples the intended victim to death. I will not consider these curiosities further. Psychologists (as distinct from lawyers, philosophers or even theologians) are more interested in the 'acts of man' than in the so-called 'acts of God'.

Common among the acts of humans are moments of absent-mindedness when we become aware that our actions have strayed from their intended path. Two conditions appear to be necessary for the occurrence of these slips of action: the performance of some largely automatic task in familiar surroundings and a marked degree of attentional 'capture' by something other than the job in hand (see Reason, 1979; Norman, 1981).

4.2.2. Intended actions and mistakes

Even when the intended actions proceed as planned, they can still be judged as erroneous if they fail to achieve their intended outcome. In this case, the problem resides in the adequacy of the plan rather than in the conformity of its constituent actions to some prior intention. Errors of this kind are termed *mistakes* (Norman, 1981, 1983; Reason & Mycielska, 1982).

Norman (1983) summarised the distinction between mistakes and slips (or lapses) very succinctly: "If the intention is not appropriate, this is a mistake. If the action is not what was intended, this is a slip." Mistakes involve a mismatch between the prior intention and the intended consequences. For slips and lapses, however, the discrepancy is between the intended actions and those that were actually executed.

Another way of distinguishing these two basic error forms is as *planning failures* (mistakes) and *execution failures* (slips and lapses). This categorization emerges not only from the logic of the three-question algorithm, but also from a consideration of cognitive levels. Planning failures are likely to arise from higher-level processes than either slips or lapses.

5. Some working definitions

We are now in a position to sketch out some working definitions of error and its principal types. A working definition is serviceable rather than ideal. It tries to embody the essential psychological characteristics of the phenomena without struggling too hard to mark out their exact semantic boundaries. The study of error, being largely an inductive mode of enquiry, does not demand precise axioms and definitions at the outset, as do the deductive sciences. The following working definitions have proved their utility in a psychological rather than a philosophical sense.

Error will be taken as a generic term to encompass all those occasions in which a planned sequence of mental or physical activities fails to achieve its intended outcome, and when these failures cannot be attributed to the intervention of some chance agency.

As we have seen, a series of planned actions may fail to achieve their desired outcome because the actions did not go as planned or because the plan itself was inadequate. It is also possible that both types of error could occur within the same sequence of planning, storage and execution. This distinction gives rise to two further working definitions.

Slips and lapses are errors which result from some failure in the execution and/or storage stage of an action sequence, regardless of whether or not the plan which guided them was adequate to achieve its objective.

Whereas *slips* are potentially observable as externalised actions-not-as-planned (slips of the tongue, slips of the pen, slips of action), the term *lapse* is generally reserved for more covert error forms, largely involving failures of memory, that do not necessarily manifest themselves in actual behaviour and may only be apparent to the person who experiences them.

Mistakes may be defined as deficiencies or failures in the judgemental and/or inferential processes involved in the selection of an objective or in the specification of the means to achieve it, irrespective of whether or not the actions directed by this decision-scheme run according to plan.

It is evident from this definition that mistakes are likely to be more subtle, more complex and less well understood than slips. As a result, they generally constitute a far greater danger. By their nature, mistakes are also far harder to detect. Consciousness is specifically tuned to picking up departures of action from intention (Mandler, 1975), but mistakes can pass unnoticed for lengthy periods (Woods, 1984), and even when detected they sometimes remain a matter of debate. Not only is the quality of the plan open to a diversity of opinion, it is also something that can be judged at two distinct stages: before and after it has been implemented. Prior to its execution, it can be assessed according to whether or not it has sufficient contingencies, displays soundness of judgement, imagination, flexibility, awareness of detail and the like. But once put into action, we judge it primarily according to how well it achieved its stated objectives.

Unfortunately, the results of these two sets of judgements do not necessarily correspond. Plans rated as good prior to their execution can fail to attain their objectives; whereas plans judged as inadequate by any reasonable criteria can turn out successfully, though not necessarily to the credit of their originators. Consider, for example, the relative qualities and eventual outcomes of the German and French plans for waging the First World War. By most a priori standards, the Schlieffen Plan was a masterpiece of military thinking. It was bold, imaginative and worked out to the last logistic detail; but it ultimately failed. The corresponding Plan XVII was, by comparison, crude and ill-considered, but it eventually succeeded. Janis (1972, p. 11) put the matter succinctly in a discussion of high-level policy making: "Defective decisions based on misinformation and poor judgement sometimes lead to successful outcomes . . . we must acknowledge that chance and the stupidity of the enemy can sometimes give a silk-purse ending to a command decision worth less than a sow's ear."

6. The classification of errors

A central problem in error classification is the difficulty of reconciling the often highly specific contextual triggers of a particular error form with the fact that it may also manifest the influence of some very general adaptive process or basic error tendency. A classification that emphasises the former at the expense of the latter is likely to overlook the broad regularities in the more predictable forms of error. Yet one that neglects the local contextual factors (e.g., task and situational considerations) will not only be of limited use to the practitioner, it will also fail to accommodate the theoretically important causal interactions between basic error tendencies and immediate task features.

There is no universally agreed classification of human error, nor is there one in prospect. A taxonomy is usually made for a specific purpose, and no single scheme is likely to satisfy all needs. Nearly everyone who has published in this field has devised some form of error classification. Consequently, the literature abounds with such taxonomies, reflecting a variety of practical concerns and theoretical orientations and ranging from the highly task specific to broad statements of underlying error tendencies.

Notwithstanding the number and diversity of existing error taxonomies, it is possible to penetrate beyond their surface idiosyncrasies to distinguish three levels at which classifications are attempted: the behavioural, contextual and conceptual levels. These correspond approximately to the "What?", "Where?" and "How?" questions about human errors.

6.1. The behavioural level of classification

At the most superficial level, errors may be classified according to some easily observable feature of the erroneous behaviour. These can include either the formal characteristics of the error (omission-commission, repetition, misordering), or its more immediate consequences (nature and extent of damage, injury). Classifications dealing with applied data at this behavioural level may also be concerned with such things as recoverability, human versus machine attribution, and operator versus design responsibility.

Most human behaviour is essentially serial in character, and there are only a limited number of purely formal ways in which a sequence of words or actions can deviate from intention. Therefore, it is not surprising that classifications of verbal and action slips framed at this level show a high degree of uniformity. There is also a large measure of agreement between judges in their allocation of slips to these limited behavioural categories (Reason, 1984a).

Despite the parsimony of such schemes and the appealing conformity of error-to-category assignment, there are strong grounds for believing that there is no simple and direct mapping of these behavioural error types onto more theoretical categories of cognitive failure. Rather, the evidence indicates that members of the same behavioural error class can arise from quite different causal mechanisms and that members of different behavioural categories can share common aetiologies (see Norman, 1981; Reason & Mycielska, 1982; Reason, 1984a).

6.2. The contextual level of classification

This level goes beyond the formal error characteristics and includes limited assumptions about causality. In most cases, these assumptions do not stray far from the 'surface' data. Many of the slips of the tongue and pen taxonomies are constructed at this level and include reference to such contextual triggering features as anticipations and perseverations.

Such categorizations are valuable because they draw attention to the complex interaction between 'local' triggering factors and the underlying error tendencies. They address themselves to the issue of what prompts an error to appear at a particular point in the behavioural sequence and so stress the importance of recording as much information as possible regarding the surrounding circumstances, both internal and external to the perpetrator of the slip. In short, they acknowledge the critical relationship between error type and the character of the situation or task in which it appears.

Yet even this useful level of classification has serious limitations. By themselves, contextual factors cannot explain why the same or very similar circumstances do not always trigger the same error forms. Freud (1922, p. 36) was well aware of this problem, as the following passage reveals:

The influence of sound-values, resemblances between words, and common associations connecting words, must also be recognized as important. They facilitate the slip by pointing out a path for it to take. But if there is a path before me, does it necessarily follow that I must go along it? I also require a motive determining my choice and, further, some force to propel me forward. These sound-values and word associations are, therefore, just . . . the facilitating causes of slips of the tongue, and cannot provide the real explanation for them.

To accept Freud's point does not necessarily require agreement with his theory of unconscious determination, but it does indicate the necessity of plumbing comparable 'depths' within the cognitive system in order to find a more solid bedrock upon which to construct a classificatory framework.

6.3. The conceptual level of classification

This third level is predicated on assumptions about the cognitive mechanisms involved in error production. In contrast to the other two, these classifications are based more upon theoretical inferences than on the observable characteristics of the error or its context. With each successive level of classification, we move further from the immediate 'surface' data and deeper into the realm of assumption and conjecture. Despite these problems, classifications based upon conceptual considerations are potentially the most fruitful because they seek to identify underlying causal mechanisms. At this point, it would be helpful to introduce the distinction between *error types* and *error forms*.

7. A distinction between error types and error forms

7.1. Error types

The term *error type* relates to the presumed origin of an error within the stages involved in conceiving and then carrying out an action sequence. These stages can be described under three broad headings: planning, storage and execution. Planning refers to the processes concerned with identifying a goal and deciding upon the means to achieve it. Since plans are not usually acted upon immediately, it is likely that a storage phase of some variable duration will intervene between formulating the intended actions and running them off. The execution stage covers the processes involved in actually implementing the stored plan. The relationship between these three stages and the primary error types is shown in Table 1.1.

For reasons that will be discussed later, mistakes can be further subdivided into (a) *failures of expertise*, where some preestablished plan or problem solution is applied inappropriately and (b) a *lack of expertise*, where the individual, not having an appropriate 'off-the-shelf' routine, is forced to work out a plan of action from first principles, relying upon whatever relevant knowledge he or she currently possesses. These two types of mistakes correspond close-ly to the rule-based and knowledge-based levels of performance as described by Rasmussen (1983).

Table1.1. Classifying the primary error types according to the cognitive stages at which they occur.

Cognitive stage	Primary error type
Planning	Mistakes
Storage	Lapses
Execution	Slips

7.2. Error forms

Whereas *error types* are conceptually tied to underlying cognitive stages or mechanisms, *error forms* are recurrent varieties of fallibility that appear in all kinds of cognitive activity, irrespective of error type. Thus, they are evident in mistakes, lapses and slips. Error forms are so widespread that it is extremely unlikely that their occurrence is linked to the failure of any single cognitive entity. Rather, this omnipresence suggests that they are rooted in universal cognitive processes, particularly the mechanisms involved in knowledge re-trieval. Two such error forms will be considered at some length in this book: *similarity* and *frequency biases* (see Chapters 4 and 5).

8. Methods of investigating human error

8.1. Naturalistic methods or 'corpus gathering'

For well over a 100 years, psycholinguists in particular and, more recently, cognitive psychologists in general have been collecting, analysing and class-ifying naturally occurring slips and lapses. The rationale for this type of inves-tigation was eloquently expressed by Bawden (1900, p. 5) as follows.

Just as little irregularities in the road enable one accustomed to it to make his way in the dark, so to the student of human nature little in-advertencies of expression, aberrations in speech, lapses of thought, confusion of ideas, hitches or slips in speaking or writing are some-times most useful and unerring guides in the understanding of mental process. Neglected trifles are sometimes suggestive of most fruitful problems for research.

Corpus gathering is concerned with the identification and description of naturally occurring phenomena, and is the first step in the process of classification. It has the merit of portraying the richness and variety of real-world phenomena and, given a large enough corpus, it provides a reasonably comprehensive qualitative account of the available species of error. From this analysis, it is possible to identify recurrent pattern of error across aspects of mental life that are often treated in relative isolation. Not only does corpus gathering satisfy the criterion of ecological validity, it also offers a much broader perspective on the mental landscape than can be obtained from necessarily focused laboratory studies.

But it is also clear that corpus gathering is not enough. The errors so noted may be natural and spontaneous, but these very qualities also mean that the investigator has little or no control over the circumstances of their occurrence. Without the possibility of systematically manipulating the various predisposing factors, it is difficult to achieve scientifically satisfactory causal explanations. In short, natural history techniques are excellent for providing a wide-angle view of the phenomena, but they often raise more questions than they can answer.

Methods used in the collection of naturalistic error data range from the kind of inspired self-observation employed by Freud (1914), to the more quantitative *extended diaries* of recent times (Reason, 1979, 1984a; Reason & Lucas, 1984b), as well as ingenious attempts to bring the rigour of laboratory measurement into the realm of everyday life (Wilkins & Baddeley, 1978).

8.2. Questionnaire studies

Another way of obtaining data about everyday errors is through self-report questionnaires. Most commonly, they present subjects with descriptions (and/or examples) of different slips and lapses and ask them to rate approximately how often they have experienced each one during some specified time period. Of course, the subjects can only respond with general impressions, and these are liable to various types of distortion. Nevertheless, such methods can yield interesting data with regard to individual differences in error proneness, the relatedness of various error types and the organisation of the underlying control mechanisms. In addition, they can provide a rough indication of how people perceive the relative frequencies of particular kinds of cognitive failure. As such, they offer a valuable supplement to the extended diary mode of naturalistic investigation (for a detailed evaluation of these questionnaire methods, see Herrmann, 1982, 1984; Morris, 1984).

As indicated in the Preface, these studies have been recently reviewed elsewhere (Reason, 1988) and will not be discussed in any detail in this book. However, the principal conclusions of this review are summarised later in the chapter.

Self-reported liability to minor cognitive failures is a relatively stable and enduring feature of the individual (Broadbent, Cooper, FitzGerald & Parkes, 1982; Herrmann, 1982; Reason & Lucas, 1982b, 1984b). Responses to questionnaire items asking about the incidence of a wide variety of minor cognitive failures remain fairly consistent over several months. Moreover, self-assessments are usually confirmed by marital partners. These findings suggest that there is some genuine correspondence between self-reports of error proneness and everyday behaviour.

Responses to questionnaire items are generally positively correlated. Thus, those people who confess to being particularly liable to one kind of cognitive failure (e.g., memory lapses) also tend to report a high degree of susceptibility to other types as well (e.g., action slips), and conversely. This suggests that error proneness is not specific to any one cognitive domain, but operates more or less uniformly across all types of mental function (see Broadbent et al., 1982; Reason & Mycielska, 1982). The implication is that susceptibility to these usually inconsequential slips and lapses is governed by some global factor relating to the characteristic way in which an individual manages his or her cognitive affairs.

Observations taken from a wide range of samples, in which people were exposed to different stresses (nurses under training, women facing breast surgery, students preparing for important examinations), support Broadbent's *stress-vulnerability hypothesis*: namely, that relatively high levels of cognitive failure in normal everyday life are associated with increased vulnerability to externally imposed stresses. Whatever governs general proneness to everyday slips and lapses also appears to contribute to stress vulnerability. This factor eludes capture by most simple laboratory measures, but it seems to relate closely to the deployment of limited attentional resources in the face of competing task demands. The evidence so far assembled suggests that it is not so much that stress induces a high rate of cognitive failure, but that certain styles of cognitive management can lead to *both* absent-mindedness *and* to the inappropriate matching of coping strategies to stressful situations.

8.3. Laboratory studies

The relative merits of naturalistic and experimental modes of enquiry and their mutual interdependence were concisely stated by Baars (1980): "Without naturalistic facts, experimental work may become narrow and blind: but without experimental research, the naturalistic approach runs the danger of being shallow and uncertain."

Undoubtedly, the most powerful technique for studying underlying mechanisms is through the deliberate elicitation of particular error types under controlled laboratory conditions. Such investigations follow in the footsteps of Helmholtz, Mach and the other great German 'illusionists' of the nineteenth century. Some of the most impressive modern studies have involved the deliberate elicitation of speech errors (see Baars, 1980; Fromkin, 1980).

There are at least two problems associated with the experimental investigation of errors. First, the need to establish precise control over the possible determinants of the error often forces investigators to focus upon rather trivial phenomena (i.e., the large number of studies on the Stroop effect). Second, it is usually the case that the greater the measure of control achieved by the experimenter, the more artificial and unnatural are the conditions under which the error is elicited.

8.4. Simulator studies

An important recent development has been the use of computer-based simulations to create within the laboratory many of the dynamic features of real-life, complex decision-making tasks that were hitherto lacking in static, one-shot experimental studies. The pioneers in this field have been Berndt Brehmer and his associates at the University of Uppsala (Brehmer, Allard & Lind, 1983; Brehmer, 1987) and Dietrich Doerner at the University of Bamberg (Doerner, 1978; Doerner & Staudel, 1979; Doerner, 1987).

The Swedish research has examined the effects of complexity and feedback delay upon decision making in highly dynamic situations, such as directing the fighting of a forest fire. The Bamberg group has been primarily concerned with charting the 'pathologies' of individual decision making in complex situations (e.g., being mayor of a small middle-European town). The work of these two groups is discussed further in Chapter 3.

8.5. Case studies

As in other branches of psychology, the intensive study of the single case can yield valuable information about the circumstances leading up to catastrophic errors. Where sufficient evidence is available regarding both the antecedent and the prevailing circumstances of a particular event or accident, we are able to study the interaction of the various causal factors over an extended time scale in a way that would be difficult to achieve by other means. Although any one catastrophe may result from the unhappy conjunction of several distinct causal chains, and hence be a truly unique happening, the precise effects of this particular combination of contributing factors teaches us something about the limits of human performance that could not be obtained from either the laboratory or from naturalistic observations.

Inevitably there are problems. The primary sources of data are accident reports. Not only are these mostly concerned with attributing blame, they also tell a story that may be inaccurate or incomplete, even when the reports are prepared by experienced and relatively open-minded investigators. There are two main difficulties. First, an accident report will always contain less information than was potentially available. Second, a written account has the effect of 'digitizing' what in the original was a complex and continuous set of 'analogue' events.

One of the important lessons of these case studies is that disasters are very rarely the product of a single monumental blunder. Usually they involve the concatenation of several, often quite minor, errors committed either by one person or, more often, by a number of people. In general, the errors contributing to human-made disasters recognizably belong to the familiar body of slips, lapses and mistakes to which all of us are prone in the normal course of daily life. Any one of them might have had negligible consequences; but their effects accumulate, each compounding the mischief of its predecessors, so that in retrospect the whole series seems to move inexorably towards its calamitous conclusion. The aetiology of accidents is considered at length in Chapter 7.

But hindsight, as Fischhoff (1975) has demonstrated, does not equal foresight. Simply knowing how past disasters happened does not, of itself, prevent future ones. However, by combining the knowledge obtained from case studies with a more adequate theory (or theories) of error production, we not only extend our knowledge of cognitive function, we can also begin to assemble a body of principles that, when applied to the design and operation of high-risk technological systems, could reasonably be expected to reduce either the occurrence of errors or their damaging consequences.

9. Summary

The more predictable varieties of human fallibility are rooted in the essential and adaptive properties of human cognition. They are the penalties that must be paid for our remarkable ability to model the regularities of the world and then to use these stored representations to simplify complex information-handling tasks. They represent the debit side of the cognitive 'balance sheet', where each entry also carries significant advantages.

Error is intimately bound up with the notion of intention. The term 'error' can only be meaningfully applied to planned actions that fail to achieve their desired consequences without the intervention of some chance or unforeseeable agency. Two basic error types were identified: *slips* (and lapses), where the actions do not go according to plan, and *mistakes*, where the plan itself is inadequate to achieve its objectives.

Errors may be classified at any one of three levels: behavioural, contextual and conceptual. But only the last provides a satisfactory foundation, since there is no direct mapping of the surface forms of error onto their underlying cognitive mechanisms. The same mental process may produce quite different behavioural error types; conversely, a particular surface form (e.g., the omission of an intended act) may arise from a variety of underlying mechanisms.

A distinction was made between *error types* and *error forms*. Error types (as will be discussed in Chapter 3) can be distinguished according to the performance levels at which they occur. On the other hand, error forms are evident at all levels of human performance and appear to originate in universal cognitive processes. In Chapters 4 and 5, we will identify these as the automatic retrieval mechanisms, *similarity-matching* and *frequency-gambling*, by which long-term memory locates and delivers its products, either to consciousness or as actions in the outside world.

2 Studies of human error

This chapter examines some significant contributions to the study of human error. Its primary aim is to outline the major influences upon the arguments presented later in this book, particularly in Chapters 3 to 5. But I also hope that it will convey something of the current state of cognitive theorising to those readers who are not themselves working in this field.

The first part of the chapter attempts to provide a modest historical vantage point from which to view contemporary treatments of error. It is necessarily selective because a complete account would encompass the entire history of psychological ideas. For our purposes, however, it is sufficient to consider the major influences of the past hundred years.

The second part deals mainly with the resource-limited aspects of human cognition: attention and 'primary' (or short-term) memory. This work has largely been carried out in the laboratory within the *natural science tradition* of experimental psychology. As such, the material discussed in these sections bears the characteristic hallmarks of this mode of investigation: a restricted focus upon well-defined, manipulable phenomena; limited, data-bound models and an abiding concern with resolving differences between theoretical contenders on the basis of their predictive performance.

The third part is concerned with the representation and deployment of stored knowledge and with the vast 'community' of specialist processors governing the more automatic aspects of perception, thought and action. Much of this work has been carried out within the more recent *cognitive science tradition*. This is too youthful and diverse an enterprise for there to be any universally accepted definition of its aims and methods. But most people who now style themselves as cognitive scientists (or cognitive engineers) would probably agree that if there is a common theme, then it has to do with devising, either in reality or in some notional form, information-processing machines that at least partly mimic the essential properties of human cognition.

The final two parts set the scene for Chapters 3 to 5, which present this book's particular view of human error mechanisms. One discusses the principal differences between 'local' and 'framework' models of cognition. The other outlines some basic assumptions regarding human cognition. These constitute the point of departure for the next three chapters.

1. Early psychological observers of human error

Since this is a psychological not a philosophical enquiry, I will focus upon those writers and early investigators who were directly concerned with the mental and behavioural aspects of error, specifically upon turn-of-the-century psychologists who sought to describe the variety of its forms and explain the processes underlying its production.

1.1. Sully's *Illusions*

In 1881, James Sully, later Grote Professor of Mind and Logic at University College London, published a largely forgotten book entitled *Illusions* in which he undertook "a wide survey of the field of error, embracing in its view not only the illusions of sense dealt with in treatises on physiological optics, etc., but also other errors familiarly known as illusions, and resembling the former in their structure and mode of origin" (Sully, 1881, preface). These 'other errors' included systematic anomalies of memory, belief, thinking and insight.

Sully defined 'illusion' (p. 6) as "any species of error which counterfeits the form of immediate, self-evident, or intuitive knowledge, whether as sense-perception or otherwise." In the first instance, he sought to separate all knowledge into two regions: primary or intuitive knowledge, and secondary or inferential knowledge. Illusions are thus false or spurious knowledge of the first kind, and fallacies are false or spurious knowledge of the second kind. However, as he points out (p. 6), "the same error may be called a fallacy or an illusion, according as we are thinking of its original mode of production or of the form which it finally assumes; and a thorough-going psychological analysis of error may discover that these two classes are at bottom very similar."

Having construed illusion as the counterfeiting of immediate knowledge, Sully based his error classification upon the kind of knowledge that these illusions simulate. Using what were then fashionable philosophical terms, he distinguished two forms of immediate knowledge: *presentative* and *representative*. The former variety is obtained through direct perception of external objects or, through introspection, of inner states. Representative knowledge was obtained through the agencies of memory and belief (insofar as this simulates direct knowledge). These four modes of cognition – external perception, introspection, memory and belief – constituted the major dimension of Sully's error taxonomy. A second dimension, active-passive, was employed to distinguish those errors arising out of spontaneous activity within the individual from those due primarily to external factors. However, along neither of these dimensions did Sully attempt to make rigid categorical distinctions.

Sully's treatment of perceptual and memory illusions provides an illustration of the way he sought common features among errors arising from different cognitive domains. Sully identified three major classes of memory illusions:

(a) False recollections to which there correspond no real events or personal history.

(b) Recollections that misrepresent the manner of the happening of real events.

(c) Recollections that falsify the date of the events remembered.

For each of these, there is a corresponding perceptual analogue: (a) perceptions for which there are no external counterparts (e.g., ocular spectra, sensations of light and hallucinations); (b) perceptions that distort the shape of the external object (e.g., the effects of haze and refracting media) and (c) perceptions that falsify size and distance (e.g., when clear air causes distant mountains to seem far closer than they are, or when intervening 'clutter' makes objects appear more distant).

Sully was probably the first psychologist to attempt to classify the broad spectrum of human error and to seek common explanatory principles. His book, though little known, is a classic in the field of error studies. If its impact had been more widely felt, Charles Spearman, a subsequent Grote professor at University College London, would have had no cause to complain, nearly 50 years later, that: "Whoever would seek for any well-digested information about (errors) may make the whole round of current psychological textbooks ... for all this, he will become but little the wiser for his pains" (Spearman, 1928, p. 30).

Actually, Spearman's complaint was not entirely justified. The 20 years or so straddling the turn of the century saw a number of significant attempts to understand the psychological origins of human fallibility. The most widely known of these was Freud's investigation of the psychopathology of everyday life. No less important were the pioneering studies of speech errors conducted by Meringer in Vienna and the contributions of psychologists in the United States, notably William James and Hugo Munsterberg (a refugee from Wundt's laboratory) at Harvard and the long-lived Joseph Jastrow at the University of Wisconsin.

1. 2. The Freudian slip

Freud first became aware of the meaningfulness of certain everyday slips and lapses in 1896. In a letter to his colleague, Fliess, he wrote that he had "at last grasped a little thing I had long suspected", namely, the reason why a known name sometimes eludes retrieval and wrong names are dredged up in its place. In this instance, he had been unable to recall the last name of the poet, Joseph Mosen: "I was able to prove (i) that I had repressed the name Mosen because of certain associations; (ii) that material from my infancy played a part in the repression; and (iii) that the substitute names that occurred to me arose, just like a symptom, from both recent and infantile groups of material" (Bonaparte, 1954).

Having established the significance of this apparently trivial lapse, he began to collect examples of many different forms of everyday error: misreadings, slips of the tongue and pen, misquotations, bungled actions and so on. Gradually he became convinced that all of these normally inconsequential slips and lapses betrayed the presence within the unconscious of repressed impulses. Most of the time they remained hidden, but occasionally they seized upon an opportune moment – in speech, memory retrieval or action – to make themselves known through some error or 'parapraxis'.

The Psychopathology of Everyday Life first appeared as a separate volume in 1904 and was subsequently enlarged over the next 20 years. It became one of Freud's most popular books, running into many editions. It is said that Freud first became aware that he was famous when he discovered his cabin steward reading this book on his voyage to America in 1909. The core ideas and many of the best examples were later expressed more succinctly (and more convincingly) in the *Introductory Lectures on Psychoanalysis*, given at the University of Vienna between 1915 and 1917 and later published (Freud, 1922). Thereafter, the phrase 'a Freudian slip' entered the language, and the view that errors were unconsciously determined became firmly lodged, for good and ill, in scientific and popular belief (see Reason & Mycielska, 1982, for a further discussion of the Freudian slip).

1.3. Meringer and speech errors

Although Paul (1880) was probably the first linguist to appreciate the significance of speech errors as clues to the covert mechanisms underlying speech utterance, it was Freud's compatriot, Meringer, who undertook the first major study (Meringer & Mayer, 1895). By 1908, he had assembled a corpus of over 8,000 slips of the tongue and pen, a collection that is still being picked over by contemporary researchers (see Fromkin, 1973, 1980). One reason why this corpus is still in use is that Meringer was extremely scrupulous about his methods of data collection and was at great pains to avoid selectional bias. His relentless questionings of speakers whose tongues slipped in his presence became so notorious at the University of Vienna that rooms would empty at his approach.

1.4. James, Munsterberg and Jastrow

Three important developments occurred in the United States during this turn-of-the-century period. In 1890, after 12 years of labour, William James completed *The Principles of Psychology*. Not only did these two volumes provide some unparalleled descriptions of everyday cognitive failings, they also contained, in the chapters on habit, memory and will, nearly all the necessary elements of a theory of human error. James himself did not formally attempt such an enterprise, but his thinking has had a profound influence on almost everyone that has. While preachers traditionally take their texts from the scriptures, contemporary psychologists, especially those with an interest in the cognitive failings of everyday life, frequently look for theirs in the writings of William James. One text in particular will see extensive service throughout this book: "Habit diminishes the conscious attention with which our acts are performed" (James, 1890, p. 114).

In a characteristically generous and farsighted manoeuvre, James contrived to have Hugo Munsterberg, originally a somewhat undervalued student of Wundt's at Leipzig, appointed as professor of psychology at Harvard, while he himself reverted to his earlier status as professor of philosophy. Among Munsterberg's many projects at Harvard was an investigation of the unreliability of eye-witness testimony. His book, *On the Witness Stand: Essays on Psychology and Crime* (1908), remains an early classic in this now active field of research. It is also interesting to note that research into 'the psychology of testimony' was of sufficient interest to warrant regular literature surveys in the early issues of the *Psychological Bulletin* (see Whipple, 1910, 1911).

In 1905, Joseph Jastrow, professor of psychology at the University of Wisconsin, published an analysis of some 300 'lapses of consciousness' collected from his students. This was the first systematic attempt to investigate slips of action (as distinct from slips of the tongue) and stressed the necessity of some kind of attentional intervention in order to prevent action sequences from deviating along habitual but unintended routes (see Reason, 1984a; Norman, 1981). Throughout the remainder of his long working life, Jastrow continued to be fascinated with human error and especially with those factors that lead to and sustain wishful rather than wise thinking.

1.5. The Gestalt tradition

The next major influence upon the study of error resulted from the work of Max Wertheimer, Wolfgang Kohler and Kurt Koffka, from whose exchange of ideas at Frankfurt in 1912 emerged the new Gestalt psychology. Following the example of William James, these three young men were driven by an evangelical urge to rescue psychology from the Wundtian domination of elemental sensations, feelings and images and from the associative ties that bound these 'atoms' into mental 'compounds'. They strove to replace this 'mental chemistry' with a concern for phenomenal wholes. Psychological phenomena, they argued, were always more than the sum of their constituent parts. Parts did not determine wholes, but were determined by them.

Their first demonstrations of this thesis involved various perceptual phenomena. Sense impressions, they maintained, are not passive photographic impressions; rather, they are actively shaped by the observer's interests and by his or her innate tendency to make the parts of the figure fit a uniform whole. In particular, small irregularities are overlooked. As a result, perceived objects conform more to the Gestalt principles of 'good figure' than the sense data alone would justify. Later, these principles were extended into the field of memory and gave rise to specific predictions about the ways in which remembered figures become distorted with time.

Although it was not their primary aim, the Gestalt psychologists were among the first to formulate a testable theory regarding human error mechanisms. While its specific predictions were not always borne out (Woodworth, 1938; Riley, 1962; Baddeley, 1968) and the physiological basis of the theory found little support, the influence of the Gestalt psychologists upon contemporary thinking about cognitive function has been immense. To a considerable extent, this impact resulted from the work of two later individuals: Kurt Lewin in Germany and later the United States and Sir Frederic Bartlett at Cambridge. Each carried the Gestalt tradition into somewhat different spheres: Lewin into the fields of action, decision making, motivation and personality (and through his students Zeigarnik and Luchins into memory and problem solving, respectively) and Bartlett into the study of remembering, thinking and skilled performance.

1.6. The neuropsychologists: Lashley and Head

One of the few positive outcomes of the First World War was the boost it gave to the description and assessment of psychological disorders associated with various types of brain damage. Two leading figures of this period were Karl Lashley in the United States, and Sir Henry Head in Britain.

An enduring question in psychology is how we achieve the relatively automatic performance characteristic of skilled or highly practised behaviour. William James (1890) argued for 'response-chaining' or the nonattentional control of habitual sequences by behavioural feedback. Once established, each movement in the sequence is triggered by the kinaesthetic feedback generated by the preceding movement. The only conscious involvement necessary is starting the sequence. The remaining actions were under peripheral or feedback control.

In 1917, Lashley made some clinical observations of a soldier whose spinal injury had resulted in almost complete anaesthesia for one leg. Although not perfectly coordinated, this man's leg movements showed normal accuracy in both direction and extent. Lashley argued that since the spinal injury had effectively removed proprioceptive feedback, the control of these movements must reside centrally in the brain and that these preprogrammed instructions were run off independently of feedback. This 'centralist' or feedforward theory of motor control has proved extremely influential in shaping contemporary views of the serial organisation of both skilled performance (see Keele, 1973) and of its characteristic errors (Lashley, 1951).

Head (1920) was similarly concerned with the effects of traumatic deafferentation upon postural control. His observations led to the introduction of the now widely used concept of the 'schema' to explain how postural impressions are matched against some internalised model of body position. "Every recognisable [postural] change enters consciousness already charged with its relation to something that has gone before. . . . For this combined standard, against which all subsequent changes of posture are measured before they enter consciousness, we propose the word schema" (Head, 1920, pp. 605-606). This notion was further developed by Bartlett (1932). Few concepts have proved so useful in explaining the occurrence of a wide variety of systematic error forms.

1.7. Bartlett and 'schemata'

Bartlett (1932) invoked the notion of schema (schemata in the plural) to explain systematic errors that were apparent in the recall of pictorial and textual material. He found that reproductions made from memory were more regular, more meaningful and more conventionalised than the original stories or drawings. Odd or uncommon features of the to-be-remembered material were 'banalized' to render them more in keeping with the person's expectations and habits of thought. Bartlett believed that his subjects were unconsciously attempting to relate the new material to established knowledge structures or schemata. In his enduring phrase, they manifested "effort after meaning". These reconstructions were sometimes the result of conscious strategies, but more often they were unconscious processes.

A schema was defined by Bartlett (1932, p. 201) as "an active organisation of past reactions, or of past experiences, which must always be supposed to be operating in any well-adapted organic response. That is, whenever there is any order or regularity of behaviour, a particular response is possible only because it is related to other similar responses which have been serially organised, yet which operate, not simply as individual members coming one after another, but as a unitary mass."

Bartlett emphasised three fundamental aspects of schemata: (a) that they were unconscious mental structures ("schema are active, without any awareness at all."), (b) that they were composed of old knowledge ("They are masses of organised past experiences."), and (c) that long-term memory comprised active knowledge structures rather than passive images. Thus, schemata reconstructed rather than reproduced past experiences. And this process leads to certain predictable biases in remembering, due in large part to "the tendency to interpret presented material in accordance with the general character of earlier experience."

Like his Gestalt contemporaries, Bartlett emphatically rejected the earlier atomistic view of mental processes. In particular, he opposed the view, originating with Ebbinghaus, that each memory trace retained its own essential individuality. Since this was very much the orthodoxy of the thirties, Bartlett's ideas fell largely upon stony ground. It was not until the mid-1970s that the schema notion was disinterred, and achieved its current prominence in psychological theorising as a term to describe higher-order, generic, cognitive structures that underlie all aspects of human knowledge and skill.

1.8. The doldrums

With the end of the First World War, German psychology, once the dominant tradition, was either spent or scattered (happily, it is now restored). The centre of psychological influence moved to the United States which had recently come under the sway of John B. Watson and the animal learning theorists. This marked the beginning of a 40-year 'ice-age' in which mentalism went underground or was pushed to the fringe and notions like volition, consciousness, imagery, intention and purpose largely vanished from the prestigious journals.

The upshot of this bloodless civil war — whose Fort Sumter was the publication of Watson's *Behaviourist Manifesto* in 1913 — was that psychology came to be ruled by two quite distinct and mutually hostile forces. The behaviourists dominated academic psychology, and the psychoanalysts exercised a powerful influence over the rest, particularly the lay mind and the popular press. Neither camp had much interest in the deviation of action from intention. The behaviourists would not admit of intention, at least not as something having any scientific worth, and the psychoanalysts denied the deviation, in keeping with Freud's assertion that errors are symptomatic of some unconsciously held wish.

With a few notable exceptions — Spearman, Lewin, Bartlett and the social psychologists — serious interest in the nature and origins of human error languished for nearly 20 years, until it was revived by both the needs and the 'clever' machines of the Second World War. These brought in their train the information-processing approach to human cognition. From the vantage point of the late 1980s, it is possible to distinguish two distinct variants of this general approach: the natural science and the cognitive science traditions.

2. The natural science tradition

2.1. Focused attention and 'bottleneck' theories

A major theoretical concern of the 1950s and 1960s was the location of the 'bottleneck' in human information processing. At what stage did a parallel processing system, capable of handling several inputs at the same time, become transformed into a serial system through which only one set of signals could be handled at any given moment? This question presumed that humans act as a single communication channel of limited capacity at some point in the information-processing sequence.

One group of investigators maintained that the selection occurs at an early perceptual stage (Broadbent, 1958; Treisman, 1969). Others, the 'late-selection' theorists, claimed that the bottleneck is located at the point where decisions are necessary to initiate a response (Deutsch & Deutsch, 1963; Norman, 1968; Keele, 1973). This could be either an overt motor response, or a covert response concerned with storing material in long-term memory. There were also compromise theories that argued that there could be more than one bottleneck within the processing system (Kerr, 1973; Posner & Snyder, 1975).

I will not review the current state of this rather arid debate (see Broadbent, 1982; Wickens, 1983). For our purpose, it is sufficient to note that both early and late selection theories still have their passionate advocates, though the weight of the evidence seems to favour the latter view. Needless to say, data exist that embarrass both camps.

A number of pioneering studies carried out during the early years of the century (see Woodworth, 1938) showed that people are surprisingly good at focusing their attention upon a given task and ignoring irrelevant events in their immediate surroundings. Whereas these early experiments typically compared task performance with and without distractors, modern studies of focused attention have usually employed the simultaneous presentation of two or more sources of information and examined the subjects' ability to process one of these selectively. A commonly used technique has been the *dichotic listening task*, in which two messages are presented by earphones to different ears and the person is required either to 'shadow' (to repeat every word on the attended channel) or to monitor (to detect particular target signals) the message stream emanating from a previously identified source. Other studies have employed brief presentations of visual stimuli organised in complex arrays or 'overlapping' videorecordings of two different activities (i.e., where both are visible on the screen at the same time).

These modern studies confirmed the earlier findings: that people are indeed very good at processing one of two physically distinct concurrent sources of information, particularly when there is no ambiguity about the to-be-shadowed channel. But this selectivity is not perfect. Certain types of information from the nonselected channel can break through. These 'breakthroughs' depend upon both the physical and the semantic properties of the unattended message.

With regard to *physical properties*, people can usually tell if the unattended message was a human voice or a noise, and if the former, whether the speaker was a man or a woman. They can also detect gross alterations in the physical character of the irrelevant source: sudden changes in the voice of the speaker, a switch from a voice to a tone or an isolated sound (see Moray, 1969). In addition, breakthrough rates increase as the spatial separation between the signal sources diminishes (Treisman, 1964).

Other kinds of breakthrough are clearly determined by the *content* of the unattended message. The attentional mechanism appears to be tuned to detect certain types of signals, regardless of whether they are on the selected or nonselected channel. Common intrusions are the presence of one's own name, the name of a recently visited country or the title of a book by an author known personally to the listener.

Yet other breakthroughs can occur when words on the rejected channel fit into the context of what has just been processed on the selected channel. The implication is that the content of the selected message primes the attentional mechanism so as to make subsequent words of appropriate content more likely to receive conscious processing, even when they occur on the rejected channel. But this contextual tuning does not seem to work in reverse; the content of a rejected message has no effect on later performance (Broadbent, 1971).

Finally, these selectivity experiments demonstrate that switching attention takes time. Selectivity is degraded with brief auditory messages presented dichotically. Performance is poor when people are given single pairs of words simultaneously, and are directed to attend to one ear. With longer messages, however, precueing is more advantageous. It seems likely that selection is most effective when the content of the attended message is coherently organised to permit the serial grouping of signals and some preview of future inputs (Kahneman, 1973). By the same token, time is also needed to redirect the focus of attention after a period of selective listening. Gopher and Kahneman (1971) showed that listeners are particularly susceptible to intrusions from the previously selected channel for some seconds after having been told to switch attention to the other ear. There are wide individual differences in proneness to such errors, and there is some evidence to show that characteristic switching rates, as measured by laboratory tests, are related to on-the-job proficiency and safety records of professional drivers (Kahneman, 1973).

2.2. Divided attention and resource theories

In the selective attention tasks discussed above, subjects were required to focus their attention upon one of the available sources of information and to exclude the others. In *divided attention* studies, they are expected to distribute their attention between the assigned activities and to deal with each of them to the best of their ability. This type of experimental paradigm was mainly responsible for the development of *resource theories* of attention.

Resource theory is the product of several independent strands of research (Knowles, 1963; Moray, 1969; Kahneman, 1973; Norman & Bobrow, 1975; Navon & Gopher, 1979). In its basic form, this theory — or, more accurately, set of theories — assumes that attention can be usefully regarded as a single reservoir of information-processing resources that is equally available to all mental operations. More sophisticated variants invoke a multiplicity of non-overlapping reservoirs (see Wickens, 1983).

This view of attention as a finite but highly flexible control resource removes the need to postulate some specialised filterlike mechanism to account for selection. In resource theory, selection is implicit in the restricted nature of the attentional commodity; it can only be deployed in relation to a limited set of entities, though the possible claims upon it are legion. Thus, only those events, task elements or ideas that receive some critical allocation of this resource will achieve deeper levels of processing.

As stated earlier, a large part of the experimental literature underpinning resource theory has been concerned with people's ability to divide attention between two concurrent tasks. It is possible to envisage a continuum of dual-task situations, running from one extreme at which both tasks are wholly automatic, and thus make little or no claim upon attention, to an opposite extreme where the demands imposed by each task are so high that they can hardly be performed adequately, even in isolation. Most studies have been concerned with the middle ground. Within this region, the crucial factor is task similarity. The greater the similarity between the components of the two tasks, the more likely they are to call upon the same processing resources at the same time, and thus produce mutual interference.

However, the more practised people are at handling the two activities at the same time, the more proficient they become at responding to just those features that differentiate the two tasks, thus reducing their initial similarity and, with it, the likelihood of interference. As Kinsbourne (1981, p. 66) stated: "Over time, processing will descend the hierarchy from limited problem solving towards a more automatic, less attention requiring mode. Thus it is in the nature of the attentive processes to generate their own extinction."

The results of several studies (see Wickens, 1980) indicate that interference can occur at several different stages of the information-handling sequence rather than at a single critical point. As Broadbent (1982) put it: "The main interference between two tasks occurs at the point where they compete most for the same functions."

Dual-task interference can show itself in a variety of ways: as a complete breakdown of one of the activities, as a lowering of performance and/or slowing in the rate of responding of one or both activities and as 'cross-talk' errors in which elements of one task either bias responses in the other or actually migrate from one activity to the other (Long, 1975; Kinsbourne & Hicks, 1978).

2.3. Multichannel processor theories

A number of studies have demonstrated that highly skilled individuals performing essentially different concurrent tasks show minimal interference (Allport, Antonis & Reynolds, 1972; Shaffer, 1976; Spelke, Hirst & Neisser, 1976; Hirst, Spelke, Reves, Caharack & Neisser, 1980). These results have given rise to a view of human information processing known as the *multichannel processor theory*. Alan Allport has been one of the most active proponents of this viewpoint. He presented an early version of it as follows:

> In general, we suggest, any complex task will depend on the operation of a number of independent, specialised processors, many of which may be common to other tasks. To the extent to which the same processors are involved in any two particular tasks, truly simultaneous performance of these two tasks will be impossible. On the other hand, the same tasks paired respectively with another task requiring none of the same basic processors can in principle be performed in parallel with the latter without mutual interference. (Allport, Antonis & Reynolds, 1972)

More recently, Allport (1980a, 1980b) has criticised cognitive theories (especially bottleneck and resource theories) that assume the existence of a general-purpose, limited-capacity central processor, or GPLCCP for short. The largely tacit belief underlying the research described earlier, namely that there are 'hardware' constraints upon the amount of information that can be processed by the cognitive system at any given time, is not, Allport maintained, the only conclusion that can be drawn from the work on divided attention. What interpretation is placed upon these findings depends largely upon the assumption held regarding cognitive 'architecture'. The greater part of the research on cognitive limitations has assumed a hierarchical, multilevel architecture in which the topmost level (the GPLCCP) needs processing constraints in order to focus selectively upon particular kinds of information.

Allport's claim was that this view of the cognitive apparatus is limited by old-fashioned notions of computer architecture. Cognitive psychologists were quick to employ a range of computer metaphors for human information processing in the 1950s and 1960s; but, Allport (1980a, p. 27) argues, these ideas were "derived from the basic design of the sequential, general-purpose digital computer itself, rather than from the potential computational processes that might be implemented on it."

Cognitive psychology, Allport demanded, should eschew models based on general-purpose digital computers and abandon its assumptions about content-independent processors. Also consigned to the dustbin should be any notion of *quantitative* limitations upon the information to be processed. In their place should be constructed models based upon distributed, heterarchical architectures in which reside a community of specialised processors, or 'experts', who are capable of managing their affairs without any overall 'boss', GPLCCP or 'central executive'. As we shall see later, such models have indeed flourished in the mid to late 1980s.

2.4. The properties of primary memory

Most of the scientific literature relating to memory is derived from laboratory studies in which people are tested on their memory for some recently learned list of items, usually comprising nonsense syllables (Ebbinghaus, 1885), digit strings or individual words. The appeal of such studies is that they permit a large measure of control over the to-be-remembered material as well as over the conditions of learning and recall. By manipulating these variables systematically and observing their effects upon memory performance, the investigator is able to make reasonably confident statements about the causes of the observed effects. The penalty paid for this degree of control is that the results of these studies tell us relatively little about the way people actually use their memories. Nevertheless, they have taught us a great deal about the properties of the 'sharp end' of the memory system: primary or short-term memory (STM).

Since Wundt's observations in 1905, it has been known that most people have an *immediate memory span* for around seven unrelated items. More recent studies have shown that this span can be altered in various ways.

Span is increased when the to-be-remembered items are grouped in a meaningful way. Miller (1956) called this *chunking*. Thus, the span for letters increases to around ten when they are presented as consonant-vowel-consonant nonsense syllables (e.g., TOK, DEX, DAS, etc.), and rises to between 20 and 30 when letters form part of sentences. Miller argued that the capacity for immediate memory was seven plus or minus two chunks, regardless of the number of individual items per chunk. In other words, STM can be thought of as comprising a limited number of expansible 'bins', each containing a variably-sized chunk of information.

Conversely, span may be dramatically reduced by the *acoustic similarity effect* (Conrad, 1964). The span for sound-alike items is markedly less than that for phonologically dissimilar items, even when the material is presented visually. In one study (Baddeley, 1966), only 9.6 per cent of similar sentences were correctly recalled, compared to 82.1 per cent for acoustically dissimilar sentences.

There is also a clear relationship between memory span and word length under normal conditions of immediate recall (Baddeley, Thomson & Buchanan, 1975). When subjects are required to recall sequences of five words of differing length, there was a 90 per cent correct recall for one-syllable words and only 50 per cent for five-syllable words. In addition, there was a close correspondence between these recall scores and reading rates. This suggested that the *word length effect* reflects the speed at which the subjects could rehearse the words subvocally.

Both the acoustic similarity and the word length effects suggest that STM relies heavily on acoustic or phonological coding. In addition, it has long been known that the latter part of a sequence presented auditorally is better recalled than one presented visually (Von Sybel, 1909). This enhanced *recency effect* for vocalised items can be eliminated by the addition of an irrelevant item to the end of the sequence. Thus, people are better able to recall the sequence 8-5-9-6-3-1-7 than 8-5-9-6-3-1-7--0, where the terminal zero does not have to be remembered, but merely acts as a recall instruction (Conrad, 1960; Crowder & Morton, 1969). To exert this influence, however, the 'suffix' has to be speechlike. A buzzer sounded at the same point has no effect, nor does the semantic character of the suffix appear to matter. However, this *suffix effect* can be greatly reduced by introducing a brief pause between the end of the to-be-remembered items and the suffix.

2.5. The concept of working memory

One view of STM that has gained wide acceptance over the past decade is that of *working memory* (Baddeley & Hitch, 1974; Baddeley, 1976; Hitch, 1980). Instead of treating STM as a temporary store intervening between the perceptual processes and long-term memory, the working memory (WM) concept is both more broadly defined and more differentiated than its predecessors (see Atkinson & Shiffrin, 1968).

In its most recent form, WM is conveniently divided into three components: a *central executive* that acts as a limited capacity control resource and is closely identified with both attention and consciousness and two 'slave systems', the *articulatory loop* and the *visuospatial scratchpad*.

Although the articulatory loop and the visuospatial scratchpad store different kinds of information, both subsystems are assumed to have an essentially similar structure. Each comprises two elements: a passive store and an active rehearsal process. While both are under the control of the central executive, they are nevertheless capable of some degree of independent function, that is, without conscious attention being given to their operations. Thus, the articulatory loop is able to store a small quantity of speechlike material – about three items in the appropriate serial order or the amount of material that can be repeated subvocally in about one and a half seconds – without involving the central executive (Baddeley & Hitch, 1974).

In the articulatory loop, the passive store is phonological and is accessed directly by any auditory speech input. This is an obligatory process; speech inputs will always displace the current contents of the passive store. The passive store can also be accessed optionally via the active-rehearsal element. The acoustic similarity effect, noted earlier, can be explained on the basis of the confusion within the passive store of phonologically-similar items. Memory span will be a function of both the durability of item traces within the passive store and the rate at which the contents can be refreshed by subvocal rehearsal. Since short words can be said 'under the breath' more quickly than longer words, more of them can be rehearsed before their traces fade from the passive store. This provides a satisfactory account of the word-length effect.

While there are still many unresolved questions concerning the precise nature of WM, it has certain features that make it congenial to the cognitive theorist. Not only does it account reasonably well for most of the basic findings of earlier STM research, it also links, albeit sketchily, the functions of the slave systems to that of the central executive (which still survives in many theories despite Allport's attack). In other words, WM plays a crucial part in controlling the current 'working database', regardless of whether the information contained therein has arrived by way of the senses or whether it has been 'called up' from long-term memory in the course of reasoning, thinking or performing mental arithmetic. In this way, it also breaks free of the dead hand of earlier 'pipe-line' models of human information processing (see Broadbent, 1984) in which the direction of the data flow is largely one way, from the sensory input through to motor output. Central to the WM concept is the idea of a mental workspace that shares its limited resources between processing and storage.

There is now considerable evidence to show that the primary constraints upon such cognitive activities as arithmetical calculation (Hitch, 1978), concept formation (Bruner, Goodnow & Austin, 1956), reasoning (Johnson-Laird, 1983; Evans, 1983) and diagnostic 'trouble-shooting' by electronic technicians (Rasmussen, 1982) stem from WM limitations. The WM concept holds that there is *competition* between the resources needed to preserve temporary data generated during processing (e.g., the intermediate stage of a mental arithmetic calculation) and those consumed by the processing itself. Many of the characteristic strategies and shortcuts employed by people during the course of protracted and demanding cognitive activities can be viewed as devices for easing the burden upon working memory; or, in other terms, as ways of minimising *cognitive strain* (Bruner et al., 1956).

3. The cognitive science tradition

3.1. Contemporary schema theorists

After nearly 30 years of lying dormant, Bartlett's schema concept reemerged in three disparate publications in the same year: Minsky (1975) writing on computer vision, Rumelhart (1975) on the interpretation of stories, and Schmidt (1975) in the context of motor skill learning. So appeared the new schema theorists.

Although they vary widely in their terminology and applications, schema theories, both ancient and modern, reject an atomistic view of mental processes, and maintain "that there are some phenomena that cannot be accounted for by a concatenation of smaller theoretical constructs, and that it is necessary to develop larger theoretical entities to deal with these phenomena" (Brewer & Nakamura, 1983). One way of catching the spirit of this revival is by looking briefly at the work of two of the most influential theorists: Minsky and Rumelhart. Minsky was primarily concerned with perception and with the way schemata guide the encoding and storage of information. Rumelhart's interest was in text comprehension and memory for stories. Both advanced essentially similar ideas.

Common to both theories is the idea that schemata are high-level knowledge structures that contain informational 'slots' or variables. Each slot will only accept a particular kind of information. If the current inputs from the world fail to supply specific data to fill these slots, they take on 'default assignments': stereotypical values derived from past transactions with the world. As will be seen in later chapters, this idea of reverting to 'default assignments' is central to the main thesis of this book.

Minsky was concerned with the computer modelling of pattern recognition. He argued that adequate recognition of three-dimensional scenes was impossible on the basis of momentary input patterns alone. He proposed that the computer, like human cognition, must be ready for each scene with preconceived knowledge structures that anticipate much of what would appear. It was only on this basis, he argued, that human perception could operate with such adaptive versatility.

In Minsky's terminology, commonly encountered visual environments, such as rooms, are represented internally by a *frame*, containing *nodes* for standard features such as walls, floors, ceilings, windows and the like, and *slots* for storing the particular items relating to a certain kind of room. Thus, if people are shown the interior of a room very briefly, their subsequent description of its layout and contents probably will be biased more towards a prototypical room than the sensory evidence would warrant. For example, if their glance took in the presence of a clock upon the wall, it is probable that, if pressed, they would report that the clock had hands, even though, on this particular occasion, none were present.

The very rapid handling of information characteristic of human cognition is possible because the regularities of the world, as well as our routine dealings with them, have been represented internally as schemata. The price we pay for this largely automatic processing of information is that perceptions, memories, thoughts and actions have a tendency to err in the direction of the familiar and the expected.

Rumelhart defined schemata as "data structures for representing generic concepts stored in memory" (Rumelhart & Ortony, 1977, p. 101). Like Minsky, he asserted that schemata have variables with constraints and that these variables (or slots) have a limited distribution of possible default values. In addition, he stressed the embedded nature of schemata. High-level schemata will have lower-level schemata as subparts, the whole nesting together like Russian dolls, one within another. Thus, an office building schema will have office schemata as sub-parts. Similarly, an office schema is likely to include desks, filing cabinets, typewriters and so on as subcomponents.

Rumelhart also attempted to clarify the nature of the interactions between incoming episodic information and the generic information embodied in the schemata: the relationships between new and old knowledge. Rumelhart and Ortony (1977) argued that "once an assignment has been made, either from the environment, from memory, or by default, the schema is said to have been *instantiated.*" Only instantiated schema get stored in memory. During the process of recall, generic information may be used to further interpret and reconstruct a particular memory from the original instantiated schema record.

In applying these notions to text comprehension, Rumelhart was concerned with the interaction between 'top-down' schema-based knowledge and 'bottom-up' text information. If a reader arrives at the schema intended by the author, then the text has been correctly comprehended. If the reader can find no schema to accept the textual information, the text is not understood. And if the reader finds a schema other than the one intended by the author, the text is misinterpreted.

Other modern variants of the schema notion include *scripts* (Abelson, 1976), *plans* (Neisser, 1976), *prototypes* (Cantor & Mischel, 1977) and *personae* (Nisbett & Ross, 1980). A script, for example, is a structure that represents a familiar episode or scenario, such as visiting the dentist or going to a restaurant. Good accounts of the current state of schema theory have been provided by Taylor and Crocker (1981), Hastie (1981) and Fiske and Taylor (1984).

The current view of schemata, then, is as higher-order, generic cognitive structures that underlie all aspects of human knowledge and skill. Although their processing lies beyond the direct reach of awareness, their products — words, images, feelings and actions — are available to consciousness. Their encoding and representational functions include lending structure to perceptual experience and determining what information will be encoded into or retrieved from memory. Their inferential and interpretative functions go beyond the given information, allowing us to supply missing data within sensory or recalled information.

As Taylor and Crocker (1981) pointed out, "virtually any of the properties of schematic function that are useful under some circumstances will be lia-

bilities under others. Like all gamblers, cognitive gamblers sometimes lose."
Systematic errors can arise (a) from fitting the data to the wrong schema, (b)
from employing the correct schema too enthusiastically so that gaps in the
stimulus configuration are filled with best guesses rather than available sensory data and (c) from relying too heavily upon active or salient schemata.
Most of these schematic error tendencies can be explained by a single principle: a schema only contains evidence of how a particular recollection or sensory input *should* appear. It has no representation of what it should *not* look
like.

3.2. Norman and Shallice's attention to action model

The Norman-Shallice model (Norman & Shallice, 1980) represents a family
of action theories (Norman, 1981; Reason & Mycielska, 1982; Reason, 1984a)
that, although they embrace aspects of the experimental literature, are derived
mainly from natural history and clinical observations of cognitive failures.
They start from the belief that an adequate theory of human action must account not only for correct performance, but also for the more predictable varieties of human error. Systematic error forms and correct performance are
seen as two sides of the same theoretical coin.

The challenge for error-based theories of human action is to specify a control system that not only allows for the relative autonomy of well-established
motor programs (as indicated by the error data), but also acknowledges that
most of our actions nevertheless go according to plan. The Norman-Shallice
model achieves this by the provision of two kinds of control structures: (a)
horizontal threads, each one comprising a self-sufficient strand of specialized
processing structures (schemas); and (b) *vertical threads*, which interact with
the horizontal threads to provide the means by which attentional or motivational factors can modulate the schema activation values. Horizontal threads
govern habitual activities without the need for moment-to-moment attentional control, receiving their triggering conditions from environmental input
or from previously active schemas. Higher-level attentional processes come
into play, via the vertical threads, in novel or critical conditions when currently active schemas are insufficient to achieve the current goal. They add to or
decrease from schema activation levels to modify ongoing action. Motivational variables also influence schema activation along the vertical threads,
but are assumed to work over much longer time periods than the attentional
resources.

3.3. The decline of normative theories

Until the early 1970s, research into human judgement and inference had a
markedly rationalist bias. That is, it assumed that the mental processes involved in these activities could be understood, albeit with minor deviations

due to human frailty, in terms of normative theories describing optimal strategies (see Kahneman, Slovic & Tversky, 1982, for a more thorough discussion of this approach). Errors were attributed either to irrationality or to unawareness on the part of the perceiver. Thus, human beings were assumed to make decisions according to Subjective Expected Utility Theory, to draw inferences from evidence in accordance with logical principles and to make uncertain judgements in the manner of 'intuitive scientists' employing statistical decision theory or Bayes Theorem. Something of the spirit of these times can be gained from the following quotations:

> In general, [our] results indicate that probability theory and statistics can be used as the basis for psychological models that integrate and account for human performance in a wide range of inferential tasks. (Peterson & Beach, 1967)

> Man, by and large, follows the correct Bayesian rule [in estimating subjective probabilities], but fails to appreciate the full impact of the evidence, and is therefore conservative. (Edwards, 1968)

In the late 1960s and early 1970s, this view came under vigorous attack from a number of quarters. The work of three groups, in particular, proved ultimately fatal to the optimizing, rationalist or normative view of human cognition: Herbert Simon and his collaborators at Carnegie-Mellon, Wason and Johnson-Laird in Britain and Tversky and Kahneman, two Israelis then recently transplanted to North America.

3.3.1. Bounded rationality and 'satisficing'

In the 1950s and 1960s, psychological research into decision making "took its marching orders from standard American economics, which assumes that people always know what they want and choose the optimal course of action for getting it" (Fischhoff, 1986). Simon (1956, 1957, 1983) and his collaborators (Cyert & March, 1963) were among the first to chart how and why the cognitive reality departs from this formalised ideal when people set about choosing between alternatives.

Subjective Expected Utility Theory (SEU) is an extremely elegant formal machine, devised by economists and mathematical statisticians to guide human decision making. Simon (1983, p. 13) described it as "a beautiful object deserving a prominent place in Plato's heaven of ideas." SEU makes four basic assumptions about decision makers.

(a) That they have a clearly defined *utility function* which allows them to assign a cardinal number as an index of their preference for each of a range of future outcomes.

(b) That they possess a clear and *exhaustive view* of the possible *alternative strategies* open to them.

(c) That they can create a *consistent joint probability distribution* of scenarios for the future associated with each strategy.

(d) That they will (or ought to) choose between alternatives and/or possible strategies in order to maximise their *subjective expected utility*.

As a few moments introspection might reveal, flesh and blood decision making falls a long way short of this ideal in a number of significant respects. Whereas SEU assumes that decision makers have an undisturbed view of all possible scenarios of action, in reality human decision making is almost invariably *focused* upon specific matters (e.g., buying a car) that from a personal perspective are seen as largely *independent* of other kinds of choice (e.g., buying a house, selecting a meal from a menu).

The formal theory requires that the decision maker comprehends the entire range of possible alternatives, both now and in the future; but the actuality is that human beings, even when engaged in important decisions, do not work out detailed future scenarios, each complete with conditional probability distributions. Rather, the decision maker is likely to contemplate only a few of the available alternatives. Moreover, there is a wealth of evidence to show that when people consider action options, they often neglect seemingly obvious candidates. In addition, they are relatively insensitive to the number and importance of these omitted alternatives (Fischhoff, Slovic & Lichtenstein, 1978). The considered possibilities are often ill-defined and not 'thought through'. This imprecision makes it difficult for decision makers to evaluate their choices subsequently, since they are unable to recollect exactly what they did and why. Such reconstructions of the decision-making process are further complicated by *hindsight bias*, the 'knew it all along' effect, or the tendency to exaggerate in hindsight what was actually known prior to the choice point (Fischhoff, 1975).

SEU assumes a well-defined set of subjective values that are consistent across all aspects of the world. Again, the reality is markedly different. Subjective utilities vary from one type of decision to the next. As Simon (1983, p. 18) put it: "particular decision domains will evoke particular values, and great inconsistencies in choice may result from fluctuating attention." In short, human decision making is severely constrained by its 'keyhole' view of the problem space, or what Simon (1975, p. 198) has dubbed *bounded rationality*:

> The capacity of the human mind for formulating and solving complex problems is very small compared with the size of the problems whose solution is required for objectively rational behaviour in the real world — or even for a reasonable approximation of such objective rationality.

This fundamental limitation upon human information processing gives rise to *satisficing behaviour*: the tendency to settle for satisfactory rather than optimal courses of action. This is true both for individual and for collective decision making. As Cyert and March (1963) demonstrated, organisational planners are inclined to compromise their goal setting by choosing minimal objectives rather than those likely to yield the best possible outcome. We will return to these notions in the next chapter.

3.3.2. Imperfect rationality

While the greater part of the cognitive world of the 1960s and early 1970s was tinkering with the nuts and bolts of short-term memory and selective attention, Wason and his students were tackling the thorny problem of how people draw explicit conclusions from evidence. In particular, they were fascinated by the fact that so many highly intelligent people, when presented with simple deductive problems, almost invariably got them wrong. And these mistakes were nearly always of a particular kind. This once lonely furrow has now yielded a rich harvest of texts documenting the various pathologies of human reasoning (Wason & Johnson-Laird, 1972; Johnson-Laird & Wason, 1977; and Evans, 1983).

Many of their observations were in close accordance with Bacon's (1620) *Idols of the Tribe*: they observed that while people are happy to deal with affirmative statements, they find it exceedingly difficult to understand negative statements ("it is the peculiar and perpetual error of the human intellect to be more moved and excited by affirmatives than by negatives"), and they show an often overwhelming tendency to verify generalisations rather than falsify them ("The human understanding when it has once adopted an opinion draws all things else to support and agree with it"). Most of these errors could be explained by one general principle: "Whenever two different items, or classes, can be matched in a one-to-one fashion, then the process of inference is readily made, whether it be logically valid or invalid" (Wason & Johnson-Laird, 1972). In short, reasoning is governed more by *similarity-matching* than by logic. We will return to this point several times in later chapters.

3.3.3. Judgemental heuristics and biases

Tversky and Kahneman (1974) directed their initial assault against Ward Edwards's claim that people made uncertain judgements on the basis of Bayesian principles. Bayes Theorem, as applied for example to the case of a physician judging whether a patient's breast lump is malignant or not, integrates three types of evidence: the *prior* or *background information* (e.g., experiential or estimated base rates influencing the doctor's subjective estimate of malignancy), the *specific evidence* concerning an individual case (e.g., the results of a mammography test) and the *known screening power* of that test (e.g., its 'false alarm' rate). On the basis of a series of ingenious studies, Tversky and Kahneman concluded: "In his evaluation of evidence, man is apparently not a conservative Bayesian: he is not a Bayesian at all."

Instead, they argued that when making judgements concerning the likeli-hood of uncertain events, "people rely on a limited number of heuristic prin-ciples which reduce the complex tasks of assessing probabilities and predicting values to simpler judgemental operations. In general, these heuristics are quite useful, but sometimes lead to severe and systematic errors" (Tversky & Kahneman, 1974). Two heuristics, in particular, exert powerful effects in a wide range of judgemental tasks: the *representativeness heuristic* (like causes like) and the *availability heuristic* (things are judged more frequent the more readily they spring to mind). These too will be considered again in later chap-ters.

3.4. Reluctant rationality

Whereas the mistakes of bounded rationality arise primarily from the limita-tions of the conscious 'workspace' and those of imperfect rationality from an overreliance on simplifying heuristics operating within the schematic knowl-edge base, the mistakes of reluctant rationality stem from human cognition's unwillingness to engage in the laborious yet computationally powerful pro-cesses involved in analytic reasoning.

As William James (1908) pointed out, these attention-demanding pro-cesses are very difficult to sustain. He was writing about the difficulties of maintaining concentration upon a boring topic; but his description also holds good for the pursuit of any novel line of thought:

> our mind tends to wander, [and] we have to bring back our attention every now and then by using distinct pulses of effort, which revivify the topic for a moment, the mind then running on for a certain number of seconds or minutes with spontaneous interest, until again some inter-current idea captures it and takes it off. (James, 1908, p. 101)

This difficulty of holding a mental course is closely bound up with what Bruner and his associates (Bruner et al., 1956) termed *cognitive strain*. This arises whenever a mental course must be steered against rather than with the prevailing currents of habit or desire. It is the cost associated with the struggle to assimilate new information.

In a now classic series of studies, Bruner and his colleagues identified some of the strategies people adopt in order to minimize cognitive strain in 'atten-tion-intensive' tasks such as problem solving and concept attainment. These strategies may be either efficient or inefficient, depending upon the task de-mands. For example, when attempting to distinguish exemplars from non-exemplars of a category, people resorted to the criterion of *verisimilitude*. That is, they tended to prefer cues that had proved useful in the past, and thus had the 'look of truth' about them, regardless of their present utility. This was part of a more general strategy called *persistence-forecasting*.

Though it continues to spring surprises, our world contains a high degree of regularity. In this respect, persistence-forecasting is an extremely adaptive way of applying prepackaged solutions to recurring problems. "What we lose in terms of efficiency or elegance of strategies employed for testing familiar hypotheses, we probably gain back by virtue of the fact that in most things persistence-forecasting does far better for us with less effort than most other forms of problem solution. It is only in unconventional or unusual situations that such an approach proves costly" (Bruner et al., 1956, p. 112).

In summary, reluctant rationality – the avoidance of cognitive strain – is likely to lead to an excessive reliance on what appear to be familiar cues and to an overready application of well-tried problem solutions. It therefore functions, as does imperfect rationality, to direct our thoughts along well-trodden rather than new pathways. And, like bounded rationality (to which it is closely related), it restricts potentially profitable explorations of the problem configuration.

3.5. Irrationality and the cognitive 'backlash'

Part of the interest in these less-than-perfect varieties of human rationality arose as a cognitive 'backlash' to earlier motivational interpretations of human fallibility. This work has shown that many of the sources of human error lie not in the darker irrational aspects of our nature, but in "honest, unemotional thought processes" (Fischhoff, 1986). So what is there left for irrationality to explain? Some theorists, notably Nisbett and Ross (1980), would claim almost nothing. Even the most apparently irrational tendencies like racial prejudice can be explained by nonmotivational factors such as the fundamental attribution error, people's readiness to overattribute the behaviour of others to dispositional causes, thus ignoring the influence of situational factors such as role or context (see Fiske & Taylor, 1984, for a detailed account of this phenomenon).

Given that even psychologists can fall prey to such fundamental errors and so impute more irrationality to humankind than is justified, are there sufficient grounds for abandoning the notion of irrational mistakes altogether? While accepting that the swing away from what was once a catch-all category is a move in the right direction, it would be unwise to allow the pendulum of psychological fashion to swing too far towards the 'cognitive-only' extreme. There still remain a number of well-documented human aberrations that cannot be readily explained by cognitive biases alone.

For example, Janis's (1972) account of the *groupthink syndrome* clearly shows that group dynamics can introduce genuine irrationality into the planning process. How else could one account for the way in which small, elite policy-making groups (e.g., the architects of the Cuban Bay of Pigs fiasco in 1961) conspire to repress adverse indications or the excessive confidence shown by these planners in the rightness of their decisions? Indeed, a definition of irrational behaviour must include something like the wilful suppression of information indicating that a particular course of action could only end in disaster. In this respect, Kennedy's advisers behaved no less irrationally than the would-be bird men who jump off high buildings with wings attached to their arms. The tragedy of the Somme in 1916 or the fall of Singapore in 1942 suggest similar processes operating among groups of military planners. Such blunders, as Dixon (1976) demonstrated in his analysis of military incompetence, require the involvement of both motivational and cognitive explanations. We will return to this question in Chapter 7 when discussing the distinction between errors and violations.

3.6. General Problem Solver

One of the most infuential contributions to our current understanding of the 'pathologies' of human problem solving has come from Newell and Simon's (1972) rule-based computer model, *General Problem Solver* (GPS). Their data on human problem solving were obtained from verbal protocols. They asked their subjects to write down any tentative solutions they had reached and to 'think aloud' as they solved a problem. From these data, they produced a general model of problem solving designed to prove theorems and to solve logical and mathematical problems. Of more concern here, however, are their analytical tools.

Newell and Simon began with the notion of a *problem space*. This consists of a set of possible *states of knowledge* about the problem, and a set of *operators* that are applied to these states to produce new knowledge. A problem is posed by giving an initial state of knowledge and then asking the subject to find a path to a final state of knowledge that includes the answer to the problem. The path to the problem solution is characterized by a *problem behaviour graph* that tracks the sequence of states of knowledge through which the subject passes on his or her way from the initial to the final state and by the operators applied to move him or her along this path.

The basic problem-solving strategy of GPS is the *means-ends analysis*. This involves setting a high-level goal, looking for differences between the current state of the world and the goal state, looking for a method that would reduce this difference, setting as a subgoal the application of that method and then recursively applying means-ends analyses until the final state is reached.

3.7. Rasmussen's skill-rule-knowledge framework

Like the Norman-Shallice model, Rasmussen's account of cognitive control mechanisms is error oriented. But there are some important differences in the provenance of these models. Whereas Norman and Shallice were primarily concerned with accounting for the usually inconsequential action slips that occur in the normal course of daily life, Rasmussen's model is primarily directed at the far more serious errors made by those in supervisory control of industrial installations, particularly during emergencies in hazardous process plants. It was also markedly influenced by GPS and its associated 'thinking out loud' methodology.

The skill-rule-knowledge framework originated from a verbal protocol study of technicians engaged in electronic 'trouble-shooting' (Rasmussen & Jensen, 1974). This tripartite distinction of performance levels has effectively become a market standard within the systems reliability community. The three levels of performance correspond to decreasing levels of familiarity with the environment or task.

3.7.1. Skill-based level

At the *skill-based* level, human performance is governed by stored patterns of preprogrammed instructions represented as analogue structures in a time-space domain. Errors at this level are related to the intrinsic variability of force, space or time coordination.

3.7.2. Rule-based level

The *rule-based* level is applicable to tackling familiar problems in which solutions are governed by stored rules (productions) of the type *if (state) then (diagnosis)* or *if (state) then (remedial action)*. Here, errors are typically associated with the misclassification of situations leading to the application of the wrong rule or with the incorrect recall of procedures.

3.7.3. Knowledge-based level

The *knowledge-based* level level comes into play in novel situations for which actions must be planned on-line, using conscious analytical processes and stored knowledge. Errors at this level arise from resource limitations ('bounded rationality') and incomplete or incorrect knowledge. With increasing expertise, the primary focus of control moves from the knowledge-based towards the skill-based levels; but all three levels can co-exist at any one time.

Rasmussen identified eight stages of decision making (or problem solution): activation, observation, identification, interpretation, evaluation, goal selection, procedure selection and activation. Whereas other decision theorists represent these or comparable stages in a linear fashion, Rasmussen's major contribution has been to chart the shortcuts that human decision makers take in real-life situations. Instead of a straight-line sequence of stages, Rasmussen's model is analogous to a step ladder, with the skill-based activation and execution stages at the bases on either side, and the knowledge-based interpretation and evaluation stages at the top. Intermediate on either side are the rule-based stages (observation, identification, goal selection and procedure selection). Shortcuts may be taken between these various stages, usually in the form of highly efficient but situation-specific *stereotypical reactions*, where the observation of the system state leads automatically to the selection of remedial procedures without the slow and laborious intervention of knowledge-based processing. The 'step-ladder' model also allows for *associative leaps* between any of the decision stages.

3.8. Rouse's 'fuzzy rule' model

Rouse's problem-solving model (Rouse, 1981; Hunt & Rouse, 1984), like Rasmussen's (from which it is partly derived), is based upon a recurrent theme in the psychological literature: "humans, if given the choice, would prefer to act as context-specific pattern recognisers rather than attempting to calculate or optimize" (Rouse, 1981). The model is a product not only of the extraordinary facility with which human memory encodes, stores and subsequently retrieves a virtually limitless set of schematic representations, but also of bounded rationality, 'satisficing', and persistence-forecasting.

The model's indebtedness to GPS is revealed in its assumption that knowledge is stored in a rule-based format (see also J. R. Anderson's, 1983, ACT* framework for cognition). Following Rasmussen (1981), Rouse distinguished two kinds of problem-solving rules: *symptomatic* and *topographic*, each of the form *if (situation) then (action)*. These rules or production systems link two schematic components: a *stored pattern of information* relating to a given problem situation, and a set of *motor programs* appropriate for governing the corrective actions. A rule is implemented when its situational component matches either the actual state of the world or some hypothesized representation of it (a mental model).

The distinction between symptomatic and topographic rules stemmed from Rasmussen's observation of two distinct search strategies adopted by electronic technicians in fault-finding tasks. With a *symptomatic strategy*, identification of the problem is obtained from a match between local system cues and some stored representation of the pattern of indications of that failure state. This, in turn, is frequently bound together in a rule-based form with some appropriate remedial procedure. In a *topographic search* the diagnosis emerges from a series of good/bad judgements relating to the location or sphere of influence of each of the system components. This mode of search depends upon some plan or mental model of the system, which provides knowledge as to where to look for discrepancies between ideal and actual states.

Thus, these two sets of rules differ in two major respects: in their dependency upon situation-specific as opposed to context-free information and in their reliance upon preexisting rules as distinct from rules derived through knowledge-based processing. *Symptom rules* (S-rules) are rapid and relatively effortless in their retrieval and application, since they only require a match between local cues and the situational component of the stored rule. An example of an S-rule for diagnosing a car fault might be: *If (the engine will not start and the starter motor is turning and the battery is strong) then (check the petrol gauge)*. *Topographic rules* (T-rules) need not contain any reference to specific system components, but they demand access to some mental or actual map of the system and a consideration of the structural and functional relationships between its constituent parts. An example might be: *If (the output of X is bad and X depends on Y and Z, and Y is known to be working) then (check Z)*.

The key feature of the model is the assertion that problem solvers *first* attempt to find and apply S-rules *before* attempting the more laborious and resource-consuming search for T-rules. Only when the search for an S-rule has failed will the problem solver seek for an appropriate T-rule.

An extremely attractive aspect of Rouse's model is that it can be expressed and modelled mathematically using fuzzy set theory. For a rule to be selected, four criteria must be satisfied in some degree.

(a) The rule must be recallable (available).

(b) The rule must be applicable to the current situation.

(c) The rule must have some expected utility.

(d) The rule must be simple.

Since, from a human problem-solving perspective, these criteria are not always distinguishable by binary-valued attributes, they are best regarded as constituting fuzzy sets. Hence, each rule must be evaluated according to the possibility of its membership in the fuzzy sets of available, applicable, useful and simple rules. Hunt and Rouse (1984) give the equations governing each rule set. The important point to emphasise is that rule selection is heavily influenced by the frequency and recency of its past successful employment (see also Anderson, 1983).

Hunt and Rouse (1984) have evaluated the model using a simulated fault-diagnosis task. The model was able to match 50 per cent of the human problem solvers' actions exactly, while using the same rules approximately 70 per cent of the time. Of particular interest was the finding that T-rules took, on average, more than twice as long as S-rules to execute. It was also found that removing S-rules brought about a marked degradation in the model's ability to mimic human performance. In addition, it was found necessary to include not only situation-action rules, but also situation-situation rules (i.e., *if (situation) then (situation)*). The latter produced no overt action, but served to update the model's knowledge base.

A qualitative variant of this model has also been used by Donnelly and Jackson (1983) to analyse the causes of eight electrical contact accidents suffered by Canadian linesmen and maintenance crews. Four of these involved errors in rule-based performance, and two involved errors in knowledge-based performance. In three accidents, there were failures in identifying hazard cues, and in two of these three cases short-term memory failures were implicated.

The model incorporates at least two error tendencies: 'place-losing' and 'strong schema capture'. Because of the intrinsically recursive nature of the process, problem solvers need a 'stack' or working memory to keep track of where they have been within the problem space and where they are going next. Since short-term memory is extremely limited in its capacity, there is the strong likelihood that problem solvers will lose items from the 'stack' along the way. This will lead to the omission of necessary steps, the unnecessary repetition of previously executed steps and tangential departures from the desired course.

The second and more predictable potential for error is the inappropriate acceptance of readily available but irrelevant patterns. As will be considered at length in the next chapter, many factors conspire together to facilitate this erroneous acceptance of 'strong-but-wrong' schemata.

3.9. The new connectionism: Parallel distributed processing

All rule-based models assume that human cognition possesses some central processor or working memory through which information must be processed serially. One of the most significant developments of the 1980s has been the appearance of radically different view of the 'architecture' of cognition: one that rejects the need for a central processor and maintains that human memory is organised as a parallel distributed processing system (Hinton & Anderson, 1981; Norman, 1985; McClelland & Rumelhart, 1985; Rumelhart & McClelland, 1986).

Parallel distributed processing (PDP) models are neurologically inspired and posit the existence of a very large number of processing units that are organised into modules. These elements are massively interconnected and interact primarily through the activation and inhibition of one another's activity. Although the processing speed of each unit is relatively slow, the resulting computations are far faster than the fastest of today's computers. As Norman (1985) put it: "Parallel computation means that a sequence that requires millions of cycles in a conventional, serial computer can be done in a few cycles when the mechanism has hundreds of thousands of highly interconnected processors."

One aim of recent PDP models (McClelland & Rumelhart, 1986) has been to resolve a central dilemma in theories of human memory: How does memory represent both the *generalised* (or prototypical) aspects of classes of objects or events and the *specific* features of individual exemplars? Norman (1985) has given an eloquent account of how the PDP modellers tackle this problem.

The PDP approach offers a very distinctive counter-approach [to rule-based or concept-based models]. Basically, here we have an adaptive system, continually trying to configure itself so as to match the arriving data. It works automatically, pre-wired, if you will, to adjust its own parameters so as to accommodate the input presented to it. It is a system that is flexible, yet rigid. That is, although it is always trying to mirror the arriving data, it does so by means of existing knowledge, existing configurations. It never expects to make a perfect match, but instead simply tries to get the best match possible at any time: The better the match, the more stable the system. The system works by storing particular events on top of one another: Aspects of different events co-mingle. The result is that the system automatically acts as if it has formed generalizations of particular instances, even though the system only stores individual instances. Although the system develops neither rules of classification nor generalizations, it *acts* as if it had these rules. It is a system that exhibits intelligence and logic, yet nowhere has explicit rules of intelligence or logic.

Although, as PDP theorists (McClelland & Rumelhart, 1986) concede, this 'headless' view of memory processing (at least in its present form) fails to explain the coherence and 'planfulness' of human cognition, it is extremely good at accounting for the 'graceful degradation' of overstretched human performance, and for the appearance of recurrent error forms. In particular, it can provide credible explanations for the similarity, frequency and confirmation biases considered in detail in later chapters (see also Norman, 1986). As will be seen, the 'spirit' of PDP theorizing, if not the precise 'letter', is a central feature of the computational model of human error production described in Chapter 5.

3.10. Baars's global workspace (GW) model

The *global workspace (GW) model* (most fully described in Baars, 1988) is concerned with explaining the many pairs of apparently similar phenomena that seem to differ only in that one is conscious and the other is not (minimally contrastive pairs). Although the model takes a predominantly 'information-processing' stance, with special attention given to cognitive failures, it also embraces both neurophysiological and clinical evidence.

Human cognition is viewed as a parallel distributed processing system (see Hinton & Anderson, 1981; Rumelhart & McClelland, 1986) made up of a large assembly of specialised processors (or specialists) covering all aspects of mental function. As in the Norman-Shallice model, these processors do not require any central mechanism to exercise executive control over them; each may decide by its own local criteria what is worth processing. But they do need a 'central information exchange' in order to coordinate their activity with regard to various nested goal structures (plans).

This role is fulfilled by the *global workspace*, a 'working memory' that allows specialist processors to interact with each other. Specialists compete for access to the global workspace on the basis of their current activation level. Once there, they can 'broadcast' a message throughout the system to inform, recruit or control other processors. The stable components of a global representation are described as a *context*, so called because they prompt other processors to organize themselves according to these local constraints. Consciousness reflects the current contents of the global workspace. As in other models, GW is closely identified with short-term memory and the limited-capacity components of the cognitive system.

4. Current trends in cognitive theorising

A little over 60 years ago, Charles Spearman felt that he could not achieve a serviceable definition of intelligence until he had first established "the framework of the entire psychology of cognition" (Spearman, 1923, p. 23). Some 40 years later, when cognition reemerged as a major field of psychological enquiry, its leading exponents turned their backs on such large-scale ambitions. Instead, they favoured an abundance of small, data-bound theories yielding specific predictions tailored to the controlled manipulation of well-defined laboratory phenomena. To get ahead in the largely academic cognitive psychology of the 1960s and 1970s, it was necessary to conduct experiments that tested between two or more (but usually two) currently fashionable theories within some well-established paradigm. The product of this pursuit of 'binarism' has been "a highly elaborated base of quantitative data over many diverse phenomena, with many local theories" (Card, Moran & Newell, 1983).

As can be seen from the preceding review, there has been a gradual change in the flavour of cognitive theorising. During the last few years, a small number of cognitive psychologists together with a newer breed styling themselves as cognitive scientists and cognitive engineers have begun producing tentative 'global' performance models which outline, in deliberately general terms, the principal characteristics of the human information-processing system. This development has gone relatively unremarked since, for the most part, these 'broad brush' models have appeared in chapters, books and technical reports, often of an applied nature, rather than in the major psychological journals.

So that global performance models should not be judged by too restricted a view of what makes a 'good' theory, it is worth spelling out some of the major differences in form and purpose between these comprehensive accounts of the cognitive system and the domain-specific models derived from conventional laboratory research (see Table 2.1). For simplicity, I will distinguish them by the terms *framework* and *local* models.

Table 2.1. A comparison of the principal characteristics of local and framework theories.

Local theories	Framework theories
Analyse	Synthesise
Predictive	Descriptive
Refutable	Subject to paradigm shifts.
Emphasise theoretical differences	Focus on agreements between theories
Laboratory-based	Derived from natural history and clinical observations
In the natural science tradition	In the engineering and clinical traditions
Use experimental techniques to establish causal relations	Make extensive naturalistic observations to derive useful working approximations
Research strategy: set up experiments to test between theoretical contenders	Research strategy: design studies to identify the conditions that limit generalisations

At another time or within another discipline, these variations in theoretical style would not need to be discussed, but I am aware that to many experimentalists the 'working approximations' embodied in broad models are of little interest (or worse) because they fail to discriminate between the available theoretical alternatives. Global assertions that could have emerged from a wide range of theoretical positions are unlikely to hold much appeal for those whose skills lie mainly in devising ways of testing between such positions. For them, the fact that many or all current theories could generate a particular assertion makes it vacuous. But it is precisely this consensual aspect that attracts the framework theorist.

For additional commentaries upon the distinctions between local and framework models, the reader is directed to Neisser (1976), Card and colleagues (1983), Broadbent (1984), Reason (1984a), and Norman and Draper (1986). The main point to be made by Table 2.1 is that although broad models have not been fashionable in the 'new' cognitive psychology, they are nevertheless in keeping with a number of honourable psychological traditions. It is also important to remind ourselves that modern psychology is a hybrid pioneered by refugees from many different disciplines with many distinct modes of enquiry. The long-standing dominance of 'binarism' sometimes causes us to feel unnecessarily apologetic about employing other legitimate means of investigating and representing cognition.

5. Conclusion: A working framework for human error

This chapter has tried to show some of the major influences upon the theoretical arguments to be presented later in this book. The review is now concluded, and it is time to take stock. The purpose of this concluding section is to draw out some of the basic assumptions about human cognition that collectively constitute the point of departure for these next few chapters.

Is there such a thing as a 'typical' framework for cognition in the late 1980s? Notwithstanding their differences with regard to structure, processing and representation, many contemporary models contain some important areas of common ground (see also Reason, 1988).

5.1. Control modes

Most frameworks make a distinction, either explicitly or implicitly, between (a) controlled or conscious processing and (b) automatic or unconscious processing. Cognitive activities are guided by a complex interplay between these two modes of cognitive control, which are discussed under the headings of the *attentional* and *schematic* modes.

5.2. Cognitive structures

For the purposes of theorising about error mechanisms it is convenient to distinguish two structural features of human cognition: the workspace or working memory and the knowledge base. The former is identified with the attentional control mode, the latter with the schematic control mode.

5.3. The attentional mode

The attentional control mode – closely identified with working memory and consciousness – is limited, sequential, slow, effortful and difficult to sustain for more than brief periods. It can be thought of as a highly restricted 'workspace' into which selected sensory inputs as well as the products of parallel search processes (carried out by the schematic mode) are delivered, and within which powerful computational operators (subsumed under the general heading of inference) are brought to bear upon a very limited number of discrete informational elements in a largely voluntary and conscious manner.

As the result of the 'work' performed upon them, these discrete informational elements may be transformed, extended or recombined. This 'work' is usually seen as deriving its 'energy' from a strictly finite pool of attentional resources.

These resource limitations confer the important benefit of selectivity, since several high-level activities are potentially available to the conscious 'workspace' at any one time. Operations within this limited workspace are largely freed from the immediate constraints of time and place. Much of this mode's work is concerned with setting future goals, with selecting the means to achieve them, with monitoring progress towards these objectives and with the detection and recovery of errors.

5.4. The schematic control mode

The cognitive system is extremely good at modelling and internalising the useful regularities of the past and then reapplying them whenever their 'calling conditions' are supplied by intentional activity or by the environment. The minutiae of mental life are governed by a vast community of specialised processors (schemata), each an 'expert' on some recurrent aspect of the world, and each operating over brief timespans in response to very specific triggering conditions (activators). This schematic control mode can process familiar information rapidly, in parallel and without conscious effort. There are no known limits to either the number of schemata that may be stored or to the duration of their retention. By itself, however, this schematic mode is relatively ineffective in the face of change.

Each schema may be brought into play by a particular set of environmental signals that match aspects of the knowledge structure's attributes or by 'descriptions' passed on from other task-related processors (see Norman & Bobrow, 1979). Since most human activities proceed roughly according to plan, it must also be assumed that the collective activation of these individual schemata is additionally orchestrated by the outputs from the workspace. It is presumed that schema activation follows automatically upon the receipt of matching 'calling conditions' produced as the result of workspace activity. It is also assumed that where several schemata might be partially matched by this 'top-down' activation, the conflict (posed by the limited capacity of the workspace) is generally resolved in favour of contextually-appropriate, high-frequency knowledge units. For this 'frequency-gambling' to occur, it is necessary that each schema should be tagged according to the approximate frequency of its prior employment (see Hasher & Zacks, 1984).

5.5. Activation

Although their framework model is prototypical in many respects, Schiffrin and Schneider (1977) were clearly wrong in asserting that the long-term store (the knowledge base) contains nodes that "are normally passive and inactive." Many cognitive theorists believe that the only way to explain the appearance of unintended yet perfectly coherent action slips is to assume (a) that specialist processors are not 'switched off' when out of use, but remain in varying states of activation; and (b) that they can receive this activation from sources other than the conscious workspace. Schemata require a certain threshold level of activation to call them into operation. The various sources of this activation can be divided into two broad classes: specific and general activators.

5.5.1. Specific activators

These activators bring a given schema into play at a particular time. Of these, intentional activity is clearly the most important. Plans constitute 'descriptions' of intended actions. For adults, these descriptions usually comprise a set of brief jottings on the mental scratchpad. The more frequently a particular set of actions are performed, the less detailed are the descriptions that need to be provided by the higher levels. But this steady devolution of control to schemata carries a penalty. To change an established routine of action or thought requires a positive intervention by the attentional control mode. The omission of this intervention in moments of preoccupation or distraction is the most common cause of absent-minded slips of action (Reason, 1979).

5.5.2. General activators

These activators provide background activation to schemata, irrespective of the current intentional state. Of these, frequency of prior use is probably the most influential. The more often a particular schema is put to work, the less it requires in the way of intentional activation. Quite often, contextual cueing is all that is needed to trigger it, particularly in very familiar environments. Other factors include recency and features shared with other schemata. It is also clear that emotional factors can play a significant part in activating specific groups of knowledge structures.

The factors involved in the *specification* of cognitive activity will be considered further in Chapter 4. There, it will be argued that error forms arise primarily as the result of *cognitive underspecification*. This can take many different forms, but its consequences are remarkably uniform; the cognitive system tends to default to contextually-appropriate, high-frequency responses. In the next chapter, however, we will look more closely at the issue of *error types*.

3 Performance levels and error types

The purpose of this chapter is to provide a conceptual framework – the *generic error-modelling system (GEMS)* – within which to locate the origins of the basic human error types. This structure is derived in large part from Rasmussen's skill-rule-knowledge classification of human performance (outlined in Chapter 2), and yields three basic error types:

> *skill-based slips (and lapses)*
> *rule-based mistakes*
> *knowledge-based mistakes*

In particular, GEMS seeks to integrate two hitherto distinct areas of error research: (a) *slips and lapses*, in which actions deviate from current intention due to execution failures and/or storage failures (see Reason, 1979, 1984a,b; Reason & Mycielska, 1982; Norman, 1981; Norman & Shallice, 1980); and (b) *mistakes*, in which the actions may run according to plan, but where the plan is inadequate to achieve its desired outcome (Simon, 1957, 1983; Wason & Johnson-Laird, 1972; Rasmussen & Jensen, 1974; Nisbett & Ross, 1980; Rouse, 1981; Hunt & Rouse, 1984; Kahneman, Slovic & Tversky, 1982; Evans, 1983).

The chapter begins by explaining why the simple slips/mistakes distinction (outlined in Chapter 1) is not sufficient to capture all of the basic error types. The evidence demands that mistakes be divided into at least two kinds: *rule-based mistakes* and *knowledge-based mistakes*. The three error types (skill-based slips and lapses, rule-based mistakes and knowledge-based mistakes) may be differentiated by a variety of processing, representational and task-related factors, as discussed in Section 2. Next, the GEMS framework is outlined and the differences in the cognitive origins of the three error types are explained, together with their switching mechanisms. The final part of the chapter looks in more detail at the failure modes possible at each of these levels and what factors may shape the resultant errors.

1. Why the slips-mistakes dichotomy is not enough

The distinction made in Chapter 1 between execution failures (slips and lapses) and planning failures (mistakes) was a useful first approximation, and can be justified on several counts. The dichotomy falls naturally out of the working definition of error; planned actions may fail to achieve their desired outcome *either* because the actions did not go as planned *or* because the plan itself was deficient. It corresponds to meaningful differences in the level of cognitive operation implicated in error production; mistakes occur at the level of intention formation, whereas slips and lapses are associated with failures at the more subordinate levels of action selection, execution and intention storage. As a consequence, mistakes are likely to be more aetiologically complex than slips and lapses.

On this basis, it is tempting to argue that slips and mistakes originate from quite different cognitive mechanisms. Slips could be said to stem from the unintended activation of largely automatic procedural routines (associated primarily with inappropriate attentional monitoring): however, mistakes arise from failures of the higher-order cognitive processes involved in judging the available information, setting objectives and deciding upon the means to achieve them. But if this were true, one would expect slips and mistakes to take quite different forms. And that is not the case. Both slips and mistakes can take *'strong-but-wrong'* forms, where the erroneous behaviour is more in keeping with past practice than the current circumstances demand.

There is also a further difficulty. Certain well-documented errors fall between the simple slip and mistake categories. They possess properties common to both. This problem is illustrated by the following errors committed by nuclear power plant (NPP) operators during five separate emergencies (Kemeny, 1979; Pew, Miller & Feeher, 1981; Woods, 1982; NUREG, 1985; Collier & Davies, 1986; USSR State Committee on the Utilization of Atomic Energy, 1986).

(a) *Oyster Creek* (1979): An operator, intending to close pump discharge valves A and E, inadvertently closed B and C also. All natural circulation to the core area was shut off.

(b) *Davis-Besse* (1985): An operator, wishing to initiate the steam and feedwater rupture control system manually, inadvertently pressed the wrong two buttons on the control panel, and failed to realise the error.

(c) *Oyster Creek* (1979): The operators mistook the annulus level (160.8 inches) for the water level within the shroud. The two levels are usually the same. But on this occasion, the shroud level was only 56 inches above the fuel elements (due to the valve-closing error described above). Although the low water level alarm sounded 3 minutes into the event and continued to sound, the error was not discovered until 30 minutes later.

(d) *Three Mile Island* (1979): The operators did not recognise that the relief valve on the pressurizer was stuck open. The panel display indicated that the relief valve switch was selected closed. They took this to indicate that the valve was shut, even though this switch only activated the opening and shutting mechanism. They did not consider the possibility that this mechanism could have (and actually had) failed independently and that a stuck-open valve could not be revealed by the selector display on the control panel.

(e) *Ginna* (1982): The operators, intending to depressurize the reactor coolant system, used the wrong strategy with regard to the pressure operated relief valve (PORV). They cycled it open and shut, and the valve stuck open on the fourth occasion.

(f) *Chernobyl* (1986): Although a previous operator error had reduced reactor power to well below 10 per cent of maximum, and despite strict safety procedures prohibiting any operation below 20 per cent of maximum power, the combined team of operators and electrical engineers continued with the planned test programme. This and the subsequent violations of safety procedures resulted in a double explosion within the core that breached the containment, releasing a large amount of radioactive material into the atmosphere.

Errors (a) and (b) are clearly slips of action. The intentions were appropriate enough, but the actions were not executed as planned. Similarly, errors (e) and (f) can be categorized fairly unambiguously as mistakes; the operators' actions went as planned, but the plans were inadequate to achieve safe plant conditions. But errors (c) and (d) do not readily fit into either category. They contain some of the elements of mistakes in that they involved improper appraisals of the system state; yet they also show sliplike features in that 'strong-but-wrong' interpretations were selected. These errors can perhaps best be described as arising from the application of inappropriate diagnostic rules, of the kind: *if (situation X prevails) then (system state Y exists)*. In both cases, rules that had proved their worth in the past yielded wrong answers in these extremely unusual emergency conditions.

One way of resolving these problems is to differentiate two kinds of mistake: rule-based mistakes and knowledge-based mistakes. Such a distinction is in accord with the *symptomatic* and *topographic* categories discussed in the previous chapter. It also allows us to identify three distinct error types, each associated with one of the Rasmussen performance levels. These are summarised in Table 3.1, and the grounds for their discrimination are considered in the next section.

2. Distinguishing three error types

The three basic error types may be distinguished along a variety of task, representational and processing dimensions. Different dimensions yield different lines of demarcation; the case for three basic error types can only be made on the basis of the total pattern of distinctions.

Table 3.1. Relating the three basic error types to Rasmussen's
three performance levels.

Performance level	Error type
Skill-based level	Slips and lapses
Rule-based level	RB mistakes
Knowledge-based level	KB mistakes

2.1. Type of activity

A key distinction, based upon Rasmussen's performance levels, is the question of whether or not an individual is engaged in *problem solving* at the time an error occurred. Behaviour at the SB level "represents sensorimotor performance during acts or activities that, after a statement of an intention, take place without conscious control as smooth, automated, and highly integrated patterns of behaviour" (Rasmussen, 1986, p. 100). Although it can also be invoked during problem solving to achieve local goals (since all three levels of performance can, and often do, occur concurrently), such behaviour is primarily a way of dealing with routine and nonproblematic activities in familiar situations.

Both RB and KB performance, on the other hand, are only called into play *after* the individual has become conscious of a problem, that is, the unanticipated occurrence of some externally or internally produced event or observation that demands a deviation from the current plan. In this sense, SB slips generally *precede* the detection of a problem, while RB and KB mistakes arise during *subsequent* attempts to find a solution. Thus, a defining condition for both RB and KB mistakes is an awareness that a problem exists.

2.2. Focus of attention

A necessary condition for the occurrence of a slip of action is the presence of attentional 'capture' associated with either distraction or preoccupation (Reason, 1979, 1984a). This means that wherever else the limited attentional resource is being directed at that moment, it will not be focused on the routine task in hand. But in the case of both RB and KB mistakes, we can be reasonably sure that the limited attentional focus will not have strayed far from some feature of the problem configuration.

2.3. Control mode

Both SB slips and RB mistakes share a predominant mode of control that is absent from KB mistakes. Performance at both the SB and RB levels is characterised by *feedforward control* emanating from stored knowledge structures (motor programs, schemata, rules). Rasmussen summarises this feature of the SB level as follows: "performance is based on feed-forward control and depends upon a very flexible and efficient dynamic internal world model" (Rasmussen, 1986, p. 101). Comparable control mechanisms operate at the RB level: "performance is goal-oriented, but structured by feed-forward control through a stored rule. Very often, the goal is not even explicitly formulated, but is found implicitly in the situation releasing the stored rules. The control is teleologic in the sense that the rule or control is selected from previous successful experiences. The control evolves by the survival of the fittest rule" (Rasmussen, 1986, p. 102).

Control at the KB level, however, is primarily of the *feedback* kind. This is necessary because the problem solver has exhausted his or her stock of stored problem-solving routines, and is forced to work 'on-line', using slow, sequential, laborious and resource-limited conscious processing. The focus of this effortful functional reasoning will be some internalised mental model of the problem space. This proceeds by setting local goals, initiating actions to achieve them, observing the extent to which the actions are successful and then modifying them to minimise the discrepancy between the present position and the desired state. It is, in essence, error-driven.

Another way of characterising these differences is in relation to the cognitive structures identified in Chapter 2. Errors at the SB and RB levels occur while behaviour is under the control of largely automatic units within the knowledge base. KB errors, on the other hand, happen when the individual has 'run out' of applicable problem-solving routines and is forced to resort to attentional processing within the conscious workspace.

2.4. Expertise and the predictability of error types

There is a good deal of evidence (see Sections 4 and 5 of this chapter) to show that at both the SB and the RB levels, errors are likely to take the form of 'strong-but-wrong' routines. At the SB level, the guidance of action tends to be snatched by the most active motor schema in the 'vicinity' of the node at which an attentional check is omitted or mistimed. Similarly, the most probable error at the RB level involves the inappropriate matching of environmental signs to the situational component of well-tried 'troubleshooting' rules. In both cases, the error forms are already available within the individual's stored repertoire of knowledge structures. But the same is not true for errors at the KB level. When the problem space is largely uncharted territory, it is less easy to specify in advance the short-cuts that might be taken in error. Thus, because they arise from a complex interaction between 'bounded rationality' and incomplete or inaccurate mental models, KB mistakes will be less predictable in their forms. At best, it is only possible to forecast the general cognitive and situational factors that will conspire to create KB mistakes.

Mistakes at the KB level have hit-and-miss qualities not dissimilar to the errors of beginners. No matter how expert people are at coping with familiar problems, their performance will begin to approximate that of novices once their repertoire of rules has been exhausted by the demands of a novel situation. The important differences between the novice and the expert are to be found at the SB and RB levels. Expertise consists of having a large stock of appropriate routines to deal with a wide variety of contingencies.

There is considerable evidence (Adelson, 1984) to show that in skilled problem solving, the crucial differences between experts and novices lie in both the level and the complexity of their knowledge representation and rules. In general, experts represent the problem space at a more abstract level than nonexperts. The latter focus more on the surface features of the problem. The classic result on the abstract representations of experts was obtained by Chase and Simon (1973), who demonstrated the marked superiority of chess masters in reconstructing meaningful midgame boards after a 5-second presentation. They found that chess masters' recall clusters frequently consisted of pieces that formed attack or defence configurations. Thus, individual chess pieces were 'chunked' as integral parts of larger meaningful units. Comparable findings have been obtained for master Go players (Reitman, 1976), physicists (Chi, Glaser & Rees, 1981), mathematicians (Lewis, 1981) and computer programmers (Adelson, 1981, 1984).

Experts, then, have a much larger collection of problem-solving rules than novices. They are also formulated at a more abstract level of representation. Taken to an unlikely extreme, this indicates that expertise means never having to resort to the KB mode of problem solving. More realistically, however, it establishes a close relationship between the predictablility of error and the degree of expertise; the more skilled an individual is in carrying out a particular task, the more likely it is that his or her errors will take 'strong-but-wrong' forms at the SB and RB levels of performance.

2.5. The ratio of error to opportunity

Virtually all adult actions, even when directed by knowledge-based processing, have very substantial skill-based and rule-based components. These are the ready-made routines of everyday life. It therefore follows that if one counts the errors made during a particular sequence of actions, the absolute numbers of SB errors and, to a lesser extent, RB errors will greatly exceed those specifically due to KB failures, simply because of the greater involvement of

SB and RB processing in human performance. Viewed in this way, SB and RB errors will be more abundant than KB errors.

This picture reverses, however, if one considers the *relative ratios* of error numbers to opportunities for error at each of the three levels of performance. Skill-based and rule-based processing are the hallmarks of expertise. They are the essence of skilled performance. When expressed as proportions of the total number of opportunities for error at each performance level, we expect that the percentage of errors in the SB and RB modes will be very much smaller than at the KB level of processing, even though their absolute numbers are very much greater.

Consider the task of driving a car. Both the numbers of discrete skill-based actions involved in controlling the vehicle and the individual rule-based decisions needed to negotiate the traffic are several orders of magnitude greater than the number of occasions requiring knowledge-based processing. Of course, these proportions vary widely with the nature of the activity. Some tasks are considerably less routinised than others; but it seems a safe generalisation to assert that all activities are likely to involve greater amounts of SB and RB processing. These are the favoured modes, and the ones at which human beings excel. And skill-based actions are needed for the implementation of any control directive, regardless of whether it comes from a prepackaged problem-solving rule or is the product of effortful on-line processing at the KB level. We will discuss this issue further in the context of error detection (Chapter 6).

2.6. The influence of situational factors

It is further evident from the preceding discussion that errors at each of the three levels will vary in the degree to which they are shaped by both intrinsic (cognitive biases, attentional limitations) and extrinsic factors (the structural characteristics of the task, context effects). In SB slips, the primary error-shaping factors are attentional 'capture' and the 'strength' of the associated action schemata—where 'strength' is, in large measure, determined by the relative frequency of successful execution. All that is required to elicit a 'strong-but-wrong' action sequence is the omission (or misapplication) of an attentional check in circumstances where some departure from previous routine was intended or necessary. For RB mistakes, the story is much the same. It is reasonable to assume that rules too are arranged in an ordered priority list (see Payne, 1982; Anderson, 1983), where the most available production system is also the one whose conditional components are most frequently satisfied by the prevailing state indications. In this case, however, we need to know more about the nature of the task in order to predict which rule an individual is most likely to apply in error. With RB mistakes, it is necessary to understand what other rules could be satisfied, either wholly or partially, by the current situational cues, and for this a detailed knowledge of both the task and the person's training is required.

At the KB level, however, mistakes can take a wide variety of forms, none of which is necessarily predictable on the basis of the individual's past experience and acquired 'knowledge stock'. Of particular importance here is the way in which both the task and other situational variables direct the limited attentional resource to relevant or nonrelevant areas of the problem space (see Payne, 1982). Most evidence relating to activity at this level stresses the extent to which cognitive performance depends upon "seemingly minor changes in tasks" (Einhorn & Hogarth, 1981). This is hardly surprising since, in the absence of suitable preprogramming, performance must of necessity be shaped primarily by extrinsic factors.

2.7. Detectability

The claim that mistakes are harder to detect than slips (see Chapter 1) receives clear support from studies in which experienced nuclear power plant (NPP) operators were exposed to a number of simulated plant failures. Woods (1984) reviewed the data from 99 test scenarios, using 23 crews in 8 different failures (or events). Nearly two-thirds of all errors went undetected. Whereas half of the execution failures (slips and lapses) were detected by the crews themselves, none of the state identification failures (RB and KB mistakes) were discovered by unaided crews. Mistakes were corrected only through the intervention of some external agent. This observation accords closely with what actually occurred during both the Three Mile Island (Kemeny, 1979) and the Oyster Creek (Pew et al., 1981) NPP emergencies.

2.8. Relationship to change

Change in one guise or another is a regular feature of error-producing situations. It will be argued here that each error type differs from the others in its relationship to change.

In SB slips and lapses, the error-triggering changes generally involve a necessary departure from some well-established routine. They may be occasioned either by an intended deviation from normal practice or by an alteration in the physical circumstances in which a routine is customarily executed. In both cases, these variants are usually known about in advance. Two domestic examples will illustrate the point.

Imagine that you have a visitor who has requested tea, while you only drink coffee. You go to the kitchen intending to prepare both coffee and tea, but return with two cups of coffee. The reason for this slip is clear; you failed to make an attentional check on your plan at the point where the initial common pathway, boiling a kettle, branches into its separate tea- and coffee-making components. As a result, you proceeded along the habitual coffee route. Imagine now that you intended to make coffee simply for yourself, but that in the recent past you had reorganised your kitchen so that the coffee was no longer in its accustomed place. You go to the kitchen and begin searching vainly for the coffee jar in its original location. Only then do you remember the changes that you yourself have made.

In one case, the slip arose from a failure to monitor the current intention; in the other, it was due to a failure to recall earlier situational changes in the kitchen. In both instances, however, the actor possessed knowledge of the precise nature of the change in advance and could, in theory at least, have been forewarned of its slip-making potential. The slips arose because knowledge relating to these changes was not accessed at the appropriate time, due almost invariably to attentional 'capture'.

In RB mistakes, the situation is subtly different. Here the nature of the likely changes are, in some degree, anticipated, either as the result of past encounters or because they are considered as likely possibilities by instructors or designers. In either case, some contingency routines for handling these troublesome variations will have been established within the individual's knowledge base or written into his or her operating procedures. What is lacking, however, is adequate knowledge of when such changes will occur and what precise forms they will take.

At the KB level, on the other hand, mistakes result from changes in the world that have neither been prepared for nor anticipated. By definition, errors arise from the fact that the problem solver has encountered a novel situation for which he or she possesses no contingency plans or preprogrammed solutions.

The three error types can therefore be discriminated according to the degree of preparedness that exists prior to the change. At the SB level, the nature and the time of the change are potentially knowable and the actor possesses routines for dealing with them. What is missing is the timely investment of an attentional check to ensure that these alternative routines are called into play. At the RB level, the changes have been anticipated, but the time of their occurrence is not known in advance. Here, the mistake arises from the application of a 'bad' rule or the misapplication of a 'good' rule. At the KB level, however, the encountered change falls outside the scope of prior experience or forethought and has to be dealt with by error-prone 'on-line' reasoning.

A summary of the distinctions made in this section between the three basic error types is given in Table 3.2.

3. A generic error-modelling system (GEMS)

As will become evident, the rule-based and knowledge-based operations of this system owe much to the models of Rasmussen (1986) and Rouse (1981)

Table 3.2. Summarising the distinctions between skill-based, rule-based and knowledge-based errors.

DIMENSION	SKILL-BASED ERRORS	RULE-BASED ERRORS	KNOWLEDGE-BASED ERRORS
TYPE OF ACTIVITY	Routine actions	Problem-solving activities	
FOCUS OF ATTENTION	On something other than the task in hand	Directed at problem-related issues	
CONTROL MODE	Mainly by automatic processors (schemata)	(stored rules)	Limited, conscious processes
PREDICTABILITY OF ERROR TYPES	Largely predictable "strong-but-wrong" errors (actions)	(rules)	Variable
RATIO OF ERROR TO OPPORTUNITY FOR ERROR	Though absolute numbers may be high, these constitute a small proportion of the total number of opportunities for error		Absolute numbers small, but opportunity ratio high
INFLUENCE OF SITUATIONAL FACTORS	Low to moderate; intrinsic factors (frequency of prior use) likely to exert the dominant influence		Extrinsic factors likely to dominate
EASE OF DETECTION	Detection usually fairly rapid and effective	Difficult, and often only achieved through external intervention	
RELATIONSHIP TO CHANGE	Knowledge of change not accessed at proper time	When and how anticipated change will occur unknown	Changes not prepared for or anticipated

that were outlined briefly in the previous chapter. The main difference between GEMS and these earlier models lies in its attempt to present an integrated picture of the error mechanisms operating at all three levels of performance: SB as well as RB and KB. It is, in effect, a composite of two sets of error theories: those of Norman (1981) and Reason and Mycielska (1982) and the General Problem Solver (see Chapter 2) tradition of theorising that has been applied by Rasmussen and Rouse to operator failures in high-risk technologies, most notably in the aircraft and nuclear power industries.

Its operations divide conveniently into two areas: those that *precede* the detection of a problem (the SB level) and those that *follow* it (the RB and KB levels). Errors (slips and lapses) occurring prior to problem detection are seen as being mainly asociated with *monitoring failures*, while those that appear subsequently (RB and KB mistakes) are subsumed under the general heading of *problem-solving failures*. The 'mechanics' of GEMS are summarized in Figure 3.1.

3.1. Monitoring failures

Well-practised actions carried out by skilled individuals in familiar surroundings comprise segments of preprogrammed behavioural sequences interspersed with attentional checks upon progress. These checks involve bringing the higher levels of the cognitive system (the 'workspace') momentarily into the control loop in order to establish (a) whether the actions are running according to plan and (b) more complexly, whether the plan is still adequate to achieve the desired outcome. The former kind of deviation, as has been shown, is detected far more readily than the latter kind.

It is also meaningful to regard routine action sequences as involving a series of nodes or choice points beyond which subsequent actions can take a number of possible routes. Harking back to our earlier example of making a beverage, it can be appreciated that the initial step of boiling a kettle can lead to a variety of outcomes: making tea or coffee, speeding up the cooking of vegetables, making instant soups, filling hot-water bottles, and so forth. For a given individual, these post-nodal routes will vary widely in their frequency and recency of prior employment. In order to ensure that actions are carried out as planned, attentional checks should occur in the region of these choice points, particularly — as we have discussed — when the current intention is *not* to take the most 'popular' post-nodal route.

Naturalistic studies of everyday slips and lapses (Jastrow, 1905; Reason, 1977, 1979, 1984a; Norman, 1981) clearly indicate the dependence of slips and lapses upon failures of attentional checking. For the most part, these involve *inattention*, omitting to make a necessary check. But a significant number of action slips are also due to *overattention*, making an attentional check at an inappropriate point in an automatised action sequence. Both could be termed

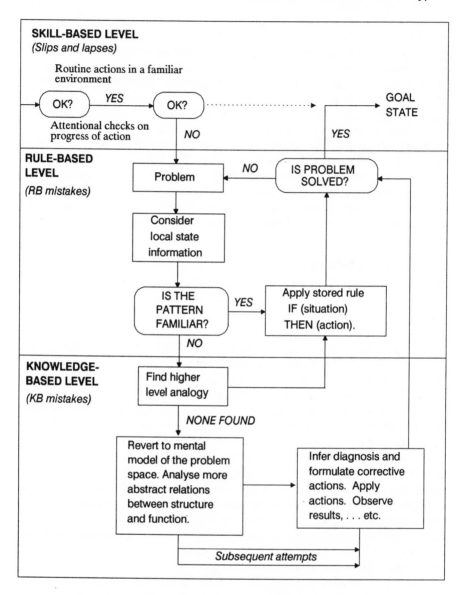

Figure 3.1. Outlining the dynamics of the generic error-modelling system (GEMS).

control mode failures in that errors arise from being in the wrong control mode with respect to the current demands of the task. That is, the higher levels of the cognitive system are running open-loop (in relation to the moment-to-moment control of the actions) when they should have been closed-loop, and conversely. A more detailed consideration of these mechanisms will be given in Section 4.

3.2. Problem-solving failures

As indicated earlier, a problem can be defined as a situation that requires a revision of the currently instantiated programme of action. The schematic mode of control can only operate satisfactorily when the current state of the world conforms to the regularities of the past. The departures from routine demanded by these situations can range from relatively minor contingencies, swiftly dealt with by preestablished corrective procedures, to entirely novel circumstances, requiring new plans and strategies to be derived from first principles.

The problem solving elements of GEMS are based upon a recurrent theme in the psychological literature, namely that "humans, if given a choice, would prefer to act as context-specific pattern recognizers rather than attempting to calculate or optimize" (Rouse, 1981).

The key feature of GEMS is the assertion that, when confronted with a problem, human beings are strongly biased to search for and find a prepackaged solution at the RB level *before* resorting to the far more effortful KB level, even where the latter is demanded at the outset. In relation to Figure 3.1, this means that they are inclined to exit from the decision box (Is the pattern familiar?) along the affirmative route. They do this by matching aspects of the local state information (the problem configuration) to the situational elements of stored problem-handling rules of the kind: *if (situation) then (system state), if (system state) then (remedial action).*

Only when people become aware that successive cycling around this rule-based route is failing to offer a satisfactory solution will the move down to the KB level take place. And even here problem solvers are likely, at least initially, to be using 'workspace' processing to search for cues that remind them of previously successful rules, which could then be adapted to the present situation. As Schank (1982) has pointed out, such analogical 'remindings' stem from an awareness that the current situation shares a common 'deep structure' with something already in memory. He gives as an example the thematic similarities between the 'scripts' of *Romeo and Juliet* and *West Side Story*. At a purely surface level, the differences between the two are enormous: one is set in Renaissance Italy the other is a musical about gang warfare in modern-day New York. Yet both – intentionally – share the same 'deep structure'. To note the similarity between the two, "one must be not only processing the normal complement of scripts and goals. One must also be, in a sense, summarising the overall plot to oneself, because that is where the match occurs" (Schank, 1982, p. 34). Schank (1982, p. 25) explains this phenomenon as follows: "We are reminded of a particular experience because the structures we are using to process the new experience are the same structures we are using to organize memory. We cannot help but pass through the old memories while processing a new input."

Also relevant to this discussion is Shepard's (1964, p. 263) summary of a very large literature on the limitations displayed by human beings when attempting to combine factors in problem solving and decision making:

> At the level of the perceptual analysis of raw sensory inputs, man evinces a remarkable ability to integrate the responses of a vast number of receptive elements according to exceedingly complex nonlinear rules. Yet once the profusion and welter of this raw input has been thus reduced to a set of usefully invariant conceptual objects, properties, and attributes, there is little evidence that they can be juggled and recombined with anything like this facility. On the contrary, the contention that they can belies the obvious disparity between the effortless speed and surety of most perceptual decisions and the painful hesitation and doubt characteristic of these subsequent higher level decisions.

In short, human beings are furious pattern matchers. They are strongly disposed to exploit the parallel and automatic operations of specialized, pre-established processing units: schemata (Bartlett, 1932), frames (Minsky, 1975), scripts (Schank & Abelson, 1977) and memory organizing packets, or MOPs (Schank, 1982). These knowledge structures are capable of simplifying the problem configuration by filling in the gaps left by missing or incomprehensible data on the basis of 'default values'. This, in turn, is derived from the memory system's remarkable ability to keep track of the 'frequency of encounter' of these 'slot' values without conscious effort (see Chapter 5 and Hasher & Zacks, 1984). Higher-level manipulations, however, create 'cognitive strain' (Bruner et al., 1956) and require the slow, laborious, resource-limited involvement of the attentional control mode.

3.3. What determines switching between levels?

3.3.1. Between the SB and RB levels

The SB level of GEMS relates to the performance of highly routinised activities in familiar circumstances. The RB level is engaged when an attentional check upon progress detects a deviation from the planned-for conditions. A primary feature of GEMS is that RB attempts at problem solution will always be tried first. If the deviation is minor and appropriate corrective rules are readily found, this phase will be terminated by a rapid return to the SB level. With more difficult problems, the rule-based cycle (scanning local signs and symptoms, rule implementation and evaluating the outcome) may be repeated several times.

3.3.2. Between the RB and KB levels

According to the simple logic of GEMS, the switch from the RB to the KB level occurs when the problem solver realizes that none of his or her repertoire of rule-based solutions is adequate to cope with the problem. In reality, however, the factors determining this transition are less clear-cut.

In the first place, affective factors are likely to play an important role. Duncan (personal communication) has suggested that the decision to resort to the more effortful KB consideration of structure-function relations will depend upon the complex interaction between subjective uncertainty and concern. Both will increase rapidly as successive rule-based solutions are recognized as being inadequate.

Second, even when this point has been reached, it is likely that the largely unconscious search for analogous problem-solving 'packets' will proceed in parallel with conscious 'topographic' reasoning. The discovery of such an analogy usually brings with it a set of largely preformed remedial possibilities (e.g., *if [it's like situation X] then [I should try action Y]*). A well-understood analogy is likely to entail a set of remedial rules that will switch the focus of activity back to the RB level so long as that particular analogy continues to be entertained. This cycling between the KB and RB levels can be repeated several times as various similarities are explored.

3.3.3. Between the KB and the SB levels

Activity at the KB level can be stopped by finding an adequate (or apparently so) problem solution. This will constitute a new plan of action requiring the execution of a fresh set of SB routines. It is unlikely that this recovery plan will have the integrated or precompiled character of a familiar action sequence. Rather, it will probably comprise routines borrowed from a variety of activities and will require considerable closed-loop control from the conscious workspace to guide these routines. In other words, there will be rapid switching to and from the SB and KB levels until performance is back on some familiar track.

This shift from the KB to the SB level is shown in Figure 3.1 by the affirmative route from the 'Is the problem solved?' decision point. There will be powerful cognitive and affective forces conspiring to encourage the problem solver to accept inadequate or incomplete solutions as being satisfactory at this point.

A plan of action represents a revised theory of the world, and confirmation biases will lead to its continued retention, even in the face of contradictory evidence. Such 'secondary errors' may also be rendered more likely by the reduction in anxiety that accompanies the discovery of an apparent solution.

But once this error is eventually detected (by an OK? check at the SB level), the problem solver will again switch back into the RB mode. By this time, the local state indicators will have changed as a consequence of the previous activity, allowing the possibility of new RB solutions being applied and so on. In this way, the focus of control will shift continuously between the three performance levels.

4. Failure modes at the skill-based level

As indicated earlier, most of the failure modes observed at the SB level (the top level of Fig. 3.1) can be grouped under two headings: *inattention*, omitting to perform the necessary attentional monitoring at critical (OK?) nodes, particularly when the current intention is to deviate from common practice; and *overattention*, making an attentional check at an inappropriate moment during a routine action sequence. Each of these two control-mode failures can take different forms, as discussed below. (To give an overall picture of where the remainder of this chapter is going, the main headings for the failure modes at each of the three levels of performance are listed in Table 3.3.)

4.1. Inattention (omitted checks)

4.1.1. Double-capture slips

Perhaps the commonest consequences of an omitted check (see Reason, 1979; Reason & Mycielska, 1982; Norman, 1981) are various forms of 'double-capture' slips. These are so named because they involve two distinct, though causally related, kinds of capture. First, the greater part of the limited attentional resource is claimed either by some internal preoccupation or by some external distractor at a time when a higher-order intervention (bringing the workspace into the control loop momentarily) is needed to set the action along the currently intended pathway. As a result, the control of action is usurped by the strongest schema leading onwards from that particular point in the sequence.

Such slips are lawful enough to permit reasonably firm predictions regarding when they will occur and what form they will take. The necessary conditions for their occurrence appear to be (a) the performance of some well-practised activity in familiar surroundings, (b) an intention to depart from custom, (c) a departure point beyond which the 'strengths' of the associated action schemata are markedly different, and (d) failure to make an appropriate attentional check. The outcome, generally, is a *strong habit intrusion*, that is, the unintended activation of the strongest (i.e., the most contextually frequent) action schema beyond the choice point.

Some actual examples, obtained in various natural history diary studies (see Reason & Mycielska, 1982; Reason 1984c), are given below.

Table 3.3. Summarising the main headings for the failure
modes at each of the three performance levels.

Skill-based performance

Inattention	*Overattention*
Double-capture slips	Omissions
Omissions following interruptions	Repetitions
Reduced intentionality	Reversals
Perceptual confusions	
Interference errors	

Rule-based performance

Misapplication of good rules	*Application of bad rules*
First exceptions	Encoding deficiencies
Countersigns and nonsigns	Action deficiencies
Informational overload	Wrong rules
Rule strength	Inelegant rules
General rules	Inadvisable rules
Redundancy	
Rigidity	

Knowledge-based performance

Selectivity
Workspace limitations
Out of sight out of mind
Confirmation bias
Overconfidence
Biased reviewing
Illusory correlation
Halo effects
Problems with causality
Problems with complexity
    Problems with delayed feed-back
    Insufficient consideration of processes in time
    Difficulties with exponential developments
    Thinking in causal series not causal nets
    Thematic vagabonding
    Encysting

(a) "I had decided to cut down my sugar consumption and wanted to have my cornflakes without it. But the next morning, however, I sprinkled sugar on my cereal, just as I always do."

(b) "We now have two fridges in our kitchen, and yesterday we moved our food from one to the other. This morning, I repeatedly opened the fridge that we used to have our food in."

(c) "On starting a letter to a friend, I headed the paper with my previous home address instead of my new one."

(d) "I intended to stop on the way to work to buy some shoes, but 'woke up' to find that I had driven right past."

(e) "I brought the milk in to make myself a cup of tea. I had put the cup and saucer out previously. But instead of putting the milk into the cup, I put the bottle straight into the fridge."

(f) "I meant to get my car out, but as I passed through the back porch on the way to the garage, I stopped to put on my wellington boots and gardening jacket as if to work in the garden."

(g) "I have two mirrors on my dressing table. One I use for making up and brushing my hair, the other for inserting and removing my contact lenses. On this occasion, I intended to brush my hair, but sat down in front of the wrong mirror, and removed my contact lenses instead."

(h) "I went to my bedroom to change into something more comfortable for the evening, and the next thing I knew I was getting into my pyjama trousers, as if to go to bed."

(i) "I meant to take off only my shoes, but took my socks off as well."

(j) "I was making shortbread and decided to double the amounts shown in the recipe. I doubled the first ingredient — butter — but then failed to double anything else."

(k) "I decided to make pancakes for tea. Then I remembered we didn't have any lemons, so I decided not to bother. Five minutes later, I started getting together the ingredients for pancakes having completely forgotten my change of mind."

(l) "I was putting cutlery away in the drawer when my wife asked me to leave it out, as she wanted to use it. I heard her, but continued to put the cutlery away."

Examples (a), (b) and (c) are clearly similar. Each involved a change of routine that led to an old-habit intrusion because of a checking omission. Examples (d) and (e) also show clear signs of strong-habit capture during a moment of inattention: but in these cases, the inattention led to a *strong-habit exclusion*, rather than to an intrusion. Examples (f) and (g) are instances of *branch-*

ing errors, in which an initial common action sequence leads to different outcomes, and the attentional check at the choice-point is omitted. Examples (h) and (i) are conceptually very similar except that they involved *overshooting a stop rule* that was not regularly imposed. Slips (j), (k) and (l) share a failure to attend to the need for change at a critical moment. In (j) and (k), this resulted in the unwanted reversion to an earlier plan; whereas in (l), it led to the continuation of an habitual sequence of actions. This last slip is interesting because it reveals something about the actor's attentional state. He clearly heard and remembered his wife's request, but failed to act upon it. This suggests that the wife's request was noted and recorded by the 'fringes' of consciousness, but was not acted upon because the man's focal attention was directed elsewhere.

4.1.2. Omissions associated with interruptions

In some instances, the failure to make an attentional check is compounded by some external event. For example:

(a) "I picked up my coat to go out when the phone rang. I answered it and then went out of the front door without my coat."

(b) "I walked to my bookcase to find the dictionary. In the process of taking it off the shelf, other books fell onto the floor. I put them back and returned to my desk without the dictionary."

(c) "While making tea, I noticed that the tea caddy was empty. I got a fresh packet of tea from the shelf and refilled the caddy. But then I omitted to put the tea in the pot, and poured boiling water into an empty kettle."

Lapses (b) and (c) suggest that secondary corrective routines (rule-based solutions to regularly encountered 'hiccups' in a routine) can get 'counted in' as part of the planned sequence of actions, so that when the rule-based activity is over, the original sequence is picked up at a point one or two steps further along. These have been termed *program counter failures* (Reason & Mycielska, 1982)

4.1.3. Reduced intentionality

It frequently happens that some delay intervenes between the formulation of an intention to do something and the time for this activity to be executed. Unless it is periodically refreshed by attentional checks in the interim, this intention probably will become overlaid by other demands upon the conscious workspace. These failures of prospective memory lead to a common class of slips and lapses that take a wide variety of forms. These include *detached intentions* ("I intended to close the window as it was cold. I closed the cupboard door instead."), *environmental capture* ("I went into my bedroom intending to fetch a book. I took off my rings, looked in the mirror and came out again —

without the book.") and *multiple sidesteps* ("I intended to go to the cupboard under the stairs to turn off the immersion heater. I dried my hands to turn off the switch, but went to the larder instead. After that, I wandered into the living room, looked at the table, went back to the kitchen, and then I remembered my original intention.").

Sometimes these errors take the form of states rather than actions i.e., lapses rather than slips): the *what-am-I-doing-here* experience ("I opened the fridge and stood there looking at its contents, unable to remember what it was I wanted.") and the even more frustrating *I-should-be-doing-something-but-I-can't-remember-what* experience.

4.1.4. Perceptual confusions

The characteristics of these fairly common errors suggest that they occur because the recognition schemata accept as a match for the proper object something that looks like it, is in the expected location or does a similar job. These slips could arise because, in a highly routinised set of actions, it is unnecessary to invest the same amount of attention in the matching process. With relatively unusual or unexpected stimuli, attentional processing brings noncurrent knowledge to bear upon their interpretation. But with oft-repeated tasks, it is likely that the recognition schemata, as well as the action schemata, become automatised to the extent that they accept rough rather than precise approximations to the expected inputs. This degradation of the acceptance criteria is in keeping with 'cognitive economics' and its attendant liberation of attentional capacity.

Thus, perceptual slips commonly take the form of accepting look-alikes for the intended object ("I intended to pick up the milk bottle, but actually reached out for the squash bottle."). A closely-related variety involves pouring or placing something into a similar but unintended receptacle ("I put a piece of dried toast on the cat's dish instead of in the bin." "I began to pour tea into the sugar bowl.").

4.1.5. Interference errors: blends and spoonerisms

Two currently active plans or, within a single plan, two action elements, can become entangled in the struggle to gain control of the effectors. This results in incongruous blends of speech and action ("I had just finished talking on the phone when my secretary ushered in some visitors. I got up from behind the desk and walked to greet them with my hand outstretched saying 'Smith speaking'." "I was just beginning to make tea, when I heard the cat clamouring at the kitchen door to be fed. I opened a tin of cat food and started to spoon the contents into the teapot instead of his bowl.") or in the transposition of actions within the same sequence, producing a behavioural spoonerism ("In a hurried effort to finish the housework and have a bath, I put the plants meant for the lounge in the bedroom and my underwear in the lounge window.").

4. Failure modes at the skill-based level

4.2. Overattention: Mistimed checks

When an attentional check is omitted, the reins of action
likely to be snatched by some contextually appropriate s
schema) or expected pattern (recognition schema). What
vious, however, is that slips can also arise from exactly the opposite p
that is, when focal attention interrogates the progress of an action sequence
at a time when control is best left to the automatic 'pilot'. Any moderately
skilled person who has tried to type or play the piano while concentrating on
the movements of a single finger will know how disruptive this can be.

Making tea is a good example of the kind of activity that is especially susceptible to place-losing errors arising from superfluous checks. This a *test-
wait-test-exit* type of task (see Harris & Wilkins, 1982), in which a series of
largely automatic actions need to be carried out in the right order and where
there are periods of waiting for something to happen: the kettle to boil, the
tea to brew in the pot. It is also an activity in which a quick visual check on
progress does not always provide the right answer.

Consider the situation in which one interrupts some reverie to enquire
where one is in the tea-making sequence. Mistimed checks such as these can
produce at least two kinds of wrong assessment. Either one concludes that the
process is further along than it actually is, and, as a consequence, omits some
necessary step like putting the tea in the pot or switching on the kettle
(omission). Or, one decides that it has not yet reached the point where it actually is and then repeats an action already done, such as setting the kettle to
boil for a second time or trying to pour a second kettle of water into an already
full teapot (repetition). The intriguing thing is that if these checks had not
been made, the automatic tea-making schemata would probably have performed their tasks without a hitch.

A rare but revealing kind of slip can appear in bi-directional sequences. An
inappropriately timed check can cause an action sequence to double back on
itself (reversal), as in the following cases.

(a) "I intended to take off my shoes and put on my slippers. I took my
shoes off and then noticed that a coat had fallen off a hanger. I hung
the coat up and then instead of putting on my slippers, I put my shoes
back on again."

(b) "I got the correct fare out of my purse to give to the bus conductor. A few moments later I put the coins back into the purse before the
conductor had come to collect them."

Like omitted checks, inappropriate monitoring is associated with attentional capture. Mistimed monitoring is most likely to occur immediately following a period of 'absence' from the task in hand. Suspecting that one has
not performed necessary checks in the immediate past can prompt an inop-

rtune interrogation of progress that falls, not at the node, but in the middle of a preprogrammed sequence.

5. Failure modes at the rule-based level

A useful conceptual framework within which to identify the possible modes of failure at the RB level has been provided by Holland, Holyoak, Nisbett and Thagard (1986):

> In assembling a [mental] model of the current situation (often, in fact, a range of models, which are allowed to compete for the right to represent the environment), the [cognitive] system combines existing rules — which are themselves composed of categories and the relations that weld the categories into a structure providing associations and predictions. The assembly of a model, then, is just the simultaneous activation of a relevant set of rules. The categories are specified by the condition parts of the rules; the (synchronic) associations and predictive (diachronic) relations are specified by the action parts of the rules. (Holland et al., 1986, p. 29)

In any given situation, a number of rules may compete for the right to represent the current state of the world. The system is extremely 'parallel' in that many rules may be active simultaneously. Success in this race for instantiation depends upon several factors:

(a) A prerequisite for entering the race at all is that the condition part (the *if* part) of the rule should be *matched* either to salient features of the environment or to the contents of some internally generated message.

(b) Matching alone does not guarantee instantiation; a rule's competitiveness depends critically upon its *strength*, the number of times a rule has performed successfully in the past.

(c) The more *specifically* a rule describes the current situation, the more likely it is to win.

(d) Success depends upon the degree of *support* a competing rule receives from other rules (i.e., the degree of compatibility it has with currently active information).

A central feature of this model concerns the manner in which rules are organised. Models of complex environments comprise a layered set of transition functions that Holland and his co-workers term *quasi-homomorphisms*, or *q-morphisms* for short. In effect, rules are organised into default hierarchies, with the most general or prototypical representations of objects and events given at the top level. These allow approximate descriptions and predictions of the basic recurrences of everyday life, but with many exceptions. Whenever exceptions are encountered, increasingly more specific rules are created at lower levels of the hierarchy. As Holland and his coauthors (1986, p. 36) explain: "Each additional layer in the hierarchy will accommodate additional exceptions while preserving the more global regularities as default expectations." The necessary condition for creating a more specific rule is a failed expectation based upon the instantiation of an overly-general (higher-level) rule. The addition of these more specific rules at lower and lower levels of the hierarchy increases both the complexity and the adaptability of the overall model.

The main reason for selecting this rather than another detailed rule-based framework (e.g., Anderson, 1983) as a basis for the present discussion is because of the close attention that Holland and his colleagues have given to possible failure modes. We will return to their treatment of error mechanisms at various points in this section.

As a first approximation, it is convenient to divide the possible varieties of rule-based errors into two general categories: RB mistakes that arise from the *misapplication of good rules*, and those due to the *application of bad rules*. It should be noted that while much of what follows is consistent with the Holland group's framework, there are some significant departures. These arise in part from differences of emphasis; Holland and his colleagues were primarily concerned with inductive learning, the process by which knowledge is expanded to accommodate changes in the world. Our interest is in the ways in which rule-based operations can go wrong.

5.1. The misapplication of good rules

As used here, a 'good rule' is one with proven utility in a particular situation. However, both the error data and the internal logic of default hierarchies indicate that such rules, though perfectly adequate in certain circumstances, may be misapplied in environmental conditions that share some common features with these appropriate states, but also possess elements demanding a different set of actions.

If one accepts that rules are organised in default hierarchies (with rules for dealing with more prototypical situations towards the top and with successively lower levels comprising rules for coping with increasingly more specific or exceptional circumstances), then there are several factors that conspire to produce the misapplication of higher-level rules, or *strong-but-wrong* rules.

5.1.1. The first exceptions

It is highly likely that on the first occasion an individual encounters a significant exception to a general rule, particularly if that rule has repeatedly shown itself to be reliable in the past, the *strong-but-now-wrong* rule will be applied. It is only through the occurrence of such errors that these 'parent' rules will develop the more specific 'child' rules necessary to cope with the range of situational variations.

A good example of this was the error made by the Oyster Creek operators when they took the water level in the annulus as an indication of the level in the shroud. Nothing in their previous experience had given them any reason to doubt the invariance of this relationship, and they had no knowledge of the prior slip that had caused the dangerous discrepancy on this particular occasion. Nor, for that matter, had the system designers anticipated such a possibility, since they omitted to provide a direct indication of the water level in the shroud. The only thing revealing that the two levels were no longer the same was the insistent ringing of an alarm, indicating that the shroud water level had dropped below a fixed point dangerously close to the top of the core. However, since the operators let this ring for a full half hour before taking appropriate corrective action, they probably interpreted it as a false alarm.

Another more homely example was recently recounted to me by a friend (Beveridge, 1987). He was about to pull out into the traffic flow after having been parked at the side of the road. He checked his wing mirror and saw a small red car approaching. He then made a cursory check on his rear-view mirror (which generally gives a more realistic impression of distance) and noted a small red car still some distance away. He then pulled out from the kerb and was nearly hit by a small red car. There were two of them, one behind the other. He had assumed they were one and the same car. The first car had been positioned so that it was only visible in the wing mirror.

5.1.2. Signs, countersigns and nonsigns

As the Oyster Creek example demonstrates, situations that should invoke exceptions to a more general rule do not necessarily declare themselves in an unambiguous fashion, particularly in complex, dynamic, problem-solving tasks. In these circumstances, there are likely to be at least three kinds of information present:

(a) *Signs*, inputs that satisfy some or all of the conditional aspects of an appropriate rule (using Rasmussen's terminology).

(b) *Countersigns*, inputs that indicate that the more general rule is inapplicable.

(c) *Nonsigns*, inputs which do not relate to any existing rule, but which constitute noise within the pattern recognition system.

The important point to stress is that all three types of input may be present simultaneously within a given informational array. And where countersigns do manage to claim attention, they can be 'argued away', as at Oyster Creek, if they do not accord with the currently instantiated view of the world.

5.1.3. Informational overload

The difficulty of detecting the countersigns is further compounded by the abundance of information confronting the problem solver in most real-life situations (see Billman, 1983). The local state indications almost invariably exceed the cognitive system's ability to apprehend them. Only a limited number will receive adequate processing. And these are likely to match the conditional components of several rules.

5.1.4. Rule strength

The chances of a particular rule gaining victory in the 'race' to provide a description or a prediction for a given problem situation depends critically upon its previous 'form', or the number of times it has achieved a successful outcome in the past. The more victories it has to its credit, the *stronger* will be the rule. And the stronger it is, the more likely it is to win in future races. Some theorists – notably Anderson (1983), though not Holland and coauthors (1986) – allow the possibility of partial matching; a rule may enter the race if some but not all of its conditions are satisfied. This idea of partial matching is the one preferred here, since it allows for a trade-off between the degree of matching and the strength of the rule. The stronger a rule, the less it will require in the way of situational correspondence in order to 'fire'. In other words, the cognitive system is biased to favour strong rather than weak rules whenever the matching conditions are less than perfect.

5.1.5. General rules are likely to be stronger

Implicit in the idea of a default hierarchy is that situations matching higher-level rules will be *stronger* than those lower down by virtue of their greater frequency of encounter in the world. Exceptions are, by definition, exceptional. Although it is possible to imagine situations in which lower-level rules acquire greater strength than higher-level ones, it is more likely that there will be a positive relationship between level and rule strength.

5.1.6. Redundancy

Related to the notion of partial matching is the fact that certain features of the environment will, with experience, become increasingly significant, while others will dwindle in their importance. By the same token, particular elements within the conditional part of a rule will acquire greater *strength* relative to other elements (i.e., they will carry more weight in the matching process). It has long been known that the acquisition of human skills depends critically upon the gradual appreciation of the *redundancy* present in the informational input. Repeated encounters with a given problem configuration allow the experienced troubleshooter to identify certain sequences or groupings of signs that tend to cooccur. Having 'chunked' the problem space, the problem solver learns that truly diagnostic information is contained in certain key signs, the remainder being redundant. An inevitable consequence of this learning process is that some cues will receive far more attention than others, and this deployment bias will favour previously informative signs rather than the rarer countersigns.

5.1.7. Rigidity

Rule usage is subject to intrinsic 'cognitive conservatism'. The most convincing demonstration of the rigidity of rule-bound problem solving was provided by Luchins and Luchins (1950) in their famous Jars Test. There can be little doubt of the robustness of these findings since the data were obtained from over 9,000 adults and children. Luchins was concerned with the blinding effects of past experience and with what happens when a habit "ceases to be a tool discriminantly applied but becomes a procrustean bed to which the situation must conform; when, in a word, instead of the individual mastering the habit, the habit masters the individual" (Luchins & Luchins, 1950).

The Jars Test and comparable techniques revealed a strong and remarkably stubborn tendency towards applying the familiar but cumbersome solution when simpler, more elegant solutions were readily available. This mechanisation of thinking is quick to develop and hard to dislodge. If a rule has been employed successfully in the past, then there is an almost overwhelming tendency to apply it again, even though the circumstances no longer warrant its use. To a person with just a hammer, every problem looks like a nail.

5.1.8. General versus specific rules

On the face of it, these arguments run counter to the claim of Holland and his coauthors (1986, p. 205) that: "People have a preference for using rules at the lowest, most specific hierarchical level; they customarily use rules at higher, more general levels only when no more specific rule provides an answer at a satisfactory level of confidence." But these positions are not so far apart as they might initially appear.

The first thing to appreciate is the difference of emphasis. Holland and coauthors wished to highlight the ease with which people modify their rule structure to cope with novel situations. Our concern is with explaining recurrent error forms.

Another point relates to the kinds of evidence adduced to support these apparently contradictory positions. Holland and his coworkers' case rests primarily upon laboratory studies that reveal that "individuating information, whether diagnostic or nondiagnostic, has substantial power to override default assumptions based on category membership" (p. 219). Our error-related assertions derive, for the most part, from naturalistic observations of problem-solving errors in complex, real-life environments. The difference is a crucial one; in the laboratory, the specific or individuating signs are presented in a way that largely guarantees their reception by the subjects. The same is not necessarily true of the real world.

A possible compromise position is as follows. Let us concede that where the individuating information is detected and where the 'action' consequences do not conflict with much stronger rules at a higher level, then people will operate at the more specific level. However, the conditions prevailing in complex, dynamic problem solving, such as handling an emergency in a nuclear power plant, rarely satisfy these criteria. Countersigns can either be submerged in a torrent of data or else explained away. In addition, there are likely to be substantial differences between the strengths of rules at different levels in the hierarchy. Such marked variations in rule or habit strength are rarely reproducible in the laboratory.

To summarise: several features of human information processing such as bounded rationality, 'conservatism', partial matching, the identification of key signs, explaining away countersigns and strength differences favouring more commonly encountered (unexceptional) problems conspire to yield strong-but-wrong rule selections in real-life situations. It is accepted, however, that more specific rules may be preferred in the relatively uncomplicated world of the psychological laboratory.

In Chapter 4, the cognitive processes implicated in the *underspecification* of rules and other knowledge structures are considered in some detail. Also discussed are the mechanisms by which the knowledge base resolves conflicts between partially matched 'candidates' in favour of contextually-appropriate, high-frequency responses.

5.2. The application of bad rules

It is convenient to divide 'bad rules' into two broad classes: *encoding deficiencies*, in which features of a particular situation are either not encoded at all or are misrepresented in the conditional component of the rule; and *action deficiencies*, in which the action component yields unsuitable, inelegant or inadvisable responses. In each case, we are interested in both the origins of such suboptimal rules and in the means by which they are preserved. Before examining these failure modes, however, it would be instructive to take a developmental perspective on the issue of rule construction.

5.2.1. A developmental perspective

Studies of children's problem solving at various developmental stages provide important insights into the ways in which rule structures develop. Particularly interesting is the somewhat puzzling observation (see Karmiloff-Smith, 1984) that older children are more likely, at least for a period, to make certain rule-based grammatical errors than younger children. A few months after they begin to employ the regular English past tense form, *-ed*, children start making errors with irregular past tense forms that they had previously used correctly. Thus, they say 'goed' and 'breaked', where they had previously said 'went' and 'broke'.

Karmiloff-Smith viewed these and other language errors as indicative of the way children grapple with problems in general. Drawing upon observations of a variety of problem-solving behaviours, she formulated a three-stage, process-orientated framework to describe how children acquire adequate problem-solving routines. A key feature of this theory is the existence of an intermediate phase giving rise to highly predictable error forms.

Phase 1. *Procedural phase*: At an early developmental stage, the behavioural output of the child is primarily data-driven. Actions are shaped mainly by local environmental factors. In Rasmussen's terms, control resides for the most part at the knowledge-based level. The procedures children generate are feedback driven and success-orientated. In effect, the child fashions, 'on-line', a specific rule for each new problem. The result is a largely unorganised mass of problem-solving routines. According to Karmiloff-Smith (1984, p. 6): "The adult observer may interpret the child's behaviour as if it were generated from a single representation, but for the child the behavioural units consist of a sequence of isolated, yet well-functioning procedures which are recomputed afresh for each part of the problem."

Phase 2. *Metaprocedural phase*: So called because at this stage "children work on their earlier procedural representations as problem spaces in their own right." In contrast to Phase 1, environmental features may be disregarded altogether. Behaviour is guided predominantly (though not exclusively) by rather rigid 'top-down' knowledge structures. The child is engaged in organising the one-off procedural rules (acquired in Phase 1) into meaningful categories. Karmiloff-Smith (1984, p. 7) continues: "There is thus a loss of the richness of the phase 1 adaptation to negative feedback but a gain in that the simplified single approach to all problem parts affords a unifying of the isolated procedures of phase 1." One consequence of this inner-directed sorting of specific rules into general categories is that these more global rules are applied overenthusiastically and rigidly, with too little regard for local cues signalling possible exceptions.

Phase 3. *Conceptual phase*: Here, performance is guided by subtle control mechanisms that modulate the interaction between data-driven and top-down processing. A balance is struck between environmental feedback and rule-structures; neither predominates. Like Phase 1 (but unlike Phase 2), performance is relatively error-free. But this success is mediated by quite different knowledge structures. Instead of the mass of piecemeal procedures characteristic of Phase 1, at Phase 3, the child can benefit from the extensive reorganisation that occurred in Phase 2. These new structures can accommodate environmental feedback without jeopardising the overall organisation of the rule-based system.

5.2.2. Encoding deficiencies in rules

(a) *Certain properties of the problem space are not encoded at all.* Siegler (1983) found that 5-year-old children consistently failed at balance-beam problems, even though they understood the importance of the relative magnitudes of the weights on either side of fulcrum. They appeared to be unaware of the significance of the distance of a weight from the fulcrum. This continued even after they had received training designed to focus their attention upon the distance factor. These difficulties were not apparent in a group of 8-year-olds. Since the younger children failed to attend to distance, it could not be encoded and was thus absent from their rules for dealing with the balance-beam problem.

The difficulty in this instance is that 5-year-olds cannot cope with manipulating two relationships at the same time. Adults, of course, do not generally retain these developmental limitations. Nevertheless, there are phases during the acquisition of complex skills when the cognitive demands of some component of the total activity screen out rule sets associated with other, equally-important aspects. At these intermediate levels, the task of learning to drive a car or fly an aeroplane is still managed at the RB and KB levels of performance. It constitutes a set of problems for which the relevant rule structures are either missing or fragmented.

Ellingstadt, Hagen and Kimball (1970) compared the control performance of experienced drivers with two groups of novices, those with fewer than 10 hours' experience and those with more than 10 hours. Experienced drivers showed, as might be expected, very little variability in either of the two main aspects of driving: speed control and steering.

The novices with fewer than 10 hours of driving experience tended to simplify the task of managing the vehicle by virtually ignoring one aspect of it, namely speed control. By 'load-shedding' in this way, they succeeded in keeping their vehicles in the correct lane for about 70 per cent of the test drive. But their speed never rose above a steady crawl.

However, the more experienced novices showed a pattern of performance somewhere midway between the experienced and the very inexperienced drivers. Although they steered the car in much the same way as the inexperienced novices, their speed control was wildly erratic. Sometimes they moved at a snail's pace, while at other times they careered around the track at breakneck speed. At this intermediate level of driving skill, vehicle control would appear to be governed by two competing sets of rules: one for managing speed and the other for direction. Only with continued practice do they become integrated into a single coherent set of control structures. When this integration occurs, vehicle management is focused at the skill-based level. Rule-based activity is primarily concerned with coping with the problems posed by the existence of other road users and with maintaining the desired route.

(b) *Certain properties of the problem space may be encoded inaccurately.* In this case, the feedback necessary to disconfirm bad rules may be misconstrued or absent altogether. Many examples have been provided by recent research on 'intuitive' or 'naive' physics: the erroneous beliefs people hold about the properties of the physical world (Champagne, Klopfer & Anderson, 1980; McCloskey & Kaiser, 1984; Kaiser, McCloskey & Proffitt, 1986; reviewed by Holland et al., 1986).

Intuitive physics pays little heed to Newton's laws of motion: "It is better characterized as Aristotelian, or perhaps as medieval. The central concept of intuitive physics is that of *impetus*" (Holland et al., 1986, p. 209). For example, McCloskey (1983) asked college students to judge the trajectory followed by a ball emerging from a coiled tube after it had been injected there with some force. Two alternatives were offered: one showing the ball following a straight path, the other a curved trajectory. Forty per cent of the students chose the curved path. This wrong choice is entirely in accord with fourteenth-century thinking: "A mover in moving a body impresses on it a certain impetus, a certain power capable of moving this body in the direction in which the mover set it going, whether upwards, downwards, sideways or in a circle" (Buridan, cited in Kaiser et al., 1986).

As Holland and his coauthors point out, one reason why these erroneous rules arise in the first place is that the human visual system is extremely poor at detecting the acceleration of objects: the key to Newtonian physics. On the other hand, people are good at judging velocity: the basis of intuitive physics. Such flawed rules persist because they go largely unpunished. Furthermore, impetus theory provides a reasonably good basis for predicting the motion of objects in conditions of constant friction, which are often encountered in everyday life.

(c) *An erroneous general rule may be protected by the existence of domain-specific exception rules.* This is likely when the problem solver encounters relatively few exceptions to the general rule, as in the case of the impetus-based assumptions of naive physics. In this case, the exception proves the rule. In a social context, similar mechanisms can operate to preserve stereotypes: "the very existence of multitudinous specific-level hypotheses, many of which operate as exceptions to higher-level rules, will serve to protect erroneous stereotypes from disconfirmation. Some of my best friends are . . ." (Holland et al., 1986, p. 222).

5.2.3. Action deficiencies in rules

The action component of a problem-solving rule can be 'bad' in varying degrees. At one extreme, it could be plain wrong. At an intermediate level, it could be clumsy, inelegant or inefficient, but still achieve its aims. Or it could simply be inadvisable; that is, it could lead to the solution of a particular problem in a reasonably efficient or economic fashion, but its repeated use may expose its user to avoidable risks in a potentially hazardous task or environment. Examples of each of these failure modes are considered below.

(a) *Wrong rules.* Some of the best-documented examples of errors arising from the use of wrong rules have been obtained from studies of mathematical procedures (Brown & Burton, 1978; Brown & VanLehn, 1980; Young & O'Shea, 1981). One such study will illustrate their employment.

Young and O'Shea have shown convincingly that most children's errors in subtraction sums arise not from the incorrect recall of number facts, but from applying incorrect strategies. They analysed a corpus of over 1,500 subtractions done by 10-year-olds (Bennett, 1976). Errors were classified into three groups: algorithm errors (36 per cent), pattern errors (16 per cent) and number-fact errors (37 per cent).

The most popular type of algorithmic (or wrong rule) errors revealed a systematic misunderstanding of when 'borrowing' was needed. Some had reversed the rule entirely, borrowing when the subtrahend digit was less than the minuend digit and not borrowing when subtrahend was greater than the minuend. Some children never borrowed; others borrowed when it was not necessary. Many errors involved the zero digit. The most common mistake was of the '0-N = 0' class (e.g., 70-47 = 30), where in the 'two-up-two-down' configuration common to subtraction sums in English children, the seven subtracted from the zero was given as a zero rather than three.

The conclusion drawn from this analysis was that "it is more fruitful to regard the child as faithfully executing a faulty algorithm than as wrongly following a correct one." In short, most of these wrong solutions arise from 'bugs' in the subtraction program.

At the other end of the spectrum were the mistakes made by the Chernobyl operators (Collier & Davies, 1986). One of these in particular suggests the application of a wrong rule. In order to carry out their assigned task of testing a turbine-driven voltage generator that would supply electricity to the emergency core cooling system's (ECCS) pumps for a brief period after an off-site power failure, the operators switched off the ECCS. Later, they increased the water flow through the core threefold. The operators appeared to be working in accordance with the following inferential rule: *if (there is more water flowing through the core) then (the reactor will have a greater safety margin, and hence there will be less risk of requiring ECCS cooling, which would be unavail-*

able). In the dangerously low power regime in which they were then operating, the reverse was actually the case; more water equalled less safety. We will look at this incident in greater detail in Chapter 7.

(b) *Inelegant or clumsy rules*: Many problems afford the possibility of multiple routes to a solution. Some of these are efficient, elegant and direct; others are clumsy, circuitous and occasionally bizarre. In a forgiving environment or in the absence of expert instruction, some of these inelegant solutions become established as part of the rule-based repertoire.

Sometimes these procedures become enshrined at the skill-based level. I have noticed, for instance, that certain elderly British drivers operate their vehicles predominantly in a 'fuel-saving' mode. Raised in a time of economic austerity or fuel rationing, they remain as long as possible in fourth gear, even when their car is labouring painfully. Approaching a traffic light, they will slip into neutral and 'coast' to a halt, unconcerned by the loss of control this entails. To a younger generation, it seems as though they would rather murder the engine than increase its rate of fuel consumption, even when the economies of the past are no longer strictly necessary. Indeed, 'false' economies are prime exemplars of procedures that satisfy certain goals, yet bring even more acute problems in their wake.

(c) *Inadvisable rules*: Here, the rule-based solution may be perfectly adequate to achieve its immediate goal most of the time, but its regular employment can lead, on occasions, to avoidable accidents. The behaviour is not wrong (in the sense that it generally achieves its objective, though it may violate established codes or operating procedures), it does not have to be clumsy or inelegant, nor does it fall into the 'plain crazy' category; it is, in the long run, simply inadvisable.

Quite often, these behaviours arise when an individual or an organisation is required to satisfy discrepant goals, among which the maintenance of safety is often a very feeble contender. Accidents are rare events. For most people, their possibility is fairly remote. And in any case, the needs of safety are often apparently satisfied by the routine observance of certain procedures like wearing a safety belt, carrying out vehicle maintenance, holding regular fire drills and the like. For a driver in a hurry, the dangers of following too close to the vehicle in front are far harder to imagine and much less compelling than the consequences of a missed appointment. To the land-locked directors of Townsend Thoresen, the need to keep their shareholders happy was a more immediate and understandable objective than the safe running of their ferries, whose day-to-day operation they were not qualified to understand. We will explore this notion of conflicting goals further in Chapter 7, which considers what lessons can be learnt from the Chernobyl and Zeebrugge disasters.

A maritime example of inadvisable rule usage was provided by a recent study of avoidance behaviour in qualified watchkeeping officers (Habberley, Shaddick & Taylor, 1986). These observations revealed the very subtle distinctions that can exist between elegant and inadvisable problem solutions. The investigators examined the way experienced ships' officers handled potential collision situations in a nocturnal ship's bridge simulator.

The watch-keeping task was categorised using Rasmussen's performance levels:

> In bridge watchkeeping, the detection and routine plotting of other ships is an example of skill-based performance, not requiring much conscious effort once well learned, and forming a continual part of the task. The watchkeeper uses rule-bases behaviour to manage the large majority of encounters with other ships (not only with reference to the formal Rules, but in accordance with what is customary practice on his ship). It is only in rather exceptional circumstances, such as the very close-quarters situation, that he needs to switch to knowledge-based behaviour, in order to find a safe solution to the problem which has developed. (Habberley, et al., 1986, p. 30)

These performance levels were defined operationally: the transition between SB and RB occurring at the 6-to-8-mile range, and that between SB and KB at the 2-to-3-mile range.

The most surprising finding was the way in which subjects consistently allowed oncoming ships to approach within close range before taking avoiding action. This had little or nothing to do with their inability to detect the approaching vessel, though they showed a tendency to wait until their lights were clearly visible before doing anything. But avoiding action was frequently left until the range was much smaller, "for no apparent reason, and without any sense on the subject's part that this was an error" (Habberley et al., 1986, p. 47).

All watchkeepers are taught to use the available sea-room to stay several miles away from other ships, only coming closer when traffic density makes it unavoidable. In contrast, most of these officers adopted the strategy of coming equally close to other ships regardless of traffic density. Both the advisable and the inadvisable rules have their own logic. The former is founded on the clear fact that closeness is a precursor to collision; while the latter asserts that since closeness is not a sufficient cause for collision, neither is it so in other less crowded conditions.

Despite their employment of the 'close encounter' strategy, these officers showed a high degree of competence in the way they manoeuvred their ships. In only 5 of the 141 test runs was it necessary for the simulator operator to intervene in order to prevent a 'collision' caused by a subject's actions; a serious error rate of just 3.5 per cent. Assuming that 'other ships' had the same error rate, a collision could occur on 0.1 per cent of such close encounters.

In accident avoidance, experience is a mixed blessing. Operators learn their avoidance skills not so much from real accidents as from near-misses. However, Habberley and coauthors (1986, p. 50) note: "if near-accidents usually involve an initial error followed by an error recovery (as marine near-misses seem to do), more may be learned about the technique of successful error recovery than about how the original error might have been avoided. Watch-keepers who become successful shiphandlers may see no reason to avoid close-quarters situations, from which on the basis of their past experience they know that they can extricate themselves."

The confidence these and other experienced operators have in their ability to get themselves out of trouble can maintain inadvisable rule behaviour. This is particularly so when a high value is attached to recovery skills and where the deliberate courting of a moderate degree of risk is seen as a necessary way of keeping these skills sharp.

6. Failure modes at the knowledge-based level

The failures that arise when the problem solver has to resort to computationally-powerful yet slow, serial and effortful 'on-line' reasoning originate from two basic sources: 'bounded rationality' and an incomplete or inaccurate mental model of the problem space. Evidence relating to the former has already been presented in the early sections of Chapter 3. The problems of incomplete knowledge are discussed at length in Chapters 5 and 7. For the moment, we will confine ourselves to listing some of the more obvious 'pathologies' of knowledge-based processing. But first it is necessary to outline the nature of KB processing and to distinguish three different kinds of problem configuration.

A useful image to conjure up when considering the problems of knowledge-based processing is that of a beam of light (the workspace) being directed onto a large screen (the mental representation of the problem space). Aside from the obvious fact that the knowledge represented on the screen may be incomplete and/or inaccurate, the principal difficulties are that the illuminated portion of the screen is very small compared to its total extent, that the information potentially available on the screen is inadequately and inefficiently sampled by the tracking of the light beam and that, in any case, the beam changes direction in a manner that is only partially under the control of its operator. It is repeatedly drawn to certain parts of the screen, while other parts remain in darkness. Nor is it obvious that these favoured portions are necessarily the ones most helpful in finding a problem solution. The beam will be drawn to salient but irrelevant data and to the outputs of activated schema that may or may not bear upon the problem.

It is also helpful to distinguish three main types of problem configuration (see Figure 3.2). A 'problem configuration' is defined as the set of cues, indicators, signs, symptoms and calling conditions that are immediately available to the problem solver and upon which he or she works to find a solution.

Static configurations: These are problems in which the physical characteristics of the problem space remain fixed regardless of the activities of the problem solver. Examples of this problem type are syllogisms, the Wason card test and cannibals-and-missionaries problems. These static configurations may also vary along an abstract-concrete dimension, that is, in the extent to which they are represented to the problem solver in recognisable real-world terms.

Reactive-dynamic configurations: Here, the problem configuration changes as a direct consequence of the problem solver's actions. Examples are jigsaw puzzles, simple assembly tasks, and the Tower of Hanoi. Such problems can also vary along a direct-indirect dimension. At the direct end, the effects of the problem solver's actions are immediately apparent to the problem solver's unaided senses. Indirect problems require additional sensors and displays so that the relevant feedback might reach the problem solver.

Multiple-dynamic configurations: In these problems, the configuration can change both as the result of the problem solver's activities and, spontaneously, due to independent situational or system factors. An important distinction here is between bounded and complex multiple-dynamic problems. In the former, the additional variability arises from limited and known sources (e.g., the other player's moves in a game of chess). In the latter, however, this additional variability can stem from many different sources, some of which may be little understood or anticipated (e.g., coping with nuclear power plant emergencies or managing a national economy).

It is important to recognise that different configurations require different strategies and, as a consequence, elicit different forms of problem-solving pathology. When confronted with a complex multiple-dynamic configuration, it makes some adaptive sense to rely primarily upon the strategy (often seen in NPP emergencies) of 'putting one's head into the data stream and waiting for a recognisable pattern to come along' (see Reason, 1988).

6.1. Selectivity

There is now a wealth of evidence (see Evans, 1983) to show that an important source of reasoning errors lies in the selective processing of task information. Mistakes will occur if attention is given to the wrong features or not given to the right features. Accuracy of reasoning performance is critically depend-

(a) Static

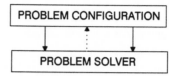

(b) Reactive-dynamic: Feedback

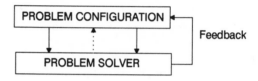

(c) Multiple-dynamic: Feedback + external influences

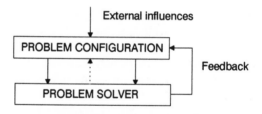

Figure 3.2. Outlining the distinguishing characteristics of the three types of problem configuration. The dashed-line arrow indicates that the problem solver can scan selected aspects of the problem configuration, but it does not produce any physical change in that configuration.

ent upon whether the problem solver's attention is directed to the *logically important* rather than to the *psychologically salient* aspects of the problem configuration.

6.2. Worskpace limitations

Reasoners at the KB level interpret the features of the problem configuration by fitting them into an integrated mental model (Johnson-Laird, 1983). In order to check whether a given inference is valid it is necessary to search for different models of the situation that will explain the available data. This activity of integrating several possible models places a heavy burden upon the finite resources of the conscious workspace. The evidence from a variety of laboratory-based reasoning studies indicates that the workspace operates by a 'first in-first out' principle. Thus, it is easier to recall the premises of a syllogism in the order in which they were first presented than in the reverse order. Similarly, it is easier to formulate a conclusion in which the terms occur in the order in which they entered working memory. Thus, the load or 'cognitive strain' imposed upon the workspace varies critically with the form of problem presentation.

6.3. Out of sight out of mind

The *availability heuristic* (see Kahneman et al., 1982) has two faces. One gives undue weight to facts that come readily to mind. The other ignores that which is not immediately present. For example, Fischhoff and coauthors (1978) presented subjects with various versions of a diagram describing ways in which a car might fail to start. These versions differed in how much of the full diagram had been pruned. When asked to estimate the degree of completeness of these diagrams, the subjects were very insensitive to the missing parts. Even the omission of major, commonly-known components (e.g., the ignition and fuel systems) were barely detected.

6.4. Confirmation bias

This works upon the criteria that allow a current hypothesis to be relinquished in the face of contradictory evidence. Confirmation bias has its roots in what Bartlett (1932) termed *effort after meaning*. In the face of ambiguity, it rapidly favours one available interpretation and is then loath to part with it.

Several studies have shown that preliminary hypotheses formed on the basis of early, relatively impoverished data, interfere with the later interpretation of better, more abundant data (see Greenwald, Pratkanis, Leippe & Baumgardner, 1986). The possible mechanics of this process have been discussed at length elsewhere (see Nisbett & Ross, 1980) and will be considered further in Chapter 5.

6.5. Overconfidence

Problem solvers and planners are likely to be overconfident in evaluating the correctness of their knowledge (Koriat, Lichtenstein & Fischhoff, 1980). They will tend to justify their chosen course of action by focusing on evidence that favours it and by disregarding contradictory signs. This tendency is further compounded by the confirmation bias exerted by a completed plan of action. A plan is not only a set of directions for later action, it is also a theory concerning the future state of the world. It confers order and reduces anxiety. As such, it strongly resists change, even in the face of fresh information that clearly indicates that the planned actions are unlikely to achieve their objective or that the objective itself is unrealistic.

This resistance of the completed plan to modification or abandonment is likely to be greatest under the following conditions:

(a) When the plan is very elaborate, involving the detailed intermeshing of several different action sequences.

(b) When the plan was the product of considerable labour and emotional investment and when its completion was associated with a marked reduction in tension or anxiety (see Festinger, 1954).

(c) When the plan was the product of several people, especially when they comprise small, elite groups (see Janis, 1972).

(d) When the plan has hidden objectives, that is, when it is conceived, either consciously or unconsciously, to satisfy a number of different needs or motives.

6.6. Biased reviewing: the 'check-off' illusion

Even the most complacent problem solver is likely to review his or her planned courses of action at some time prior to their execution. But here again, distortions creep in. One question problem solvers are likely to ask themselves is: 'Have I taken account of all possible factors bearing upon my choice of action?' They will then review their recollections of the problem-solving process to check upon the factors considered. This search will probably reveal what appears to be a satisfactory number; but as Shepard (1964, p. 266) pointed out: "although we remember that at some time or another we have attended to each of the different factors, we fail to notice that it is seldom more than one or two that we consider at any one time." In retrospect, we fail to observe that the conscious workspace was, at any one moment, severely limited in its capacity and that its contents were rapidly changing fragments rather than systematic reviews of the relevant material. We can term this the 'check-off' illusion.

6.7. Illusory correlation

Problem solvers are poor at detecting many types of covariation. Partly, they have little understanding of the logic of covariation, and partly they are disposed to detect covariation only when their theories of the world are likely to predict it (Chapman & Chapman, 1967).

6.8. Halo effects

Problem solvers are subject to the 'halo effect'. That is, they will show a predilection for single orderings (De Soto, 1961) and an aversion to discrepant orderings. They have difficulty in processing independently two separate orderings of the same people or objects. Hence, they reduce these discrepant orderings to a single ordering by merit.

6.9. Problems with causality

Problem solvers tend to oversimplify causality. Because they are guided primarily by the stored recurrences of the past, they will be inclined to underestimate the irregularities of the future. As a consequence, they will plan for fewer contingencies than will actually occur. In addition, causal analysis is markedly influenced by both the *representativeness* and the *availability* heuristics (Tversky & Kahneman, 1974). The former indicates that they are likely to judge causality on the basis of perceived similarity between cause and effect. The latter means that causal explanations of events are at the mercy of arbitrary shifts in the salience of possible explanatory factors. This is also compounded by the belief that a given event can only have one sufficient cause (see Nisbett & Ross, 1980). As indicated in Chapter 3, problem solvers are also likely to suffer from what Fischhoff has called 'creeping determinism' or *hindsight bias*. Knowledge of the outcome of a previous event increases the perceived likelihood of that outcome. This can also lead people to overestimate their ability to influence future events, what Langer (1975) has termed 'the illusion of control'.

6.10. Problems with complexity

6.10.1. The Uppsala DESSY studies

For several years now, Brehmer and his research group (Brehmer, Allard & Lind, 1983; Brehmer, 1987) at the University of Uppsala have used the *dynamic environmental simulation system* (or DESSY for short) to investigate problem solving in realistically complex situations. Much of their work has focused upon a fire-fighting task in which subjects act as a fire chief who obtains information about forest fires from a spotter plane and then deploys his various fire-fighting units to contain them. The complexity arises from the fact that while fires spread exponentially, the means to combat them can only travel in a linear fashion.

To date, they have concentrated primarily upon the effects of two task variables: complexity (the number of fire-fighting units the 'fire chief' has at his disposal, and their relative efficiency) and feedback delay. The results are reasonably clear-cut. So long as the relative efficiency of the units is kept constant, the number deployed at any one time has little effect upon the performance of the 'fire chief'. However, subjects fail to differentiate between the more efficient and less efficient fire-fighting units, even when the former put out fires four times as fast as the latter. They do hold strong beliefs about the efficiency of these units, but they bear virtually no relationship to their actual performance.

The other major finding is that feedback delay has a truly calamitous effect upon the 'fire chief's' performance. Even when the delay is minimal, virtually no improvement occurs with practice. These results indicate that the subjects fail to form any truly predictive model of the situation. Instead (like Karmiloff-Smith's Phase 1 children), they are primarily data-driven. This works well enough when the feedback is immediate, but it is disastrous with any kind of delay, because the subjects lose synchrony with the current situation and are then always lagging behind actual events.

An adaptive response to delayed feedback would be to give more freedom of action to local unit commanders; which the 'fire chiefs' rarely do. Such failures to 'distribute' the decision-making process become even more evident towards the end of the session, when most of the forest has burned down and the fire chief's own base is about to be engulfed. This suggests that the tendency to overcontrol increases as a function of stress, a finding consistent with the work of Doerner and his associates that is discussed below.

6.10.2. The Bamberg *Lohhausen* studies

Like Berndt Brehmer, Dietrich Doerner and his associates (Doerner, 1978; Doerner & Staudel, 1979; Doerner, 1987) at the University of Bamberg have used computer simulations to map out the strengths and weaknesses of human cognition when confronted with complex problem-solving environments. In one series of studies, subjects were given the task of running a small mid-European town (Lohhausen) as mayor. Lohhausen had approximately 3,500 inhabitants, most of whom worked in a municipal factory producing watches. Subjects were able to manipulate several variables: the production and sales policy of the town factory, rates of taxation, jobs for teachers, the number of doctors' practices, housing construction, and so on. A major concern was to document the 'pathologies' exhibited by all subjects initially and by a few persistently. Doerner divided these mistakes into two groups: *primary mistakes*, made by almost all subjects, and the *mistakes of subjects with poor performance*. Primary mistakes included:

(a) *Insufficient consideration of processes in time*: Subjects were more interested in the way things are now than in considering how they had developed over previous years. For example, they concentrated on the amount of money currently in the city treasury without regard for the ups and downs of its previous financial fortunes.

(b) *Difficulties in dealing with exponential development:* Processes that develop exponentially have great significance for systems in either growth or decline, yet subjects appeared to have no intuitive feeling for them. When asked to gauge such processes, they almost invariably underestimated their rate of change and were constantly surprised at their outcomes. This means, for example, that they had virtually no appreciation of what was meant by, say, a 6 per cent annual growth in the number of cars registered to citizens.

(c) *Thinking in causal series instead of in causal nets:* When dealing with complex systems, people have a marked tendency to think in linear sequences. They are sensitive to the main effects of their actions upon the path to an immediate goal, but remain unaware of their side effects upon the remainder of the system. In a highly-interactive, tightly-coupled system, the consequences of actions radiate outwards like ripples in a pool, but people can only 'see' their influences within the narrow sector of their current concern (see also Rasmussen, 1986; Brehmer, 1987).

Among the poor performers, two maladaptive styles were especially noteworthy:

(a) *Thematic vagabonding:* This involves flitting from issue to issue quickly, treating each one superficially. No one theme is pursued to its natural conclusion. In some cases, they pick up topics previously abandoned, apparently forgetting their earlier attempts. Doerner (1987, p. 101) interpreted this as escape behaviour: "Whenever subjects have difficulties dealing with a topic, they leave it alone, so that they don't have to face their own helplessness more than necessary."

(b) *Encysting:* On the surface, this seems to be the exact opposite of vagabonding. Topics are lingered over and small details (e.g., school meals) attended to lovingly. Other more important issues are disregarded. In reality, however, both vagabonding and encysting are mediated by the same underlying tendencies: bounded rationality, a poor self-assessment and a desire to escape from the evidence of one's own inadequacy.

Of particular interest was the way subjects behaved when things went badly wrong. Critical situations provoked what Doerner has termed an *intellectual emergency reaction*, geared to produce rapid responses. Overall, this could be characterised as a reduction in intellectual level: thinking reduces to reflexive behaviour. There is a marked diminution in phases of self-reflection in which subjects pause to evaluate their progress and previous actions. Planful thinking degrades into the production of disconnected and increasingly stereotyped actions.

The experience of repeated failure on the part of poor performers brings with it a further set of 'pathologies'. They take greater risks, apparently driven by the need to master the situation at any price. There is a marked increase in their willingness to bend the rules: whether a particular course of action involves violating some acceptable practice becomes subordinate to the achievement of the immediate goal. Their hypotheses become increasingly more global in character: all phenomena are attributed to a single cause. Doerner (1987, p. 107) states: "Such reductive hypotheses are very attractive for the simple reason that they reduce insecurity with one stroke and encourage the feeling that things are understood."

Confirmation biases become more marked with the experience of failure. In the beginning of the test run, all subjects looked for confirming rather than disconfirming evidence. Later, however, the good subjects would adopt strategies designed to provoke the refutation of their current hypotheses. Poor subjects, on the other hand, grew increasingly more single-minded in their search for confirmation.

6.11. Problems of diagnosis in everyday situations

In a recent and highly ingenious set of studies, Groenewegen and Wagenaar (1988) investigated people's ability to diagnose problems in real-life situations at the knowledge-based level of performance. The subjects were asked to perform two kinds of task: they diagnosed what had gone wrong in some everyday problem situation or they identified the symptoms for which some explanation was needed.

A number of recurrent difficulties were observed. People were not at all good at the diagnosis task. On their first attempts, only 28 per cent of the subjects produced complete diagnoses. The major difficulty appeared to lie in the identification of symptoms rather than in the ability to generate plausible event scenarios. Part of the trouble arose from people's efforts to search for symptoms and to create possible event scenarios at the same time. They identify a few symptoms and then use these as a basis for generating explanatory stories. In so doing, they are frequently unaware that some of the symptoms they have incorporated into their scenarios do not require an explanation. The process is one of continual interchange between observed symptoms and story elements and the two become increasingly confused.

Groenewegen and Wagenaar reasoned that if the initial symptom identification was the main problem, diagnoses should be significantly improved by providing support for the diagnostic phase of the task. They did this in two ways. In one case, they gave subjects a list of the relevant symptoms. This increased the number of correct diagnoses from 28 to 48 per cent. The second type of support involved directed questions that forced people to make explicit how their initial diagnoses explained the symptoms supplied by the experimenters. Inducing this 'active verification' frame of mind increased the number of correct diagnoses to 69 per cent. Those who were not helped by this type of support failed to see that their diagnoses conflicted with the facts of the situation, originally described.

The root of the problem in everyday diagnoses appears to be located in the complex interaction between two logical reasoning tasks. One serves to identify critical symptoms and those factual elements of the presented situation needing an explanation. The other is concerned with verifying whether the symptoms have been explained and whether the supplied situational factors are compatible with the favoured explanatory scenario. Difficulties arise not because people lack the necessary creativity to generate scenarios, they can do this well enough, but because they fail to apply strictly logical thinking to both the initial facts and to the products of scenario generation. This, as we have seen earlier, is a familiar theme in accounts of knowledge-based processing.

7. Summary and conclusions

This chapter began by presenting evidence for the existence of three basic error types: skill-based slips and lapses, rule-based mistakes and knowledge-based mistakes. It was argued that these could be variously differentiated along several dimensions: type of activity, focus of attention, predominant control mode, predictability, relative abundance, the influence of situational factors, detectability, mode of error detection and relationship to change.

The possible origins of these basic error types were then located within the Generic Error Modelling System, or GEMS. Errors at the skill-based level were attributed mainly to *monitoring* failures. Most usually, these involved inattention: the omission of a high-level check upon behaviour at some critical point beyond which routine actions branched towards a number of possible end states. The failure to bring the conscious workspace 'into the loop' at these critical points generally causes actions to run, by default, along the most frequently travelled route when the current intention was otherwise. Slips and lapses also arise from overattention: when a high-level enquiry is made as to the progress of an ongoing action sequence, and the current position is assessed as either being further along or not as far as it actually is.

Mistakes at the rule-based and knowledge-based levels are associated with problem solving. A key feature of GEMS is the assertion that problem solvers always confront an unplanned-for change by *first* establishing (often at a largely automatic pattern-matching level) whether or not the local indications have been encountered before. If the pattern is recognised – and there are powerful forces at work to establish some kind of match – a previously established *if (condition) then (action)* rule-based solution is applied. Only when this relatively effortless pattern-matching and rule-applying procedure fails to provide an adequate solution will they move to the more laborious mode of making inferences from knowledge-based mental models of the problem space and, from these, go on to formulate and try out various remedial possibilities.

It was argued that rule-based mistakes fell into two broad categories: those associated with the *misapplication of good rules* (i.e., rules of proven worth) and those due to the *application of bad rules*. In the case of the former, several factors conspire to yield *strong-but-wrong* rules: exceptions to general rules are truly exceptional, countersigns may be missed in a mass of incoming data or explained away and higher-level, more general rules will be stronger than more specific ones. Bad rules, on the other hand, can arise from encoding difficulties or from deficiencies in the action component. The latter were considered under three headings: wrong rules, inelegant or clumsy rules and inadvisable rules.

Knowledge-based mistakes have their roots in two aspects of human cognition: bounded rationality and the fact that knowledge relevant to the problem space is nearly always incomplete and often inaccurate. Several specific 'pathologies' associated with knowledge-based problem solving were then considered: selecting the wrong features of the problem space, being insensitive to the absence of relevant elements, confirmation bias, overconfidence, biased reviewing of plan construction, illusory correlation, halo effects, and problems with causality, with complexity and with diagnosis in everyday life.

By now, we have reviewed a wide variety of data relating to the more systematic varieties of human error. We have also attempted to integrate the basic error types within a broad theoretical framework, the generic error-modelling system. In the next chapter, we will examine in more detail how cognitive operations are specified and why it is that various forms of *under-specification* lead to contextually-appropriate, high-frequency error forms. In particular, we will seek to link the widespread occurrence of these forms to the 'computational primitives' of the cognitive system: *similarity-matching* and *frequency-gambling*.

4 Cognitive underspecification and error forms

In Chapter 1, a distinction was made between error types and error forms. *Error types* are differentiated according to the performance levels at which they occur. *Error forms*, on the other hand, are pervasive varieties of fallibility that are evident at all performance levels. Their ubiquity indicates that they are rooted in universal processes that influence the entire spectrum of cognitive activities.

The view advanced in this chapter is that error forms are shaped primarily by two factors: similarity and frequency. These, in turn, have their origins in the automatic retrieval processes — *similarity-matching* and *frequency-gambling* — by which knowledge structures are located and their products delivered to consciousness (thoughts, words, images, etc.) or to the outside world (action, speech or gesture). It is also argued that the more cognitive operations are in some way underspecified, the more likely it is that error forms will be shaped by the frequency-gambling heuristic.

If the study of human error is to make a useful contribution to the safety and efficiency of hazardous technologies, it must be able to offer their designers and operators some workable generalizations regarding the information-handling properties of a system's human participants (see Card, Moran & Newell, 1983). This chapter explores the generality of one such approximation:

When cognitive operations are underspecified, they tend to default to contextually appropriate, high-frequency responses.

Exactly what information is missing from a sufficient specification, or which controlling agency fails to provide it, will vary with the nature of the cognitive activity being performed. The crucial point is that notwithstanding these possible varieties of underspecification, their consequences are remarkably uniform: what emerge are perceptions, words, recollections, thoughts and actions that recognisably belong to an individual's well-established repertoire for a given situation. Or, to put it another way, the more often a cognitive routine achieves a successful outcome in relation to a particular context, the more likely it is to reappear in conditions of incomplete specification.

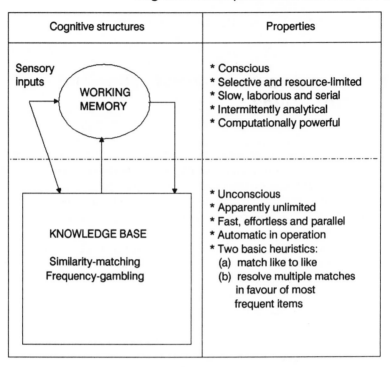

Cognitive structures	Properties
Sensory inputs WORKING MEMORY	* Conscious * Selective and resource-limited * Slow, laborious and serial * Intermittently analytical * Computationally powerful
KNOWLEDGE BASE Similarity-matching Frequency-gambling	* Unconscious * Apparently unlimited * Fast, effortless and parallel * Automatic in operation * Two basic heuristics: (a) match like to like (b) resolve multiple matches in favour of most frequent items

Figure 4.1. The two modes of cognitive control: attentional control associated with working memory (or the conscious workspace) and schematic control derived from the knowledge base (long-term memory).

Frequency biasing gives predictable shape to human errors in a wide variety of activities and situations (see Norman, 1981; Reason & Mycielska, 1982; Rasmussen, 1982). The psychological literature is replete with terms to describe this pervasive error form: 'conventionalization' (Bartlett, 1932), 'sophisticated guessing' (Solomon & Postman, 1952), 'fragment theory' (Neisser, 1967), 'response bias' (Broadbent, 1967), 'strong associate substitution' (Chapman & Chapman, 1973), 'inert stereotype' (Luria, 1973), 'banalization' (Timpanaro, 1976), 'strong habit intrusions' (Reason, 1979) and 'capture errors' (Norman, 1981). But irrespective of whether or not the consequences are erroneous, this tendency to 'gamble' in favour of high-frequency alternatives when control statements are imprecise is generally an adaptive strategy for dealing with a world that contains a great deal of regularity as well as a large measure of uncertainty.

1. The specification of mental operations

Correct performance in any sphere of mental activity is achieved by activating the right schemata in the right order at the right time. Cognitive processes receive their guidance from a complex interaction between the conscious workspace and the schematic knowledge base, as summarised in Figure 4.1 (see also Chapter 2). The former specifies the strategic direction and redirection of action (both internal and external), while the latter provides the fine-grained tactical control.

Schemata require a certain threshold level of activation to call them into operation. The various sources of this activation can be divided into two broad classes: specific and general activators (see Figure 4.2).

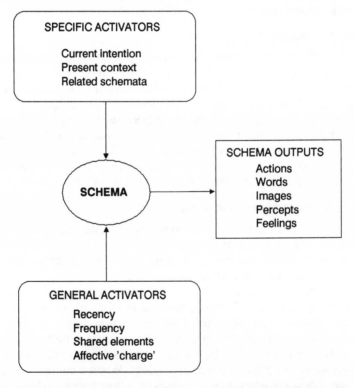

Figure 4.2. The combined influence of specific and general schema activators. Schemata are brought into play by both sets of activators, but only the specific activators are directly related to the current intention.

1.1. Specific activators

Specific activators bring a given schema into play at a particular time. Of these, intentional activity is clearly the most important. Plans constitute 'descriptions' of intended actions. For adults, these descriptions usually comprise a set of brief jottings on the mental scratchpad (e.g., "Go to the post office and buy some stamps."). There is no need to fill in the 'small print' of each detailed operation; these low-level control statements are already present within the constituent schemata. The more frequently a particular set of actions is performed, the less detailed are the descriptions that need to be provided by the higher levels. But this steady devolution of control to schemata carries a penalty. To change an established routine of action or thought requires a positive intervention by the attentional control mode. The omission of this intervention in moments of preoccupation or distraction is the most common cause of absent-minded slips of action (see Chapter 3).

1.2. General activators

A number of general factors provide background activation to schemata irrespective of the current intentional state or context: recency, frequency, attributes shared with other schemata and emotional or motivational factors (see Norman & Shallice, 1980; Reason 1984a). Of these, frequency of prior use is probably the most influential. The more often a particular schema is put to work, the less it requires in the way of intentional activation. Quite often, contextual cueing is all that is needed to trigger it, particularly in very familiar environments. The issue of priming by active schemata possessing common elements will be considered in detail in Section 1.4.

1.3. Specifications are context-dependent

As Bobrow and Norman (1975, p. 133) pointed out, descriptions are context-dependent. "We suggest that descriptions are normally formed to be unambiguous within the context in which they were first used. That is, a description defines a memory schema relative to a context."

Even the most ill-formed or high-flown intention must boil down to a selection of ways and means if it is to be considered at all seriously. Sooner or later, the planner must move down the abstraction hierarchy (Rasmussen, 1984) from a vague statement of some desired future state to a detailed review of possible resources and situations. And as soon as that occurs, the intentional activity becomes context-dependent. When a context is identified, the range of possible schema candidates is greatly restricted. Whenever a person moves from one physical location to another, either in action or in thought, the schemata within the contextual frame change accordingly. Comparatively little in the way of additional specification is needed to retrieve the appropriate schemata once this contextual frame has been established.

Each schema was originally acquired in relation to a particular context. That contextual information forms an intrinsic part of the schema's 'knowledge package'. Any subsequent encounter with that context will raise the schema's level of activation; thus, another way of looking at the idea of a contextual frame is as a cognate set of currently active schemata.

While individual schemata are 'context-dependent', the cognitive system as a whole is not 'context-bound'. As indicated earlier, one of the central properties of the attentional control mode is its power to transcend these immediate contextual constraints. But this demands processing resources that are not always available.

1.4. Contexts are semantic as well as physical locations

The idea of a semantic context is not novel. The notion was clearly expressed by Hotopf (1980) in his analysis of whole-word slips of the tongue:

> If the word we intend to speak is highly associated with another word that meets the contextual constraints operating within the utterance, then, given a certain time limit, that other word may be produced instead. The error word needs to be a word of high frequency or one whose threshold for production is lowered by other events occurring at the same time for it to have the necessary short latency in response. (Hotopf, 1980, p. 106)

Some recent studies (Reason & Mackintosh, 1986), using phonological priming to manipulate 'thresholds of production', also provide strong evidence for the existence of semantic contextual constraints, at least in one rather specific verbal domain. As is well known to children, same-sound priming can be a very effective way of tricking people into producing what is immediately recognised as the wrong answer to a simple question. The example investigated was that described by Kimble and Perlmuter (1970):

Q. What do we call the tree that grows from acorns?

A. Oak.

Q. What do we call a funny story?

A. Joke.

Q. What sound does a frog make?

A. Croak.

Q. What is another word for cape?

A. Cloak.

Q. What do you call the white of an egg?

A. Yolk (sic!).

In the first of three very simple studies, we investigated the effects of varying the number of 'oak-yolk' primes upon the naming of the white of an egg (Reason & Mackintosh, 1986). A total of 80 subjects were used in the first study, divided into four groups of 20 subjects. Each subject was questioned individually, and no testing session lasted more than about 3 minutes. To establish a baseline, one group was simply asked the key question: "What do you call the white of an egg?" (zero primes). The remaining groups received either one, three or five 'oak-yolk' primes (selected randomly from the set of primes listed above) before being asked to name the white of an egg. Subjects were instructed to respond as quickly as possible with the first word that came to mind, and that single word answers were needed throughout.

The results confirmed the potency of the 'oak-yolk' priming effect, and showed that erroneous 'yolk' answers increased with the number of prior rhyme primes. The frequency of the primes, as well as the presence of common phonological elements, clearly played an important part in determining the likelihood of a 'yolk' response. This is in general agreement with the schema-activating assumptions shown in Figure 4.2.

Now that we have shown that the effects of phonological priming were incremental, at least within the 'oak-yolk' game, the next question concerns the selectivity of this priming. Was it restricted to a particular semantic subdomain, such as the contents of the egg, or could it spread to other parts of the 'egg' semantic context? An egg could be regarded as having several semantic subdomains. Only two, however, are of interest here: that relating to the contents (yolk, white, albumen) and that relating to the exterior (shell).

In the second study, involving three groups of 20 students, subjects received either three, five, or seven 'shell' primes, and were asked the same key question ("What do you call the white of an egg?"). These primes consisted of a series of simple questions eliciting monosyllabic answers rhyming with 'shell' (e.g., "What rings in a belfry and on a bicycle?", "From where did people once draw water?", "The Swiss folk hero that shot an apple off his son's head was called William . . . ?")

The most important finding was that only 2 of the 60 subjects produced an erroneous, priming-induced, 'shell' response to the key question, despite the fact that 'shell' is almost as strongly associated with 'egg' as 'yolk' (Palermo & Jenkins, 1962; Rubin, 1983). These findings are consistent with the notion that the phonological priming effects were confined to the 'egg contents' subdomain (as directed by the semantics of the key question).

An alternative way of testing the relative impermeability of the contextual frame was to prime 'yolk' and then direct the semantics of the key question not to the white of an egg, but to the outside of an egg. In the third study, two groups of ten students were used. One group was simply asked the question: "What do you call the outside of an egg?" The other group was asked the same question after first receiving five 'oak-yolk' primes. The results were very clear-cut. All the subjects in both groups produced the correct 'shell' answer. Taken as a whole, the results of these three studies provided a clear demonstration of (a) the incremental potency of phonological or 'shared-element' priming within the appropriate semantic context and (b) the relative absence of any 'spillover' of these priming effects from one contextual frame to another. This suggests that although prior priming may initially activate all words in the mental lexicon sharing the same phonetic and structural characteristics, these effects are only 'delivered' to a very specific semantic context by the final key question. This is also borne out out by the absence of any interference from one priming question to the next: each addressed a different semantic context, and none had any high-frequency competitors sharing common elements.

2. Similarity and frequency: Cognitive 'primitives'

Such fundamental aspects of experience as the degree of likeness between events or objects and their frequency of prior occurrence have been termed intuitive concepts. Similarity and frequency information appear to be processed automatically without conscious effort, or perhaps even without awareness, regardless of age, ability, cultural background, motivation or task instructions (see Wason & Johnson-Laird, 1972; Schweder, 1977; Tulving, 1983; Hasher & Zacks, 1984). There is a strong case for regarding them as being the computational 'primitives' of the cognitive system. This argument will be developed further in Chapter 5.

3. Demonstrations of underspecification

3.1. Word identification

The large volume of literature dealing with the recognition of words presented for very brief durations or in noise has been discussed elsewhere (see Howes & Solomon, 1951; Solomon & Postman, 1952; Pollack, Rubinstein & Decker, 1960; Savin, 1963; Spence, 1963; Newbigging, 1961; Neisser, 1967; Broadbent, 1967; Catlin, 1969; Nakatani, 1973). A number of theories have been advanced to explain the *word frequency effect*, the repeated finding that common words are more readily recognised than infrequent ones when presentation is rapid or attenuated. Newbigging (1961) has provided a useful summary statement: "When a word is presented at a short duration, only a few letters or a fragment of the word is seen by the subject. This fragment may be common to a number of words, and if the subject is instructed to guess the word presented he will respond with the word of the greatest frequency of occurrence (response strength) which incorporates the fragment" (quoted by Neisser, 1967; see also Neisser's discussion of 'fragment theory', pp. 115-118).

An important corollary to this view is that seen fragments of low-frequency words are prone to being erroneously perceived as high-frequency words sharing the same features (Broadbent, 1967). Both are in keeping with the cognitive underspecification generalization.

3.2. The recall of verbal list items

The word frequency effect also appears in the recall of word lists. Commonly occurring words tend to have a higher probability of recall than less frequent words. Likewise, high-frequency words are more common as intrusions when the subject is attempting to recall a previously presented list. (see Gregg, 1976, for an excellent review of this and the related 'frequency paradox' literature).

3.3. Category generation

In continuous recall tasks, the only specification offered to subjects is the name of a semantic category, whereupon they are asked to generate as many exemplars as they can without repetition. Beginning with Bousfield and Barclay (1950), several investigators have found substantial correlations between the dominance of a particular item (the number of times a given exemplar is generated by a group of individuals) and its average position in the output order. The most popular exemplars appear earliest. In the case of Bousfield and Barclay's categories, these correlations ranged between 0.97 and 0.88. In a later study involving 56 semantic categories, Battig and Montague (1969) obtained dominance/output order correlations (for the Maryland sample, $N = 270$) ranging between 0.252 and 0.857. When these correlations are averaged using Fisher's z-transformations, the mean dominance-order correlation is 0.64. When the same correlations are computed for only the 20 most dominant types in each category, this mean value rises to 0.76. Such findings are in keeping with the predictions of the 'spew hypothesis' (Underwood & Schulz, 1960), of Zipf's Law (Zipf, 1945, 1949) and of Hull's habit strength postulate (see Bousfield & Barclay, 1950).

The dominance of a particular exemplar within a semantic context (e.g., dog, within the category 'four-footed animals') reflects its 'salience-in-the-world' for that particular subculture. This, in turn, is likely to correspond to its frequency of encounter by the subculture as a whole. The dominance orders of categories whose types are subject to the influences of fashion or location will vary according to time and place. Thus, when American college students of a generation ago were asked to produce exemplars of 'a type of dance', the first seven types in the dominance order were: waltz, frug, twist, fox-trot, cha-cha, monkey and jerk (Battig & Montague, 1969). It is doubtful whether many, or even any, of these types would appear high in a contemporary listing. The dominance-orders of other categories (e.g., precious stones, units of time, relatives, metals, etc.), being universals, are extremely stable across groups within the same broad culture.

In a recent category generation study carried out in our laboratory, the relationship between output order and frequency of encounter was assessed directly, rather than via dominance assumptions. Different groups of undergraduates were each asked to produce up to 20 exemplars of nine categories, varying in their degree of search specification. The data were collected in individual interviews, lasting about 30 minutes. After they had generated their items, subjects were asked to make metacognitive ratings, on a scale of one to seven, of the following features of each exemplar (fed back to them in random order): recency of encounter, frequency of encounter, feeling of knowing about the item, strength of affect and effort required to elicit the item. The average correlations with output order (computed across all nine categories using Fisher's z-transforms) were: -0.70 for recency, -0.73 for frequency of encounter, -0.66 for feeling of knowing, -0.55 for strength of affect and + 0.87 for effort. Negative correlations indicated that the most highly rated items were generated soonest.

This pattern of correlations clearly indicates that items produced early in the output sequence are judged as more recent, more frequent, more known about and more affectively 'charged' than those produced later. In general, these data provide strong support for the assertion that underspecification causes the most activated schema to be called to mind first. Although these correlations do not provide unambiguous evidence for the primacy of frequency, it is not unreasonable to assume that factors like recency, knowledge and affective tone depend heavily upon the number of times a particular item has been encountered in the past (see also Matlin, Stang, Gawron, Steedman & Derby, 1979).

3.4. Recurrent intrusions in blocked memory searches

Freud (1901) noted that when we are laboriously searching memory for a known name or word whose retrieval is temporarily blocked (the target), other items, "although immediately recognised as false, nevertheless obtrude themseves with great tenacity." This observation provoked Reason and Lucas (1984a) to test the hypothesis that these 'recurrent intruders' in tip-of-the-tongue states (TOTs) were analogous to the strong habit intrusions observed in action slips.

Sixteen volunteers kept diaries of their TOT states over a period of four weeks. For each resolved TOT, they were required to make a set of standardised ratings. The study yielded data for 40 TOTs. Twenty-eight of these (70 per cent) involved the presence of recurrent intruders: recognisably wrong names or words that continued to block access to the target during deliberate search periods.

These recurrent intruders were judged by the diarists as being more frequently and recently used than both the related targets and the nonrecurrent intermediate solutions. The diarists also rated recurrent intermediates as being more closely associated with the target than other intermediates generated during that particular TOT state. In 50 per cent of the TOT states with recurrent intruders, the blocking word/name was ranked higher than the target for frequency and recency in the context of the search. In 77 per cent of the blocked TOTs, the recurrent 'blocker' was ranked higher than the target on either frequency, recency, or both. Comparisons of these recurrent intruders with the eventually-retrieved target revealed that they almost invariably shared some common phonological, syllabic, structural or semantic features.

These data are consistent with the view that recurrent intruders emerge in TOT states when the initial fragmentary retrieval cues are sufficient to locate the general context of the sought-for item, but not to provide a unique specification for it. Two conditions need to be satisfied for 'blockers' to appear. The first is that the recurrent 'blocker' has a high level of activation at the time of the search, where this is probably due to the high frequency of its prior use. The second is that its close structural and/or phonological resemblance to the target make it compatible with some of the incomplete 'calling conditions' (or retrieval cues) available at the outset of the search. These, in turn, supply the additional activation necessary to bring it to mind. Subsequently, this 'blocker' is likely to recur due to the incrementing effects of the frequency/recency general activators. This unprofitable retrieval cycle will also gain added momentum from the continued sense that its products – the recurrent blockers – are 'warm' with respect to the target word. Usually, the only way to break this deadlock is to deliberately discontinue the search. Over 30 per cent of the targets thus blocked were recovered as spontaneous 'pop-ups', most often during the execution of some routine activity like washing up or driving.

3.5. Slips of the tongue

As with TOT states, slips of the tongue show marked similarities between the actual and target (intended) utterances (see Fromkin, 1973, 1980). According to Dell and Reich (1980, p. 281): "The more similar a given unit is to an intended unit, the more likely the given unit or a part of it will replace the intended unit or a corresponding part of it."

Different kinds of similarity effect are likely to operate at the various stages of formulating and executing the articulatory program. Fromkin (1971) has suggested that semantically-related substitutions may occur because of underspecification of the semantic features. At the more detailed level of phoneme specification, however, substitutions are facilitated by a phonological similarity between word segments (Nooteboom, 1969; MacKay, 1970).

3.6. Slips of action

Diary studies of naturally-occurring slips of action (see Chapter 3) reveal that they are most likely to be committed during the performance of highly automatised tasks in very familiar surroundings while experiencing some form of attentional 'capture' (preoccupation or distraction). A large proportion of these slips (40 per cent in one study) took the form of well-organised action sequences that were judged by their makers to belong to some other task or activity not then intended. These 'other activities' were rated as being recently and frequently executed and as sharing similar locations, movements and objects with the intended actions. The largest single category of action slips were strong habit intrusions, possessing structural or contextual elements in common with the planned actions.

3.7. Failures of prospective memory

Except in the case of spontaneous action (see Chapter 1), there is usually an interval between the formulation of an intention and the moment planned for its execution. During this time, the intention must be held in prospective memory. Relatively little is known about the properties of this 'intention store' (Harris & Wilkins, 1982; Baddeley & Wilkins, 1984; Harris, 1984). What is certain, however, is that it constitutes one of the more vulnerable parts of the memory system and is thus a major source of cognitive underspecification. Failures of prospective memory—forgetting to remember to carry out intended actions at the appointed time and place—are among the most common forms of human fallibility (Reason & Mycielska, 1982).

3.8. Planning for uncertain futures

Plans are, of necessity, based upon 'best guesses' about the future state of the world. These emerge from a complex interaction between the perception of its current state and the recall of previous states. Both the perceptual and the knowledge elements of this appraisal can be incomplete or incorrect. Whatever the precise source of the underspecification, however, the outcome tends to favour the selection of either salient (vivid) or familiar (frequently encountered) scenarios for future action (see Nisbett & Ross, 1980; Kahneman, Slovic & Tversky, 1982; Fischhoff, Lichtenstein, Slovic, Derby & Keeney, 1981). We will be looking in some detail at the effects of incomplete and inaccurate knowledge in Sections 5 and 6.

Barbara Tuchman (1962, p. 38), writing about the German plan for waging the First World War, stated: "Dead battles, like dead generals, hold the military mind in their dead grip, and Germans, no less than other peoples, prepare for the last war." These words capture a universal truth about human planners. Our cognitive systems make us prisoners of the past, and this offers only a very approximate guide to the future.

3.9. Pathological underspecification

Erroneous behaviours associated with various kinds of mental disorders and brain damage can also be viewed as arising from underspecification. Three examples will serve to illustrate this point.

3.9.1. Frontal lobe damage

Luria described the disturbances of planning and the difficulties of sustaining intentional activity that stem from massive lesions of the frontal lobes; for example: "One such patient . . . when asked to light a candle struck a match correctly but instead of putting it to the candle which he held in his hand, he put the candle in his mouth and started to 'smoke' it like a cigarette. The new and relatively unstabilized action was thus replaced by a more firmly established inert stereotype. I have observed such disturbances of a complex action program and its replacement by elementary, basic behaviour in many patients with a clearly defined frontal syndrome" (Luria, 1973, pp. 199-200).

With such extensive damage, it is difficult to pinpoint any one type of underspecification; but the problem seems to lie mainly in the inability of the damaged frontal lobes to formulate or sustain an organized plan of future action. The goal-directed linkages between one action schema and the next seem to be weakened, or perhaps were never properly established, so that the course of action is readily 'captured' by the presence of well-trodden actions paths in the 'vicinity'. Similar observations have been made by Tim Shallice (1986) and Brenda Milner (1986). These pathological behaviours closely resemble the slips of normal individuals in conditions of 'reduced' or 'suspended' intentionality (see Chapter 3).

3.9.2. Schizophrenic thought and language

Also working in a clinical context, but this time with schizophrenics, Chapman and Chapman (1973) have argued that many of these patients' apparently bizarre utterances reflect an excessive yielding to normal biases, in particular to the tendency to substitute strong associates for appropriate responses. As an illustration, they cite Bleuler's woman patient who, when asked to list the members of her family, began with 'Father, son,' but then concluded with, 'and the Holy Ghost'. They provided an impressive body of experimental evidence in support of this idea (see Chapman & Chapman, 1973, pp. 119-136).

The Chapmans have also shown that these tendencies towards strong associate substitutions are present to a lesser degree among normal controls, and show up most clearly when the correct response selection is underspecified, or when the task is too difficult. For example, normal subjects were found to choose associative alternatives on multiple-choice vocabulary items when they did not know the correct answer (Boland & Chapman, 1971; Willner, 1965; see also Section 5, this chapter).

Many authors have offered attentional deficiencies as the basis for the prevalence of these *strong-associate substitutions* in schizophrenic thought and language. Thus, Jung (1906) proposed that schizophrenics suffer 'diminished' or 'relaxed' attention that leads them to produce familiar rather than appropriate associates. Similarly, Broen and Storms (1966) and Venables (1964) have argued that schizophrenics are characterized by 'narrowed' attention, which in turn may be due to heightened drive (Easterbrook, 1959). There is clearly a close correspondence between these notions and the idea of attentional underspecification at critical points in an action sequence (see Chapter 3). In the case of normal people, these monitoring failures are transitory and relatively infrequent. In certain kinds of schizophrenia, however, the mechanisms directing such attentional checks appear to be chronically impaired.

3.9.3 Limb apraxias

Roy (1982) was struck by the similarities between the slips of action observed in normals and those exhibited by patients with limb apraxias, due to cortical lesions in the motor system. He identified three error types common to both normal and pathological states, though occurring far more frequently in the latter. The most common type is the tendency to repeat (perseverate) actions. The second major type is one in which the actions are performed correctly, but in relation to the wrong objects (e.g., using a pencil as a comb). A third type involves the omission of an action altogether. The patient may be aware of what he must do, and can describe how to perform the action, but he is unable to initiate the action on command.

The precise nature of the underspecification in these patients is not clear. Roy's (1982) view is that these errors are multiply determined, that is, many different agencies are likely to be involved in their production. In some cases, the underspecification arises at the level of intention; in others, it appears to originate in the mediating neural mechanisms. In both, however, there is a tendency for the actions to be overspecified by local, situational factors. One of the consequences of brain damage is that it often leaves the patient excessively context-dependent (Goldstein, 1942; Luria, 1973)

4. Taking stock

My purpose so far has been to present sufficient evidence to demonstrate the possible varieties of cognitive underspecification. An inadequate specification may arise for several reasons and implicate a number of different cognitive mechanisms: incomplete or ambiguous inputs, fragmentary retrieval cues, incomplete or inaccurate knowledge, losses from prospective memory, spillage from the conscious workspace, intentional limitations and either normal or pathologically-induced failures of attentional monitoring. But regardless of this diversity of the possible kinds of underspecification, the outcomes are remarkably similar. The cognitive system tends to generate responses that (a) are more familiar, more expected and more frequently-encountered than those that might have been intended or judged correct and (b) are context-bound in two senses: they conform both to the current physical situation and to the 'semantic context' of the prevailing intention. Another way of expressing this generalisation is to say that when cognitive operations are underspecified, they manifest both frequency and similarity biases to a greater degree than would have occurred had the 'small print' of the activity been more precisely stated by either 'top-down' or 'bottom-up' processes.

Whereas the effects of frequency are relatively clear-cut, those of similarity are more subtle. Error forms can resemble the properties of both the current intentional specification and the prevailing environmental cues in varying degrees. The most obvious tendency in mistakes — particularly those in which the problem solver has been limited by an incomplete or incorrect knowledge base — is for the error forms to be shaped by salient features of the problem configuration. In both lapses and slips, however, there can be matching to both intentional and contextual cues. The forms of these execution failures may show close similarities to the intended word or action, as well as, on occasions, being appropriately matched to the situation in which they occur. Exactly what is matched by the error form appears to be related to the extent to which the correct response is, or could be, specified at the outset of the thought or action sequence. Difficulties encountered at the level of formulating the intention or plan tend to create errors that are moulded primarily by immediate contextual considerations; those that occur at the level of storage or execution may reflect the influences of both intentional and environmental 'calling conditions' (specifiers). But irrespective of the precise nature of the matching, similarity effects are evident across all error types.

5. Convergent and divergent memory searches

In the remainder of this chapter, we shall be concerned with the effects of underspecification upon the retrieval of semantic knowledge items. It is useful to preface this discussion with a brief consideration of two different kinds of memory search: convergent and divergent searches.

If a person were to be asked: What has four legs, barks, wags its tail, is usually friendly, has an acute sense of smell, cocks its leg and is called man's best friend? — there is little doubt that he or she would answer 'a dog'. If the same person were asked to generate exemplars of the category 'four-legged animal', there is also a very strong possibility (see Battig & Montague, 1969) that the response 'dog' would occur very early in the output list, probably in the first position.

Although these two requests yield very much the same initial response, it is clear that they are mediated by two quite different kinds of search. In the first case, sufficient cues (calling conditions) were supplied to identify unique-ly a single knowledge structure: dog. In this convergent mode of search, the response was produced entirely by the similarity-matching of supplied cues to stored attributes. In the category generation example, however, only one very imprecise cue was given: the class of animals having four legs. Under these divergent and underspecified search conditions (as seen above), the output is largely determined by frequency-gambling. The first items to be retrieved have been most often encountered in the past. These differences are illus-trated diagrammatically in Figure 4.3.

Convergent and divergent search processes can be thought of as the ex-tremes of a continuum. At the convergent end, the similarity-matching heur-istic is dominant, whereas frequency-gambling prevails at the divergent end.

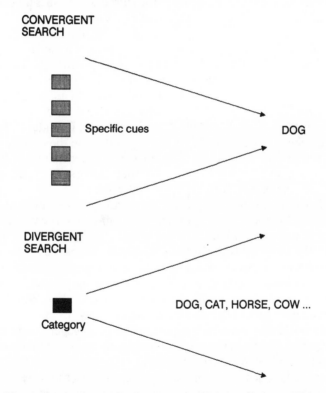

Figure 4.3. Contrasting two extremes of memory search: *convergent* search, in which the supplied cues uniquely specify a particular knowledge item, and *divergent* search, in which only the category is given at the outset.

In everyday life, however, many searches for stored knowledge items tend to lie somewhere between these two extremes. The calling conditions generated during the course of planning or decision making, for instance, are neither as precise as those in the convergent example nor as vague as in the divergent case. These intermediate searches are likely to produce partial matches between the calling conditions and a limited number of knowledge items. This 'fuzziness' is due to either imprecise or fragmentary retrieval cues or to incomplete stored knowledge. These two sources of underspecification will, for theoretical purposes, be treated as functionally equivalent.

6. The retrieval of incomplete semantic knowledge

A cognitive activity in which it is possible to vary both the specificity of the 'calling conditions' and the adequacy of the stored schemata is that of answering general knowledge questions. Given some approximate idea of how much (or how little) information a group of individuals has about a particular knowledge domain, and providing the questions are posed in a way that encourages guessing, the answers obtained tend to be highly predictable. For example, ask any British lecture audience to identify the source of the following quotation: "The lamps are going out all over Europe; we shall not see them lit again in our lifetime," and there is a strong probability that most of them will attribute it to Winston Churchill. Neville Chamberlain and Franklin D. Roosevelt will also receive a few mentions. Hardly any will name the correct source of this far-sighted observation: Sir Edward Grey, British Foreign Secretary, spoken at dawn on 3 August 1914 to the Italian ambassador as the gas lamps were being extinguished on Horse Guards Parade.

Aside from the fact that the person who actually made this eerily familiar remark is now a fairly obscure figure, it is not difficult to see why such a predictable misattribution occurs. The topic and style of the quote point to a statesman, the language is English and the sense locates it on the eve or during the early days of a world war. For most people questioned, this combination of cues inexorably signifies just one person and one period: Churchill, the great speechmaker, at the outset of the Second World War. With the exception of those with specialist knowledge, the category 'English statesman on the eve of a world war' contains, for most British people, perhaps three or four names, of whom Churchill's is the most frequently encountered (even though he did not hold office in September 1939).

This section is concerned with the cognitive processes that yield such common but wrong answers to general knowledge questions, particularly in domains where the information in semantic memory is both relatively sparse and unevenly distributed. We begin by sketching out the processes involved in knowledge retrieval, and then discuss the findings of three studies that test certain hypotheses derived from this view.

6.1. Retrieval mechanisms

It is argued that knowledge retrieval involves at least four kinds of cognitive activity: a metacognitive assessment of whether or not the sought-for item is likely to be available in semantic memory; the similarity-matching of retrieval cues to the attributes of stored knowledge structures; resolving conflicts created by the partial matching of several 'candidates' by gambling in favour of high-frequency alternatives and the inferential work performed by the conscious workspace, the product of which is a revised set of 'calling conditions'.

6.1.1. Frequency information as the basis of epistemic awareness

A major determinant of the effort that will be invested in searching for the answer to a general knowledge question is what Klatzky (1984) has termed *epistemic awareness*: the feelings of knowing (FOK) about what one knows. There is now a considerable body of evidence to show that adults are able to make reasonably accurate judgements of their subsequent success in an effortful memory search (Hart, 1965; Arbuckle & Cuddy, 1969; Blake, 1973; Gruneberg & Sykes, 1978; King, Zechmeister & Shaughnessy, 1980; Zechmeister & Nyberg, 1982; Reason & Lucas, 1984a).

A substantial proportion of everyday memory work can be likened to directing a very small 'access window' through an enormous knowledge base in an effort to locate stored items of information that satisfy current demands. Without the ready availability of something akin to an index or knowledge map, this would be an exceedingly difficult task. If it were necessary to search in an undirected and serial fashion for every item of sought-for knowledge, an unacceptably large part of mental life would be consumed in retrieval activities. Metamemoric FOK assessments clearly play a critical role in the management of cognitive affairs. But upon what basis are these assessments made?

Of special relevance to this question is how a person decides that he or she does not know something. Glucksberg and McCloskey (1981) proposed a two-stage model of question-answering to account for different types of 'don't know' decisions: the one rapid and confident, the other slow and uncertain. In the first stage, a preliminary search of memory is conducted to locate any stored information that may be relevant to the question. If nothing is found, a rapid 'don't know' decision is made. But if relevant facts are found, these are examined in detail to determine whether they indicate an answer to the question. If these retrieved facts fail to provide an answer, a slow 'don't know' decision results. In either case, however, the discovery of relevant facts is expected to delay the outcome.

Unfortunately, this account begs the question of how the preliminary memory search is made. Consistent with this chapter's general theme, it is proposed that initial appraisals of the knowledge base depend critically upon the immediate availability of crude frequency data regarding the number of times particular stored items have been encountered in the past or have co-occurred with other items. This view rests on two well-founded assumptions regarding the status of frequency information within the memory system. First, frequency-of-encounter information appears to be stored in memory by "an implicit or automatic encoding process" (Hasher & Zacks, 1984). Second, most of the experimental evidence favours a multiple trace hypothesis in which each encounter with a given item is recorded as an additional trace on a 'pile' of like traces (Hintzman, 1976; Hintzman, Nozawa & Irmscher, 1982). According to this notion, frequency information is represented in a privileged analogue form (i.e., by the 'height' of the 'pile' of like traces). It is also assumed that each individual trace preserves episodic information regarding both the context of the encounter and connections with co-occurrent items.

What is being proposed here, then, is that people are able to make more or less instant 'frequency maps' of particular semantic regions in a way that is analogous to brain heat scans. The metamemorial information so obtained, though crude and relative, forms the basis of a memory management system by which the limited 'access window' is steered (or drawn) towards promising areas of the knowledge base. By the same token, if a 'scan' throws up little or no frequency information – either in regard to the previous occurrence of single knowledge items or concerning the co-occurrence of multiple items – then there is little to be gained by searching further. The crucial point is that frequency-derived epistemic awareness of the 'fatness' of a particular knowledge 'file' appears to be available to the memory searcher before he or she has had an opportunity to examine its contents in any detail. This is in keeping with Oldfield and Wingfield's (1964) notion that crude assessments of frequency are as immediate as the act of recognition itself. When we recognise something, we not only know that we have it in memory, we also know approximately how much is known.

6.1.2. Similarity-matching

According to William James (1908, pp. 118-119): "Whatever appears in the mind must be introduced. . . . This is as true of what you are recollecting as it is of everything else you think of." This section is concerned with the way in which these 'introductions' are effected in question-answering: by the matching of the calling conditions present in a question to the attributes of knowledge items stored in semantic memory.

Similarity-matching is a recurrent theme across a wide variety of memory theories. It is the primary basis of memory search. The view adopted here is that the form of a general knowledge question delivers a set of retrieval cues to long-term memory (the knowledge base). These cues then automatically activate stored items possessing attributes that match either wholly or partially the 'calling conditions' communicated by the question. This is assumed to be an extremely rapid and efficient process, once the cues have been set loose within the knowledge base.

How these calling conditions are perceived plays a critical part in determining the course of the subsequent act of retrieval. For example, many Britons, when encouraged to persevere with the question 'Who was the tall watcher on the tor?', produce one of two sensible answers, depending upon how they interpret the available cues. One group correctly responds with Sherlock Holmes, the other with Heathcliffe. Both groups assume from the linguistic style of the question that it refers to a dated English literary figure; the difference in outcome hinges on how they understand the term 'tor'. Those that say Sherlock Holmes recognise that 'tor' usually refers to a rocky outcrop on Dartmoor, from which they make the connection to Sherlock Holmes in the *Hound of the Baskervilles*. The others interpret 'tor' as a hilly place on any moor and conjure up the ready image (among educated Britons at least) of the brooding Yorkshireman (or of Olivier, his screen counterpart) in *Wuthering Heights*.

These reactions to the 'watcher' question also illustrate a further point: not all of the available calling conditions need be active at the outset. The more subtle clues to an answer may only be uncovered as the result of sustained inferential activity. Thus, a critical calling condition could remain concealed for some time, and only when its possible relevance has been established will it be loosed upon its automatic matching quest. Many questions will release all of their calling conditions immediately, but others will leak them only gradually into the retrieval system.

6.1.3. Frequency-gambling

The calling conditions supplied by a general knowledge question frequently fail to find an immediate right answer, either because the retrieval cues are insufficiently specified or because the relevant stored knowledge is incomplete. (These two possibilities are treated as being functionally equivalent within the model.) As a result, a number of partially matched 'candidates' can be activated at various stages of the search. The essence of frequency-gambling is that selection from among these candidates is biased in favour of the more frequently-encountered items, and that these are more likely to be called to mind for additional serial processing. Selection is necessary because the workspace available to handle the products of parallel search is extremely limited in its capacity.

The extent to which frequency-gambling plays a part in the retrieval process depends upon the quality of the match between the calling conditions and a specific knowledge item or restricted set of items. The less precise the 'description' of a stored fact provided by the calling conditions at the outset of the search and the more patchy the relevant knowledge held in memory, the greater will be the involvement of frequency-gambling. This is simply a reiteration of the underspecification principle stated earlier.

6.1.4. Inference

As used here, the term 'inference' embraces a number of different serial search procedures. Collectively, they involve the directed application of selected pieces of knowledge and various operators to the products of parallel search. Similarity-matching and frequency-gambling are the automatic processes by which various candidates are brought to mind. They operate in the realms of unawareness beyond the "intensively active gap" in consciousness described by William James (1890). Inference, on the other hand, refers to the work done upon these items within the limited workspace, once they have been 'called to mind'.

In regard to the nature of this 'mindwork', it has been suggested that inferences fulfill two general functions (Warren, Nicholas & Trabasso, 1979). First, they establish connections between the propositions available in a question (calling conditions) and stored knowledge items. This not only guides the retrieval process, it also allows for the integration of both new and old information into a coherent body of knowledge. Second, since knowledge is always incomplete, inferences help the memory user to fill in the missing pieces (see Bartlett, 1932; Schank, 1982).

Even when people feel certain that a particular item of knowledge is not available in memory, they can sometimes piece together what they do not know by making plausible inferences from other kinds of stored knowledge. Consider the following question: "Which president of the United States was the first to travel in an aeroplane?" Although this is hardly a well known fact, most of us can make an educated guess at who it was, even though we may possess very little relevant knowledge. Our inferences might go along the following lines: The first manned flight was in the early 1900s; but until the end of the First World War aircraft were far too small and precarious for a president to be allowed to fly in one. Commercial aviation began in earnest sometime in the early 1920s. Who were the presidents of that time? Wilson, Harding and Coolidge. Wilson was probably too sick to fly even if there were aircraft large and safe enough to carry him and his retinue. So the most likely candidates are either Harding or Coolidge. Since presidents, being politicians, are quick to seize upon new ways of reaching the voters, it was probably Harding rather than Coolidge.

This may not be the right answer (which is still unknown to the writer), but the way it was reached shows how a feasible guess can be constructed by doing 'inference work' on scraps of knowledge drawn from two fairly disparate domains: aviation history and U.S. presidents. Although this chain of inference was presented as if it were a wholly conscious process, it will actually have involved several intermittent bursts of nonreportable parallel search: for the approximate date of the first manned flight, for the condition of early aircraft, for the beginnings of commercial aviation, for the presidents of the early to mid-1920s and so on. Thus, what might be recounted by the searcher as a coherent linear sequence is, in reality, a complex cycling of (a) items thrown up by unconscious retrieval mechanisms and (b) conscious inferential work, with the latter yielding fresh calling conditions for the former. Only the products of the parallel activity and a certain amount of the serial problem-solving are accessible to introspection.

6.2. Serial and parallel search processes

The distinction made above between the parallel and serial aspects of memory search corresponds in many important respects to that made by other theorists. For example, it has been argued (Atkinson & Juola, 1973; Mandler, 1980) that memory representations may be accessed in two ways: the one direct and rapid; the other slower and indirect, involving a laborious search along relatively unfamiliar associative pathways. Since these two search mechanisms differ in their demands upon conscious attention, Klatzky (1984, p. 75) suggested that they can be described in terms of their positions along an attentional continuum: "as a search relies more on nonhabitual, novel associations in the memory structure, it demands more attention. Direct search is achieved by activation of well established memory pathways and lies at the low end of the continuum. Associative search uses attention in varying amounts." This proposal avoids the need to make hard and fast distinctions between conscious and unconscious processes, which are in any case hard to substantiate.

6.3. "The buck stops here"

Who said (or, more accurately, had a sign on his desk saying): "The buck stops here"? The answer is Harry S Truman. If this quotation is not in your Truman 'file' (i.e., a stored attribute of Truman), then you might reason along the following lines. Quotation questions usually relate to famous people. The word 'buck' suggests an American. The most famous Americans are presidents. In three short and largely intuitive steps, the possible search set has been reduced from many millions to the (then) 39 American presidents. But which president?

The retrieval theory outlined above would predict that people who did not actually know the answer, but were willing to guess, would attempt to make a match with the first president that came to mind, probably the then incumbent, Ronald Reagan. If this did not 'feel right', they might then proceed down the frequency-of-encounter gradient . . . Kennedy, Carter, Nixon, Franklin D. Roosevelt, Lincoln, Washington, Ford . . . until they came to a name that seemed to match the quotation.

If one asked this question of a large number of people who knew little of American presidents, it should be possible to obtain some idea of the relative influences of the various search strategies in providing the guessed answer. If only frequency-gambling prevailed, then their attributions would correspond precisely to the frequency gradient. If other processes also played a part, then the attributions would deviate in some degree from this correspondence, with less salient presidents receiving a larger number of attributions than the more frequently encountered ones. This was what actually happened when I put the question to 126 British psychology students who, on average, knew the names of only 9 of the 39 presidents. The results are shown in Figure 4.4.

"The buck stops here"

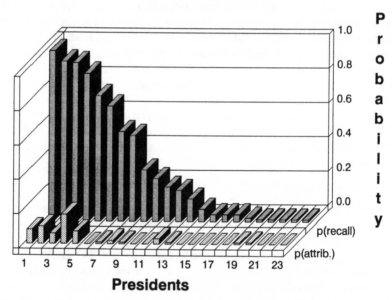

Figure 4.4. Two distributions are plotted: *p(recall)*, the probability of recall of 23 American presidents; and *p(attribution)*, the probability of attributing the "buck" quotation to a particular president. In descending *p(recall)* order, the first eight presidents are: Reagan, Kennedy, Carter, Nixon, FDR, Lincoln, Washington and Ford. Truman (the correct answer) is number 12.

In this case, the 'salience gradient' (the rear distribution) was derived from the probability of a president being recalled when the students were asked to generate as many exemplars as possible of the category 'American president' in five minutes (see also Roediger & Crowder, 1976). The quotation attributions are shown by the front distribution. The first point to notice is that over 80 per cent of these attributions were assigned to the five most salient presidents. The second point is that the number of attributions per president does not correspond to the salience order. Nixon received more than his fair share. Further probing yielded the following explanation. The subjects did not equate 'buck' with responsibility (not knowing the story of Mississippi gamblers and buck-handled knives); instead, they took it to mean a dollar. While they knew relatively little of the facts of Richard Nixon's presidency, many of them thought he had been involved in some kind of shady dealing. On this basis, they interpreted the quotation to mean 'The buck (the dollar) stops here (in my pocket)', and Nixon as the likely source.

Although inaccurate, these assumptions clearly indicate the involvement, in certain subjects at least, of a matching process that overrode the dictates of the frequency gradient. Taken as a whole, this simple demonstration reveals something of the complex interaction between the three search mechanisms: similarity-matching, frequency-gambling and inference. We will explore further aspects of this interaction below.

6.4. The quotations study

This section describes a recent Manchester study (Reason, Horrocks & Bailey, 1986) designed to test the following prediction from the cognitive underspecification hypothesis: The amount of frequency-gambling (i.e., the tendency to emit high-frequency candidates) evident in the responses to general knowledge questions will be inversely related to the degree of relevant knowledge possessed by the respondent. The knowledge domain was American presidents, and the study was carried out in two separate stages: a mapping phase and a test phase.

The mapping phase was in two parts. In the first, two separate groups of psychology undergraduates (totalling 126 subjects) were asked, on separate occasions, to recall as many presidents as they could in a 5-minute period. In the second part, again on separate occasions, they were given a list of all (the then) 39 presidents and were required to make frequency-of-encounter ratings (on a scale of one to seven) for each one. These lists were in random rather than chronological order.

In the test phase, a questionnaire was given to 114 undergraduates, none of whom had been involved in the mapping phase. Each questionnaire was in two main parts:

(a) A *recognition test*, comprising the names of the (then) 39 incumbents mixed together with those of 78 famous contemporaries. These were in random order and the subjects were asked to underline the names of those presidents they could identify as such. The score, corrected for guessing, was assumed to give an approximate indication of the individual's domain knowledge.

(b) *Multiple-choice quotation attribution*, in which four quotations were presented, each with an attribution selection of eight presidential names beneath (one of whom was the true source). For each quotation, subjects were required simply to underline their 'best guess' as to the source. The dependent variable was the frequency score for the selected president in each case. These scores were derived from the ratings obtained in the mapping phase.

The subjects were split into approximately equal quartile groupings according to their recognition scores – indicating their degree of domain knowledge. As predicted, the results revealed a highly significant inverse relationship between domain expertise and the tendency to frequency-gamble. The more people knew, the less inclined they were to attribute quotations to contextually appropriate, high-frequency presidents.

A more immediate 'feel' for these data is provided by Figure 4.5, which shows the pattern of attributions for the 'low knowledge' (LK) and 'higher knowledge' (HK) groups (a median split) in relation to the Teddy Roosevelt quotation: "A man who is good enough to shed his blood for his country is good enough to be given a square deal afterwards. More than that no man is entitled to, less than that no man shall have."

The implicit cueing directs subjects to consider end-of-war or postwar presidents. In both groups, the majority guessed the correct source, but probably for the wrong reasons: a confusion between Franklin and Theodore Roosevelt that was further compounded by the similarity between Teddy's 'square deal' and Franklin's 'New Deal'. Other data indicate that FDR is known by these undergraduates to be a wartime president, so, even allowing for the confusion, it is an intelligent choice. Of more interest, however, was the difference between the groups in the Kennedy attributions. To Manchester psychology students, John F. Kennedy remains a very salient president, being second only in rated frequency-of-encounter to Ronald Reagan. But since his term of office was some 15 years after World War Two and nearly a decade after the Korean conflict, he is not a particularly good match to the calling conditions supplied by the quote. For the LK group, therefore, he was an 'ignorant' guess; whereas the popular choices among the HK group reveal a fairly 'educated' pattern of guessing. Roosevelt (whichever one), Truman, Grant and Nixon all had good cause to be concerned about the welfare of veterans.

Cued: "...shed his blood."

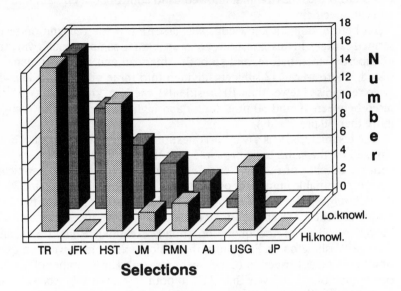

Figure 4.5. Comparing selections for the low- and high-knowledge subjects in regard to the "shed his blood ..." quotation. Most interesting are the differences for JFK between the two groups (see text).

6.5. The presidential recognition study

The underspecification hypothesis makes a number of predictions regarding the relative usage of similarity-matching and frequency-gambling. It postulates that similarity-matching will be the predominant strategy when (a) the 'calling conditions' (retrieval cues) are adequate to specify a unique knowledge item and (b) when there is a large number of stored items. In contrast, frequency-gambling will predominate (a) when the cues are insufficient or ambiguous and (b) when there is impoverished domain knowledge (i.e., low expertise). Thus, domain knowledge and cue sufficiency are seen as functionally equivalent in their effects upon the degree of retrieval underspecification; a degradation of one or both would decrease the specification of the knowledge item, and would therefore increase the level of frequency-gambling.

In the quotation study, we were able to test the knowledge strand of this hypothesis. I found, as predicted, that the less subjects knew about American presidents, the more likely they were to attribute the quotes to high-frequency presidents. However, the use of quotations as test material did not permit the systematic manipulation of the specificity of the retrieval cues. A second study was therefore conducted that allowed us to control both domain knowledge and cue specificity.

As before, domain knowledge was assessed by the recognition test (described earlier). In this case, however, we sought to sample a much wider range of expertise than before, and so both American and British students were tested. There were 112 subjects, divided into three groups: low knowledge (who recognised fewer than 10 presidents); medium knowledge (who recognised between 10 and 30 presidents) and high knowledge (who recognised more than 30 presidents).

The test material was a two-part questionnaire, where both parts were constructed on the same basic principles. At the top of each page were listed a variable number of retrieval cues, each one relating to a biographical fact covering a variable number of presidents. Below were listed the same 20 presidents, but in a different order for each retrieval task. These were the 20 most frequently-encountered presidents (as shown by the ratings obtained from the 'mapping' phase of the quotation study), excluding Ronald Reagan and George Washington. In Section A, these biographical facts were unique to a single president. In Section B, they were possessed by a number of presidents (more than one, but fewer than 11). In both cases, the subjects were simply asked to underline those listed president(s) who best fitted the retrieval cues. In addition, they were required to rate their confidence in the selection (0-100%), and to indicate (in percentage values) what strategies they used in making their choice. They were offered four possibilities: pure guesswork, process of elimination, direct identification and other means (none used this last category).

In both sections of the questionnaire, the test material was designed to vary both the number of supplied retrieval cues and the 'set sizes' covered by each cue (i.e., the number of listed presidents who fitted each 'calling condition'). It was assumed that cue specificity would increase as a function of cue number and decrease with set size.

Taken together, the findings from both Sections A and B provided qualified support for the notion that a decrease in search specificity, whether due to impoverished knowledge or imprecise cueing, leads to an increase in the employment of the frequency-gambling strategy and a corresponding diminution in the use of similarity-matching. It was also evident that people were unaware of this process. Thus, low-knowledge subjects, when asked how they made their choices, said they were guessing. In reality, however, their selections were heavily influenced by presidential salience, or, as operationally defined here, by a president's frequency of encounter in the world.

These three studies confirmed the predictions of the underspecification hypothesis, at least with regard to the retrieval of knowledge relating to American presidents. It will, of course, be necessary to explore a much wider range of knowledge domains before we can claim that we are dealing with a universal knowledge retrieval phenomenon. Nevertheless, when the results of these 'presidential' studies are considered alongside those summarised in the earlier part of the chapter, a strong case can be made for the ubiquity of the underspecification principle in human cognitive processing.

7. Concluding remarks

This chapter has presented evidence to support the generalization that the cognitive system is disposed to select contextually appropriate, high-frequency responses in conditions of underspecification, and that this tendency gives predictable form to a wide variety of errors. There is little new in this assertion (see Thorndike, 1911). What is more unusual is that the evidence has been drawn from a broad range of cognitive activities.

Howell (1973) offered two reasons to explain why the general significance of frequency in cognition has been largely unappreciated. The first is that most investigators who were interested in frequency have preferred not to deal in cognitive concepts. The second is that "frequency has become tied to the particular vehicle by which it is conveyed (e.g., words, numbers, lights, etc.) and the particular paradigm in which it occurs (e.g., paired-associate learning, decision making, information transmission)" (Howell, 1973, p. 44).

The revival of the schema concept in the mid-1970s (due in large part to developments in artificial intelligence) has created a theoretical climate in which it is possible to regard frequency in a less paradigm-bound fashion. Common to the schema concept, in all its many contemporary guises (scripts, frames, personae, etc.), is the notion of high-level knowledge structures that contain informational 'slots' or variables. Each slot will only accept information of a particular kind. When external sources fail to provide data to fill them, they take on 'default assignments', where these are the most frequent (or stereotypical) instances in a given context.

By its nature, frequency is intimately bound up with many other processing and representational factors, of which 'connectedness' is probably the most important. How can we be sure that frequency rather than the degree of association with other schemata is more important in determining 'default assignments'? The short answer is that we can never be certain, and this probably does not matter. Frequency and connectedness are inextricably linked. The more often a particular object or event is encountered, the more opportunity it has to form episodic and semantic linkages with other items. Just as all roads lead to Rome, so all – or nearly all – associative connections within a given context are likely to lead to the most frequently-employed schema. Such a view is implicit in recent computer models of parallel distributed processing (see McClelland & Rumelhart, 1985; Rumelhart & McClelland, 1986; Norman, 1985). But irrespective of whether it is frequency-logging or connectional weighting that is the more fundamental factor, the functional consequences are likely to be very similar.

In recent years, a number of authors have made strong cases for the largely automatic encoding of event frequency (see Hasher & Zacks, 1984), and for its privileged representation in memory (Hintzman & Block, 1971; Hintzman, 1976; Hintzman, Nozawa & Irmscher, 1982). These observations prompt the question: If frequency information is so important, what is it good for? This chapter has attempted to provide one very general answer.

5   A design for a fallible machine

This chapter sketches out one possible answer to the following question: *What kind of information-handling device could operate correctly for most of the time, but also produce the occasional wrong responses characteristic of human behaviour?* Of special interest are those error forms that recur so often that any adequate model of human action must explain not only correct performance, but also these more predictable varieties of fallibility.

Most of the component parts of this 'machine' have been discussed at earlier points in this book. The purpose of this chapter is to assemble them in a concise and internally consistent fashion.

It is called a 'fallible machine' rather than a theoretical framework because it is expressed in a potentially computable form. That is, it borrows from Artificial Intelligence (AI) the aim of making an information-handling machine do "the sorts of things that are done by human minds" (Boden, 1987, p. 48). As Boden (1987, p. 48) indicates, the advantages of this approach are twofold: "First, it enables one to express richly structured psychological theories in a rigorous fashion (for everything in the program has to be precisely specified, and all its operations have to be made explicit); and secondly, it forces one to suggest specific hypotheses about precisely how a psychological change can come about."

The description of the 'fallible machine' is in two parts. In the first seven sections of the chapter, it is presented in a notional, nonprogrammatic form. The remaining sections consider how these ideas may be embodied in a suite of computer programs designed to model the cognitive processes involved in the retrieval of incomplete knowledge. More specifically, these programs are intended to emulate (a) the way our human subjects generated exemplars of the category 'American presidents', and (b) their responses to Section B of the presidential quiz (see Chapter 4).

1. The structural components of the 'machine'

The 'machine' has two principal components: *working memory* (WM) and the *knowledge base* (KB). WM is subdivided into two parts: focal WM and peripheral WM. The primary interconnections between these components are shown in Figure 5.1.

These two aspects of the memory system communicate with the outside world via the input function (IF) and the output function (OF). The IF comprises an array of specialised sensors whose activity is fed into peripheral WM. The OF consists of a set of effectors for transforming stored instructions into speech or motor action, and for directing sensory orientation. The OF acts upon outputs from the knowledge base. There are also feedback loops connecting the output and input functions (not shown in Figure 5.1).

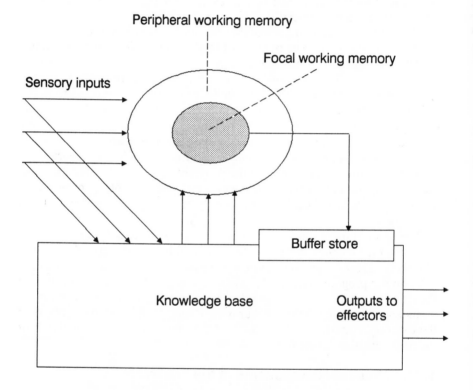

Figure 5.1. The principal structural components of the *fallible machine* and their interconnections: peripheral and focal working memory, the knowledge base and its associated buffer store.

2. The functional properties of the parts

2.1. Focal working memory (FWM)

This is a limited capacity 'workspace' that receives inputs continuously from both the outside world (sensory inputs) and the knowledge base. It has a cycle time of a few milliseconds, and each cycle contains around two or three discrete informational elements. During a run of consecutive cycles, these elements may be transformed, extended or recombined as the result of 'work' performed upon them by powerful operators that function only within this highly restricted domain.

A useful image for FWM is that of a slicer. Information, comprising elements from both the sensory inputs and the KB, is cut into 'slices' (corresponding to the few milliseconds of cycle time) that are then dropped into the buffer store of the KB. The width of these 'slices' may vary according to the type of 'work' that is done upon them during their transition through FWM.

2.2. Peripheral working memory (PWM)

The primary function of PWM is to govern access to FWM. It receives inputs directly from the IF and KB, and holds this information briefly while a selection is being made. Only a very small proportion of the contents of the peripheral WM reach focal WM. Access to FWM is decided according to a variety of prioritising principles.

2.2.1. Visual dominance

Visual information has priority access to FWM at all times. So long as the visual sensors are working, their outputs will constitute the 'foreground' of FWM activity.

This dominance of vision among the sensory modalities has been demonstrated in many situations. Studies of divided attention show that when a light and a tone are presented simultaneously, the light is likely to be detected first (Colavita, 1974; Posner, Nissen & Klein, 1976).

Visual prepotence is perhaps revealed most dramatically in conditions of sensory rearrangement in which the normally harmonious relations between the spatial senses are deliberately distorted so that visual information is at odds with the inputs from the vestibular and muscle-skin-joint systems (see Reason, 1974). Uniform movement of large parts of the visual scene is usually an accompaniment of self-motion, and this is the way the brain interprets such large-scale movements, even when the immediate environment is being moved and the body is actually stationary. Notwithstanding the fact that these visual inputs are at variance with the veridical information derived from the other spatial senses, they still come to dominate visual perception. Ernst Mach, for example, described one form of these visually-derived illusions of self-motion (or vection): "If we stand on a bridge, and look at the water flowing beneath, we usually feel ourselves at rest, whilst the water seems in motion. Prolonged looking at the water, however, commonly has for its result to make the bridge with the observer and its surroundings suddenly seem to move the direction opposed to that of the water, whilst the water itself assumes the appearance of standing still" (cited by James, 1880). Similar effects can be obtained by the movement of a train on the next track whilst our own is stationary, or from looking up at scudding clouds over the edge of a house or tree.

2.2.2. Change detection

Inputs indicating a step change in the conditions of the outside world have privileged access to FWM. All sensory systems are biased to accentuate the differences in the immediate environment and to attenuate its constant features. In short, the nervous system is essentially a change-detector, and this general principle appears to hold good throughout the animal kingdom for all sensory modalities.

2.2.3. Coherence principle

Access to FWM is biased to favour information that corresponds to its current contents. This principle preserves the consistency of successive FWM elements. In this way, FWM maintains a coherent 'picture' of the world. The coherence principle also contributes to confirmation bias: the tendency to hold on to initial hypotheses in the face of contradictory evidence (see Johnson-Laird & Wason, 1977).

2.2.4. Activation principle

Access to FWM of informational elements from the KB is determined by the level of activation of the knowledge units from which they originate (the concept of activation and the factors that determine it will be discussed below). The higher this level of activation, the greater the chances of admission to FWM.

2.2.5. Dedicated processors

The PWM also contains dedicated 'slave systems' such as the *articulatory loop* and the *visuo-spatial scratch pad* (see Baddeley & Hitch, 1974; Hitch, 1980). These provide limited 'holding facilities' for specialised information currently being processed by FWM.

2.3. Knowledge base

This is a vast repository of knowledge units. These originate, in the first instance, from WM activity. The KB is effectively unlimited in either its storage capacity or the length of time for which knowledge units may be stored. However, it has relatively little in the way of intrinsic organisation; it is more like a tip than a library. Any outward appearance of categorical organisation is due to the way the retrieval system operates, not to any hierarchical structure or modularity within the knowledge base itself (see Kahneman & Miller, 1986). What organisation it possesses derives from shared context or co-occurrence. That is, FWM slices that repeatedly recur in consistent sequences (e.g., routine actions, arithmetical procedures, logical operators, etc.) tend to be compiled into procedural knowledge units.

A similar kind of process operates for declarative knowledge units. Individual knowledge slices become compiled into larger units as a consequence of their continual recycling through focal WM. Compilation of declarative knowledge is achieved through forging (within FWM) 'is-a', 'has-a', 'means' linkages between shared-element slices. Consider how the machine might develop a knowledge unit representing, say, a raven. At some point, the machine will have in FWM a visual image of a largish, black feathered creature together with the supplied information 'is-a raven'. In the same way, further connections will be made with 'is-a bird', 'is-a member of the crow family', 'is-a feathered vertebrate', 'is-to-be-found-on Tower Green', 'is-the title of a poem by Edgar Allan Poe', and so on. To the extent that these various slices share the label 'is-a raven', they will be compiled as a discrete knowledge unit. In this way, the KB develops a 'unitised' and distributed organisation rather than a categorical one (see McClelland & Rumelhart, 1985). Each unit is a 'content-addressable' knowledge file (see Alba & Hasher, 1983).

3. The dynamics of the system: Activation

It is now time to assemble these various components into a working machine and imbue it with some driving force. This is supplied by the notion of activation.

Each knowledge unit within the KB, whether declarative or procedural, has a modifiable level of activation. When this level exceeds a given threshold, the knowledge unit will emit a product. These products may be instructions for action, words or images, depending upon the character of the unit. They are delivered either to the effectors (if procedural units) or to PWM. It is important to emphasise that it is the products of these units and not the units themselves that are so despatched.

Knowledge units receive their activational charge from two principal sources, the one obtained from activity within FWM (to be described in a moment) and the other deriving from a number of nonspecific sources. These two sources will be labelled specific and general activators.

3.1. Specific activators

These activators give the machine its purposive character and are the most influential of all the triggering factors. The mechanism is very simple. The most recent 'run' of FWM slices is held briefly in a buffer store (see Figure 5.1). All stored knowledge units possessing attributes that correspond to those held in the buffer will increase their activation by an amount related to the goodness of match. The closer the match, the greater will be the received activation. In short, specific activators operate on the basis of graded similarity-matching.

3.2. General activators

These allow knowledge units to 'fire off' without continual direction from the FWM. Perhaps the single most important general activator derives from the frequency of prior use. The more often a particular unit, or related set of units, has been triggered in the past, the greater is its 'background level' of activation, and the less additional activation is necessary to call it into play. As a consequence of the activation principle, the products of well-used units will have an advantage in the competition for FWM access.

Whereas the activational resources supplying stored knowledge units are virtually unrestricted, the attentional activators serving both parts of working memory (but especially FWM) are drawn from a strictly limited 'pool'. Certain types of directed processing make heavy demands upon this limited attentional resource. When this happens, control falls by default to active knowledge units, which are likely to be contextually-appropriate, high-frequency units. This, together with the coherence principle, gives the machine its characteristic conservatism.

4. Retrieval mechanisms

For the most part, the basic dynamics of the retrieval process have already been described above. However, a number of points need to be elaborated further. The machine has three mechanisms for bringing the products of stored knowledge units into FWM. Two of them, similarity-matching and frequency-gambling, constitute the computational primitives of the system as a whole and operate in a parallel, distributed and automatic fashion within the KB. The third retrieval mechanism, serial or directed search (analogous to human inference), derives from the sophisticated processing capabilities of FWM. Within this restricted workspace, through which informational elements must be processed slowly and sequentially, speed, effortlessness and unlimited capacity have been sacrificed in favour of selectivity, coherence and computational power.

4.1. Similarity-matching

As indicated earlier, this process entails the continuous matching of the recent output of FWM (termed the 'calling conditions') to attributes of knowledge units. To avoid exhaustive searches of the entire knowledge base, the first 'pass' is directed at those stored units sharing similar contextual elements to the recent contents of FWM (i.e., those currently in the KB's buffer store). Such elements may be said to define the contextual frame of the search. If this first pass fails to produce a satisfactory match, then other frames must be found through FWM activity.

Note also that retrieval is initiated automatically by the products of FWM activity. No special fiat or directive is required. But the products of this automatic similarity-matching need not necessarily arrive in FWM. They may be excluded by the selection criteria currently operative within PWM, or they may simply be pre-empted by higher priority inputs. The greater the activational charge of the knowledge units emitting the search products, the greater is their chance of reaching FWM.

4.2. Frequency-gambling

In many situations, the calling conditions emerging from FWM are insufficient to provide a unique match for a single knowledge unit, because either the calling conditions or the stored elements are incomplete. These two possibilities are functionally equivalent. When searches are underspecified, a number of partially matched 'candidates' may arrive in PWM. Where these contenders are equally matched to the calling conditions, the conflict is resolved in favour of the most frequently-encountered item by the activation principle. An oft-triggered knowledge unit will have a higher 'background' activation level than one that is less frequently employed. This is generally an adaptive heuristic because the most contextually typical search products will be dealt with first by FWM. In other words, the machine responds to the statistical properties of the world it inhabits.

4.3. Directed search

FWM has no direct access to the stored knowledge units, only to their products. Its sole means of directing knowledge retrieval is through the manipulation of calling conditions. The actual search itself is carried out automatically by the similarity-matching and frequency-gambling heuristics. All that FWM can do, therefore, is to deliver the initial calling conditions, assess whether the search-product is appropriate and, if not, to reinstate the search with revised retrieval cues. FWM thus has the power to reject the high-frequency candidates thrown up by underspecified matches, but only when sufficient processing resources are available.

5. Intentional characteristics

As we have seen, actions can be set in train and knowledge products propelled into FWM as an automatic consequence of (a) prior processing in FWM and (b) knowledge unit activation. But these properties alone are not sufficient to guarantee the successful execution of goal-directed behaviour. What gives the machine its intentional character? How does it initiate deliberate actions or knowledge searches?

As with many other questions, William James (1890, p. 561) provided an answer: "The essential achievement of the will . . . is to attend to a difficult object and hold it fast before the mind. The so doing is the fiat; and it is a mere physiological incident that when the object is thus attended to, immediate motor consequences should ensue."

This statement maps readily onto the properties of our machine. The 'holding-fast-before-the-mind' translates into a sustained run of same-element FWM slices (see Figure 5.2.). Once in the KB buffer, the consistency of these slices will generate a high level of focused activation within a restricted set of knowledge units. This will automatically and advantageously release their products, either to the output function or to WM. But such an 'act of will' places heavy demands upon the limited attentional resources available to working memory. The perseveration of specific elements has to be maintained in the face of continual pressure from other claimants to FWM attention. And such an 'effort' can only be sustained for short periods, particularly when the object being attended to is less than compelling. As James (1908, p. 101) put it: "When we are studying an uninteresting subject, if our mind tends to wander, we have to bring back our attention every now and then by using distinct pulses of effort, which revivify the topic for a moment, the mind then running on for a certain number of seconds or minutes with spontaneous interest, until again some intercurrent idea captures it and takes it off." Like the human mind, the 'fallible machine' is naturally prone to "intercurrent ideas."

As the machine's recurrent actions become compiled into preprogrammed instructional sequences, FWM need only focus upon (i.e., sustain an image of) the desired consequences, not upon the detailed movements. To overcome the difficulty of having the effects of an action precede the action itself, James's ideomotor theory maintained that the imagined consequences of voluntary movements are derived originally from the experience of reflex behavioural units: "When a particular movement, having once occurred in a random, reflex or involuntary way, has left an image of itself in the memory, then the movement can be desired again, proposed as an end, and deliberately willed" (1890, p. 487). Similarly, our machine could begin its working life with a limited stock of 'hard-wired' action, ideational and perceptual programs. Acquired knowledge units would develop as increasingly elaborated variants of this basic 'starter-kit'.

6. Concurrent processing

The principal achievement of human cognition is its extraordinary ability to internalise the recurrences of the world in long-term memory (as schemata, scripts, frames, rules and so on), and then to bring the products of these stored knowledge structures into play whenever the current situational calling conditions demand them. What is even more remarkable is that these retrieval

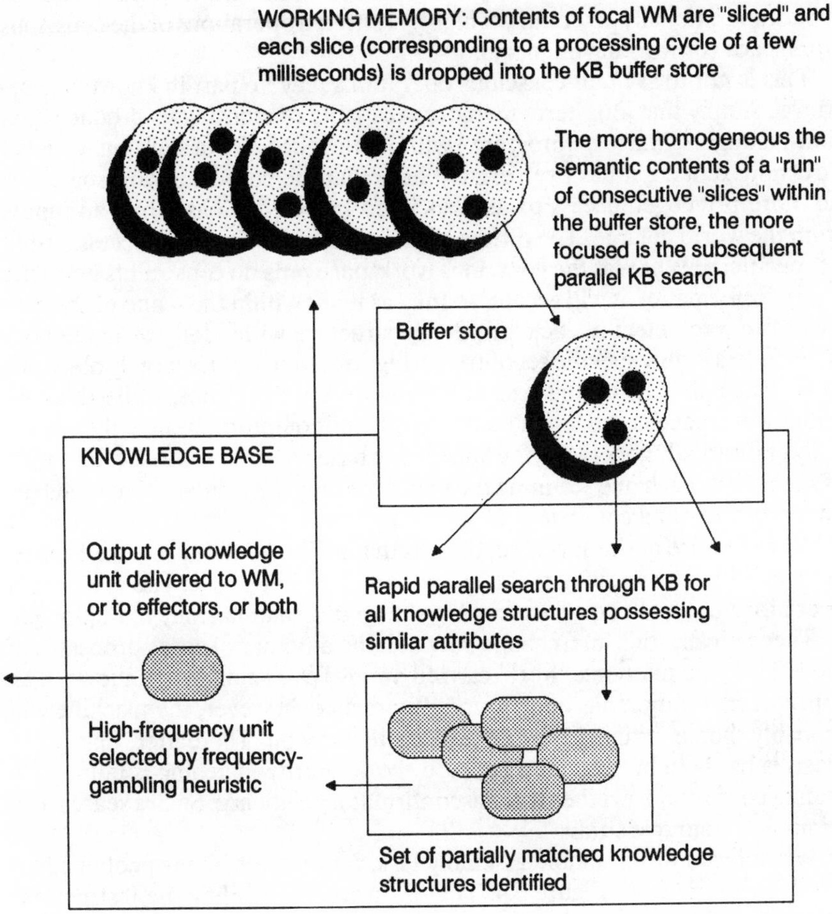

WORKING MEMORY: Contents of focal WM are "sliced" and
each slice (corresponding to a processing cycle of a few
milliseconds) is dropped into the KB buffer store

The more homogeneous the
semantic contents of a "run"
of consecutive "slices" within
the buffer store, the more
focused is the subsequent
parallel KB search

Buffer store

KNOWLEDGE BASE

Output of knowledge
unit delivered to WM,
or to effectors, or both

Rapid parallel search through KB for
all knowledge structures possessing
similar attributes

High-frequency unit
selected by frequency-
gambling heuristic

Set of partially matched knowledge
structures identified

Figure 5.2. The role of intention in the fallible machine.
Intentional activity involves the allocation of limited attentional resources to sustaining a *run* of same-element
slices within FWM. The consistency of these *slices* creates
a high level of focused activation within a restricted set of
knowledge structures. This, in turn, helps to preserve the
coherence of FWM activity.

activities are performed in a largely automatic fashion, without recourse to the computationally powerful yet highly restricted operations of the conscious workspace (or working memory).

This is not to say that conscious operations play no part in knowledge retrieval, simply that long-term memory is capable of emitting its products (actions, thoughts, images, words, etc.) without the necessity of such higher-level direction. Indeed, it has been argued here that the conscious workspace has no more privileged access to its associated knowledge base than do inputs from the world at large. The difference lies not in the degree of access, but in its specificity. Whereas the conscious workspace puts no constraints upon the type of information it will accept, so long as it lies within the scope of the sensory system to detect it, each knowledge structure within long-term memory is tuned to a highly specific set of triggering conditions and is largely oblivious to all that falls outside this exceedingly narrow range. Thus, while the conscious workspace keeps 'open house' to all kinds of information, either externally or internally generated, the knowledge base constitutes a vast community of specialists, each one scanning the world for only those inputs that match its own very parochial concerns.

A key feature of this machine, then, is that information is processed simultaneously by both working memory and the knowledge base. The concurrent operations of these two structures are shown diagrammatically in Figure 5.3.

Theoretically, this interchange between the automatic search processes of the KB and the inference 'work' carried out by FWM could continue until an appropriate solution has been found. In practice, however, the machine will probably 'home in' upon a hypothesis quite early on. Thereafter, that hypothesis is likely to be sustained because the similarity-matching is tailored to finding confirmatory rather than disconfirmatory evidence. Such a search also minimises cognitive strain.

When faced with a simple assembly task, for instance, many people adopt the strategy shown in Figure 5.4. That is, instead of reading the instructions carefully and then following them step-by-step, they frequently just 'fiddle' with the problem configuration until a recognisable pattern (idea) comes along, and then act upon it. This creates a new configuration . . . and so on. In other words, they act (a) to minimise cognitive strain and (b) to maximise the chances of automatic pattern recognition. Likewise, children (or adults), when set an apparently difficult problem will search their questioner's face, the situation or other people's expressions for a clue to act upon, even though they have been provided with sufficient information to derive the solution deductively.

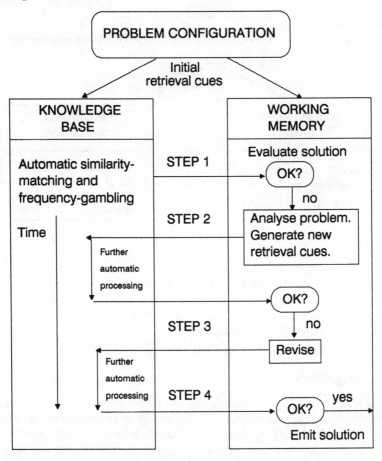

Figure 5.3. Concurrent processing by the knowledge base and working memory during problem
solution. Step 1. The first solution is delivered to
WM as the result of automatic similarity-matching and frequency-gambling acting upon the initial retrieval cues. Step 2. The solution is
evaluated by WM and found inadequate. Analytical processes generate revised retrieval cues.
These are processed automatically within the KB,
and a second solution is delivered to WM. Step 3.
Again the solution is judged as inadequate, and
further cues are generated by WM processing.
Step 4. The third solution is found to be satisfactory and emitted.

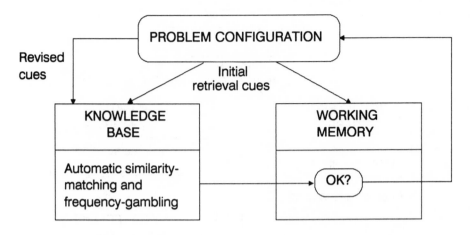

Figure 5.4. An everyday problem-solving strategy.
Instead of doing inference work, default solutions
are continuously emitted until a familiar pattern
comes along. The problem is worked out in action
rather than in thought.

7. Taking stock

Any attempt to model the fundamentals of human cognition must address two
basic issues: (a) the properties of the knowledge base and its modes of representation, and (b) a set of rules or heuristics for selecting which stored knowledge structure will be activated in any given situation. This response-selection
element not only provides the model with its human information-handling
characteristics, but also creates and shapes the recognisably human error
forms.

In an ideal world, each particular problem configuration would elicit one
appropriate stored solution. But the reality is usually far from ideal and contains two major sources of 'fuzziness': (a) The calling conditions associated
with any particular problem configuration can match several stored structures
or none at all; or they can be degraded, not attended to, or absent and (b)
knowledge structures can be incomplete (not all facts known), wrong or missing altogether. As far as the cognitive system is concerned, these two kinds
of 'fuzziness' are functionally equivalent. Both represent sources of underspecification (see Chapter 4). These varieties of underspecification create the
conditions under which similarity and frequency biases are most likely to show
themselves.

Inevitably, this design for a fallible machine dodges many crucial issues and skates over others. In particular, it says very little about inference, and nothing at all about the way FWM decides that it has found an appropriate problem solution. What it tries to do, however, is to convey a picture of an information-handling 'machine' that, though capable of internalising the complexity of the world around it, is in essence driven by a small number of simple computational principles. In the next part of this chapter, we will examine one attempt to implement these notions within a computer model designed to simulate the retrieval of incomplete knowledge.

8. Modelling the retrieval of incomplete knowledge

8.1. Category generation

This section describes the basic features of a computer model (implemented in Prolog) designed to emulate the way in which people with a relatively sparse knowledge of United States presidents respond to the request to generate exemplars of that category. All the computer models described in this chapter were written by Philip Marsden of the University of Manchester.

8.1.1. What the model 'knows'

The model's knowledge base comprised 32 frames, corresponding to each of 32 individuals who have occupied the office of president of the United States, from Washington through to Reagan. (Why this should be 32 rather than the (then) complete list of 39 presidents will be explained later.) Each frame contained two pieces of information: (a) the president's name, and (b) an actual frequency of encounter value (ACTFOE).

The ACTFOE values were obtained from a diary study (Marsden, 1987) in which 10 volunteers kept a daily tally over a period of 13 weeks of the number of times they encountered (in the media, in books, in conversation, etc.) any one of the 39 presidential names. The ACTFOE value for each president constituted the sum of all the encounters over the record-keeping period for all diarists. These ACTFOE values are listed in rank order in Table 5.1.

The following presidents were not logged in the diary study and consequently did not appear in the knowledge base for the category generation simulation: Harding, Madison, Fillmore, Pierce, Andrew Johnson and Zachary Taylor.

8.1.2. How the model works

On each run, the program was designed to simulate the output of a single human subject when the latter was asked to generate as many names of American presidents as possible within a time span of approximately 5 minutes. The structure of the program is most conveniently described in three sections:

Table 5.1. Actual frequency of encounter (ACTFOE) values
for U.S. presidents.

Ronald Reagan: 1822	Calvin Coolidge: 11
John F. Kennedy: 176	Thomas Jefferson: 10
Richard Nixon: 145	Benjamin Harrison: 6
Abraham Lincoln: 93	John Tyler: 6
Franklin D. Roosevelt: 75	John Adams: 6
George Washington: 63	William H. Harrison: 4
Lyndon B. Johnson: 61	John Quincy Adams: 3
Jimmy Carter: 57	James A. Garfield: 3
Woodrow Wilson: 56	Rutherford B. Hayes: 3
Dwight D. Eisenhower: 53	William McKinley: 3
Theodore Roosevelt: 47	James K. Polk: 3
Gerald Ford: 43	Grover Cleveland: 2
Harry S. Truman: 40	James Buchanan: 2
Ulysses S. Grant: 31	William H. Taft: 2
Herbert Hoover: 21	Martin van Buren: 1
	Chester A. Arthur: 1

Section 1: This is the control section and contains the executive rule for generating presidential exemplars. Ultimately the rule fails; but, in the process, it outputs the results of the search as a side-product.

Section 2: This section converts the ACTFOE values into calculated frequencies-of-encounter (CALCFOEs). The CALCFOE is a random number between unity and the ACTFOE value for each president. These values differ on each run. However, the larger the original ACTFOE, the greater the chance that the CALCFOE will also be relatively large.

Section 3: This section deals with the knowledge base search procedures, and contains the following components:

(a) *search* is the mechanism that guides the scanning process. It has three parameters: *upper* (the upper limit of the search scan – defined as a CALCFOE value), *lower* (the lower limit) and *time* (a crude time interval flag). Following each instantiation of scan, search checks to see if the noise threshold (a CALCFOE value below which no presidents are retrieved – analogous to the subject's knowledge level) has been reached before altering the scan parameters and adjusting the time interval. It then initiates a further search.

(b) *set band* is a sequence which sets the width of the search process in CALCFOE units. With each successive search, the band becomes narrower, thus retrieving progressively fewer items. This simulates the increasing difficulty experienced by subjects in generating new exemplars as the output progresses.

(c) *check band* checks the new bandwidth to ensure that its value never falls below unity.

(d) *scan* is the search band. It checks the presidential knowledge base to establish if the CALCFOE falls within its range. If it does, then it returns the president's name, the CALCFOE value and the time interval.

(e) *set noise* establishes a different noise threshold for each run. This varies randomly between 11 and 49 CALCFOE units and is intended to simulate the fact that within a given population of subjects there will be differences in the level of knowledge (i.e., a value of 11 corresponds to relatively high knowledge, and a value of 49 represents a very low knowledge level).

(f) *noise* is the noise threshold, a value (in CALCFOE units) below which no items can be retrieved.

The model thus has two sources of quasi-random fluctuation from run to run: the variable CALCFOE value for each president within the knowledge base, and the noise threshold, varying between 11 and 49 CALCFOE units. Since it scans downwards from high CALCFOE values to lower ones in increasingly smaller 'bites', it will show a marked but not invariant tendency to output high CALCFOE presidents first. This, in turn, will be positively (but not perfectly correlated) with the ACTFOE values. That is, there is a built-in tendency for items to be generated in an order corresponding roughly to presidential frequency of encounter in the world, as determined by the diary study. This tendency corresponds to well-established findings (Bousfield & Barclay, 1950; Battig & Montague, 1969; Reason, 1984, 1986).

8.1.3. The model's output

The program was run 100 times to simulate the performance of 100 'virtual' subjects. The number of presidential names generated per run ranged between 2 and 17. The mean output was 9.95 presidential names. This corresponds reasonably closely to the level of output of 128 British psychology students, whose mean output was 10.4 names.

This group constituted the main comparison sample. As part of an earlier study (see Chapter 4), they had performed the following tasks:

(a) They were asked to generate exemplars of the category 'American presidents'.

(b) One week later they were presented with a list of all 39 presidents in random order and asked (i) to indicate whether or not they recognised each name as belonging to an American president, and (ii) to rate each president on a frequency-of-encounter scale, ranging from 1 (hardly ever encountered) to 7 (encountered very frequently indeed).

Additional comparisons were made between the model's output and that of 159 Yale and Purdue students (Roediger & Crowder, 1976). These U.S. students were given 5 minutes to write down, in any order, the names of all the presidents of the United States whom they could recall.

Overall, these model/subject comparisons yielded the following six measures for each of the 39 presidents: (a) total number of model returns (model), (b) per cent recall, British sample, (c) per cent recall, U.S. sample, (d) per cent recognition, British sample, (e) mean frequency rating, British sample and (f) actual encounters, 10 subjects over 13 weeks. The intercorrelations for these values are shown in Table 5.2.

The highly significant concordance between the model's output and the responses of the human subjects indicates that the program has captured some essential features of human category generation. It is also consistent with the existence of a common factor controlling a substantial proportion of the variance across all six measures. Several considerations point to presidential 'salience-in-the-world', or relative frequency-of-encounter, as the principal basis for this common variance.

The first and most obvious fact is that the only systematic parameter influencing the model's performance from run to run is the CALCFOE value. This, in turn, is constrained and thus shaped by the ACTFOE values.

Table 5.2. Product-moment correlations between the model's output and data from U.K. and U.S. students.

Human subject measure	Correlation with model output
U.K. recall data	0.93 **
U.S. recall data	0.78 **
U.K. recognition data	0.87 **
U.K. frequency ratings	0.93 **

$** = p < .001$

Interestingly, the ACTFOE measure, by which the model was actually 'tuned', correlated less well with the program's performance than did the rated frequencies of encounter obtained from the British psychology students. One interpretation of this finding is that these actual encounters by 10 individuals over a period of 13 weeks in the autumn of 1986 constituted a less reliable mapping of presidential salience than the more global and impressionistic ratings made by the larger undergraduate sample. Certainly these estimates corresponded more closely to the performance of the U.S. students 10 years earlier (r = 0.94, as opposed to 0.324 between ACTFOE and U.S. recall). This suggests that although relative presidential salience differs slightly from one side of the Atlantic to the other (Americans are more knowledgeable about the early presidents than their British counterparts), there is nevertheless a good deal of commonality across the two cultures.

The results for both the model and the humans were consistent with the theoretical assumptions spelled out earlier in the chapter. That is, when a retrieval task is minimally specified, as is the case in category generation, the responses will show maximum influence of the frequency-gambling retrieval heuristic.

8.2. Recognition from limited factual cues

This section describes a computer simulation (again implemented in Prolog by Philip Marsden) of the ways in which people with varying knowledge of the domain of U.S. presidents respond to the task of identifying an appropriate subset of 20 listed presidents on the basis of one to three biographical facts (retrieval cues). The model is built upon the foundations of the category generation program and is designed specifically to respond to section B of the presidential quiz described in Chapter 4.

8.2.1. The normative knowledge base

In the recognition model, the normative knowledge base (NKB) contains a specific number of true facts about each president. These facts are represented as an entity/attribute matrix of the kind shown in Figure 5.5. The entities in this case are the presidents, each of whom has a number of binary attributes relating to selected autobiographical facts. Each presidential frame thus contains the following items of information:

(a) A president's name.

(b) An actual frequency of encounter (ACTFOE) value, derived from either actual observations or ratings by individuals within the common sub-culture.

(c) True binary values for each of 11 attributes, including whether completed (or did not) term of office, Republican or Democrat, was

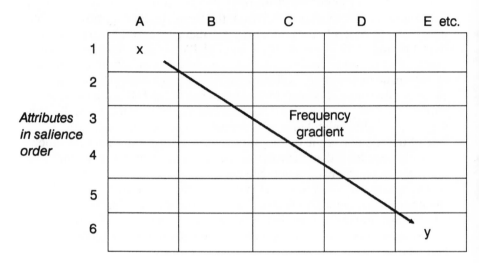

Figure 5.5. The basic features of the entity/attribute
matrix. This is the knowledge format used in the recognition program. The entities in this case are U.S.
presidents (ranked from left to right according to
frequency of encounter) and the attributes are biographical facts (ranked from top to bottom according to their salience) relating to one or more of these
presidents. Thus, x is the most salient fact about the
most frequently encountered president and y is the
least salient fact about the least frequently encountered president. The attributes (e.g., Democrat,
assassinated, etc.) vary in their *diagnosticity*, that is,
their ability to discriminate between entities (presidents). For example, being a Democrat has relatively low diagnosticity, since it is an attribute shared by
approximately half the presidents. Having been assassinated, on the other hand, is highly diagnostic
since it is an attribute common to only four presidents.

(or was not) a lawyer, was (or was not) a vice-president), did (or did not) have an overseas war during presidency.

(d) Salience weightings (0–100) for each attribute value. These reflect empirically-determined co-occurrence ratings between a president and a given fact.

As before, each run of the model represents the performance of one human subject. A different descriptive knowledge base (DKB) is created on each run. Only the DKB has any influence on the model's output for that run.

8.2.2. The descriptive knowledge base (DKB)

Each DKB is an incomplete (but not distorted) version of the NKB, representing a single individual's domain knowledge. Over many runs, the contents of the DKB will approximate to the NKB, but will never achieve the same completeness.

The conversion from NKB to DKB always involves quasi-random adjustments of the 'tuning' factors: ACTFOE and attribute salience values. These, in turn, determine a fact's probability of appearing in the DKB. The basic assumption is: the more salient-in-the-world the president, the more will be known about him.

On each run, the model converts ACTFOEs into calculated frequency-of-encounter values (CALCFOEs). These are random numbers lying between 1 and the ACTFOE for each president. The values differ on each run. Since the presence or absence of facts depends, in part, upon these CALCFOEs, these run-by-run variations will cause changes in the degree of completeness (relative to the NKB) of the DKB.

The detailed steps in the creation of the DKB on each run are as follows:

(a) Program generates a CALCFOE for each presidential frame.

(b) The presidential frame is assigned to one of four knowledge bands on the basis of this CALCFOE value. The higher the band, the more facts will be 'known' about each president. Each president has a different probability of band assignment, depending upon his ACTFOE value.

(c) The program makes a quasi-random adjustment to the salience weights (attached to the attribute values) in each presidential frame. These salience weights take a value between 50 per cent and 100 per cent of the original NKB weighting (derived empirically). The 50 per cent lower cut-off is set to prevent facts from disappearing too readily.

(d) Each knowledge band has a threshold salience value. If a fact's salience value exceeds this threshold, it is included in the DKB and could be used in making a recognition match.

8.2.3. The role of working memory

Working memory (WM) controls the retrieval sequence by executing various procedures (search, comparison and decision—see below). It also collects, collates and holds the products of these processes. WM memory engages in three types of activity.

(a) It elicits information from DKB relating to the current calling conditions. The information from this stage is held in three units: calling conditions, negative instances (contraindications) and number of cues present.

(b) WM then executes a more detailed search. It requests presidential names with attributes corresponding to the current retrieval cues. Note that WM has no influence over the actual search, but it can reject search products and/or reactivate the search processes.

(c) On receipt of a suitable candidate, WM begins to accumulate evidence both for and against the returned name. Having done this, it activates the decision-making procedure (see below). This results in either an output or a non-output. In the case of the latter, the search is reactivated.

8.2.4. The search processes

WM has no direct access to the DKB. Interactions between WM and the DKB are mediated by the basic search processes: similarity-matching and frequency-gambling.

Search is invoked by WM following the presentation of a set of calling conditions. Its termination follows acceptance by WM of a search product.

Similarity-matching seeks high-context (well-matched) exemplars of the calling conditions. Frequency-gambling looks for high-frequency exemplars.

8.2.5. Comparative processes

Once a candidate has been returned to WM (along with its CALCFOE and attribute list), the comparative process is initiated. The program accumulates two kinds of evidence: (a) confirmatory evidence—confirming a match between calling conditions and returned attributes, and (b) contradictory evidence—indicating the presence of disconfirming facts.

Each calling condition is examined in turn to see whether it can be matched to a known fact. When all possible evidence has been collated, the decision-making phase is initiated.

8.2.6. The decision-making processes

The function of this procedure is to weigh all the evidence and to select the most appropriate strategy for that particular configuration of calling conditions and recovered facts. Four basic strategies are available.

(a) *Direct identification*: This entails the direct matching of attribute values to calling conditions. Defined formally, it is where the degree of confirmatory evidence equals the number of calling conditions. When this occurs, the presidential name currently being considered is output to the list of exemplars with a confidence value of 100 per cent.

(b) *Elimination*: This involves the recognition of a mismatch between the attribute values and the calling conditions. It is the converse of direct identification, but comes in two forms: (i) strong elimination, leading to a confident rejection of the president under consideration, and (ii) weak elimination, where the contradictory evidence comprises a single item. Most often, the candidates in this position will be eliminated. Occasionally, however, a president will be returned with a single contradictory fact and a confidence of 0 per cent. The process determining which president will be returned in this manner is a randomiser. A random number is generated in the range of 1 to 100, and the threshold for return is set at greater than or equal to 95.

(c) *Partial identification*: Here there is partial matching of attribute values to calling conditions with no contradictory evidence. This, too, functions in a strong and a weak form, the major determinant being the degree of uncertainty. When it is low, the president under consideration will be returned with an associated confidence of 50 per cent. A low degree of uncertainty is defined as an identification count equal to one less than the number of calling conditions. The weak form of partial identification comes into play when the confirmatory evidence is greater than or equal to a single item, but not equal to one less than the number of calling conditions. The criterion for selection is a random number (ranging from 1 to 100) greater or equal to 40. When successful, this process returns a weak partial identification with a confidence of 10 per cent.

(d) *Guessing*: This strategy may be invoked following a major knowledge failure in which no evidence for or against a particular president can be found. Defined formally, it operates when the degree of uncertainty equals the number of calling conditions. Two quite distinct forms of guessing can be used: calculated guessing and frequency-gambling guessing. Calculated guesses produce only 'unknown' presidents — presidents of whom the 'subject' has no knowledge, but accepts their presidential status because their names appear on the list of presidents. In contrast to this, frequency-gambling guesses produce only high-salience presidents.

8.2.7. Evaluating the model's output

The model was evaluated against the human data presented in Section 5.5. of Chapter 4. The comparison sample comprised 126 U.K. and U.S. students. These subjects were further subdivided into two samples, matched for knowledge of U.S. presidents: sample A (N = 90) and sample B (N = 91). The model's output (selected presidents), over 100 runs, for each of the six presidential quiz questions was correlated with the selections made by the evaluation samples A and B. To provide some criterion of how good this match was, the selections of sample A were correlated with those for sample B.

There was a high degree of correspondence between the model's output and the responses of samples A and B. The mean correlation coefficients (averaged over all six questions) were 0.85 and 0.87 respectively. This was not significantly less than the degree of correspondence between the two human samples (r = 0.96). These findings suggest that the model has indeed captured some of the fundamental knowledge retrieval processes involved in this particular recognition test. It remains to be seen how well this agreement holds up over other domains of knowledge, both declarative and procedural.

9. Summary and conclusions

This chapter has addressed the following question: What kind of information-handling device could produce both the correct performance and the recurrent error forms characteristic of human beings? Its starting point was the general observation, considered at length in Chapter 4; when cognitive operations are underspecified (at the planning, storage or execution phases), they tend to 'default' to contextually appropriate, high-frequency responses. Its basic assumption was that these responses were rooted in the processes by which stored knowledge items are retrieved in response to situational calling conditions.

The first part of the chapter described a notional model of human cognition having two structural components: a resource-limited, but computationally-powerful, serial workspace interacting with an effectively unlimited, parallel knowledge base. This model has three ways by which knowledge structures are brought into play in response to a set of calling conditions (retrieval cues), generated either by the environment or within the workspace. Two of them, similarity-matching (activating knowledge structures on the basis of similarity between calling conditions and stored attributes) and frequency-gambling (resolving conflicts between partially-matched 'candidates' in favour of high-frequency items), constitute the computational primitives of the system as a whole and operate automatically within the knowledge base. A third retrieval mechanism, inference, is the exclusive property of the workspace.

A key feature of the model is the assertion that the workspace can only direct knowledge retrieval through the inferential manipulation of the calling conditions. The actual search within the knowledge base is always performed by the similarity and frequency mechanisms. The only part that working memory can play in the retrieval of the products of knowledge structures (actions, images, words, etc.) is to deliver the calling conditions, to assess whether the search product is appropriate and, if not, to reinstate the search with revised cues. The workspace can reject default search products, but only when it has sufficient resources available to sustain directed inference. Such resources are severely rationed in conditions of high workload and stress. Consequently, the computational primitives will exert a powerful and pervasive influence upon all types of performance, both correct and erroneous.

The model predicts that, when retrieval operations are underspecified either as the result of impoverished domain knowledge or because of incomplete or ambiguous calling conditions, human subjects will manifest increased frequency-gambling (i.e., they will show a greater tendency to select high-frequency candidates). Thus, the degree of expertise and cue specificity are seen as functionally equivalent; diminution of either will lead to increased frequency-gambling.

The second part of the chapter described a suite of computer programs (implemented in Prolog) that (a) embodies the cognitive theory set out above; and (b) attempts to simulate the ways in which people with only a partial knowledge of the domain of U.S. presidents respond to the tasks of generating exemplars, and recognising listed presidents who fit supplied facts. The outputs of the category generation and recognition programs were evaluated against the performance of human subjects and were found to have between 60 to 80 per cent shared variance in their respective selections for the domain of U.S. presidents. These findings provide (as yet domain-specific) support for the basic assumptions of the notional model and indicate that it is possible to create an information-processing device capable of simulating both the correct and incorrect choices of human beings.

6 The detection of errors

So far, we have focused mainly upon the causes of errors, that is, upon the conditions that precede their occurrence and on the cognitive mechanisms that shape their more predictable forms. For the remaining chapters, the emphasis will shift towards their consequences, beginning here with a consideration of the processes involved in the detection and recovery of errors.

To err is human. No matter how well we come to understand the psychological antecedents of error or how sophisticated are the cognitive 'prostheses' — devices to aid memory or decision making — we eventually provide for those in high-risk occupations, errors will still occur. Errors are, as we have seen, the inevitable and usually acceptable price human beings have to pay for their remarkable ability to cope with very difficult informational tasks quickly and, more often than not, effectively. In conditions where "machines botch up, humans degrade gracefully" (Jordan, 1963). But, as we shall discuss further in the ensuing two chapters, the centralised supervisory control of complex, hazardous, opaque, tightly-coupled and incompletely understood technologies can, on occasions, transform these normally adaptive properties into dangerous liabilities.

If it is impossible to guarantee the elimination of errors, then we must discover more effective ways of mitigating their consequences in unforgiving situations. Many have suggested that this is really the only sensible way of combating the human error problem in high-risk technologies. The first step along this path is to consider what is known about the means by which slips, lapses and mistakes can be detected and recovered.

Despite the obvious importance of the topic, the psychological literature contains very little in the way of empirical studies of error detection or of theories to explain the processes by which people catch and correct errors made either by themselves or by others. What studies there are usually relate to very specific tasks such as reading (Carpenter & Daneman, 1981), writing (Hayes & Flower, 1980) or solving statistical problems (Allwood & Montgomery, 1981, 1982; Allwood, 1984). Only a few investigators have looked at error detection in real-life settings. Among these, the most important findings have been obtained by Woods (1984), who observed how nuclear power plant operators discover their errors in real and simulated emergencies, and by Rizzo, Bagnara and their co-workers (Rizzo, Bagnara & Visciola, 1986; Bagnara, Stablum, Rizzo, Fontana & Ruo, 1987), who investigated the use of a computer database by novices and the production plans made by experienced operators in a steel mill. Other investigators have carried out naturalistic studies of specific error types: slips of action (Norman, 1981) and slips of the tongue (Nooteboom, 1980). Despite the paucity of this error detection research, however, it is possible to give a preliminary account of human error detection and of the factors likely to impede it — though such a discussion will undoubtedly raise more questions than it answers. We begin by considering the various agencies that could be involved in discovering an error.

1. Modes of error detection

Both everyday observation and common sense have shown that there are probably only three ways in which people's errors are brought to their attention. Most directly, they can find out for themselves through various kinds of self-monitoring. Second, something in the environment makes it very clear that they have gone astray. Or third, the error is discovered by another person who then tells them. Each of these three detection modes is considered further below.

2. Self-monitoring

Just as the control of behaviour resides at several different levels within the nervous system, from spinal nerve reflexes at one extreme to the effortful 'online' conscious guidance of unpractised actions at the other, so also are error detection mechanisms located at various points across this multilevel control structure. They range in complexity from the automatic correction of postural deviations to the thought-intensive direction of knowledge-based performance.

The essence of feedback control (as opposed to feedforward control) is that it is error driven. Deviations of output from some ideal or desired state are fed back to the controlling agency, which then acts to minimise these discrepancies. This basic loop structure (see Figure 6.1) is present at all levels of action control. What differs between the levels is the means by which discrepancies are detected and the extent to which attentional (as opposed to automatic) processes are involved in their correction. This, in turn, carries implications for the various ways in which the 'ideal or desired state' can be defined and represented.

Although we may not know a great deal about the precise operation of these various error detection mechanisms, one thing is clear: the higher the 'level' at which they operate, the more they are themselves error prone. Selected examples of error detection processes are considered below, beginning at a relatively low level with posture control.

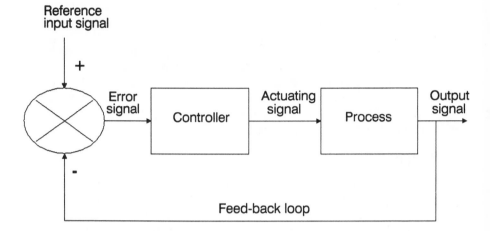

Figure 6.1. A basic feed-back loop in which the output signal is compared to a reference input signal. The difference between the output and input signals (the error signal) constitutes the input to the controller, which then acts to minimise the discrepancy. The system is thus error driven.

2.1. The automatic correction of postural deviations

Virtually all animals, even very primitive ones, possess some means to keep themselves oriented with respect to gravity. Unstable bipeds such as human beings could not maintain their upright posture without the continuous activity of these wholly automatic mechanisms. For the most part, they do their job extremely well; our dependence upon them only becomes apparent when one or other of their components is damaged. Then the consequences, in the case of sudden onset, are catastrophic. Aside from being unable to stay upright, the sufferer experiences violent dizziness, nausea, vomiting and something very akin to acute depression – like a prolonged case of the worst kind of seasickness (see Reason & Brand, 1975).

That which we mostly take for granted, postural stability, depends upon the complex interaction of the spatial senses – peripheral vision, the semicircular canals and otoliths (together comprising the vestibular system) and the muscle-skin-joint system – with the cerebellum and the spinal reflexes. The subtle orchestration of this multipart stabilising system only becomes apparent when it is abused by disease, by drugs (e.g., alcohol) or, most informatively, by a variety of laboratory manipulations. Among the latter, some potent effects can be achieved by presenting people with large-scale, moving visual

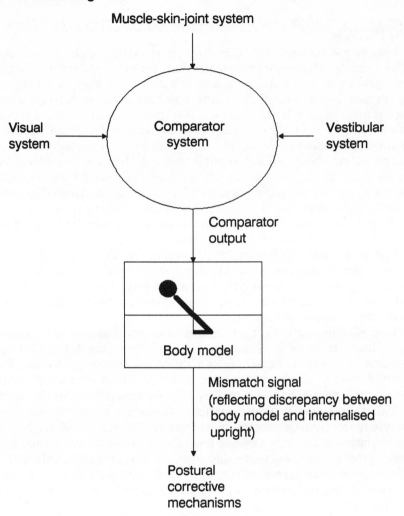

Figure 6.2. The possible mechanisms governing automatic postural corrections. Inputs from the various spatial senses are checked for their degree of correspondence, one with another, within the comparator system. The output from this comparison process adjusts the position of an internalised body model relative to the primary spatial coordinates. Where discrepancies exist between the inputs from the spatial senses, those from the visual modality override the others. Only the output from the model (the mismatch signal) acts directly upon the corrective musculature.

scenes in which all the structural elements move in unison – the technique called 'vection'.

Imagine the following situation: You are standing upright in front of a striped display that occupies the greater part of your visual field. The stripes now begin to move at a steady velocity in a downward direction while your eyes remain fixed on a target light in the centre of the display. After a few seconds, you will begin to lean forward quite involuntarily, only maintaining your balance (if at all) by fairly strenuous work on the part of your ankle and leg muscles. After about a minute, the visual motion is stopped, and the 'force' that caused your body to lean forward is removed. However, instead of drifting back to the upright position, you will now find yourself leaning backwards – to such an extent that you may be forced to hold on to something solid to avoid falling over. But, if instead of the visual motion being stopped, you simply close your eyes, then there is no tilt-back effect. Your body merely returns to the upright position and stays there.

This simple and largely irresistible lean-forward effect, together with its sequelae (see Reason, Wagner & Dewhurst, 1981), tells us a great deal about the covert processes involved in maintaining balance. A diagrammatic representation of the possible interrelationships between these various postural mechanisms is shown in Figure 6.2.

To explain these effects, it is necessary to assume that each of the spatial senses feeds its inputs to a comparator that checks for the degree of correspondence between their descriptions of the body's position and motion. The central feature of this theory, however, is that the output from this comparison process is not passed directly to the corrective musculature; instead, it acts to adjust the orientation of some internalised representation of the body's position in space. Thus, only the position of this 'body model' can direct the corrective musculature. In the example given above, the model was 'fooled' into thinking that the body was tilting backwards. As a result, it instituted postural adjuments designed to return the body to the upright position. But since the body was upright to begin with, their effect was to tilt it forwards. How could this happen?

Under natural conditions, large-scale movements of the visual field are an invariable accompaniment of self-locomotion. A uniform downward motion of the entire visual scene (relative to some fixed point on the retina) is something that normally goes along with a backward tilt. Vision is the dominant sense. Even when the other senses (as was the case in the tilt effect) are signalling veridical information, peripheral vision, although wrong, has the power to override them and to modify – in this case erroneously – the position of the 'body model' so that it adopts a tilt-back orientation. This should not be interpreted as a failure of the postural correction system. Like any biological mechanism, it is precisely attuned to a particular set of environmental conditions. And these do not include the psychological laboratory.

Why does the body overshoot the upright position when the motion is switched off? Having been driven forward by the automatic correction mechanisms, the muscle-skin-joint system has to work very hard to prevent the body from falling flat on its face. These inputs, via the comparator, to the 'body model' serve to counteract some of the effects of the visual motion. In effect, the body model reorients itself near to the apparent vertical, even though it is actually tilted forward. When the visual motion is stopped, the lean-forward force is suddenly removed and the effect of this is to 'flip' the body model to an apparent upright that lies somewhere behind the true vertical. The body then aligns itself with this apparent upright position rather than with the true vertical, putting its physical reality (as distinct from its cerebellar representation) into a tilt-back position. It does not do this when the eyes are shut during the motion because that signals 'no vision' rather than 'no motion'. Since the eyes are capable of shutting, the comparator is designed to accommodate the simple absence of vision.

The simplest way to understand this process is to imagine an elastic band, knotted in the middle and held at either end. The position of the knot represents the forward or backward tilt of the body model. When the visual motion begins, one end of the band is pulled forward, shifting the knot towards the pulling force. The compensating proprioceptive inputs then start to 'pull' at the other end, causing the knot to move back towards the central position. Now the knot is held steady by tension at either end of the band. When the visual motion stops, the force from the forward end of the band is suddenly removed, and the knot now shifts to the backward position. As the body drifts back to the upright, the proprioceptive counterforces are gradually released, but not fast enough to prevent it from adopting a backwards lean in accord with the knot (the body model). Eventually, the knot stabilises in the centre of the rubber band with little or no tension at either end. At that point, the physical body is restored to the true upright. In the case where the eyes are shut, one can think of the forces at either end of the elastic band being reduced at an approximately equal rate.

This is not the place to discuss these mechanisms further. The interested reader is directed to the relevant literature: Dichgans and Brandt (1978), and Reason, Wagner and Dewhurst (1981). The point of this discussion has been to reveal the exquisite machinery of the postural correction mechanisms, even though, paradoxically, we have had to demonstrate this by their failures in a nonecological situation. When intact under normal conditions, they function as a near-perfect piece of biological engineering without any recourse to cognitive processes. Indeed, they are only rendered fallible when forced by these high-level control agencies to operate within atypical force environments, such as are found in almost all kinds of human transport.

2.2. The detection and correction of simple motor responses and perceptual discriminations

From the mid-1960s onwards, Patrick Rabbitt and his collaborators at the University of Oxford conducted a series of studies designed, in the first instance, to identify the mechanisms by which errors in simple choice-response tasks were so rapidly and accurately corrected (Rabbitt, 1966, 1967, 1968; Rabbitt & Phillips, 1967; Rabbitt & Vyas, 1970). The investigation began with the observation that error-correcting responses tend to be faster than correct responses (Rabbitt, 1966), or even correct response repetitions (Burns, 1965), in tasks where people were required to press as quickly as possible one of a series of keys at the onset of one of a matching number of signal lamps.

It was found that people could catch and recover nearly all of their errors in these simple keyboard tasks, even though the apparatus itself gave them no indication of whether their responses were correct or not. The efficiency of this detection and correction process was unaffected by the degree to which the signals and the required responses were compatible. Moreover, error corrections occurred, on average, much more quickly than responses to other signals within the task.

The most parsimonious explanation for these results was that people detect their execution errors by comparing what they felt or saw of the wrong response with a record of what they had intended. Expressed in control theory terms, one could say that these execution errors were detected by monitoring the feedback from each response and checking it against some internal model of the correct response. Evidence for the existence of such a response 'template' comes from physiological recordings showing the existence of anticipatory muscle tension some 100 milliseconds before any overt limb movement occurs (Megaw, 1972). The fact that movement errors are detected so rapidly after their execution suggests that something like an 'echo' of the correct motor program persists after the response has been made, allowing comparison between the actual and intended responses.

Although it is clear from these data that most errors of this kind are caught and corrected by feedback-checking, there are good reasons for doubting that this is the only possible detection mechanism. It is quite possible, for example, that some motor errors in choice-reaction tasks arise not because of the misselection of the response, but because of a misperception of the signal. If a person mistook signal A for signal B, and made a response appropriate to B, there is no way that monitoring the feedback could reveal the error. Discrimination errors of this kind would require a different detection mechanism.

A further set of studies were conducted by this Oxford group to determine whether such perceptual errors can be corrected, and, if so, to identify the means of detection and correction (Rabbitt & Vyas, 1977; Rabbitt, Cumming & Vyas, 1978). The problem with the choice-reaction task, however, is that it is virtually impossible to discover retrospectively whether a particular error was due to a failure in response execution or to a failure in perceptual discrimination. To overcome this difficulty, they employed a visual search task in which subjects inspected one display of letters at a time and were required to respond differently depending upon whether the target set of letters was present or absent in a given display. Two kinds of errors could then be identified, indicating that a target was present when it was not (false identification error) or failing to respond to a target that was actually present (omission error).

It was found that omission errors were much more common than false identifications, but that many more of them were corrected. In addition, omissions were detected and corrected more rapidly than false identifications.

The general conclusion was that as well as correcting execution errors by feedback-checking, people can also correct some of the perceptual identification errors they make during visual search tasks. The differences in the relative ease of detection of omissions and false identifications could best be explained by assuming that the perceptual analysis of a display persisted for some time after an incorrect response had been made to it.

2.3. The detection and correction of speech errors

Speech, which is made up of readily identifiable linguistic units, allows for a more fine-grained analysis of error detection and correction than do other less easily segmented skill-based activities. Most psycholinguists (see Fromkin, 1980) now accept the existence of an internal monitor or 'editor' that checks speech outputs both before and immediately after their utterance. These theorists differ, however, in the degree of detail with which they specify the workings of this error-detection mechanism (see Nooteboom, 1980; Laver, 1980; Garrett, 1980).

Nooteboom (1980) analysed all the errors in Meringer's 1908 corpus (see Chapter 2) that were discovered and corrected by the speakers. Sixty-four per cent of all the errors in the corpus were corrected by their perpetrators. For both lexical and phonological errors, anticipations were detected more often than perseveration or transposition slips. The detection rate for anticipation slips was between 80 per cent and 90 per cent; for perseverations it was between 55 per cent and 66 per cent; while for transpositions it was between 14 per cent and 18 per cent. This low figure for transposition detections is readily accounted for by the method of classification. If a transposition like 'heft hemisphere' is corrected after the first phonemic error and before the spoonerism is complete, it would be classified as an anticipation error. Classifying the first halves of transpositions as anticipation errors could well explain the latter's relatively high detection rate within the corpus.

Another interesting finding was that phonological errors of all kinds were corrected at least as often as lexical errors. This tells us something about the criteria for detection and correction. Nooteboom (1980, p. 89) states:

> If possible harm to communication were the main criterion for correction, one would expect lexical errors to be corrected far more often than phonological errors. If, on the other hand, possible harm to linguistic orthodoxy were the main criterion, one would expect that phonological errors, which often lead to nonwords, would be corrected more often. If there is a difference it is rather in favour of the second possibility, but apparently the mental strategy (Laver's Monitor) dealing with the detection and correction of overt speech errors strives both for successful communication and linguistic orthodoxy.

The fact that not all errors are corrected indicates that the output editing is not perfect. Two factors are likely to be in competition immediately following the detection of a speech error: (a) an urge to correct the error immediately, and (b) an urge to complete the word being uttered. When the detection occurs before the next word boundary, the first force sometimes prevails; but when detection occurs later than this, the second force always overcomes the first. No stop occurs in the middle of a word, and the chance of detection after about five words is nil (Nooteboom, 1980).

In an ingenious set of laboratory studies designed to investigate artificially-induced spoonerisms, Baars, Motley and MacKay (1975) and Baars (1980) observed that people could be made to produce lexically possible spoonerisms (e.g., saying 'barn door' for 'darn bore') significantly more often than transpositions resulting in nonwords ('bart doard' for 'dart board'). They also noted that it was hard to get people to produce salacious spoonerisms (i.e., they show a marked reluctance to spoonerise phrases like 'fuzzy duck' or 'plucking pheasants').

These findings suggest that we edit spoken output at a number of levels, and that errors obeying lexical rules are more likely to evade the scrutiny of the 'editor', particularly if the latter is occupied elsewhere. Except, that is, when the lexically appropriate output is socially unacceptable. But, as most of us know, embarrassing speech errors still occasionally emerge, indicating that sufficient 'custodial attention' is not always available (see Chapter 3 and Reason & Lucas, 1984b).

2.4. The detection of action slips

As argued in Chapter 3, the occurrence of many actions-not-as-planned result directly from the failure of high-level attentional monitoring. Although

2. Self-monitoring

the tasks in which these moments of inattention occur are mostly run off automatically under feedforward control, some attentional investment is needed at intervals to ensure that the actions conform to current intentions, particularly when they demand a deviation from routine practice. This means bringing the conscious workspace into the control loop momentarily to check that things are running as intended. Even notoriously abstracted individuals like Archimedes or G. K. Chesterton would have needed to perform these checks fairly often in order to live anything like normal lives. In short, the process by which slips are detected has already been presented in the earlier discussion of their causes. Slips occur through the absence of necessary attentional checks and can be detected by their later occurrence.

But this is not the whole story. Making a postslip attentional check does not of itself ensure the detection of the error. Detection must also depend upon the availability of cues signalling the departure of action from current intention. When the slip involves pouring tea into a sugar bowl, the evidence is immediately apparent. But when it is something like doubly salting a stew, the error may remain undetected for a long time, particularly if the stew is destined for the freezer. The same is also true for omissions. We only realise that something we had intended to bring from home to the office was forgotten when we open our brief-cases on the following morning. As will be seen in the next chapter, undetected errors of this kind make a major contribution to system catastrophes.

Unlike speech errors, the possibility of detecting slips of action extends well beyond actual occurrence of the error. At one extreme, they may be 'caught in the act', as in Norman's (1980) example: "I was about to pour the tea into the opened can of tomatoes that was just next to the teacup. ... Not yet an error – but certainly a false movement"; while, at the other extreme, discovery may be delayed for days, weeks or months, as in the case of omitted actions. Slips are apparently detected at many levels, ranging from immediate feedback processes embedded within the action schemata (see Norman, 1981; Reason & Mycielska, 1982; Norman & Shallice, 1986) to conscious and effortful feats of memory performed after a long delay.

2.5. The detection of errors during problem solving

So far, we have been considering the detection of errors at the skill-based level of performance where any discrepancy between the current and desired state is, in principle at least, fairly easy to determine. Thus, the spatial senses (particularly the otoliths and peripheral vision) are specifically designed to register significant deviations of the body from the upright position; for speech and routine action, the goal is represented by some internally formulated intention. In the latter case, errors may go undetected if the cues signalling a departure of current action from intention are insufficiently salient and/or if the intention itself is underspecified (Norman, 1981). Usually, however, both of these conditions are satisfied, so that most speech or action slips are discovered by their perpetrators. But this is clearly not the case at the rule-based and knowledge-based levels. For the moment, we will take 'problem solving' as a blanket term to cover the various activities involved at the RB and KB performance levels (i.e., reasoning, judgement, diagnosis and decision making).

In the skill-based activities considered hitherto, the criteria for successful performance are, to a large extent, directly available within the head of the individual, ranging from automatic body tilt indicators and their associated corrective reflexes to an awareness of what is being done and what is currently intended. For problem solvers, however, the correct solution may only be present in the external world.

In knowledge-based performance, an adequate path to a desired goal is something that lies 'out there', waiting to be discovered by the problem solver. Aside from inspired guesses, the only way forward is by trial and error, where success depends upon (a) defining the goal correctly, and (b) being able to recognise and correct deviations from some adequate path towards that end. These are the strategic and tactical aspects of problem solving, and each has different implications for error detection. It is likely to be much harder to discover a strategic mistake (selecting the wrong goal) than a tactical one (taking the wrong path), since the feedback information regarding the former will be less readily specified and interpreted than that relating to the latter for several reasons. First, the success of strategic decisions can only be judged over a much longer time scale than tactical ones, and then only in reference to some superordinate or more distant goal. Second, the criteria for success or failure can often only be judged with the benefits of hindsight. Third, the identification of a goal constitutes a theory about the future state of the world and is thus subject to the 'blinkering' of confirmation bias and anxiety reduction. So, not only is there less objective information upon which to base an adequate strategic decision, there are also powerful subjective influences at work to restrict the search for cues bearing upon the inadequacy of this choice. It follows from this, therefore, that the task of error detection will be easier in those problems for which the correct solution is clearly recognisable in advance, so that present performance is judged only at the tactical level.

2.5.1. The Swedish studies

One of the most detailed investigations of error detection during problem solving was carried out by Allwood (1984) of the University of Gothenberg. He asked subjects to think aloud while attempting to solve statistical problems. For the purposes of analysis, this task was divided into two phases: (a) a progressive phase, when the subject works towards the goal state of the problem, and (b) an evaluative phase, when the subject checks upon some completed part of the problem. The latter may be either affirmative (the subject is satisfied with current progress) or negative. Error detection always occurs during negative evaluations and involves two stages: the triggering of the error detection mechanisms and later steps taken to discover and correct the error.

Analysis of the subjects' verbal protocols suggested that negative evaluation episodes may be classified into three types:

(a) *Standard check* (SC). These are initiated independently of the specific properties of the previous work: the subject simply decides to carry out a general check on progress.

(b) *Direct error-hypotheses formation* (DEH). These episodes are triggered by an abrupt detection of a presumed error. They need not occur immediately after the error was made, nor do they necessarily discover actual errors.

(c) *Error suspicion* (ES). Here the subject notices something unusual, and suspects that an error has been made. Whereas with the DEH mode, the subject's remarks always relate to a specific, though possibly only presumed, error; ES episodes relate to some property of the produced solution without initially identifying the precise cause for concern.

These findings support two kinds of theories concerning error detection. The SC episodes, identified in the protocols, are evidence for the centrally-invoked mechanisms suggested by Hayes and Flower (1980), Sussman (1975) and Allwood and Montgomery (1982). These are not initiated by any feature of the problem solution, rather they emerge as a characteristic part of the subject's problem-solving technique. Other theories about error detection emphasise the spontaneous, data-driven nature of the process. Errors may be discovered either because of a match between stored representations of past errors and currently observed ones (see Hayes & Flower, 1980; Sussman, 1975), or the detection process may be triggered between the subject's general expectations and the results of his or her problem-solving efforts (see Baars, 1980; Carpenter and Daneman, 1981). DEH episodes conform to the first kind of triggering, while ES episodes are compatible with the second kind.

Taken overall, Allwood's results may be summarised as follows:

(a) Only one-third of the undetected errors were relevant to some evaluation phase. Subjects clearly had difficulty in reacting to the effects of their errors.

(b) Among the various kinds of evaluation, DEH and ES episodes occurred most frequently. Ninety-five per cent of the former and 66 per cent of the latter were triggered by erroneous solution parts.

(c) Execution errors (slips) were detected far more readily than solution method errors (mistakes). A much higher proportion of the slips

were detected by DEH episodes, which did not seem to be particularly well suited to picking up mistakes. The results also highlighted the
importance of ES episodes for the detection of solution method errors.

(d) The chances of a successful error detection occurring during ES
episodes diminished rapidly as time elapsed between the error and the
episode. This effect was more apparent for execution slips than for solution method errors.

2.5.2. The Italian studies

In two separate studies, Rizzo and his collaborators (Rizzo, Bagnara & Visciola, 1986; Bagnara, Stablum, Rizzo, Fontana & Ruo, 1987) examined the relationship between the three basic error types (outlined in Chapter 3) and the
three self-monitoring detection processes discussed above (Allwood, 1984).

In the first study, 16 'naive' subjects were trained to use a database system
(Appleworks) in two sessions. A third session instructed them in the 'talk
aloud' technique to be used in the experiment proper. Subsequently, there
were four successive experimental sessions, each more complex than the last.
These sessions involved (a) finding a given item and reporting its values, (b)
finding three items and changing their values, (c) creating a new file from information already present within the database and (d) creating three new files
and printing them out. No time limits were imposed upon these activities.
Overall, the subjects made 924 errors and detected 780 of them.

Most skill-based slips were detected during DEH episodes, whereas the
bulk of the knowledge-based mistakes were picked up during ES episodes.
Rule-based mistakes, however, were discovered primarily by either DEH or
ES episodes.

A very similar pattern of error types and detection modes was observed in
a second study carried out in a steel works. Eight experienced operators were
required to carry out a simulated production planning exercise relating to a
hot strip mill. The subjects' work was videorecorded and subsequently analysed by the experimenters and by task experts. The subjects made 95 errors
and detected 74 of them.

In both studies, a reasonably consistent association was found between
error types and detection modes. Slips were detected mainly by direct error
hypothesis episodes; rule-based mistakes by a mixture of DEH and error suspicion episodes; and knowledge-based mistakes were discovered largely as the
result of standard check behaviour. These findings provide further support for
the differentiation of the three basic error types set out in Chapter 3, and for
Allwood's categorisation of self-monitoring processes. They also carry important implications for designing future systems that provide the maximum
opportunity for error detection and recovery.

3. Environmental error cueing

3.1. Forcing functions

The most unambiguous way by which the environment can inform us that we have made an error is to block our onward progress. If we have failed to turn the appropriate keys in all the locks or not drawn all the bolts, the door will not open. If we attempt to drive away a car without first switching on the ignition, it will not move. If we have not made all the appropriate connections in the wiring of an electrical applicance, it will not work. These are what Norman has termed *forcing functions*: "something that prevents the behaviour from continuing until the problem has been corrected" (Lewis & Norman, 1986, p. 420).

The existence of appropriate forcing functions guarantees error detection. Sometimes they are a natural property of the task (as in the case of the locks and bolts). In other cases, they are deliberately built in by the system designer. Most word processing packages, for example, will not allow you to return to the operating system until you have saved the current text file. Some computer manufacturers go one stage further and physically prevent the removal of the diskette until the file has been saved. Note that in both cases, however, these forcing functions are not proof against the user simply switching off the computer prematurely.

A harsh fact of life, and one that contributes to a large proportion of maintenance errors (see Chapter 7), is that there are usually many more forcing functions available in dismantling a piece of equipment than there are in reassembling it. In stripping down a tap or a part of an engine to its component parts, each step in the process is cued by the physical characteristics of the item. It is simply not possible, for example, to remove the washer from most taps without first taking off the handle. Unfortunately, these cues are hardly ever present when it comes to putting the pieces back together again, hence, the 'garage floor phenomenon', captured by cartoons in which the oil-covered male figure turns to the woman saying 'That'll fix it', and she replies, eyeing the ground beneath the car, 'How clever of you to save all those pieces'.

Like good advice, a forcing function is most valuable if it does not come too late. Forcing functions encountered long after the commission of an error provide little diagnostic help. Indeed, they may actually promote the occurrence of further errors. The process of back-tracking from a forcing function creates additional opportunities for deviation and can lead to total confusion on the part of the fault finder.

People's reactions to forcing functions are not always entirely rational. How many of us, for example, have stood continuously rattling the handle of a door we have failed to unlock? Some individuals see forcing functions not as an indication of past correctable errors, but as a physical barrier to be overcome

by other more direct means: jumping over, driving through, or something —
quite literally — to be forced open. Responses to forcing functions, particularly those designed to guide emergency action (i.e., barriers across basement
stairs blocking a non-escape route), are clearly worth closer investigation.

In the course of their investigation of error detection in steel mill operators,
Bagnara and coauthors (1987) examined the extent to which forcing functions
contributed to the discovery of various error types. They identified three levels of mismatch or 'failed expectation': (a) forcing functions, when errors lead
to a blocking of further progress; (b) external feedback, when information relating to the error is available in the environment; and (c) internal feedback,
when error-related information is available within the subject's working memory, but not in the environment.

It was found that the efficiency of forcing function mismatches was greater
for the recovery of slips than it was for mistakes, particularly knowledge-based
ones. In the latter case, the operators had considerable difficulty in moving
from mismatch detection to appropriate diagnosis to effective error recovery.
This, in turn, derived from a complex interaction between the inadequacy of
the operators' system knowledge (even though their working experience
ranged from 13 to 17 years) and the inflexibility of the system itself. We will
return to the difficulty of recovering knowledge-based mistakes later on in this
chapter.

3.2. Cued discovery

Sometimes a piece of problem-solving behaviour is not so much wrong as plain
foolish — foolish, that is, when you come to realise that a far simpler solution
was readily available. Occasionally, the world allows you to discover your foolishness by accident, as in the following personal example.

The right front tyre of my car was badly worn, so I decided to exchange
the wheel for the spare. I jacked up the car and attempted to loosen
the nuts securing the wheel. But these had been tightened by some
muscle-bound mechanic and refused to budge. I tried various ways to
shift them: brute force, penetrating oil, and more brute force. Then I
tried hammering at the end of the spanner. Nothing worked. Not only
were the nuts seized tight, but the wheel turned whenever I tried to
get a purchase on the spanner. This, I concluded, was the root of the
problem. If I could prevent the wheel from turning, the nuts would
surely be unable to resist my efforts.

My subsequent thinking went along these lines. Putting on the hand-
brake won't help because that only works on the rear wheels, and the
same applies to putting the car in gear. So I'll have to use the brake
pedal. But I can't do that and work the nuts at the same time. What
about using something heavy to keep the brake pedal depressed? No,

I don't have anything handy that is heavy enough. I know. I'll get my wife to sit in the car with her foot on the brake pedal. Ah! She won't be able to get in through the driver's door because the jack is preventing it from opening. And if she gets in on the passenger's side, she might rock the car off the jack. I'll have to bring the car down and take away the jack so she can get in . . . So, I lowered the jack, and it was only when all four wheels were firmly back on the ground that I realised I had accidentally discovered the solution to the problem of the turning wheel. (Reason & Mycielska, 1982, pp. 81-82)

A more proficient tyre changer would never have jacked up the car without first loosening the nuts. But that is not the point. The problem here was not faulty logic. The error lay in following a blinkered line of thought from one difficulty to the next without considering the total 'problem space'. And then, quite serendipitously, the answer appeared beneath my nose, revealing the earlier foolishness. I did not encounter a forcing function exactly. The environment simply provided an opportunity for rejoining the correct path.

3.3. System responses to error

Lewis and Norman (1986) identified six possible ways in which a system can respond to its operators' errors. The actual examples are taken from human-computer interactions, but their underlying principles are applicable to a wide range of systems.

3.3.1. 'Gagging'

A 'gag' is a forcing function that prevents users from expressing unrealisable intentions. In a human-computer interaction, this could take the form of locking the keyboard to prevent further typing until the terminal has been reset. Raskin (1974), cited by Lewis and Norman (1986), inserted such 'gags' within his tutorial language system FLOW. If a user attempts to key in a character that does not form a legal command, it is not accepted.

3.3.2. Warnings

Whereas the 'gag' presents a block to anything but appropriate responses from users, warnings simply inform them of potentially dangerous situations. The user is left to decide the correct course of action. Thus, the Macintosh interface provides menus that cover all possible actions, including those that are not legal at that particular time. These illegal actions are distinguished by a grey shading. As Lewis and Norman put it, such warnings are error messages before the fact.

3.3.3. "Do nothing"

As the name implies, the system simply fails to respond to an illegal input. It quite literally does nothing, and the user is left with the task of sorting out what went wrong. Such a device is only helpful when adequate feedback information is available.

3.3.4. Self-correct

Whereas the 'do nothing' method is the simplest error-preventing technique, 'self-correct' devices can be extremely sophisticated. Here, once an error (usually a programming error) is detected, the system tries to guess some legal action that corresponds to the user's current intentions. A particularly 'intelligent' example is 'DWIM: Do What I Mean' (Teitelman & Masinter, 1981), available on the InterLisp system. Teitelman, the designer of the system, gave its rationale as follows: "If you have made an error, you are going to have to correct it anyway. I might as well have DWIM try to correct it. In the best case, it gets it right. In the worst case it gets it wrong and you have to undo it: but you would have had to make a correction anyway, so DWIM can't make it worse" (quoted by Lewis & Norman, 1986, p. 423).

3.3.5. "Let's talk about it"

Some systems respond to user errors by beginning a dialogue. A useful example cited by Lewis and Norman (1986) is the way that many Lisp systems react to user-induced problems. The user receives a message describing as far as possible the source of the difficulty. He or she is then automatically switched into the 'Lisp Debugger', which allows the user to interact directly with system so as to locate the error.

2.3.6. "Teach me"

On detecting an unknown or inexact input, the system quizzes the user as to what it was he or she had in mind. In short, the system asks the user to teach it. For instance, when one natural language inquiry system (Clout) encounters a word it does not understand, it asks the user for a definition. If the system fails to understand one of the words making up the definition, that too is queried and so on until the definition is comprehended. The new words or phrases are then stored by the system and are accepted without question in future interactions.

4. Error detection by other people

At Three Mile Island (see Chapter 7 for a more detailed discussion of this accident), the operators failed to recognise that the power operated relief valve (PORV) had not automatically closed, as it was designed to do in the course of recovery from a reactor trip. They were misled by the control panel indications showing that the valve was 'commanded' shut; they failed to appreciate that this did not, by itself, signify that the valve was actually closed (see also Chapter 4). This error was further compounded by two other crew failures. First, they twice misread a 285 degrees Fahrenheit temperature as being only

235 degrees. Second, they wrongly assumed that the observed high temperature was due to a chronically leaking valve. As a consequence, they did not identify the true state of the plant for more than two hours. The resulting water loss caused significant damage to the reactor.

The stuck-open PORV was only discovered two and a half hours into the incident when the shift supervisor of the oncoming shift noticed that the PORV discharge temperature was about 25 degrees hotter than the code safety discharge temperature. He correctly interpreted the reading as showing a stuck-open PORV. The associated block valve was shut, thus isolating the malfunctioning PORV. Only at this point did effective recovery actions begin.

At Oyster Creek (a General Electric boiling water reactor) on 2 May 1979, an operator erroneously closed four pump discharge valves instead of two. This effectively shut off all natural circulation in the core area. The error was only discovered 31 minutes later, when the engineering supervisor entered the control room and noticed a precipitous decline in the water level after a discharge valve had been opened. He noted the unintended closure of the B and C discharge valves while walking to check the pump seal display.

That these are not isolated incidents has been shown by Woods (1984), who analysed 99 simulated emergency scenarios, using 23 experienced nuclear power plant crews in 8 different events. He categorised operator errors into two groups: (a) state identification problems (misdiagnoses), and (b) execution failures (slips). Whereas half the execution failures were detected by the crews themselves, none of the diagnostic errors were noticed by the operators who made them. They were only discovered by 'fresh eyes' (i.e., by some external agent). Nearly three-fourths of all the errors remained undetected. Woods concluded that the most common cause of the failure to correct system state errors was 'fixation' on the part of the operators. Misdiagnoses tended to persist regardless of an accumulation of contradictory evidence.

These observations are very much in keeping with what we know of knowledge-based processing in particular, and of mistakes in general. When the diagnostic hypothesis is incorrect, feedback that is useful for detecting slips is unavailable. There is no discrepancy between action and intention, only between the plan and the true state of affairs.

5. Relative error detection rates

We have now considered a number of studies specifically concerned with error detection. Each examined a different task or activity. In most cases, these studies also differentiated between errors detected at different levels of performance: skill-based, rule-based and knowledge-based. From these data, it is possible to make crude comparisons between the error detection rates associated with (a) various degrees of task difficulty, and (b) different performance levels.

5.1. Detection rates and task complexity

The overall detection rates for these studies (irrespective of error type) is listed below.

Speech errors (Nooteboom/Meringer, 1908): 64 per cent minimum. (Note: This is the correction rate. Detection rate would presumably have been much higher.)

Statistical problem solving (Allwood, 1984): 69 per cent.

Database manipulation (Rizzo et al., 1986): 84 per cent to 92 per cent. (Note: These two values are from the two conditions employed in the study. Only condition 1 was discussed earlier.)

Steel mill production planning (Bagnara et al., 1987): 78 per cent.

Simulated nuclear power plant emergencies (Woods, 1984): 38 per cent.

Thus, the detection rates for all but one of these tasks were relatively high, ranging from just below 70 per cent to over 90 per cent. The clear exception was recovery from simulated nuclear power plant emergencies: 38 per cent. Against this relatively low figure, however, should be set the fact that the overall error rate among these operators was extremely low: only 39 recorded errors in 99 test scenarios (though this may say more about the investigators' ability to detect errors than their actual commission by the operators).

This comparison by itself does not really provide sufficient grounds to infer that error detection rates decline as the task becomes more complex, though the performance of the nuclear power plant operators provides some hint that it does. The one legitimate conclusion to be drawn from these scanty data is that cognitive detection mechanisms succeed in catching most errors, though by no means all.

5.2. Detection rates and error types

Three of the studies (Allwood, Rizzo and colleagues, and Bagnara and colleagues) allowed a direct comparison between the detection rates for the three basic error types. In the Allwood study, the error types could be inferred from his descriptions; in the Italian studies the distinctions were made by the investigators themselves. Averaging over all three studies (with two conditions for Rizzo et al., 1986), we find the relative proportions of the three error types to be 60.7 per cent for skill-based errors, 27.1 per cent for rule-based errors, and 11.3 per cent for knowledge-based errors. The corresponding overall detection rates are 86.1 per cent (SB), 73.2 per cent (RB) and 70.5 per cent (KB). The detailed analyses of these data are shown in Figures 6.3 to 6.5.

On the face of it, the relative incidence of the three error types appears to conflict with the assertion, made in Chapter 3, that performance at the knowledge-based level was intrinsically more error prone than at the other two levels. It should be recalled, however, that this claim was made in relation to the relative opportunities for making these three types of errors, not to their absolute incidence. The latter will always be greater at the SB level than at the RB level, and likewise greater in RB performance than in KB performance. Not only does the SB level predominate in routine, problem-free environments, it is also extensively employed at both the RB and KB levels as well. Similarly, RB performance, albeit in a somewhat fragmented form, will also be used during KB processing. It is thus hardly surprising that SB slips occurred on average more than twice as often as RB mistakes, which in turn were almost three times more frequent than KB mistakes.

Although the averaged detection data from the Swedish and Italian studies (see Figures 6.3 to 6.5) differentiate between the error types with regard to their likelihood of discovery, the range of variation is quite small, from 87 per cent for SB slips to 71 per cent for KB mistakes. The differences between them, however, are considerably more marked when it comes to making an effective correction. Allwood's data showed that the chances of properly recovering from an SB slip were twice those for an RB mistake and three times better than for a KB mistake. Moreover, whereas the correction rates for SB and RB errors were only slightly less than their respective detection rates, only half of the detected KB mistakes (i.e., the higher-level mathematical errors) were satisfactorily corrected.

Interestingly, one kind of slip — those that Allwood called 'skip errors' involving the omission of a necessary step in calculation — were the most resistant of all to detection. None of the 29 skip errors were discovered by the subjects, and only one of them was associated with an evaluative episode. This suggests we should be cautious in claiming that all skill-based errors are readily detected. Certain omissions stand apart as being largely 'invisible' to the detection mechanisms.

6. Cognitive processes that impede error detection

Lewis and Norman (Norman, 1984; Lewis & Norman, 1986; Lewis, 1986) describe three processes that can prevent or impede the discovery of one's own mistakes: relevance bias, partial explanation and the overlap of the mental model and the world.

6.1. Relevance bias

'Bounded rationality' means that human problem solvers often have only a 'keyhole' view of all the factors that could lead to an adequate solution (see Chapter 2). As a result, they are forced to select evidence from a problem

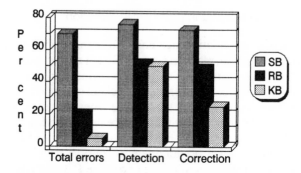

Figure 6.3. A comparison of the rates of error detection and correction in statistical problem solving for skill-based, rule-based and knowledge-based errors (data from Allwood, 1984).

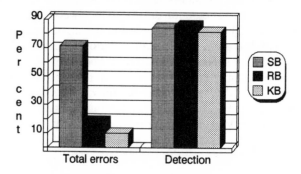

Figure 6.4. A comparison of detection rates in a database-handling task when subjects were required to find a given item and report its values (data from Rizzo, Bagnara & Visciola, 1986).

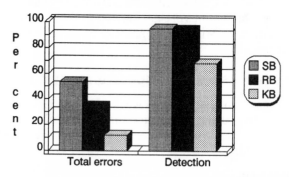

Figure 6.5. A comparison of detection rates in a database-handling task in which subjects were required to find three items and change their values (data from Rizzo, Bagnara & Visciola, 1986).

space that is generally too large to permit an exhaustive exploration. The most immediate guide to this selection is likely to be the problem solver's current hypothesis about what constitutes a likely solution. Another way of looking at confirmation bias, therefore, is to suggest that it is a selective process that favours items relevant to the presently held view. According to Lewis (1986): "If disconfirming evidence is less likely to seem relevant than confirming evidence, the bias can be explained not as a bias toward confirming evidence, but as a bias toward relevant-appearing evidence."

In complex systems like nuclear power plants, this problem is further exacerbated by the fact that the plant is continually changing its state spontaneously, and these alterations may not be known to the operators. In short, troubleshooting in something like a nuclear power plant presents a multiple dynamic problem configuration (see Chapter 3). Under these circumstances, it is natural that operators should cling tenaciously to their hunches. Even when wrong, they confer order upon chaos and offer a principled way of guiding future action. In a situation as rich in information as a control room, confirming evidence is not hard to find. The more entrenched the hypothesis, the more selective becomes the working definition of what is relevant. But those who enter the situation afresh at some later point are not so theory-bound, at least initially. The nakedness of the emperor is readily seen by those who have not come to believe him clothed.

6.2. Partial explanations

Errors are not detected because people are willing to accept only a rough agreement between the actual state of the world and their current theory about it. Indeed, the forming of partial explanations is an essential part of the learning process. But what promotes learning can delay error detection.

Lewis (1986) described the case of someone learning a word-processing package who misread the instructions for a typing exercise. Instead of entering text, as the exercise intended, she simply executed a series of cursor movements around an empty screen. The learner was surprised to find that no text appeared, but rationalised her actions by telling herself that the cursor movements were defining a screen area into which text would later be entered. As a result of this partial explanation she wrongly concluded that she had done the exercise correctly.

6.3. Overlap of world and mental model

A person's mental model of a particular problem space is likely to correspond in large part to the reality, even though it may be wrong in some respects. Lewis and Norman (1986) state: "If one's model were too far off it would have to be adjusted. As a result of this rough agreement, finding points of disagreement is hard. Most of the things that one does will produce the results predicted by one's model, which is thus supported." Having expectations frequently confirmed reduces the sensitivity of the error detection mechanisms.

6.4. The difficulty of detecting high-frequency error forms

Errors may take such familiar, high-frequency forms that they slip past the mechanism that monitors discrepancies between intention and performance. This 'disguise-by-familiarity' factor falls somewhere between Norman and Lewis's 'partial explanation' and 'overlap' categories. It is, however, very much in accord with the theoretical arguments of this book. Error detection processes may fail because they too are subject to similarity and frequency biases.

Consider the following personal example. I had been writing about unsafe act auditing which I referred to throughout the text by the acronym UAA. It cropped up several times in the passage, but in one instance I had typed USA instead of UAA. Although I proofread the section several times, I failed to spot the USA error. It was pointed out to me by someone else. It seems likely that the same frequency bias that caused me to type USA in the first place was also responsible for my failure to detect it subsequently.

Alice Healy (1976, 1980) has carried out a number of studies investigating the effects of familiarity upon detection, both of letter targets and proofreading errors. Her investigation began with the observation by Corcoran (1966) that when people are required to search for and mark the letter e in a printed prose passage, they are most likely to miss it when it occurs within the word *the*. One explanation offered by Corcoran was that *the*, being a highly redundant word, is not scanned in reading. Healy, however, had a different idea: the unitization hypothesis, which she expressed as follows (Healy, 1976, p. 235): "*The* is a word with an extremely high frequency in the language which should make it especially likely to be read as a unit or chunk rather than in terms of its component letters."

To test this view, she carried out four experiments in which students read 100-word passages and circled instances of the letter t. It was found that they missed a disproportionate number of t's in the word *the*, and this effect could not be explained by either the redundancy of *the* or by factors involving the location and pronunciation of the t in *the*. Rather, it was the high frequency of *the* that appeared to be critical. She concluded that high-frequency words such as *the* are read in terms of units larger than individual letters. Further support for this idea came from a demonstration that, in a passage of scrambled nouns, letter-detection errors occurred more frequently on common nouns than on rare nouns.

In a second series of experiments, Healy (1980) looked at the task of proofreading in which subjects were required to detect misspelled words in a passage of text. In the first experiment, the misspellings were introduced by transposing two adjacent letters. In two subsequent studies, involving prose passages and scrambled nouns, the misspellings were created by replacing the letter *t* with the letter *z*. The results revealed quite a different pattern of errors. "Whereas subjects made an inordinate number of errors on *the* in letter detection, the number of errors on *the* was no greater than chance in proofreading. . . Likewise, whereas subjects made more errors on common than rare words in letter detection, a small difference in the opposite direction was found in proofreading" (Healy, 1980, pp. 54-55).

These findings failed to support Corcoran's redundancy hypothesis. People do not skip over the word *the* when it is misspelled. Instead the data fit more readily with the unitization hypothesis. In reading normal prose, people process automatically common words, especially *the*, in units larger than single letters. However, when the formation of common words is distorted by misspellings, the subjects switch to a more detailed letter-by-letter processing and thus detect printing errors.

It should be noted, however, that these results do not cover the USA-UAA case discussed above. In Healy's studies, the misspelled words were not lexically possible ones. But USA is not only part of the English lexicon, it is also a very commonly-encountered acronym. In this instance, the error-to-be-detected is highly unitized and, as such, is likely to evade the eye during proofreading for the reasons offered by Healy to explain her letter detection differences. Obviously, a more detailed investigation of this 'disguise-by-familiarity' effect is needed before making any confident generalizations. It is worth remembering, though, that Healy herself was more interested in the size of the units used in reading than in the mechanisms of error detection per se.

7. Summary and conclusions

Error detection processes form an integral part of the multilevel mechanisms that direct and coordinate human action. Although their precise operation is little understood, there are grounds for believing that their effectiveness relates inversely to their position in the control hierarchy. Unless they are damaged or required to function in ecologically invalid circumstances, low-level postural corrections operate with a very high degree of reliability. At the other extreme, high-level cognitive processes concerned with setting of goals and selecting the means to achieve them are far less sensitive to potential or actual deviations from some optimal path towards a desired state.

The relative efficiency of these detection mechanisms depends crucially upon the immediacy and the validity of feedback information. At low levels, this is supplied directly and automatically by 'hard-wired' neural mechanisms. At the highest levels, however, this information is at worst unavailable and at best open to many interpretations.

There are basically three ways in which an error may be detected. It may be discovered by one of a variety of self-monitoring processes. These, as noted above, are most effective at the physiological and skill-based levels of performance. It may be signalled by some environmental cue, most obviously a forcing function that prevents further progress. Or it may be discovered by some other person. Detection by others appears to be the only way in which certain diagnostic errors are brought to light in complex and highly stressful situations.

Although skill-based errors are detected more readily than either rule-based or knowledge-based mistakes, the laboratory data so far obtained do not suggest that there are wide differences in their relative ease of discovery. Such evidence as there is indicates that approximately three out of every four errors are detected by their perpetrators. The chances of making an effective correction, however, appear to be highest at the skill-based level of performance and lowest at the knowledge-based level.

7   Latent errors and systems disasters

In considering the human contribution to systems disasters, it is important to distinguish two kinds of error: *active errors*, whose effects are felt almost immediately, and *latent errors* whose adverse consequences may lie dormant within the system for a long time, only becoming evident when they combine with other factors to breach the system's defences (see Rasmussen & Pedersen, 1984). In general, active errors are associated with the performance of the 'front-line' operators of a complex system: pilots, air traffic controllers, ships' officers, control room crews and the like. Latent errors, on the other hand, are most likely to be spawned by those whose activities are removed in both time and space from the direct control interface: designers, high-level decision makers, construction workers, managers and maintenance personnel.

Detailed analyses of recent accidents, most particularly those at Flixborough, Three Mile Island, Heysel Stadium, Bhopal, Chernobyl and Zeebrugge, as well as the *Challenger* disaster, have made it increasingly apparent that latent errors pose the greatest threat to the safety of a complex system. In the past, reliability analyses and accident investigations have focused primarily upon active operator errors and equipment failures. While operators can, and frequently do, make errors in their attempts to recover from an out-of-tolerance system state, many of the root causes of the emergency were usually present within the system long before these active errors were committed.

Rather than being the main instigators of an accident, operators tend to be the inheritors of system defects created by poor design, incorrect installation, faulty maintenance and bad management decisions. Their part is usually that of adding the final garnish to a lethal brew whose ingredients have already been long in the cooking.

There is a growing awareness within the human reliability community that attempts to discover and neutralise these latent failures will have a greater beneficial effect upon system safety than will localised efforts to minimise active errors. To date, much of the work of human factors specialists has been directed at improving the immediate human-system interface (i.e., the control room or cockpit). While this is undeniably an important enterprise, it only addresses a relatively small part of the total safety problem, being aimed primarily at reducing the 'active failure' tip of the causal iceberg. One thing that has been profitably learned over the past few years is that, in regard to safety issues, the term 'human factors' embraces a far wider range of individuals and activities than those associated with the front-line operation of a system. Indeed, a central theme of this chapter is that the more removed individuals are from these front-line activities (and, incidentally, from direct hazards), the greater is their potential danger to the system.

Other attempts to minimise errors have been purely reactive in nature, being concerned with eliminating the recurrence of particular active failures identified post hoc by accident investigators. Again, while it is sensible to learn as many remedial lessons as possible from past accidents, it must also be appreciated that such events are usually caused by the unique conjunction of several necessary but singly insufficient factors. Since the same mixture of causes is unlikely to recur, efforts to prevent the repetition of specific active errors will have only a limited impact on the safety of the system as a whole. At worst, they merely find better ways of securing a particular stable door once its occupant has bolted.

This chapter considers the contribution of latent errors to the catastrophic breakdown of a number of different complex systems. Since the notion of latent error is intimately bound up with the character of contemporary technology, I begin by summarising some of the significant changes that have occurred in the control of high-risk systems over the past few decades. I also consider some of the psychological problems associated with the supervisory control of complex systems.

1. Technological developments

Over the past 30 to 40 years, a technological revolution has occurred in the design and control of high-risk systems. This, in turn, has brought about radical (and still little understood) changes in the tasks that their human elements are called upon to perform. Some of the more important factors affecting human performance are outlined below.

1.1. Systems have become more automated

One of the most remarkable developments of recent years has been the extent to which operators have become increasingly remote from the processes that they nominally control. Machines of growing complexity have come to intervene between the human and the physical task.

In the beginning, operators employed direct sensing and manipulation. They saw and touched what they controlled or produced. Then came the intervention of remote sensing and manipulation devices. Either the process was too dangerous or too sensitive to handle directly, or there was a need to

1. Technological developments

extend human muscle power or the operator's unaided senses v
cient to detect important physical changes.

But the most profound changes came with the advent of cheap computing
power. Now the operator can be separated from the process by at least two
components of the control system. At the lowest level, there are task-interactive systems controlling the various detailed aspects of the operation. And intervening between the specialised task-interactive systems and the operators
is the human-system interface, where the control system presents various selected pieces of information to the operators. This interface generally permits
only a very prescribed degree of interaction between the human and the now
remote process.

This is the situation termed supervisory control, defined by Sheridan and
Hennessy (1984) as "initiating, monitoring, and adjusting processes in systems
that are otherwise automatically controlled." The basic features of human
supervisory control are shown in Figure 7.1.

According to Moray (1986), true supervisory control is achieved through
four distinct levels. The lowest two levels comprise the task-interactive system (TIS). This exercises closed-loop control over the hardware components
of the task (e.g., propellers, engines, pumps, switches, valves and heaters)
through automatic subsystems (e.g., thermostats, autopilots, governors, preprogrammed robots and packaged subroutines). The TIS can trim the system
to predetermined set points, but it is incapable of adjusting these set points or
of initiating any kind of adaptive response. The TIS is controlled by the human-
interactive system (HIS). This comprises the top two levels of the control hierarchy. The HIS is an 'intelligent' computer that intercedes between the human
operator and the lower-level controllers. This is the distinctive feature of
human supervisory control. The HIS communicates the state of the system to
the operator through its displays. It also receives commands from the operator regarding new goals and set points. Its intelligence lies in the fact that it
can use its stored knowledge to issue tactical commands to the TIS that will
optimise various performance criteria.

Such a control system has brought about a radical transformation of the
human-system relationship. As Moray (1986, pp. 404-405)) has pointed out:

> There is a real sense in which the computer rather than the human
> becomes the central actor. For most of the time the computer will be
> making the decisions about control, and about what to tell or ask the
> operator. The latter may either pre-empt control or accept it when
> asked to do so by the computer. But normally, despite the fact that the
> human defines the goals for the computer, the latter is in control. The
> computer is the heart of the system.

We have thus traced a progression from where the human is the prime
mover and the computer the slave to one in which the roles are very largely

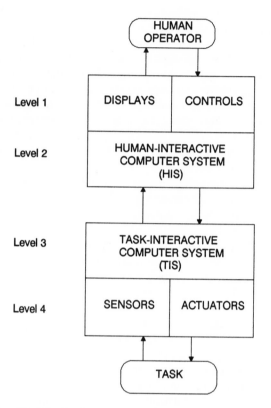

Figure 7.1. The basic elements of supervisory control (after Moray, 1986).

reversed. For most of the time, the operator's task is reduced to that of monitoring the system to ensure that it continues to function within normal limits.
The advantages of such a system are obvious; the operator's workload is substantially reduced, and the HIS performs tasks that the human can specify but
cannot actually do (see Moray, 1986, for a complete list of the advantages of
supervisory control). However, the main reason for the human operator's continued presence is to use his still unique powers of knowledge-based reasoning to cope with system emergencies. And this, as will be discussed in Section
2, is a task peculiarly ill-suited to the particular strengths and weaknesses of
human cognition.

1.2. Systems have become more complex and more dangerous

One of the accompaniments of the increasing computerisation has been that
high-risk systems such as nuclear power plants and chemical process installa-

tions have become larger and more complex. This means that greater amounts of potentially hazardous materials are concentrated in single sites under the centralised control of fewer operators. Catastrophic breakdowns of these systems pose serious threats not only for those within the plant, but also for the neighbouring public. And, in the case of nuclear power plants and weapons systems, this risk extends far beyond the immediate locality.

Complexity can be described in relation to a number of features. Perrow (1984) has identified two relatively independent system characteristics that are particularly important: complexity of interaction and tightness of coupling.

Systems may be more or less linear in their structure. Relatively complex, nonlinear systems possess the following general features (adapted from Perrow, 1984):

(a) Components that are not linked together in a production sequence are in close proximity.

(b) Many common-mode connections (i.e., components whose failure can have multiple effects 'downstream') are present.

(c) There is only a limited possibility of isolating failed components.

(d) Due to the high degree of specialisation, there is little chance of substituting or reassigning personnel. The same lack of interchangeability is also true for supplies and materials.

(e) There are unfamiliar or unintended feedback loops.

(f) There are many control parameters that could potentially interact.

(g) Certain information about the state of the system must be obtained indirectly, or inferred.

(h) There is only a limited understanding of some processes, particularly those involving transformations.

In addition, the elements of a system may be coupled either tightly or loosely. The characteristics of a tightly-coupled system are listed below (adapted from Perrow, 1984):

(a) Processing delays are unacceptable.

(b) Production sequences are relatively invariant.

(c) There are few ways of achieving a particular goal.

(d) Little slack is permissible in supplies, equipment and personnel.

(e) Buffers and redundancies are deliberately designed into the system.

It should be stressed that interactiveness and tightness of coupling are tendencies, not hard-and-fast properties. No one system is likely to possess all the characteristics of complexity outlined above. Nuclear power plants, nuclear weapons systems, chemical process plants and large passenger aircraft are examples of systems that possess both a high degree of interaction and tightness of coupling. Dams, power grids, rail and marine transport have tight coupling but linear interactions. Mining operations, research and development companies, universities, and multigoal public agencies (such as the Department of Health and Social Security in Britain) have loose coupling and complex interactions. Trade schools, assembly-line production and most manufacturing plants have loose coupling and linear interactions.

1.3. Systems have more defences against failure

Because of the increasing unacceptability of a catastrophic disaster, and because of the widespread availability of intelligent hardware, designers have sought to provide automatic safety devices (ASDs) sufficient to protect the system against all the known scenarios of breakdown. According to Perrow (1984, p. 43): "The more complicated or tightly coupled the plant, the more attention is paid to reducing the occasion for failures."

The design of a modern nuclear power station is based upon the philosophy of 'defence in depth'. In addition to a large number of 'back-up' subsystems, one line of defence is provided by ASDs: devices that, having sensed an out-of-tolerance condition, automatically 'trip' the reactor, and/or switch off the turbines and/or release excess pressure. Not only are they programmed to shut down various aspects of the process, they also call in automatic safety systems, such as the emergency core cooling system (ECCS) or safety injection (SI), should there be the danger of a core melt. A further line of defence is provided by the containment, a massive concrete structure that prevents the accidental release of radioactive material to the outside world in the event of a failure of the ASDs. If all of these defences fail, and dangerous materials are released to the exterior, then it is hoped that their harmful consequences would be minimised by the general (though not universal) practice of siting nuclear power stations in sparsely populated areas.

For a catastrophe to happen, therefore, a number of apparently unlikely events need to occur in combination during the accident sequence (see Rasmussen & Pedersen, 1984). First, the ASDs must fail to restore the disturbed system to a safe state. Second, the containment must fail to prevent the release of toxic material to the exterior. But such disasters still happen. One of the most obvious reasons is that the safety systems themselves are prey to human error, particularly of the latent kind. We are thus faced with a paradox: those specialised systems designed solely to make the plant safe are also its points of greatest weakness.

1.4. Systems have become more opaque

One of the consequences of the developments outlined above is that complex, tightly-coupled and highly defended systems have become increasingly opaque to the people who manage, maintain and operate them. This opacity has two aspects: not knowing what is happening and not understanding what the system can do.

As we have seen, automation has wrought a fundamental change in the roles people play within certain high-risk technologies. Instead of having 'hands on' contact with the process, people have been promoted "to higher-level supervisory tasks and to long-term maintenance and planning tasks" (Rasmussen, 1988). In all cases, these are far removed from the immediate processing. What direct information they have is filtered through the computer-based interface. And, as many accidents have demonstrated, they often cannot find what they need to know while, at the same time, being deluged with information they do not want nor know how to interpret. In simpler, more linear systems, it was always possible for an operator or manager to go out and inspect the process at first hand, to examine directly the quality of the product, to look at the leaky valve or to talk to the experienced man or woman on the job. But these alternatives are not available in chemical and nuclear plants where an unapproachable and only partially understood process is largely hidden within a maze of pipes, reinforced vessels and concrete bunkers.

There is also another important factor contributing to system opacity: the system's own defences. Rasmussen (1988, pp. 3-4) has called this 'the fallacy of defence in depth'.

Another important implication of the very nature of the 'defence in depth' philosophy is that the system very often does not respond actively to single faults. Consequently, many errors and faults made by the staff and maintenance personnel do not directly reveal themselves by functional response from the system. Humans can operate with an extremely high level of reliability in a dynamic environment when slips and mistakes have immediately visible effects and can be corrected. Survival when driving through Paris during rush hours depends on this fact.

Compare this to working in a system designed according to the 'defence in depth' principle, where several independent events have to coincide before the system responds by visible changes in behaviour. Violation of safety preconditions during work on the system will probably not result in an immediate functional response, and latent effects of erroneous acts can therefore be left in the system. When such errors are allowed to be present in a system over a longer period of time, the probability of coincidence of the multiple faults necessary for release of an accident is drastically increased. Analyses of major accidents typically show that the basic safety of the system has eroded due to latent errors. A more significant contribution to safety can be expected from efforts to decrease the duration of latent errors than from measures to decrease their basic frequency.

1.5. The ironies of automation

Lisanne Bainbridge (1987) of University College London has expressed in an elegant and concise form many of the difficulties that lie at the heart of the relationship between humans and machines in advanced technological installations. She calls them 'the ironies of automation'.

Many systems designers view human operators as unreliable and inefficient and strive to supplant them with automated devices. There are two ironies here. The first is that designers' errors, as discussed later in this chapter, make a significant contribution to accidents and events. The second is that the same designer who seeks to eliminate human beings still leaves the operator "to do the tasks which the designer cannot think how to automate" (Bainbridge, 1987, p. 272).

In an automated plant, operators are required to monitor that the automatic system is functioning properly. But it is well known that even highly motivated operators cannot maintain effective vigilance for anything more than quite short periods; thus, they are demonstrably ill-suited to carry out this residual task of monitoring for rare, abnormal events. In order to aid them, designers need to provide automatic alarm signals. But who decides when these automatic alarms have failed or been switched off?

Another operator task is to take over manual control when the automatic control system fails. Manual control is a highly skilled activity, and skills need to be practised continuously in order to maintain them. Yet an automatic control system that fails only rarely denies operators the opportunity for practising these basic control skills. One of the consequences of automation, therefore, is that operators become de-skilled in precisely those activities that justify their marginalised existence. But when manual takeover is necessary something has usually gone wrong; this means that operators need to be more rather than less skilled in order to cope with these atypical conditions. Duncan (1987, p. 266) makes the same point: "The more reliable the plant, the less opportunity there will be for the operator to practise direct intervention, and the more difficult will be the demands of the remaining tasks requiring operator intervention."

These ironies also spill over into the area of training. Conscious of the difficulties facing operators in the high-workload, high-stress conditions of a plant emergency, designers, regulators and managers have sought to proceduralise operator actions. These frequently involve highly elaborate branching structures or algorithms designed to differentiate between a set of foreseeable faults. Some idea of what this means in practice can be gained from the following extract from the U.S. Nuclear Regulatory Commission's report on the serious loss of main and auxiliary feedwater accident at Toledo Edison's Davies-Besse plant in Ohio (NUREG, 1985). The extract describes the actions of the crew immediately following the reactor and turbine trips that occurred at 1.35 a.m. on 9 June 1985.

The primary-side operator acted in accordance with the immediate post-trip action, specified in the emergency procedure that he had memorized. . . . The secondary-side operator heard the turbine stop valves slamming shut and knew the reactor had tripped. This 'thud' was heard by most of the equipment operators who also recognized its meaning and two of them headed for the control room. . . . The shift supervisor joined the operator at the secondary-side control console and watched the rapid decrease of the steam generator levels. . . . The assistant shift supervisor in the meantime opened the plant's looseleaf emergency procedure book (It is about two inches thick with tabs for quick reference. . .). As he read aloud the immediate actions specified, the reactor operators were responding in the affirmative. After phoning the shift technical advisor to come to the control room, the administrative assistant began writing down what the operators were saying, although they were speaking faster than she could write.

[Later] The assistant shift supervisor, meanwhile, continued reading aloud from the emergency procedure. He had reached the point in the supplementary actions that require verification that feedwater flow was available. However, there was no feedwater, not even from the Auxiliary Feedwater System (AFWS), a safety system designed to provide feedwater in the situation that existed. Given this condition, the procedure directs the operator to the section entitled, 'Lack of Heat Transfer'. He opened the procedure at the tab corresponding to this condition, but left the desk and the procedure at this point, to diagnose why the AFWS had failed. He performed a valve alignment verification and found that the isolation valve in each AFW train had closed. [Both valves had failed to reopen automatically.] He tried unsuccessfully to open the valves by the push buttons on the back panel. . . . The AFW system had now suffered its third common-mode failure, thus increasing the number of malfunctions to seven within seven minutes after the reactor trip. . . . At this point, things in the control room were hectic. The plant had lost all feedwater; reactor pressure and temperature were increasing; and a number of unexpected equipment problems had occurred. The seriousness of the situation was appreciated." [It should be added that despite the commission of a number of slips and mistakes, the plant was restored to a safe state within 15 minutes. This was a very good crew!]

This passage is worth quoting at length because it reveals what the reality of a serious nuclear power plant emergency is like. It also captures the moment when the pre-programmed procedures, like the plant, ran out of steam, forcing the operators to improvise in the face of what the industry calls a 'beyond design basis accident'. For our present purposes, however, it highlights a further irony of automation: that of drilling operators to follow written instructions and then putting them in a system to provide knowledge-based intelligence and remedial improvisation. Bainbridge (1987, p. 278) commented: "Perhaps the final irony is that it is the most successful automated systems, with rare need for manual intervention, which may need the greatest investment in operator training."

1.6. The operator as temporal coordinator

French (Montmollin, 1984) and Belgian (De Keyser, Decortis, Housiaux & Van Daele, 1987) investigators have emphasised the importance of the temporal aspects of human supervisory control. One of the side effects of automation has been the proliferation of specialised working teams acting as satellites to the overall process. These include engineers, maintenance staff, control specialists and computer scientists. In many industrial settings, the task of orchestrating their various activities falls to the control room operator. De Keyser and her colleagues are currently documenting the errors of temporal judgement that can arise in these circumstances (De Keyser, 1988).

2. The 'Catch 22' of human supervisory control

As indicated earlier, the main reason why humans are retained in systems that are primarily controlled by intelligent computers is to handle 'non-design' emergencies. In short, operators are there because system designers cannot foresee all possible scenarios of failure and hence are not able to provide automatic safety devices for every contingency.

In addition to their cosmetic value, human beings owe their inclusion in hazardous systems to their unique, knowledge-based ability to carry out 'on-line' problem solving in novel situations. Ironically, and notwithstanding the Apollo 13 astronauts and others demonstrating inspired improvisation, they are not especially good at it; at least not in the conditions that usually prevail during systems emergencies. One reason for this is that stressed human beings are strongly disposed to employ the effortless, parallel, preprogrammed operations of highly specialised, low-level processors and their associated heuristics. These stored routines are shaped by personal history and reflect the recurring patterns of past experience.

The first part of the catch is thus revealed: Why do we ha[...]
complex systems? To cope with emergencies. What will the[y]
deal with these problems? Stored routines based on previous [...]
a specific environment. What, for the most part, is their experience w[...]
control room? Monitoring and occasionally tweaking the plant while it performs within safe operating limits. So how can they perform adequately when
they are called upon to reenter the control loop? The evidence is that this task
has become so alien and the system so complex that, on a significant number
of occasions, they perform badly.

One apparent solution would be to spend a large part of an operator's shift
time drilling him or her in the diagnostic and recovery lessons of previous system emergencies. And this brings us to the second part of the catch. It is in the
nature of complex, tightly-coupled, highly interactive, opaque and partially
understood systems to spring nasty surprises. Even if it were possible to build
up – through simulations or gameplaying – an extensive repertoire of recovery routines within operating crews, there is no guarantee that they would
be relevant, other than in a very general sense, to some future event. As case
studies repeatedly show, accidents may begin in a conventional way, but they
rarely proceed along predictable lines. Each incident is a truly novel event in
which past experience counts for little and where the plant has to be recovered
by a mixture of good luck and laborious, resource-limited, knowledge-based
processing. Active errors are inevitable. Whereas in the more forgiving circumstances of everyday life, learning from one's mistakes is usually a beneficial process, in the control room of chemical or nuclear power plants, such
educative experiences can have unacceptable consequences.

The point is this: Human supervisory control was not conceived with humans in mind. It was a by-product of the microchip revolution. Indeed, if a
group of human factors specialists sat down with the malign intent of conceiving an activity that was wholly ill-matched to the strengths and weaknesses of
human cognition, they might well have come up with something not altogether
different from what is currently demanded of nuclear and chemical plant operators. To put it simply: the active errors of stressed controllers are, in large
part, the delayed effects of system design failures.

Perrow (1984, p. 9), having noted that between 60 and 80 per cent of systems accidents are attributed to 'operator error', went on to make the following telling comment: "But if, as we shall see time and time again, the operator
is confronted by unexpected and usually mysterious interactions among
failures, saying that he or she should have zigged instead of zagged is only
possible after the fact. Before the accident no one could know what was going
on and what should have been done."

3. Maintenance-related omissions

By their nature, it is generally difficult to quantify the contribution made by latent errors to systems failures. An interesting exception, however, are those committed during the maintenance of nuclear power plants. Two independent surveys (Rasmussen, 1980; INPO, 1984) indicate that simple omissions – the failure to carry out some of the actions necessary to achieve a desired goal – constitute the single largest category of human performance problems identified in the significant event reports logged by nuclear plants. Moreover, these omission errors appear to be most closely associated with maintenance-related tasks. Here, the term maintenance-related includes preventive and corrective maintenance, surveillance testing, removal and restoration of equipment, checking, supervision, postmaintenance testing and modifications.

3.1. The Rasmussen survey

Drawing upon the Nuclear Power Experience compilation of significant event reports in NPPs, Rasmussen (1980) analysed 200 cases classified under the heading of 'Operational problems'. Omissions of functionally isolated acts accounted for 34 per cent of all the incidents, and a further 8.5 per cent involved other kinds of omission. The complete error distribution is shown in Table 7.1.

Table 7.1. The distribution of error types in 200 NPP incidents (from Rasmussen, 1980).

Breakdown of error types
Absent-mindedness: 3
Familiar association: 6
Alertness low: 10
Omission of functionally isolated acts: 68
Other omissions: 17
Mistakes among alternatives: 11
Strong expectation: 10
Side effect(s) not considered: 15
Latent conditions not considered: 20
Manual variability, lack of precision: 10
Spatial orientation weak: 10
Other, unclassifiable: 20
TOTAL: 200

3. Maintenance-related omissions

The 85 omission errors were further broken down according to (a) the kind
of task involved, and (b) the type of mental activity implicated in the phase of
the task at which the error occurred. These two analyses are shown in Tables
7.2 and 7.3.

Two aspects of these data are of particular importance. First, they reveal
the significance of omission errors in test, calibration and maintenance activities. Second, the mental task analysis shows a close association between
omissions and the planning and recalling of procedures. This point is further
highlighted by the INPO root cause analysis discussed below.

Table 7.2. The distribution of omissions across tasks (from
Rasmussen, 1980).

Omissions per task
Monitoring and inspection: 0
Supervisory control: 2
Manual operation and control: 5
Inventory control: 8
Test and calibration: 28
Repair and modification: 35
Administrative task: 1
Management, staff planning: 1
Other (not mentioned): 5
TOTAL: 85

Table 7.3. The distribution of omissions across mental task
phases (from Rasmussen, 1980).

Omissions per mental task
Detection of demand: 2
Observation/communication: 2
Target: tactical system state: 1
Procedure: plan, recall: 77
Execution: 3
TOTAL: 85

3.2. The INPO root cause analysis

The root causes of 87 significant events reported to the Institute of Nuclear Power Operations (INPO is the U.S nuclear industry's own organization, located in Atlanta, Georgia) in 1983 were analysed using the Root Cause Record Form. Of the 182 root causes identified, 80 (44 per cent) were classified as human performance problems (see Figure 7.2).

The event descriptions provided were sufficient to allow omissions to be distinguished from other behavioural error forms. Forty-eight of the 80 (60 per cent) human performance root causes were classified as involving either single or multiple omissions.

The following points are of interest: (a) Ninety-six per cent of the deficient procedures involved omissions (31.3 per cent of all human performance root causes). (b) Omissions were most frequently associated with maintenance-related activities: 64.5 per cent of the errors in this task category involved omitted acts. These made up a quarter of all human performance root causes, (c) Seventy-six per cent of the human errors in the operation task category were omissions, representing 20 per cent of all human performance root causes.

3.3. General conclusions

Clearly, there are some differences between the Rasmussen and INPO analyses regarding the distribution of omissions over tasks. But these are more likely to reflect discrepancies in categorization and emphasis than real

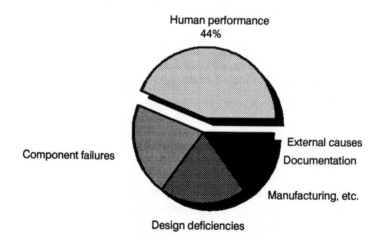

Figure 7.2. INPO analysis of the 182 root causes identified in 87 significant events occurring within nuclear power plants in 1983.

changes in the pattern of NPP errors over time (the Rasmussen study sampled the period up to 1978; the INPO data related to 1983). Of greater importance, however, is that both studies highlighted maintenance-related activities as being the most productive source of event root causes and both identified omissions as the most prevalent error form. The former conclusion is further supported by the more extensive NUMARC study (INPO, 1985a), while the latter is in close accord with the relative incidence of error types in everyday life (Reason & Mycielska, 1982; Reason, 1984a), where forgetting intentions was the most common form of lapse.

4. Operator errors

In a subsequent INPO report (INPO, 1985b), the classificatory scheme was modified in two ways: to eliminate 'component failure' (preferring to seek more assiduously for the cause of these failures), and to include 'construction and installation deficiencies' in the human performance category. This revised scheme was then applied to 180 significant event reports issued in both 1983 and 1984, in which a total of 387 root causes were identified. This analysis is summarised in Figure 7.3.

The human performance problems were further broken down into subcategories, as shown in Table 7.4. There are two important conclusions to be drawn from these data. First, at least 92 per cent of all root causes were manmade (see Figure 7.3). Second, only a relatively small proportion of the root causes were actually initiated by front-line personnel (i.e., failure to follow procedures). Most originated in either maintenance-related activities or in bad decisions taken within the organizational and managerial domains.

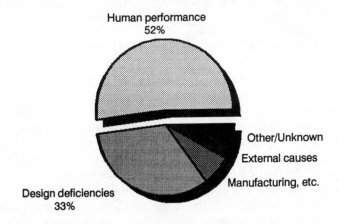

Figure 7.3. INPO analysis of the 387 root causes identified in 180 significant event reports in both 1983 and 1984.

Table 7.4. Breakdown of human performance problems (from INPO, 1985b).

Human performance problems
Deficient procedures or documentation: 43% Lack of knowledge or training: 18% Failure to follow procedures: 16% Deficient planning or scheduling: 10% Miscommunication: 6% Deficient supervision: 3% Policy problems: 2% Other: 2%

5. Case study analyses of latent errors

This section attempts to show something of the nature and variety of latent errors through case study analyses of six major accidents: Three Mile Island, Bhopal, *Challenger*, Chernobyl, Zeebrugge and the King's Cross underground fire. These events were not chosen because of the unusually critical part played by latent failures. Other disasters like Flixborough, Seveso, Aberfan, Summerland, Tenerife, Heysel Stadium and the Bradford and Piper Alpha fires would have demonstrated the significance of these dormant factors equally well. Three criteria influenced this particular selection: (a) all the events are comparatively recent so that their general nature will be familiar to the non-technical reader, (b) they are all well documented, indeed many have been the subject of high-level governmental investigations, and (c) they cover a range of complex, high-risk systems.

In view of the diversity of the systems considered here, it is unlikely that any one reader will be conversant with all of their technical details. Accordingly, the major part of each case study will be presented in the form of a summary table indicating some of the major contributory latent failures – not all because, by their nature, many remain undiscovered. A latent failure in this context is defined as an error or violation that was committed at least one to two days before the start of the actual emergency and played a necessary (though not sufficient) role in causing the disaster. Accompanying each table will be a short description of the accident sequence and, where appropriate, some additional commentary on the general 'health' of the system.

As always in such analyses, there is the problem of defining the explanatory time frame. Any catastrophic event arises from the adverse conjunction of several distinct causal chains. If these are traced backwards in time, we encounter a combinatorial explosion of possible root causes, where the elimination of any one could have thwarted the accident sequence. There are no clear-cut rules for restricting such retrospective searches. Some historians, for example, trace the origins of the charge of the Light Brigade back to Cromwell's Major-Generals (see Woodham-Smith, 1953); others are content to begin at the outset of the Crimean campaign, still others start their stories on the morning of 24 October 1854.

In the present context, there are two obvious boundary conditions. The combined constraints of space, information and the reader's patience place severe limits on how far back in time we can go. Yet the immediate need to demonstrate the significance of antecedent events makes it essential to focus upon those human failures that were committed prior to the day of the actual catastrophe. As it turns out, these antecedent time frames vary in length from around 2 years for Three Mile Island to 9 years for the *Challenger* disaster, their precise extents being determined by the particular histories of each disaster and the available sources.

The point is that these starting points are fairly arbitrary ones. However, no particular significance is being placed on the quantities of latent and active errors; given their relative timescales, the former will always be more numerous than the latter. Rather, our purpose is to illustrate the insidious and often unforeseeable ways in which they combine to breach the system's defences at some critical moment.

5.1. Three Mile Island

At 0400 on 28 March 1979, one of the turbines stopped automatically (tripped) in Unit No. 2 of Metropolitan Edison's two pressurized water reactors (PWRs) on Three Mile Island (TMI) in the Susquehanna River, 10 miles south of Harrisburg (principal source: Kemeny, 1979). This was due to a maintenance crew attempting to renew resin for the special treatment of the plant's water. A cupful of water had leaked through a faulty seal in the condensate polisher system and had entered the plant's instrument air system. The moisture interrupted the air pressure applied to two valves on the two feedwater pumps, and 'told' them something was wrong (which was not actually the case in this particular subsystem). The feedwater pumps stopped automatically. This cut the water flow to the steam generator and tripped the turbine. But this automatic safety device was not sufficient to render the plant safe. Without the pumps, the heat of the primary cooling system (circulating around the core) could not be transferred to the cool water in the secondary (nonradioactive) system.

At this point, the emergency feedwater pumps came on automatically. They are designed to pull water from an emergency storage tank and run it through the secondary cooling system to compensate for the water that boils off once it is not circulating. However, the pipes from these emergency feedwater tanks were blocked by closed valves, erroneously left shut during maintenance two days earlier.

With no heat removal from the primary coolant, there was a rapid rise in core temperature and pressure. This triggered another automatic safety device: the reactor 'scrammed' (graphite control rods, 80 per cent silver, dropped into the core and absorb neutrons, stopping the chain reaction). But decaying radioactive materials still produce heat. This further increased temperature and pressure in the core. Such pressure is designed to be relieved automatically through a pilot-operated relief valve (PORV). When open, the PORV releases water from the core through a large pressurizer vessel and then into the sump below the containment. The PORV was supposed to flip open, relieve pressure and then close automatically. But on this occasion, still only about 13 seconds into the emergency, it stuck open. This meant that the primary cooling system had a hole in it through which radioactive water, under high pressure, was pouring into the containment area, and thence down into the basement.

The emergency lasted in excess of 16 hours and resulted in the release of small quantities of radioactive material into the atmosphere. No loss of life has been traced directly to this accident, but the cost to the operating companies and the insurers was in the region of one billion dollars. It also marked a watershed in the history of nuclear power in the United States, and its consequences with regard to public concern for the safety of nuclear power plants are still felt today. The principal events, operator errors and contributing latent failures are summarised in Case Study No.1 (see Appendix).

The subsequent investigations revealed a wide range of sloppy management practices and poor operating procedures. Subsequent inspection of TMI-1 (the other unit on the site) revealed a long-term lack of maintenance. For example, "boron stalactites more than a foot long hung from the valves and stalagmites had built up from the floor" (Kemeny, 1979) in the TMI-1 containment building. Other discoveries included:

(a) The iodine filters were left in continuous use rather than being preserved to filter air in the event of radioactive contamination. Consequently, on the day of the accident, they possessed considerably less than their full filtering capacity.

(b) Sensitive areas of the plant were open to the public. On the day before the accident, as many as 750 people had access to the auxiliary building.

(c) When shifts changed, no mechanism existed for making a systematic check on the status of the plant. Similarly, maintenance personnel were assigned jobs at the beginning of their shift, but no subsequent check was made on their progress.

(d) A retrospective review of TMI-2's licensee event reports revealed repeated omissions, inadequate failure analyses and lack of corrective actions.

(e) Pipes and valves lacked suitable means of identification. Thus, 8 hours after the start of the accident, operators spent 10 minutes trying unsuccessfully to locate three decay heat valves in a high radiation field.

Was the state of TMI-2 unusual? Was this simply the "bad apple in the nuclear barrel" (Perrow, 1984)? The evidence suggests not. Some years earlier, Morris and Engelken (1973) had examined eight loss-of-coolant (LOCA) accidents that had occurred in six different boiling water reactors over a 2-year period when there were only 29 plants operating. They looked particularly at the cooccurrence of multiple failures. Each accident involved between two to four different types of failure. In half of them there were also violations of operating procedures, but they occurred in conjunction with two to five other failures. Nor were failures limited to plant personnel. Deficient valves were found in 20 plants supplied by 10 different manufacturers. As Perrow (1984) pointed out, it is from the concatenation of these relatively trivial events in nontrivial systems that accidents such as TMI-2 are born. Generating electric power from nuclear energy is a highly technical business; but it would be naive to suppose that NPPs are managed or operated by a special breed of supermen. They are no worse than those in other industries, but neither are they significantly better.

5.2. Bhopal

On the night of 2-3 December 1984, a gas leak from a small pesticide plant, owned by a subsidiary of Union Carbide Corporation, devastated the central Indian city of Bhopal. It was the worst industrial disaster ever. At least 2,500 people were killed, and more than 200,000 were injured. Perhaps more than any other event, it revealed the hitherto largely unrealised dangers associated with the manufacture of highly toxic chemicals, in this case, methyl isocyanate (MIC).

The immediate cause of the discharge was an influx of water into an MIC storage tank. How it got there is a tangled story of botched maintenance, operator errors, improvised bypass pipes, failed safety systems, incompetent management, drought, agricultural economics and bad governmental decisions. It is too long to tell in detail here, though an inventory of the major latent failures is shown in Case Study No. 2 (see Appendix).

With such a terrible catastrophe, it is difficult to find unbiased sources. Union Carbide's own report (March, 1985) clearly has its own axe to grind, as also does the Morehouse and Subramanian account, published by the Council on International and Public Affairs (1986). Other, less comprehensive, though more balanced accounts have been written by Lihou and Lihou (1985) and Bellamy (1985). Still other accounts can be found in the general scientific press (e.g., *New Scientist*) and in the chemical journals throughout 1985.

5.3. Challenger

Described in purely physical terms, the cause of the Space Shuttle *Challenger* disaster on the morning of 28 January 1986 was brutally simple. A rubbery seal, called an O-ring, on one of the solid rocket boosters split shortly after lift-off, releasing a jet of ignited fuel that caused the entire rocket complex to explode, killing all seven astronauts. But how that item came to be there after a 9-year history of repeated erosion and faults is a complicated tale of incompetence, selective blindness, conflicting goals and reversed logic. The main protagonists were NASA's principal solid-rocket contractor, Morton Thiokol, and all levels of the NASA management. It is summarised in Case Study No. 3 (see Appendix).

More detailed accounts can be found in the Report of the Presidential Commission on the Space Shuttle *Challenger* Accident (June, 1986), and in an excellent article by Cooper (1987). A discussion of how these facts were obtained from reluctant and often devious sources has been given by Kerhli (1987), one of the presidential commission's principal investigators (his previous job had been prosecuting mafiosi).

5.4. Chernobyl

At 0124 on Saturday, 26 April 1986, two explosions blew off the 1000-tonne concrete cap sealing the Chernobyl-4 reactor, releasing molten core fragments into the immediate vicinity and fission products into the atmosphere. This was the worst accident in the history of commercial nuclear power generation. It has so far cost over 30 lives, contaminated some 400 square miles around the Ukrainian plant and significantly increased the risk of cancer deaths over a wide area of Scandinavia and Western Europe. It was an entirely man-made disaster.

The chain of events leading up to the accident together with the associated latent failures are shown in Case Study No. 4 (see Appendix). Other more detailed accounts of the accident can be found in the report of the USSR State Committee on the Utilization of Atomic Energy (1986), in *Nature* (vol. 323, 1986), and in a report prepared for the Central Electricity Generating Board (CEGB) by Collier and Davies (1986).

In the immediate aftermath of the accident, the Western nuclear industry vigorously asserted that 'it couldn't happen here' (see Reason, 1987; Baker & Marshall, 1988; Reason, 1988). Whereas the Russian analysts highlighted human errors and violations as the principal cause, their Western counterparts, and especially Lord Marshall, head of the CEGB, preferred to blame the poor design of the Russian reactor and the inadequacy of the 'Soviet safety culture' – although the latter came to sound increasingly hollow after the Zeebrugge and King's Cross disasters.

Notwithstanding the obvious design defects of the RBMK reactor, it is clear from these latent failure analyses that the main ingredients for the Chernobyl disaster were not unique to the Soviet Union. There was a society committed to the generation of energy through large-scale nuclear power plants. There was a system that was hazardous, complex, tightly-coupled, opaque and operating outside normal conditions. There was a fallible management structure that was monolithic, remote and slow to respond, and for whom safety ranked low in the league of goals to be satisfied. There were operators who possessed only a limited understanding of the system they were controlling and in any case, were set a task that made dangerous violations inevitable.

5.5. Zeebrugge

At 1805 on 6 March 1987, the 'roll-on/roll-off' passenger and freight ferry *Herald of Free Enterprise*, owned by Townsend Thoresen, sailed from the inner harbour at Zeebrugge en route to Dover with her bow doors open. As she passed the Outer Mole and increased speed, water came over the bow sill and flooded into the lower car deck (Deck G). At around 1827, the *Herald* capsized rapidly (in fewer than 2 minutes) and came to rest in shallow waters with her starboard side above the water. No fewer than 150 passengers and 38 crew lost their lives. Many others were injured. The chain of events and a limited inventory of the latent failures are shown in Case Study No. 5 (see Appendix). The single best source for more detailed information is the Department of Transport's report on the formal investigation, conducted by Mr Justice Sheen, the Wreck Commissioner (published September 1987).

Mr Justice Sheen's investigation was an interesting exception to the general tendency of postaccident inquiries to focus primarily upon active errors. It is worth quoting at some length from what he wrote about the management's part in this catastrophe (Sheen, 1987, p. 14):

At first sight the faults which led to this disaster were the aforesaid errors of omission on the part of the Master, the Chief Officer and the assistant bosun, and also the failure by Captain Kirk to issue and enforce clear orders. But a full investigation into the circumstances of the disaster leads inexorably to the conclusion that the underlying or cardinal faults lay higher up in the Company. The Board of Directors did not appreciate their responsibility for the safe management of their ships. They did not apply their minds to the question: What orders should be given to the safety of our ships? The directors did not have any proper comprehension of what their duties were. There appears to have been a lack of thought about the way in which the HER-

ALD ought to have been organised for the Dover/Zeebrugge run. All concerned in management, from the members of the Board of Directors down to the junior superintendents, were guilty of fault in that all must be regarded as sharing responsibility for the failure of management. From top to bottom the body corporate was infected with the disease of sloppiness. . . . The failure on the part of the shore management to give proper and clear directions was a contributory cause of the disaster.

5.6. King's Cross

At 1925 on 18 November 1987, discarded smoker's material probably set light to highly inflammable rubbish that had been allowed to accumulate in the running tracks of an escalator. Twenty minutes later, jets of flame shot up the escalator shaft and hit the ceiling of the ticket hall in which those evacuated via the Piccadilly and Victoria line escalators were gathering. Although a number of active failures were committed by the station staff and the emergency services in the intervening period, the primary causes of the disaster were present long before the start of the fire. These latent failures are summarised in Case Study No. 6 (see Appendix).

In the subsequent investigation (Fennell, 1988), the inspector placed the responsibility for the disaster squarely with the managements of London Regional Transport and its operating company, London Underground. Three quotations will serve to convey the flavour of his judgement.

The Chairman of London Regional Transport. . . . told me that whereas financial matters were strictly monitored, safety was not. . . . In my view, he was mistaken as to his responsibility. (Fennell, 1988, p. 17)

It is clear from what I heard that London Underground was struggling to shake off the rather blinkered approach which had characterised its earlier history and was in the middle of what the Chairman and Managing Director described as a change of culture and style. But in spite of that change the management remained of the view that fires were inevitable in the oldest most extensive underground system in the world. In my view they were fundamentally in error in their approach. (Fennell, 1988, p. 17)

I have devoted a chapter to the management of safety because the principal lesson to be learned from this tragedy is the right approach to safety. (Fennell, 1988, p. 18)

6. Distinguishing errors and violations

An important lesson to be learned from both the Chernobyl and Zeebrugge disasters is that the term 'error' does not capture all the ways in which human beings contribute to major accidents. An adequate framework for aberrant behaviours (literally 'a straying from the path') requires a distinction to be made between errors and violations. Both can be (and often are) present within the same action sequence, but they can also occur independently. One may err without committing a violation; a violation need not involve error.

Errors involve two distinct kinds of 'straying': the unwitting deviation of action from intention (slips and lapses) and the departure of planned actions from some satisfactory path towards a desired goal (mistakes). But this error classification, restricted as it is to individual information processing, offers only a partial account of the possible varieties of aberrant behaviour. What is missing is a further level of analysis acknowledging that, for the most part, humans do not plan and execute their actions in isolation, but within a regulated social milieu. While errors may be defined in relation to the cognitive processes of the individual, violations can only be described with regard to a social context in which behaviour is governed by operating procedures, codes of practice, rules and the like. For our purposes, violations can be defined as deliberate — but not necessarily reprehensible — deviations from those practices deemed necessary (by designers, managers and regulatory agencies) to maintain the safe operation of a potentially hazardous system.

The boundaries between errors and violations are by no means hard and fast, either conceptually or within a particular accident sequence. What is certain, however, is that dangerous aberrations cannot be studied exclusively within either the cognitive or the social psychological traditions; both need to be integrated within a single framework.

7. A preliminary classification of violations

7.1. The boundary categories

Violations may be committed for many reasons. One way of identifying the extremes of this range of possibilities is through the issue of intentionality. The first step is to ask: Was there a prior intention to commit this particular violation? If the answer is no, we can assign the violation to a category labelled erroneous or unintended violations. If the violation was deliberate, we need to know whether or not there was a prior intention to cause damage to the system. If there was, we can assign the violation to the general category of sabotage. Since the former category lies within the now well-defined province of error and the latter falls outside the scope of most accident scenarios, the violations of greatest interest are likely to be those occupying the middle ground, that is, violations having some degree of intentionality, but that do not involve the goal of system damage.

Within this broad hinterland of deliberate but nonmalevolent infringements, it is possible to make a further rough dichotomy between routine and exceptional violations. The former are largely habitual, forming an established part of an individual's behavioural repertoire; the latter are singular violations occurring in a particular set of circumstances. The road environment provides multiple examples of routine violations. The behaviour of the Chernobyl operators in the 20 or so minutes before the explosions offers a clear instance of an exceptional set of violations.

7.2. Routine violations

Two factors, in particular, appear to be important in shaping habitual violations: (a) the natural human tendency to take the path of least effort; and (b) a relatively indifferent environment (i.e., one that rarely punishes violations or rewards observance). Everyday observation shows that if the quickest and most convenient path between two task-related points involves transgressing an apparently trivial and rarely sanctioned safety procedure, then it will be violated routinely by the operators of the system. Such a principle suggests that routine violations could be minimised by designing systems with human beings in mind at the outset. Landscape architects are forever making the mistake of laying out pathways to satisfy aesthetic criteria rather than human needs; as a consequence, their symmetry is soon marred by muddy diagonal tracks across protected grassland.

7.3. Exceptional violations

Exceptional violations are not so clearly specified, being the product of a wide variety of local conditions. However, both the Chernobyl and the Zeebrugge disasters suggest the significance of what might loosely be called 'system double-binds' — particular tasks or operating circumstances that make violations inevitable, no matter how well-intentioned the operators might be.

8. Psychological grounds for distinguishing errors and violations

One place where errors and violations are both abundant and relatively easy to observe is on the roads. In a recent study (Reason, Manstead, Stradling, Baxter, Campbell & Huyser, 1988), a Driver Behaviour Questionnaire (DBQ) was administered anonymously to 520 UK drivers of both sexes and covering a wide age range. The DBQ was made up of 50 items, each one describing either an error (a slip or a mistake) or a violation. The latter included both infringements of the Highway Code and deviations from accepted practice (e.g., driving too slowly on a two-lane rural highway). The respondents used a 5-point rating scale to indicate how frequently (over the past year) they had committed each type of 'bad behaviour'.

   The data were analysed using a factor analytic technique involving varimax rotation. Three orthogonal factors accounted for nearly 40 per cent of the variance. Items loading highly on factor 1 were violations (e.g., drinking and driving, close following, racing with other drivers, disregarding speed limits, shooting stop lights, etc.). Factors 2 and 3, however, were clearly associated with erroneous behaviour. The items loading highly on factor 2 tended to be hazardous errors: slips and mistakes that could have adverse consequences for other road users (e.g., failing to see 'Give Way' signs, failing to check mirror before manoeuvres, misjudging the speed of oncoming vehicles when overtaking, etc.). Items associated with factor 3, on the other hand, tended to be inconsequential lapses (e.g., taking the wrong exit at a roundabout, forgetting where one's car is in a car park, driving to destination A when destination B was intended, etc.).

This analysis provided strong support for the belief that errors and violations are mediated by different cognitive mechanisms. This conclusion was further endorsed by the age and sex relationships. Violations declined with age, errors did not. Men at all ages reported more violations than women. Women were significantly more lapse-prone than men (or more honest!). These self-report data also correspond closely with what we know of the relative contributions of men and women at various ages to road accidents (Storie, 1977).

9. A resident pathogen metaphor

The case studies considered earlier, along with numerous others (Turner, 1978; Perrow, 1984), indicate that major disasters in defended systems are rarely if ever caused by any one factor, either mechanical or human. Rather, they arise from the unforeseen and usually unforeseeable concatenation of several diverse events, each one necessary but singly insufficient.

These observations suggest an analogy between the breakdown of complex technological systems and the aetiology of multiple-cause illnesses such as cancer and cardiovascular disease. More specifically, there appear to be similarities between latent failures in complex technological systems and resident pathogens in the human body.

The resident pathogen metaphor emphasises the significance of causal factors present in the system before an accident sequence actually begins. All man-made systems contain potentially destructive agencies, like the pathogens within the human body. At any one time, each complex system will have within it a certain number of latent failures, whose effects are not immediately apparent but that can serve both to promote unsafe acts and to weaken its defence mechanisms. For the most part, they are tolerated, detected and corrected, or kept in check by protective measures (the auto-immune system). But every now and again, a set of external circumstances – called here local triggers – arises that combines with these resident pathogens in subtle and often unlikely ways to thwart the system's defences and to bring about its catastrophic breakdown.

In medicine, a good deal more is known about the nature of active failures (i.e., trauma, invasive agencies, acute diseases, etc.) than about the action of resident pathogens. The same is true in the systems reliability field; single component failures or simple human errors can be foreseen and contained by built-in safety devices, but these engineered defences offer little protection against certain combinations of system pathogens and local triggers. In addition, there are interesting parallels between the aetiologies of pathogen-related diseases and the catastrophic breakdown of complex, opaque technical installations. Both seem to require the breaching of defences by a concatenation of resident pathogens and external triggering events, though in both cases the precise nature of this interaction is hard to predict.

The resident pathogen notion directs attention to the indicators of 'system morbidity' that are present prior to a catastrophic breakdown. These, in principle, are more open to detection than the often bizarre and unforeseeable nature of the local triggering events. Implicit in the metaphor is the notion that the likelihood of an accident will be some function of the number of pathogens currently present within the sociotechnical system. The greater the number of pathogens residing in a system, the more likely it will encounter just that particular combination of triggering conditions sufficient to complete an accident sequence.

Other things being equal, the more complex, interactive, tightly-coupled and opaque the system, the greater the number of resident pathogens it is likely to contain. However, while simpler systems are usually less interactive, less centralised and more transparent, they tend to be considerably less evolved with regard to built-in defences. Thus, relatively few pathogens can often wreak greater havoc in simpler systems than in more advanced ones.

An important corollary of these arguments is that the risk of an accident will be diminished if these pathogens are detected and neutralized proactively. However, like cancer and heart disease, accidents have multiple causes. The occurrence of an accident is not simply determined by the sheer number of pathogens in the system; their adverse effects have to find windows of opportunity to pass through the various levels of the system and, most particularly, through the defences themselves. In short, there are a large number of stochastic factors involved.

The resident pathogen metaphor has a number of attractive features, but it is far from being a workable theory. Its terms are still unacceptably vague. Moreover, it shares a number of features with the now largely discredited accident proneness theory, though it operates at a systemic rather than at an individual level.

Accident proneness theory had two elements. First, the purely statistical observation that certain people have more than their chance share of accidents, as determined by the Poisson model. Second, and much more controversial, there was the assumption that this unequal liability originated in some relatively enduring feature of the individual (i.e., personality traits, information-processing deficiencies, physical characteristics and the like). In the pathogen metaphor, comparable assertions are being made about systems rather than individuals. Here it is argued that some systems have a greater accident liability due to their larger accumulation of resident pathogens. The major difference, of course, lies in their respective remedial implications. Accident proneness theory, predicated as it is upon stable dispositional factors, offers no alternative other than the screening out of high-liability individuals; pathogen theory leads to a search for preaccident morbidity indicators and assumes that these are remediable.

Accident proneness theory failed because it was found that unequal accident liability was, in reality, a 'club' with a rapidly changing membership. In addition, attempts to find a clearly definable accident-prone personality proved fruitless.

The pathogen metaphor would suffer a similar fate if it were found that pathogens could only be identified retrospectively in relation to a specific set of accident circumstances in a particular system. For the pathogen metaphor to have any value, it is necessary to establish an a priori set of indicators relating to system morbidity and then to demonstrate clear causal connections between these indicators and accident liability across a wide range of complex systems and in a variety of accident conditions.

10. A general view of accident causation in complex systems

This section seeks to extend the pathogen metaphor in order to lay the foundations of a possible theoretical framework for considering the aetiology of accidents in complex technological systems. As indicated earlier, the challenge for such a framework is not just to provide an account of how latent and active failures combine to produce accidents, but also to indicate where and how more effective remedial measures might be applied. The framework has as its building blocks the basic elements of production common to any complex system (Wreathall, 1989).

10.1. The basic elements of production

The notion of production offers a reasonably uncontroversial starting point. All complex technologies are involved in some form of production. The product can be energy, a chemical substance or the mass transportation of people by road, rail, sea or air.

Figure 7.4 identifies the basic elements common to all such productive systems. These elements are represented diagrammatically as planes, one behind the other. We can think of these planes as identifying the essential, benign components of effective production.

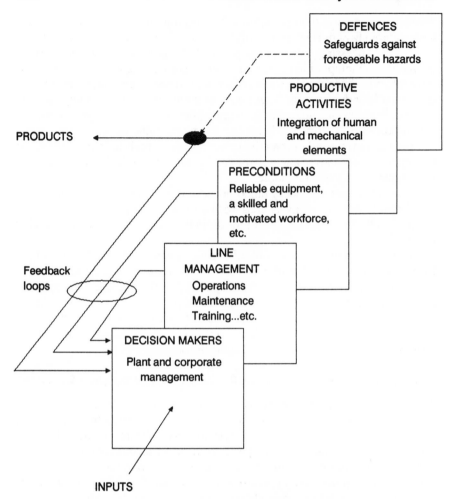

Figure 7.4. The basic elements of production. These constitute the necessary and benign components of any productive system.

10.1.1. The decision makers

These include both the architects and the high-level managers of the system.
Once in operation, they set the goals for the system as a whole in response to
inputs from the outside world. They also direct, at a strategic level, the means
by which these goals should be met. A large part of their function is concerned
with the allocation of finite resources. These comprise money, equipment,

people (talent and expertise) and time. Their aim is to deploy these resources to maximise both productivity and safety.

10.1.2. Line management

These are the departmental specialists who implement the strategies of the decision makers within their particular spheres of operation. They go by various labels: operations, training, sales, maintenance, finance, procurement, safety, engineering support, personnel and so on.

10.1.3. Preconditions

Appropriate decisions and effective line management are clearly prerequisites for successful production. But they are not of themselves sufficient. We need something between the line managers and the productive activities. These are a set of qualities possessed by both machines and people: reliable equipment of the right kind; a skilled and knowledgeable workforce; an appropriate set of attitudes and motivators; work schedules, maintenance programmes and environmental conditions that permit efficient and safe operations; and codes of practice that give clear guidance regarding desirable (safe and/or efficient) and undesirable (unsafe and/or inefficient) performance – to name but a few.

10.1.4. Productive activities

These are the actual performances of humans and machines: the precise synchronisation of mechanical and human activities in order to deliver the right product at the right time.

10.1.5. Defences

Where productive activities involve exposure to natural or intrinsic hazards, both individuals and machines should be supplied with safeguards sufficient to prevent foreseeable injury, damage or costly outages.

10.2. The human elements of accident causation

These are represented in Figure 7.5. It should be noted that a parallel diagram could equally well have been drawn for the purely mechanical or technical failures. However, our principal concern is with the human contribution to systems accidents, because accident analyses reveal that human factors dominate the risks to complex installations. Even what appear at first sight to be simple equipment breakdowns can usually be traced to some prior human failure. Nevertheless, it is important to acknowledge that any component or piece of equipment has a limited reliable life; all such items may fail for engineering rather than human reasons.

The essence of Figure 7.5 is that it portrays these human contributions as weaknesses or 'windows' in the basic productive 'planes' (shown in Figure 7.4). Here we show the dark side of the production picture. The causal sequence

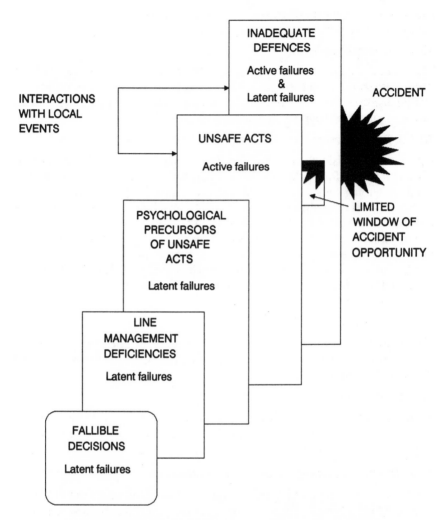

Figure 7.5. The various human contributions to the break-down of complex systems are mapped onto the basic elements of production. It is assumed that the primary systemic origins of latent failures are the fallible decisions taken by top-level plant and corporate managers. These are then transmitted via the intervening elements to the point where system defences may be breached.

moves from fallible decisions, through the intervening planes to an accident, that is, the unplanned and uncontrolled release of some destructive force, usually in the presence of victims. In what follows, I will elaborate upon the nature of each of these 'malign planes,' beginning with fallible decisions.

10.2.1. Fallible decisions

A basic premise of this framework is that systems accidents have their primary origins in fallible decisions made by designers and high-level (corporate or plant) managerial decision makers.

This is not a question of allocating blame, but simply a recognition of the fact that even in the best-run organisations a significant number of influential decisions will subsequently prove to be mistaken. This is a fact of life. Fallible decisions are an inevitable part of the design and management process. The question is not so much how to prevent them from occurring, as how to ensure that their adverse consequences are speedily detected and recovered.

In considering fallible decisions, it is important to be aware of the context in which high-level decisions are taken. Figure 7.6 summarises some of the constraints facing corporate and senior plant managers. All organizations have to allocate resources to two distinct goals: production and safety. In the long term, these are clearly compatible goals. But, given that all resources are finite, there are likely to be many occasions on which there are short-term conflicts of interest. Resources allocated to the pursuit of production could diminish those available for safety; the converse is also true. These dilemmas are exacerbated by two factors:

(a) *Certainty of outcome.* Resources directed at improving productivity have relatively certain outcomes; those aimed at enhancing safety do not, at least in the short term. This is due in large part to the large contribution of stochastic elements in accident causation.

(b) *Nature of the feedback.* The feedback generated by the pursuit of production goals is generally unambiguous, rapid, compelling and (when the news is good) highly reinforcing. That associated with the pursuit of safety goals is largely negative, intermittent, often deceptive and perhaps only compelling after a major accident or a string of incidents. Production feedback will, except on these rare occasions, always speak louder than safety feedback. This makes the managerial control of safety extremely difficult.

Furthermore, decision makers do not always interpret feedback on either the production or the safety channels accurately. Defensive 'filters' may be interposed that both protect them from bad news and encourage extrapunitive reactions. Thus, poor achievement on the production front can be blamed upon an inadequate workforce, union interference, market forces, world recession, shortages of materials

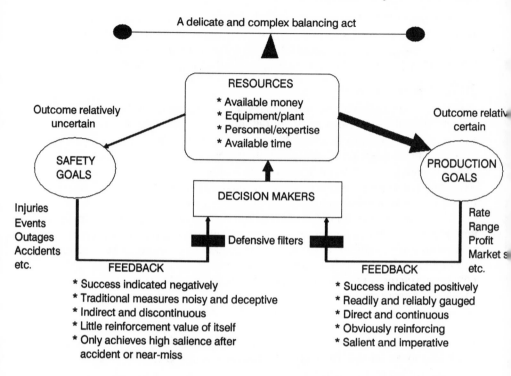

Figure 7.6. A summary of some of the factors that contribute
to fallible, high-level decision making. Resources allocated
to production and safety goals differ (a) in their certainty of
outcome, and (b) in the nature and impact of their respective
feedback.

and the like. A bad safety record can be attributed to operator care-
lessness or incompetence. This position is sometimes consolidated by
cataloguing the various safeguards, engineered safety devices and safe
operating practices that have already been implemented. Indeed,
given the almost diabolical nature of some accident sequences, these
are perfectly understandable reactions. But they nevertheless block
the discovery of effective remedies and contribute to further fallible
decisions.

10.2.2. Line management deficiencies

On this 'plane', the consequences of fallible decisions manifest themselves
differently in the various line management departments. Of course, it would

be naive to assume that the pathology or otherwise of a given line department is purely a function of higher-level decision making. The native incompetence of any set of line managers could further exacerbate the adverse effects of high-level decisions or even cause good decisions to have bad effects. Conversely, competence at the line management level could do something to mitigate the unsafe effects of fallible decisions, make neutral decisions have safer consequences, and transform good decisions into even better ones. Nevertheless, the scope for line management intervention is, in very real terms, constrained by the size of their departmental budgets or the resources at their disposal. For theoretical purposes, we will assume that these allocations will have been decided at a higher level in the system. Indeed, such allocations constitute a major part of the output of higher-level decision making.

The interaction between line management deficiencies and the psychological precursors of unsafe acts is extremely complex. There is a many-to-many mapping between possible line management deficiencies and the various psychological precursors of unsafe acts. For example, deficiencies in the training department can manifest themselves as a variety of preconditions: high workload, undue time pressure, inappropriate perception of hazards, ignorance of the system and motivational difficulties. Likewise, any one precondition (e.g., undue time pressure) could be the product of many different line management deficiencies (e.g., poor scheduling, poor procedures, deficiencies in skills, rules, or knowledge and maintenance inadequacies).

A useful way of thinking about these transformations is as *failure types* converting into *failure tokens* (Hudson, 1988). Deficient training is a pathogen type that can reveal itself, on the precondition plane, as a variety of pathogenic tokens. Such a view has important remedial consequences. Rectifying a particular failure type could, in principle, remove a wide and varied class of tokens. The type-token distinction is intrinsically hierarchical. Condition tokens at this level of analysis become types for the creation of unsafe act tokens at our next stage of analysis.

10.2.3. Preconditions for unsafe acts

Preconditions or psychological precursors are latent states. They create the potential for a wide variety of unsafe acts. The precise nature of these acts will be a complex function of the task being performed, the environmental influences and the presence of hazards. Each precursor can contribute to a large number of unsafe acts, depending upon the prevailing conditions.

At this level, the type-token distinction becomes especially significant due to the some-to-many mapping between precursors and unsafe acts. A particular psychological precursor, either alone or in combination with other precursors, can play a significant part in both provoking and shaping an almost infinitely large set of unsafe acts. But the precise nature, time, place and perpetrator of any single act are almost impossible to anticipate, though we can apply some general predictive principles.

The stochastic character of this onward mapping reveals the futility of 'tokenism' – the focusing of remedial efforts upon preventing the recurrence of specific unsafe acts. Although certain of these acts may fall into an easily recognisable subclass (e.g., failing to wear personal safety equipment in the presence of hazards) and so be amenable to targeted safety programmes and training, most of them are unforeseeable, sometimes even quite bizarre. The only sensible way of dealing with them is, first, to eliminate their preconditions as far as possible and, second, to accept that whatever the measures taken, some unsafe acts will still occur, and so provide defences that will intervene between the act and its adverse consequences.

As in the case of line management deficiencies, not all unsafe act precursors result from fallible decisions. Many of the pathogens at this level are introduced directly by the human condition. The capacities for being stressed, failing to perceive hazards, being imperfectly aware of the system and having less than ideal motivation are brought by each person into the workplace. Thus, in causal terms, there is only a loose coupling between the line management and precursor 'planes'. The point to stress is that these predispositions can either be markedly exaggerated or considerably mitigated by the character of decisions made at the top levels of the system and communicated to the individual via line departments. Even the best-run organisations cannot eliminate the harmful psychological effects of negative life events (e.g., marriage breakdowns, sickness in the family, bereavements, etc.) occurring outside the workplace. But they can anticipate the possibility if not the particular form of occurrence of negative life events and provide adequate defences against their unsafe consequences.

10.2.4. Unsafe acts

Even more than their psychological precursors, the commission of unsafe acts is determined by a complex interaction between intrinsic system influences (of the kind described for the preceding three 'planes') and those arising from the outside world. This has to do both with protean environmental factors and with the particular form of the existing hazards. Thus, an unsafe act can only be defined in relation to the presence of a particular hazard. There is nothing inherently unsafe about not wearing a safety helmet or a life jacket. Such omissions only constitute unsafe acts when they occur in potentially hazardous situations (i.e., when heavy objects are likely to fall from above, or in close proximity to deep water). An unsafe act is more than just an error or a violation – it is an error or a violation committed in the presence of a potential hazard: some mass, energy or toxicity that, if not properly controlled, could cause injury or damage. A classification of unsafe acts based upon arguments presented earlier in this book is shown in Figure 7.7.

10.2.5. Defences: The limited window of accident opportunity

A system's defences can be made up of many elements. At the lowest level of sophistication, they may consist of little more than personal safety equipment for the workforce and guards preventing direct contact with dangerous materials or moving parts. At the other extreme, there are the 'defences in depth' of nuclear power plants. These comprise both people (the control room operators) and many (both redundant and diverse) engineered features such as automatic safety devices and levels of containment.

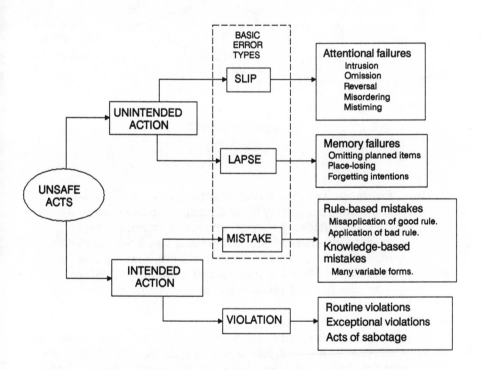

Figure 7.7. A summary of the psychological varieties of unsafe acts, classified initially according to whether the act was intended or unintended and then distinguishing errors from violations.

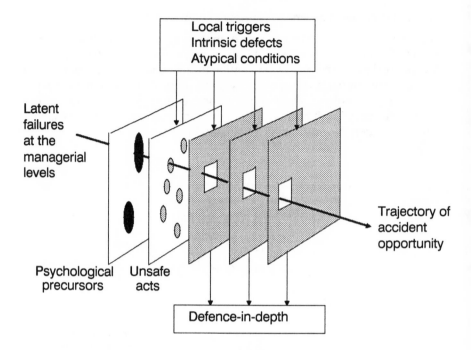

Figure 7.8. The dynamics of accident causation. The diagram shows a trajectory of accident opportunity penetrating several defensive systems. This results from a complex interaction between latent failures and a variety of local triggering events. It is clear from this figure, however, that the chances of such a trajectory of opportunity finding loopholes in all of the defences at any one time is very small indeed.

Very few unsafe acts result in actual damage or injury, even in relatively unprotected systems. And in highly protected systems, the various layers of defence can only be breached by the adverse conjunction of several different causal factors. Some of these are likely to be latent failures of pathogenic origin, others will be local triggering events such as the commission of a set of unsafe acts in a highly specific set of circumstances – often associated with some atypical system condition (i.e., the unusually low temperature preceding the *Challenger* launch, the testing carried out prior to the annual shut-down at Chernobyl-4, and the nose-down trim of the *Herald of Free Enterprise* due to a combination of high tide and unsuitable docking facilities).

Figure 7.8 tries to capture some of the stochastic features involved in the unlikely coincidence of an unsafe act and a breach in the system's defences. It shows a trajectory of opportunity originating in the higher levels of the system, passing via the precondition and unsafe act planes and then on through three successive layers of defence. Each of these planes has windows of opportunity, but they are in continual flux due to the largely unpredictable influences of both intrinsic and extrinsic factors. On each plane, the areas of permeability or windows vary over time in both their location and their size, and these changes have different time constants at different levels of the system. This picture emphasises the unlikelihood of any one set of causal factors finding an appropriate trajectory.

In a highly defended system, one of the most common accident scenarios involves the deliberate disabling of engineered safety features by operators in pursuit of what, at the time, seems a perfectly sensible goal (i.e., Chernobyl), but that fails to take account either of the side effects of these actions or of system characteristics. On other occasions, the defences are breached because the operators are unaware of concurrently created gaps in system security (i.e., at TMI-2, Bhopal, *Herald*) because they have an erroneous perception of the system state.

10.3. Controlling safer operations

The control of safe operations, like the control of production, is a continuous process. The prerequisites for adequate safety control are: (a) a sensitive multichannel feedback system, and (b) the ability to respond rapidly and effectively to actual or anticipated changes in the safety realm. These two aspects of control – feedback and response – are considered further below.

Figure 7.9 portrays the feedback loops and indicators potentially available to those responsible for the management of system safety. Together these various feedback loops and indicators constitute the safety information system (SIS).

It has been shown that an effective safety information system ranks second only to top management involvement in discriminating between safe and unsafe organisations matched on other variables (Kjellen, 1983).

Loop 1 (the reporting of accidents, lost time injuries, etc.) is the minimum requirement for an SIS. In most cases, however, the information supplied is too little and too late for effective anticipatory control. It is too little because such indices as fatalities and LTIs are simply the tip of the event iceberg. It is too late because they are retrospective; the events that safety management seeks to eliminate have already occurred.

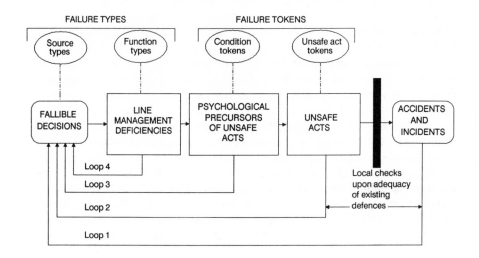

Figure 7.9. Feedback loops and indicators. The indicators are divided into two groups: *failure types* (relating to deficiencies in the managerial/organisational sectors) and *failure tokens* (relating to individual conditions and unsafe acts).

Loop 2 is potentially — though rarely actually — available through such procedures as unsafe act auditing (Shell Safety Committee, 1987). Usually the information derived from such auditing is disseminated only at the lower levels of the organisation. However, since unsafe acts are the stuff from which accidents are made, a feedback loop that samples the incidence and nature of unsafe acts in various operational spheres would provide a greater opportunity for proactive safety control.

The main thrust of this view of accident causation is towards the establishment of loops 3 and 4: *pathogen auditing*. The theory dictates that the most effective way of managing safety is by acting upon types rather than tokens, that is, by influencing system states occurring early on in the accident sequence. To identify these failure types and to find ways of neutralizing the pathogens so revealed represent the major challenges facing human factors researchers concerned with preserving the safety of complex, high-risk systems.

10.4. General indicators

The general indicators shown in Figure 7.9 cover two broad aspects of an organisation's safety functioning. The first relates to the variety and sensitivity of its feedback loops. The second deals with the decision makers' responsiveness to safety-related data. No amount of feedback will enhance an organisation's degree of safety if the information supplied is not acted upon in a timely and effective manner.

Westrum (1988) has provided a simple but meaningful classification of the ways in which organisations may differ in their reactions to safety data. His basic premise is that: "Organizations think. Like individuals, they exhibit a consciousness, a memory, and an ability to create and to solve problems. Their thinking strongly affects the generation and elimination of hazards." Organisational responses to hazards fall into three groups: denial, repair and reform actions.

Denial Actions

Suppression: Observers are punished or dismissed, and the observations expunged from the record.

Encapsulation: Observers are retained, but the validity of their observations is disputed or denied.

Repair Actions

Public Relations: Observations emerge publicly, but their significance is denied; they are sugar-coated.

Local Repairs: The problem is admitted and fixed at the local level, but its wider implications are denied.

Reform Actions

Dissemination: The problem is admitted to be global, and global action is taken upon it.

Reorganisation: Action on the problem leads to reconsideration and reform of the operational system.

The more effective the organisation, the more likely it is to respond to safety data with actions from the bottom of this list (i.e., reform), while those less adequate will employ responses from the top (i.e., denial).

Westrum then uses these reactions to define organisations along a scale of what he calls 'cognitive adequacy', or the effectiveness of their ways of thinking about hazard. These are grouped under three headings: pathological, calculative and generative organisations.

(a) *Pathological organisations* are ones whose safety measures are inadequate even under normal conditions. These organisations sacrifice safety goals in the pursuit of production goals, often under severe economic pressures, and actively circumvent safety regulations. Information about hazardous conditions is suppressed at the source by suppressing or encapsulating the messenger (e.g., the Tennessee Valley Authority's nuclear power plant management).

(b) *Calculative organisations* try to do the best job they can using 'by-the-book' methods. These are usually adequate under normal operating conditions, but often fail when they encounter unforeseen circumstances. In short, they may implement many safety practices but have little in the way of effective disaster plans (e.g., the New Jersey chemical industry, the CEGB, the U.K. Department of Energy).

(c) *Generative organisations* are characterised by a high degree of ostensibly irregular or unconventional activity in furthering their goals. They set targets for themselves beyond ordinary expectations and fulfill them because they are willing to do unexpected things in unexpected ways. They emphasise results rather than methods, and value substance more than form. Hazards tend to be quickly discovered and neutralised because lower-level personnel have both permission to see and permission to do (e.g., U.S. nuclear aircraft carrier flight deck operations – see Rochlin, LaPorte & Roberts., 1987).

11. Learning the right lessons from past accidents

It is not easy to learn the right lessons from past disasters, especially if these events are likely to further undermine public confidence in the safety of one's own similar technologies. Institutional reactions to other people's catastrophes reveal, among other things, two universal human failings: the fundamental attribution error and the fundamental surprise error.

The *fundamental attribution error* has been widely studied in social psychology (see Fiske & Taylor, 1984; see also Chapter 2, Section 3.5). This refers to a pervasive tendency to blame bad outcomes on an actor's personal inadequacies (i.e., dispositional factors) rather than attribute them to situational factors beyond his or her control. Such tendencies were evident in both the Russian and the British responses to the Chernobyl accident. Thus, the Russian report on Chernobyl (USSR State Committee on the Utilization of Atomic Energy, 1986) concluded that: "The prime cause of the accident was an extremely improbable combination of violations of instructions and operating rules." Lord Marshall, Chairman of the U.K. Central Electricity Generating Board (CEGB), wrote a foreword to the U.K. Atomic Energy Authority's report upon the Chernobyl accident (UKAEA, 1987), in which he assigned blame in very definite terms: "To us in the West, the sequence of reactor operator errors is incomprehensible. Perhaps it came from supreme arrogance or complete ignorance. More plausibly, we can speculate that the operators as a matter of habit had broken rules many, many times and got away with it so the safety rules no longer seemed relevant." Could it happen in the U.K.? "My own judgement is that the overriding importance of ensuring safety is so deeply engrained in the culture of the nuclear industry that this will not happen in the U.K."

The term *fundamental surprise* was coined by an Israeli social scientist, Zvi Lanir (Lanir, 1986), in regard to the Yom Kippur War, but it is particularly apt for both the TMI-2 and Chernobyl accidents. A fundamental surprise reveals a profound discrepancy between one's perception of the world and the reality. A major reappraisal is demanded. Situational surprises, on the other hand, are localised events requiring the solution of specific problems.

Lanir likens the difference between situational and fundamental surprise to that between 'surprise' and 'astonishment' and illustrates it with an anecdote from Webster, the lexicographer. One day, Webster returned home to find his wife in the arms of his butler. "You surprised me," said his wife. "And you have astonished me," responded Webster. Mrs Webster experienced merely a situational surprise; Mr Webster suffered a fundamental one.

The natural human tendency is to respond to fundamental surprises as if they were only situational ones. Thus, the fundamental surprise error "is to avoid any fundamental meaning and to learn the situational lessons from the surface events" (Lanir, 1986).

At the Sizewell B public inquiry (Layfield, 1987), the CEGB witnesses sought to dissociate the future station from the troubles that beset the Metropolitan Edison pressurised water reactor (PWR) on Three Mile Island on 28 March 1979. They identified various salient features of the TMI-2 accident — the steam power plant, sticky relief valves, poor control room design, inadequate operator training, etc. — and asserted that these and more would be significantly improved in the Sizewell B PWR. In his assessment of this evidence, Sir Frank Layfield hinted at broader issues: "Some aspects of the TMI accident give warnings which are of general importance," but then concluded that they were not applicable in the U.K. due to organisational differences.

This natural urge to distance U.K. installations from foreign catastrophes was even more apparent in the UKAEA's (1987) analysis of the Chernobyl disaster that concluded: "the Chernobyl accident was unique to the [Russian] reactor design and there are few lessons for the United Kingdom to learn from it. Its main effect has been to reinforce and reiterate the importance and validity of existing UK standards."

So what are the right lessons to be learned from TMI and Chernobyl? These, I believe, have been well stated for TMI-2 by David Woods, previously

214 Latent errors and systems disasters

of the Westinghouse Corporation (Woods, 1987). The same general conclusions apply equally to Chernobyl and to the Bhopal, *Challenger*, and Zeebrugge accidents (Woods, 1987):

> The TMI accident was more than an unexpected progression of faults; it was more than a situation planned for but handled inadequately; it was more than a situation whose plan had proved inadequate. The TMI accident constituted a fundamental surprise in that it revealed a basic incompatibility between the nuclear industry's view of itself and reality. Prior to TMI the industry could and did think of nuclear power as a purely technical system where all the problems were in the form of some technical area or areas and the solutions to these problems lay in those engineering disciplines. TMI graphically revealed the inadequacy of that view because the failures were in the socio-technical system and not due to pure technical nor pure human factors.

Regardless of the technology or the country that it serves, the message of this chapter is very clear: No one holds the monopoly on latent failures. And these resident pathogens constitute the primary residual risk to complex, highly-defended technological systems.

12. Postscript: On being wise after the event

This chapter has argued that most of the root causes of serious accidents in complex technologies are present within the system long before an obvious accident sequence can be identified. In theory, at least, some of these latent failures could have been spotted and corrected by those managing, maintaining and operating the system in question. In addition, there were also prior warnings of likely catastrophe for most of the accidents considered here. The Rogovin inquiry (Rogovin, 1979), for example, discovered that the TMI accident had 'almost happened' twice before, once in Switzerland in 1974 and once at the Davis-Besse plant in Ohio in 1977. Similarly, an Indian journalist wrote a prescient series of articles about the Bhopal plant and its potential dangers three years before the tragedy (see Marcus & Fox, 1988). Other unheeded warnings were also available prior to the *Challenger*, Zeebrugge and King's Cross accidents.

For those who pick over the bones of other people's disasters, it often seems incredible that these warnings and human failures, seemingly so obvious in retrospect, should have gone unnoticed at the time. Being blessed with both uninvolvement and hindsight, it is a great temptation for retrospective observers to slip into a censorious frame of mind and to wonder at how these people could have been so blind, stupid, arrogant, ignorant or reckless.

One purpose of this concluding section is to caution strongly against adopting such a judgemental stance. No less than the accident-producing errors themselves, the apparent clarity of retrospection springs in part from the shortcomings of human cognition. The perceptual biases and strong-but-wrong beliefs that make incipient disasters so hard to detect by those on the spot also make it difficult for accident analysts to be truly wise after the event. Unless we appreciate the potency of these retroactive distortions, we will never truly understand the realities of the past, nor learn the appropriate remedial lessons.

There is one obvious but psychologically significant difference between ourselves, the retrospective judges, and the people whose decisions, actions or inactions led to a disaster; we know how things were going to turn out, they did not. As Baruch Fischhoff and his colleagues have shown, possession of outcome knowledge profoundly influences the way we survey past events (Fischhoff, 1975; Slovic & Fischhoff, 1977; Fischhoff, 1989). This phenomenon is called *hindsight bias*, and has two aspects:

(a) The 'knew-it-all-along' effect (or 'creeping determinism'), whereby observers of past events exaggerate what other people should have been able to anticipate in foresight. If they were involved in these events, they tend to exaggerate what they themselves actually knew in foresight.

(b) Historical judges are largely unaware of the degree to which outcome knowledge influences their perceptions of the past. As a result, they overestimate what they would have known had they not possessed this knowledge.

The historian George Florovsky described this phenomenon very precisely: "In retrospect, we seem to perceive the logic of the events which unfold themselves in a regular or linear fashion according to a recognizable pattern with an alleged inner necessity. So that we get the impression that it really could not have happened otherwise" (quoted by Fischhoff, 1975, p. 288).

Outcome knowledge dominates our perceptions of the past, yet we remain largely unaware of its influence. For those striving to make sense of complex historical events, familiarity with how things turned out imposes a definite but unconscious structure upon the antecedent actions and conditions. Prior facts are assimilated into this schema to make a coherent causal story, a process similar to that observed by Bartlett (1932) in his studies of remembering. But to those involved at the time these same events would have had no such deterministic logic. Each participant's view of the future would have been bounded by local concerns. Instead of one grand convergent narrative, there would have been a multitude of individual stories running on in parallel towards the expected attainment of various distinct and personal goals.

Before judging too harshly the human failings that concatenate to cause a disaster, we need to make a clear distinction between the way the precursors appear now, given knowledge of the unhappy outcome, and the way they seemed at the time. Wagenaar and Groeneweg (1988) have coined the term *impossible accident* to convey the extreme difficulty of those involved to foresee any possible adverse conjunction between what seemed then to be unconnected and, in many instances, not especially unusual or dangerous happenings. They concluded their review of 100 shipping accidents with the following comment (Wagenaar & Groeneweg, 1988, p. 42):

> Accidents appear to be the result of highly complex coincidences which could rarely be foreseen by the people involved. The unpredictability is caused by the large number of causes and by the spread of the information over the participants. . . . Accidents do not occur because people gamble and lose, they occur because people do not believe that the accident that is about to occur is at all possible.

The idea of personal responsibility is deeply rooted in Western cultures (Turner, 1978). The occurrence of a man-made disaster leads inevitably to a search for human culprits. Given the ease with which the contributing human failures can subsequently be identified, such scapegoats are not hard to find. But before we rush to judgement, there are some important points to be kept in mind. First, most of the people involved in serious accidents are neither stupid nor reckless, though they may well have been blind to the consequences of their actions. Second, we must beware of falling prey to the fundamental attribution error (i.e., blaming people and ignoring situational factors). As Perrow (1984) argued, it is in the nature of complex, tightly-coupled systems to suffer unforeseeable sociotechnical breakdowns. Third, before beholding the mote in his brother's eye, the retrospective observer should be aware of the beam of hindsight bias in his own.

8 Assessing and reducing the human error risk

This book began by discussing the nature of human error and the theoretical influences that have shaped its study. It then proposed distinctions between error types based on performance levels and error forms derived from basic memory retrieval mechanisms. Chapters 4 and 5 presented a framework theory of error production, and Chapter 7 considered the various processes by which errors are detected. The preceding chapter examined some of the consequences of human error in high-risk technologies, looking in particular at the effects of latent failures.

It is clear from this summary that the bulk of the book has favoured theory rather than practice. This concluding chapter seeks to redress the balance somewhat by focusing upon remedial possibilities. It reviews both what has been done and what might be done to minimise the often terrible costs of human failures in potentially hazardous environments. More specifically, it deals with the various techniques employed or proposed by human reliability specialists to assess and to reduce the risks associated with human error.

The chapter has been written with two kinds of reader in mind: psychologists who are unfamiliar with the methods of human reliability analysis (not unsurprisingly since most of this material is published outside the conventional psychological literature), and safety practitioners of one sort or another. For the sake of the former, I have tried to make clear the model and assumptions underlying each technique. This means that relatively little space is left to tell the practitioners exactly how these methods should be applied in specific contexts. To compensate for this, I will indicate (where they are available and/or appropriate) where more detailed procedural information can be obtained. For the benefit of both types of reader, however, I will state briefly what is known of the reliability and validity of these methods, where such data exist.

The development of human reliability analysis (HRA) techniques has been intimately bound up with the fortunes and misfortunes of the nuclear power industry. This does not mean that such methods are applicable only to the design and operation of nuclear power plants – they have been pioneered and widely used in other industries and organizations – but it is certainly true that nuclear power generation has been the focus of most human reliability developments over the past two decades. Since nuclear power applications will fea-

217

ture so extensively here, it is worth dwelling briefly on why this has been the case.

The first reason has to do with the fears – neither entirely baseless nor altogether rational – excited by anything nuclear, particularly in Europe. This public concern over the safety of nuclear power generation was considerably heightened by the Chernobyl disaster. In June 1988, the industry's technical magazine, *Nuclear Engineering International*, reported the results of its annual world survey, which showed that 10 countries, mostly in Europe, had postponed or cancelled reactor orders. This occurred even in countries like Finland and Belgium, where the good operating record of their existing stations had previously created a climate favourable to the development of nuclear power.

In the United Kingdom, where the Central Electricity Generating Board (CEGB) is planning to introduce about six pressurized water reactors (PWRs) by the early years of the twenty-first century, the government and the utility have gone to considerable lengths to persuade the public of both the economic necessity and the safety of these new reactors. The public inquiry held to decide whether or not to give permission for the building of the first of these PWRs at Sizewell ran for well over 2 years (340 working days) and was the longest of its kind held in Britain. Over a year was devoted to safety issues. Despite the decision to go ahead with the Sizewell 'B' reactor and the length of these debates, the public inquiry into the CEGB's proposal to build a further PWR at Hinkley Point has attracted formal opposition from 19 local authorities, 250 organisations and over 20,000 individuals.

The second reason for the close connection between reliability analysis and the nuclear industry has to do with the fact that, in order to obtain both public acceptance and an operating licence, utilities have to demonstrate in advance that their reactor designs will satisfy certain safety targets. In Britain, for example, these are expressed as order-of-magnitude probabilities: less than one in a million per reactor year for a large uncontrolled release of radioacitivity into the environment, and a frequency of less than 1 in 10,000 per reactor year for a limited emission. As Rasmussen (1988) explains: "For hazardous large-scale installations, design cannot be based on experience gained from accidents, as it has been the case for accidents in minor separate systems. . . . The days of extensive pilot plant tests for demonstration of the feasibility of a design are over and the safety target has to be assessed by analytical means based on empirical data from incidents and near misses." One of the consequences of this shift of focus has been the rapid development over the past 20 years of a branch of reliability engineering known as probabilistic risk assessment (PRA). Since many of the developments in human reliability analysis have been designed to contribute to these overall plant risk assessments, we need to look more closely at the nature and underlying assumptions of PRA.

1. Probabilistic risk assessment

At the heart of PRA are logical 'tree' models of the plant and its functions. These trees take two basic forms: (a) fault trees that address the question: How can a given plant failure occur (e.g., a serious release of radioactive material)? and (b) event trees that answer the question: What could happen if a given fault or event occurs (e.g., a steam generator tube rupture or small loss of coolant accident)? In the case of a fault tree the starting point is usually a gross system failure (the top event) and the causes are then traced back through a series of logical AND/OR gates to the possible initiating faults. An event tree begins with an initiating fault or event and works forward in time considering the probabilities of failure of each of the safety systems that stand between the initial malfunction and some unacceptable outcome (see Figure 8.1).

PRA has thus two aims. first, to identify potential areas of significant risk and indicate how improvements can be made; second, to quantify the overall risk from a potentially hazardous plant.

The general structure of a PRA was established in 1975 with the publication of the U.S. Reactor Safety Study, a 10-kilogram document known as WASH-1400 and formally titled: *An Assessment of Accident Risks in U.S. Commercial Nuclear Power Plants*. In outline, PRA involves the following procedural steps:

(a) Identify the sources of potential hazard. In the case of a nuclear power plant, the major hazard is the release of radioactivity from a degraded core.

(b) Identify the initiating events that could lead to this hazard.

(c) Establish the possible sequences that could follow from various initiating events using event trees.

(d) Quantify each event sequence. This involves data or judgement about two things: (i) the frequency of the initiating event, and (ii) the probability of failure on demand of the relevant safety systems.

(e) Determine the overall plant risk. This will be a function of the frequency of all possible accident sequences and their consequences.

It should be noted that even in its purely engineering application (focusing only on hardware failures), this technique has been criticised on a number of grounds. The logic of event trees demands that only conditional probabilities should be used, allowing for the preceding components of an accident sequence. In practice, however, this conditionality is rarely recognised, and independence of events has normally been assumed. In short, PRAs have neglected the possibility of common-mode failures, something that is considerably enhanced by the presence of human beings at various stages in the design, installation, management, maintenance and operation of the system. Other problems arise from the need to quantify events. In many cases, the data on previous faults do not exist and so have to be estimated. Reliability data relating to component failure rates do not necessarily 'travel well' from one type of installation to another.

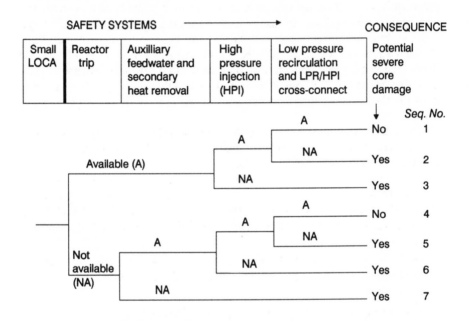

Figure 8.1. Standard event tree for a small loss of coolant accident (LOCA) in a pressurised water reactor (PWR). Sequences 2 to 7 describe logical combinations of defence-in-depth failure(s), each having

Nonetheless, the development of a standardised PRA was a major step forward in reliability engineering. In particular, its underlying logic provides an important adjunct to the design process, identifying those areas where redundant or diverse safety systems need to be installed in order to prevent the propagation of unacceptably likely accident sequences. Its major failing, however, and one that came to be widely acknowledged after the Three Mile Island accident in 1979, was its inability to accommodate adequately the substantial contribution made by human failures (and particularly mistakes) to the accident risk. This problem has been the stimulus for numerous attempts to convert human error rates into the numerical currency demanded by PRA. We will consider some of the more notable of these methods below under the general heading of Human Reliability Analysis or HRA techniques.

2. Human reliability analysis (HRA) techniques

A large number of these techniques have emerged within the last decade. Schurman and Banks (1984) reviewed nine models for predicting human error probabilities; Hannaman, Spurgin and Lukic (1984) identified ten methods (including two of their own) that have been developed for use in PRA studies; Senders, Moray and Smiley (1985) examined eight such models; and Williams (1985) compared the performance of some nine techniques. Although there are common elements in each list, none is precisely the same. Here we will focus on those techniques that are either frequently cited or that involve a relatively distinct approach. The descriptions of the methods given below draw heavily upon the excellent reviews by Hannaman, Spurgin and Lukic, (1984), Senders and coauthors (1985) and Embrey (1985, 1987), as well as upon original sources.

2.1. Technique for human error rate prediction (THERP)

THERP is a technique that has attracted superlatives of all kinds. It is probably the best known and most widely used means of providing human reliability data for PRA studies. It is also the most accessible from the practitioner's point of view; its procedures and rationale are clearly described in a 300-plus page *Handbook of Human Reliability Analysis with Emphasis on Nuclear Power Plant Applications* (Swain & Guttmann, 1983), as well as in a number of other publications (Bell & Swain, 1983; Swain & Weston, 1988). It is also one of the oldest techniques: its origins go back to the early 1960s (Swain, 1963), and its present handbook form seeks to transfer the 30-year experience of its principal architect, Alan Swain, to subsequent generations of human reliability analysts. And, probably as the result of its extensive usage and the effectiveness of its dissemination, it has also been subject to more criticism than any other HRA method. Yet it is judged by some whose opinions are worth noting (Senders et al., 1985) as "probably the best of the techniques currently available." These factors, together with its heroic aspirations, make it a technique worthy of close examination.

The basic assumption of THERP (as in most other decompositional approaches to HRA) is that the operator's actions can be regarded in the same light as the success or failure of a given pump or valve. As such, the reliability of the operator can be assessed in essentially the same way as an equipment item. The operator's activities are broken down into task elements and substituted for equipment outputs in a more-or-less conventional reliability assessment, with adjustments to allow for the greater variability and interdependence of human performance.

The object of THERP is "to predict human error probabilities and to evaluate the degradation of a man-machine system likely to be caused by human errors alone or in connection with equipment functioning, operational procedures and practices, or other system and human characteristics that influence system behaviour" (Swain & Guttman, 1983). The procedural stages involved in applying the THERP technique accord very closely to those in a PRA, described in the previous section. There are four steps:

(a) Identify the system functions that may be influenced by human error.

(b) List and analyse the related human operations (i.e., perform a detailed task analysis).

(c) Estimate the relevant error probabilities using a combination of expert judgement and available data.

(d) Estimate the effects of human errors on the system failure events, a step that usually involves the integration of HRA with PRA. When used by designers, it has an additional iterative step that involves making changes to the system and then recalculating the probabilities in order to gauge the effects of these modifications.

The basic analytical tool is a form of event tree termed a probability tree diagram. In this, the limbs represent binary decision points in which correct or incorrect performance are the only available choices. Each limb represents a combination of human activities and the presumed influences upon these activities: the so-called performance shaping factors (PSFs). The event tree starts from some convenient point in the system and works forward in time. With the possible exception of the first branching, all the human task elements depicted by the tree limbs are conditional probabilities.

The performance shaping factors are, in effect, the major concession that THERP makes to the humanity of the operators. They are used to modify the nominal human error probabilities (HEPs) according to the analyst's judgement of such factors as the work environment; the quality of the man-machine interface; the skills, experience, motivation and expectations of the individual operator; and the degree and type of the stresses likely to be present in various situations.

The core of THERP is contained in 27 tables of human error probabilities set out in Part IV of the 1983 handbook. The values given in the tables relate to nominal HEPs (the probability that when a given task element is performed, an error will occur). These numbers are generic values, based on expert opinion and data borrowed from activities analogous to those of NPP operators.

Each of these tables deals with particular errors associated with specific activities: for example, errors of commission in reading and recording quantitative information from unannunciated displays; selection errors in operating manual controls or locally-operated valves and so on. Each table is broken down into smaller task components and, for each component, two numerical values are usually given: the *nominal HEP* and either the *error factor* (the square root of the ratio of the upper to the lower uncertainty bounds), or the *uncertainty bounds* themselves (the upper and lower bounds of the given HEP, reflecting uncertainty of estimates). The upper and lower uncertainty bounds correspond to the ninety-fifth and fifth percentiles, respectively, in a lognormal scale of HEPs. As indicated earlier, the analyst is required to adjust the nominal error probability values according to his or her judgement of the effects of local performance shaping factors.

Earlier versions of THERP were widely criticised for their exclusive focus on behavioural error forms and for their corresponding neglect of mistakes such as misdiagnosis or selecting an inappropriate remedial strategy – exactly the kind of errors, in fact, that contributed so extensively to the TMI accident. More recently, Swain and his collaborators have sought to revise the original technique (Swain, 1976) so that it can accommodate diagnostic errors and other higher level 'cognitive' mistakes (Swain & Guttmann, 1983), and this process of revision is still continuing some five years after the publication of the handbook (Swain & Weston, 1988).

These latest revisions are interesting for two reasons. First, they mark a departure from nominal error probabilities, derived from expert judgement, which has been shown to be highly variable (Comer, Seaver, Stillwell & Gaddy, 1984). In his latest work, Swain favours time-dependent error frequencies based on simulator data in which NPP crews are given different types of abnormal events to deal with. These data show the time taken for each correct diagnosis and the number of control teams who fail to achieve a correct diagnosis. Second, they provide a basis for estimating the probabilities of different kinds of postevent misdiagnoses. With the exception of the confusion matrix technique (Potash, Stewart, Dietz, Lewis & Dougherty, 1981), these had hitherto not been differentiated, being commonly consigned to an 'incorrect diagnosis' category.

It is too early to say whether these modifications to the basic THERP technique will be sufficient to ward off earlier criticisms relating to both the unreliability of its underlying human performance numbers and THERP's limited focus upon external error forms (i.e., errors of omission and commission). Although Swain and his colleagues have shown considerable willingness to shift from their exclusively behaviourist stance to one that embraces more cognitive elements, it is unlikely that these moves will be sufficient to appease their mentalist critics who demand a more theoretically-driven, top-down mode of error analysis and who remain deeply sceptical about assigning meaningful probabilities to anything but highly situation-specific slips of action. For all its technical sophistication, THERP remains an art form — exceedingly powerful when employed by people as experienced as Alan Swain and his immediate collaborators, but of more doubtful validity in the hands of others.

2.2. Time-reliability techniques

This section deals with a closely related set of techniques that are concerned with quantifying postaccident errors on the basis of time-reliability curves. The first of these was the model termed operator action trees (OATS).

When OATS was first developed in the early 1980s (Hall, Fragola and Wreathall, 1982; Wreathall, 1982), THERP was the only technique that had been used to quantify human error risks contributing to possible NPP accidents. In its early form, THERP focused primarily upon procedural errors (e.g., leaving manual valves in the wrong position) which occur prior to the onset of a reactor trip and that may either cause the event or result in the unavailability of some safety system. The architects of the OATS technique saw this as neglecting other important kinds of human error: those that occur after an accident sequence has been initiated. These they called cognitive errors because they have for the most part involved mistakes in higher-level cognitive processes, such as reasoning, diagnosis and strategy selection. Procedural and cognitive errors require very different analytical techniques for both modelling and quantification. OATS was devised specifically for dealing with operator errors during accident and abnormal conditions and is designed to provide error types and associated probabilities to be used in PRAs.

A detailed account of the OATS procedures is given in NUREG/CR-3010 (Hall et al., 1982) and by Wreathall (1982). In brief, the method employs a logic tree, the basic operator action-tree, that identifies the possible postaccident operator failure modes. Three types of cognitive error are identified:

(a) Failure to perceive that an event has occurred.

(b) Failure to diagnose the nature of the event and to identify the necessary remedial actions.

(c) Failure to implement those responses correctly and in a timely manner.

These errors are quantified by applying an analytical tool called the time-reliability curve, which describes the probability of failure as a function of the time interval between the moment at which the relevant warning signals are evident to when action should be taken to achieve successful recovery. Simple modifications are made to this time-reliability curve when the analyst judges that operators would be reluctant to take certain actions. The probabilities derived from these time-relaibility relationships represent the likelihood of successful action by a team of operators. The major input to the quantification curve is the time available for thinking: $t_T = t_0 - t_I - t_A$, where t_T is the thinking interval, t_0 is the overall time from the initiation of an accident sequence to the point by which actions have to be completed, t_I is the time after initiation at which appropriate indications are given and t_A is the time taken to carry out the planned actions. The basis for these parameters are reported by Wreathall (1982). In the absence of suitable field data, they share with THERP the fundamental problem of being 'best guesses', derived either from experts or extrapolated from laboratory studies.

Hannaman and his coauthors (1984, p. A-4) list the following 'plus' points for OATS: "it provides a defined structure for assessing the operator failure modes which is independent of procedures, it is simple to use with defined dependencies, it has an application guide, and defined data." Senders and coauthors (1985, p. 44) comment: "OATS has not been formally validated, but it has been related to empirical data in a particularly interesting way by use of generic 'time-to-completion' curves. As a result, OATS can predict the probability that no response will yet have been made to the annunciation of an incident as a function of the time since the incident occurred. The resulting curves seem to provide a reasonable estimate of 'speed accuracy trade-off' in fault diagnosis when compared to (recently obtained) data."

In their original description of the OATS technique, Wreathall and his coworkers (Hall et al., 1982) tentatively suggested that different time-reliability curves could be drawn for skill-based, rule-based and knowledge-based performance on the basis of time-reliability correlations developed by Joe Fragola. This idea has been developed by Hannaman and coauthors (1984) in the form of the human cognitive reliability model, or HCR.

HCR is predicated on the assumption that different kinds of cognitive activity take different times to execute. Its outputs are the time-dependent nonresponse probabilities of NPP operators confronting an abnormal state of the plant. Whereas OATS comprises only a single time-reliability relationship, HCR provides sets of curves, each one relating to a different kind of cognitive processing (SB, RB or KB), for modelling specific situations (e.g., steam generator tube rupture). As such, it provides an assessment of the probability of error persistence against time.

Reviewers of the HCR correlational technique (Senders et al., 1985; Embrey & Lucas, 1989) have commended a number of its features:

(a) It is a quick and relatively convenient technique to apply.

(b) It takes account of the time-dependent nature of operator actions.

(c) Good fits have been found between the model and observed completion times in simulator studies.

(d) It covers knowledge-based behaviour as well as the more usually modelled skill-based and rule-based levels of performance.

(e) Its input data (times available from the onset of the emergency) are the same as those used by hardware reliability assessment techniques.

While the HCR model predicts time to task completion, it does not, of itself, constitute a model of error. As Senders and his coauthors noted (1985, p. 44): "It uses models or data on error as its input, rather than producing such data as an output. Specifically, the occurrence of error increases time to completion: but the model does not predict when or how often such an error will occur."

According to Embrey and Lucas (1989), a major shortcoming of the HCR correlation is its limited focus upon nonresponse probabilities. Many of the critical operator errors observed in NPP emergencies involve commission as well as omission errors, for example, the rapid selection of wrong courses of action or the deliberate violation of established procedures. Embrey and Lucas (1989) also point out that the rules for assigning tasks to the various performance levels (SB, RB and KB) do not take account of the rapid switching between these levels apparent during the course of actual events (see Woods, 1982). Similarly, it is not easy to determine whether the nonresponse probabilities (obtained from the HCR curves) are due to the slow processing of information, or to a failure to detect the onset of the emergency. These are psychologically different processes, and it seems unlikely that they could be described by the same time-available/nonresponse probability curves.

2.3. Empirical technique to estimate operators' errors (TESEO)

TESEO is an acronym for the Italian name: tecnica empirica stima errori operatori. It was developed by the Reliability Research Group of ENTE Nazional Idrocarburi (Bello & Colombari, 1980) from interview data collected in petrochemical process plants, but it is also applicable to nuclear process plants.

TESEO yields the probability of operator failure through the combined application of five error probability parameters, K_1 to K_5:

K_1 = type of activity (routine or not routine, requiring close attention or not): probability parameters between 0.001 and 0.1.

K_2 = a temporary stress factor for routine activities (assigned according to the time available): parameters between 10 and 0.5; a temporary stress factor for nonroutine activities (again depending upon the available time): parameters between 10 and 0.1.

K_3 = operator qualities (assigned according to selection, expertise and training): parameters between 0.5 and 3.

K_4 = an activity anxiety factor (dependent upon the situation, either a grave emergency, potential emergency or nominal conditions): parameters between 3 and 1.

K_5 = an activity ergonomic factor (according to the quality of the microclimate and plant interface): parameters between 0.7 and 10.

Kletz (1985, p. 80)) gives an example of how the technique is applied in practice: "Suppose a tank is filled once a day and the operator watches the level and closes a valve when it is full. The operation is a very simple one, with little to distract the operator who is out on the plant giving the job his full attention." Assigning values for the five parameters in this situation, we get: K_1 = 0.001; K_2 = 0.5; K_3 = 1; K_4 = 1; K_5 = 1; giving a predicted failure rate of 1 in 2,000 occasions — roughly once every six years.

Hannaman and coauthors (1984) judge the mathematical framework of this model to be generally useful for quantifying human reliability in specific process situations. It is relatively simple to use and its output compares reasonably well with the assessments of expert judges. Once again, though, its numerical basis is derived from informed guesses rather than hard data.

2.4. Confusion matrix

The confusion matrix was devised by Potash and his coworkers (1981) as a means of evaluating the errors of operators responding to abnormal plant conditions. It has been used for this purpose in two PRAs on American nuclear power plants: Oconee (Oconee PRA, 1984) and Seabrook (Pickard, Lowe & Garrick, 1983). Its relatively unique feature is that its seeks to identify various modes of misdiagnosis for a range of possible events (see Swain & Weston, 1988).

The method relies upon the judgements of experts (usually the training staff of the plant in question) as to the likelihood of different misdiagnoses of specific critical plant states. These judgements are solicited in a structured and systematic fashion, allowing for the evaluation of probabilities at different times during a given accident sequence. Thus, its outputs represent the probabilities that operators will fail to respond correctly to events A, B, C, etc., at times t_1, t_2 ...t_n after the initiation of the sequence. In giving their judgements, the experts are encouraged to take account of such factors as the overlap of symptoms between different events, the operators' expectations based on their previous experience, the effects of stress and the general ergonomic quality of the control room.

The principal advantage of this technique is that it provides a simple structure for helping analysts to identify situations not easily modelled by other HRA methods. It appears to have more value as a qualitative analytical tool than as a quantitative one. Considerable disagreements arise between the probability estimates of different experts. It also shares with other techniques the weakness of being based upon simplistic manipulations of subjective data that, in this case, are low-value absolute probabilities.

2.5. Success likelihood index methodology (SLIM)

The SLI methodology (Embrey, Humphreys, Rosa, Kirwan & Rea, 1984), like the confusion matrix, was developed to provide a means of eliciting and structuring expert judgements. The software products that support this methodology allow experts to generate models that connect error probabilities in a specific situation with the factors that influence that probability. The underlying rationale is that the likelihood of an error occurring in a particular situation depends upon the combined effects of a relatively small number of performance influencing factors (PIFs). This is a somewhat less behaviourist variant of the performance shaping factors (PSFs) used in THERP. The success likelihood index (SLI) is derived from a consideration of the typical variables known to influence error rates (i.e., quality of training, procedures and time available for action). It is also assumed that judges can give numerical ratings of how good or bad these PIFs are in a given situation. The relative importance weights and ratings are multiplied together for each PIF, and the products are summed to give the success likelihood index. This Index is presumed to relate to the probability of success that would be observed over the long run in the particular situation of interest.

The SLI methodology has a number of attractive features. It is available in the form of two comprehensive, interactive software packages: SLIM-SAM (SLIM assessment module), which derives the success likelihood indices, and SLIM-SARAH (sensitivity analysis for reliability assessment of humans), which allows additional sensitivity and cost-benefit analyses to be performed. In order to establish the independence of the PIFs (an important assumption of the underlying model), the SLIM-SAM software checks the degree of shared variance between the ratings generated by the judges and informs the user if the ratings on two PIFs are correlated. In addition, up to 10 tasks can be evaluated within a single SLIM session. This substantially reduces the call upon the expert's time.

At present, there are some difficulties with the calibration of SLIM. A basic assumption is that SLIM may be calibrated with reference to the linear equation: log HEP = a SLI + b (where HEP is human error probability). In theory, error probabilities can be obtained by reference to two calibration tasks whose error probabilities are objectively known. However, it turns out that the choice of these reference tasks is critical, and the equation underlying the linear function of calibration has not been widely accepted. In addition, as will be discussed later, SLIM has not fared particularly well in independent validation studies. But this, as we shall see, is not unique to SLIM.

Other human reliability assessment techniques that have emerged from this same prolific source include: STAHR (socio-technical assessment of human reliability), which uses influence diagrams to assess the effects upon error rates of complex sociotechnical factors such as morale, organizational features and group dynamics (Phillips, Humphreys & Embrey, 1984); and SCHEMA (system for critical human error management and assessment) which also applies the basic SLIM methodology to a wide variety of process plant operations (Embrey & Lucas, 1989). To date, both of these techniques are still in their developmental stages, but they have attracted considerable interest within the human reliability community.

2.6. Systematic human action reliability procedure (SHARP)

It must be evident from even this far from comprehensive list of HRA methods that the practitioner faces a considerable problem in deciding which technique to employ, and when and where to apply it. To ease these difficulties, Hannaman and coworkers (1984) have devised a procedure with the acronym SHARP (systematic human action reliability procedure) "to help PRA analysts incorporate human interactions into a PRA study in a systematic, comprehensive and scrutable manner." SHARP, as they point out, is neither a model nor a technique, but a means for guiding the selection of appropriate HRA models and techniques. Specifically, it indicates the available options with regard to the representation of operator actions (THERP, OATS, etc.) and indicates the kinds of models or data that underlie the various HRA techniques: human reliability data bases, time-reliability curves, mathematical models, or expert judgements of human reliability.

3. How good are HRA techniques?

3.1. Validation studies

A relatively comprehensive review of the very few studies designed to compare the validity of HRA techniques was carried out by Williams (1985). He strikes the predominant note in his opening sentence: "It must seem quite extraordinary to most scientists engaged in research into other areas of the physical and technological world that there has been little or no attempt made by human reliability experts to validate the human reliability assessment techniques which they so freely propagate, modify and disseminate" (p. 150). As one explanation for this embarrassing lack, he suggests that HRA specialists are too busy generating additional models. But there are other alternatives: "an aversion to validation in case the outcome is unattractive, political or economic pressures which dissuade modellers from exploring the validation loop, shortage of sufficient personnel to carry out validation exercises, and misguided research methodologies."

In a 'peer review' of THERP, Brune, Weinstein and Fitzwater (1983) asked 29 human factors experts to carry out human reliability analyses covering a range of possible performance scenarios in a nuclear power plant setting. For any one scenario, they found a wide variation in the problem solutions developed by the experts. There were also large differences, as much as five orders of magnitude on some occasions, between their estimated probabilities of failure. This lack of interanalyst reliability continues to be a significant problem in current attempts to apply THERP to the design of the new British PWR at Sizewell 'B' (Jackson, Madden, Umbers & Williams, 1987; Whitworth, 1987).

How can one gauge the accuracy of HRA methods? Williams (1985) suggests that we should be looking for outputs that are at least comparable to PRA methods in their predictive precision. This means that HRA methods should produce predictions that are accurate to within a factor of 4 on about 90 per cent of occasions; or, somewhat more generously, we should require predictions that are accurate on 100 per cent of occasions within 1 order of magnitude (a factor of 10).

The Williams review covered a number of the techniques discussed above (THERP, TESEO, SLIM and OATS). In addition to other methods not mentioned here, it also included the very simple technique of absolute probability judgement (APJ) in which judges assign numerical failure likelihoods directly to the tasks being assessed. It is then possible to represent the absolute probability judgement for any given task by the median for the estimates of the different judges. In essence, it means taking the average of a set of informed guesses.

The overall conclusions of the review were that if high-risk technologists are looking for an HRA method that is comparable in terms of its predictive accuracy to general reliability assessments, then APJ is probably the best. Kirwan (1982) found that median absolute probability judgements were accurate to within a factor of 2 on 30 per cent of occasions, to within a factor of 4 on about 60 per cent of occasions and to within a factor of 10 on nearly all occasions when compared to the known probabilities of events. Interestingly, in the SLIM assessment, the combined generic weightings and task weightings showed little or no relationship to actual data, whereas the 'untreated' task ratings accounted for about 50 per cent of the variance. Kirwan also found that group consensus values offered no advantage over individual estimates, no one 'expert type' performed significantly better than any other, and that calibration feedback to did not significantly improve APJ estimates.

If the analyst is looking for scrutability, THERP offers the most comprehensible form of modelling. But, as Williams (1985, p. 160) concluded, "if they are seeking methods which are scrutable, accurate and usable by nonspecialists, the short answer is that there is no single method to which they can turn. The developers of human reliability assessment techniques have yet to demonstrate, in any comprehensive fashion, that their methods possess much conceptual, let alone, empirical validity."

3.2. The human factors reliability benchmark exercise

Recently, the Joint Research Centre (Ispra) of the European Commission (Poucet, 1988) organised a systematic comparison of HRA modelling techniques in the nuclear power context. Fifteen teams from eleven countries applied selected HRA techniques to two case studies: (a) the analysis of routine testing and maintenance with special regard to test-induced failures, and (b) the analysis of human actions during an operational transient with regard to the accuracy of operator diagnosis and the effectiveness of corrective actions. The methods applied included THERP, SLIM, HCR and TESEO.

In both cases, there was considerable variability in the quantitative results. The main contribution to this lack of agreement was the problem of mapping the complex reality on to these relatively simple models. This was particularly evident in the wide variety of modelling assumptions and in the different levels of decomposition used in the analyses. There was also considerable variation in the ways in which recovery and dependency structures were included in the chosen model. Mistakes were found to be far harder to quantify than slips and lapses.

Within a particular team, the results obtained from THERP and SLIM agreed fairly well. However, this concordance was largely due to the use of THERP data in SLIM calibrations. As indicated earlier, the choice of anchoring points (the calibration error probabilities) in the SLIM application greatly influenced its output.

The exercise also revealed some of the dangers in using a large and detailed error data base, such as that associated with the THERP technique. There was a marked tendency for analysts to model only those errors that appeared in the data base and to ignore others that qualitative analyses have shown to be important. Interestingly, the performance influencing factors given the highest importance by the experts in the SLIM technique were not considered in the THERP application because the THERP handbook had made no provision for them. THERP, however, was confirmed as being the reference method for human reliability assessment of procedural tasks. But this is hardly surprising since, for the present at least, the THERP handbook is the only readily available source of data on human error probabilities.

3.3. Qualitative criteria

A number of authors have sought to make explicit the general criteria that a good HRA technique should satisfy. Schurman and Banks (1984) provided a table for assessing the merits of the nine HRA models they reviewed. The criteria included cost, breadth of applicability, ease of use, face validity, precision, acceptance by professionals of the quality of the output, sensitivity to differences in the systems under evaluation, predictive validity, replicability, scrutability (this means no hidden assumptions, no special operations and full documentation) and how closely the output of the model approximates to a true ratio-scale measure. On these criteria, Schurman and Banks found no method scoring above 50 per cent of the possible total score when a quantitative rating scale was applied to each dimension.

Hannaman and his coworkers listed eight desirable features for HRA models:

(a) They should be compatible with and complement current PRA techniques.

(b) They should be scrutable, verifiable and repeatable.

(c) Their application should result in quantification of crew success probability as a function of time.

(d) They should take account of different kinds of cognitive processing (i.e., at the skill-based, rule-based and knowledge-based levels of performance).

(e) They should identify the relationship to the model of various performance-shaping factors (e.g., design features affecting the human-machine interface, operator training and experience levels, stress factors, the time available for effective action, etc.).

(f) They should be comparable to the highest degree possible with existing data from plant experience, simulator data or expert judgement.

(g) They should be simple to implement and use.

(h) They should help to generate insights and understanding about the potential for operators to cope with the situations identified in PRA studies.

As we have seen, few techniques can satisfy the repeatability criterion; but many of the HRA models listed earlier have made effective progress towards meeting the more qualitative criteria.

John Wreathall, one of the leading figures in the development of HRA techniques, posed the question: Is human reliability analysis a fact or is it fiction? His own attempt to answer this question represents as good a summary of the current state of the HRA art as any: "There is and always has been an aversion to modelling humans; reasons range from 'it's too difficult' and 'people are too varied' to 'it reduces people to mere cogs'. Each of these has an element of truth, but no more than an element. Human reliability models have been, and still are being developed – this is a fact. However, the existing

3. How good are HRA techniques? 233

methods are very simplistic — to claim that they represent reality is a fiction" (Wreathall, 1981).

It is important to see these HRA models in the context of their development. They emerged to meet the demands upon PRA analysts to quantify the large and hitherto neglected human error contribution to systems accidents. PRAs, for their part, evolved to meet the demand for a priori assessments of the risks associated with potentially hazardous and often controversial technologies.

Some HRA methods were created by engineers already professionally engaged in general reliability analyses, Bill Hannaman and John Wreathall are two notable instances of this breed. Others have been devised by human factors specialists, Alan Swain and David Embrey fall into this category. For both of these camps, there was, at the time of greatest industry demand, the mid- to late-1970s, little or nothing in the way of an agreed theoretical framework for human error mechanisms. Rasmussen's skill-rule-knowledge classification has done an enormous service in filling this vacuum, both for the reliability engineers and for the psychologists. I hope that this book will carry this essential process some way further. Without an adequate and conceptually meaningful error classification and a workable theoretical infrastructure, there can be little or no principled basis to the business of human reliability quantification. Now that we have made some progress in that direction, we can reasonably hope for the emergence of more effective HRA techniques. Whether their predictions will ever do better than the proverbial orders of magnitude remains to be seen.

One final point: It may seem on the face of it that these HRA methods have been more concerned with assessment than error reduction. However, it should be stressed that these two aspects of PRA/HRA are intimately related. Given the inevitability of human error, there are many who would argue that the best way of protecting hazardous systems against human failure is to make them more error tolerant (see Rouse & Morris, 1985, for a cogently argued expression of this view). One way of doing this is by identifying those human failures most likely to jeopardise the integrity of the plant and to defend against them by engineered safety devices or by procedures such as the '30-minute rule' that buy operators thinking time in an emergency by demanding automatic systems capable of restoring the plant to a safe state without the need for human intervention for some fixed time after the initiating event. And where these safety devices themselves might be under threat from possible human errors, it is necessary to build in independent back-up systems or 'redundancies'. The need for such safety measures and guidance as to where they should be deployed are, in theory, the natural products of combined PRA/HRA studies. In an ideal world, good assessment should always drive effective error reduction.

4. Risk management

PRA does more than identify an acceptable level of risk. It also defines a set of conditions for the safe operation of the plant. Thus, probabilistic risk assessment constitutes a reference model to which risk management must aspire. Rasmussen and Pedersen (1984, p. 183) expressed this view as follows:

The result of the PRA is a calculated risk figure which, if accepted, covers the 'accepted risk'. If not accepted, the design has to be modified until acceptance has been achieved. Owing to incompleteness and errors during the PRA, an 'additional risk' may exist, which is not included in the accepted risk.

Sources of this unaccounted risk include: (a) the use of components and materials which fall outside the populations providing the PRA failure data, or that are substandard, (b) the fact that the real plant does not conform to the model underlying the PRA, and (c) that the plant is not operated and maintained according to the assumptions made in the PRA. The function of risk management, therefore, is to limit these additional risks through such means as quality control, inspection and continual monitoring of failure data. The latter provide crucial feedback as to whether the design preconditions are being met by the operational reality.

Rasmussen and Pedersen (1984, p. 183) also note that: "The major part of the human decision-making and administrative functions involved in operations management is not accessible to formal analyses with the present state of PRA. Errors of management may, however, be significant sources of common-mode errors and are therefore important candidates for risk management by feedback control."

5. Potential measures for error reduction

So far, we have discussed relatively well-established assessment and reduction methods, or at least ones that have been or might soon be applied to high-risk technologies. In the remainder of this chapter, we will examine reduction possibilities that are still in the early stages of research and development, but that nevertheless offer some promise for improving the current state of affairs.

Human error, as we have seen, appears in many guises and has a variety of causes. It is therefore not surprising that no single, universally applicable, error-reducing technique is either available or in prospect. Human reliability specialists will always need to rely upon a wide range of remedial tools in order to find methods best suited to their immediate needs. Considered below are some relatively new (or at least largely untried) approaches that may help to extend the utility of the future toolbag.

5.1. Eliminating affordances for error

Most human beings enjoy the experience of free will. They form intentions, make plans and carry out actions, guided by what appears to them to be internal processes. Yet these apparently volitional activities are subtly constrained by the character of the physical objects with which they interact. The term affordance refers to the basic properties of objects that shape the way in which people react to them.

In his most recent book, *The Psychology of Everyday Things* (1988), Donald Norman has explored, among other things, how man-made objects and procedures offer affordances for error. Norman's reasons for being drawn to this topic are worth quoting at some length (1988, pp 1-2):

> Over the years I have fumbled my way through life, walking into doors, failing to figure out water faucets, incompetent at working the simple things of everyday life. Just me, I mumbled, just my mechanical ineptitude. But as I studied psychology, as I watched the behavior of other people, I began to realize I was not alone. My fumblings and difficulties were mirrored by the problems of others. And everyone seemed to blame themselves. Could it be that the whole world was mechanically incompetent?

> The truth emerged slowly. My research activities led me to the study of human error and industrial accidents. I began to realize that human error resulted from bad design. Humans did not always behave so clumsily. But they do so when the things they must do are badly conceived, badly designed. Does a commercial airliner crash? Pilot error, say the reports. Does a Soviet nuclear power plant have a serious problem? Human error, says the newspaper. Do two ships at sea collide? Human error, is the official cause. But careful analysis of the events that transpired during these kinds of incidents usually gives the lie to such a story. At the famous nuclear power plant disaster, Three-Mile Island, the blame was placed on the humans, on the plant operators who misdiagnosed the problems. But was it human error? Consider the phrase operators who misdiagnosed the problems. Aha, the phrase reveals that first there was a problem, in fact a series of mechanical failures. Then why wasn't equipment failure the real cause? What about the misdiagnoses? Why didn't the operators correctly determine the cause? Well, how about the fact that the proper instruments were not available, that the plant operators did the actions that had always been the reasonable and proper ones to do. How about the pressure relief valve that failed to close. . . . To me it sounds like equipment failure coupled with serious design error.

In brief, people are not so much the possessors of 'original fallibility' as the victims of user-hostile objects. Norman's analyses of error-affording situations are directed by the argument that people underestimate the extent to which the knowledge is located in the world, rather than in their heads. There is a trade-off between these two kinds of knowledge. Knowledge in the world (KIW) is accessible. It is always there and does not need to be prompted: but it is subject to the 'out-of-sight-out-of-mind' principle. While knowledge in the head (KIH) is efficient and independent of the immediate environment, it needs to be retrieved, and this often requires reminding. KIW does not have to be learned, merely interpreted. As such, it is easier to use. But such interpretations can lead to erroneous actions.

These distinctions lead to a set of design principles for minimising error affordances:

(a) Use both knowledge in the world and in the head in order to promote a good conceptual model of the system on the part of its users: this requires consistency of mapping between the designer's model, the system model and the user's model.

(b) Simplify the structure of tasks so as to minimise the load upon vulnerable cognitive processes such as working memory, planning or problem solving.

(c) Make both the execution and the evaluation sides of an action visible. Visibility in regard to the former allows users to know what is possible and how things should be done; visibility on the evaluation side enables people to gauge the effects of their actions.

(d) Exploit natural mappings between intentions and possible actions, between actions and their effects on the system, between the actual system state and what is perceivable, between the system state and the needs, intentions and expectations of the user.

(e) Exploit the power of constraints, both natural and artificial. Constraints guide the user to the next appropriate action or decision.

(f) Design for errors. Assume their occurrence. Plan for error recovery. Make it easy to reverse operations and hard to carry out non-reversible ones. Exploit forcing functions (see Chapter 6).

(g) When all else fails, standardise — actions, outcomes, layouts, displays, etc. The disadvantages of a less than perfect standardisation are often compensated for by the increased ease of use. But standardisation for its own sake is only a last resort. The earlier principles should always be applied first.

This brief summary of Norman's book does scant justice both to its richness and scope. Psychologists and practitioners are strongly urged to read it, the former because it shows where Norman's 10-year error quest has current-ly brought him, and the latter because the book is highly readable and filled with practical illustrations of error-affording objects and situations.

For those who might feel that the *The Psychology of Everyday Things* is strong on anecdotal evidence but weak on laboratory support, this section ends with a brief account of an empirical study that more than bears out Norman's basic thesis about everyday objects. Hull, Wilkins and Baddeley (1988) asked 24 intelligent men and women to wire an electric plug. Only 5 succeeded in doing so safely, even though 23 of the subjects had wired at least one plug dur-ing the preceding 12 months. The errors were attributed to failure to read the instructions (subjects preferred "to act rather than reflect"); negative trans-fer — subjects treated new designs as though they were more familiar ones; the inability to formulate an adequate mental model of the task; and — most sig-nificantly for Norman's thesis — the failure of plug designers to provide clear physical constraints on errant actions.

5.2. Intelligent decision support systems

The Three Mile Island accident in March 1979 was, as we have seen, a water-shed in the history of nuclear power generation. Among other things, it brought home to the nuclear industry with painful clarity the marked error proneness of human decision making in emergency conditions. Similar con-clusions have been drawn from retrospective analyses of the subsequent acci-dents at Prairie Island, North Anna, Oconee, Oyster Creek and Ginna (Pew, Miller & Feeher, 1981; Woods, 1982). Following TMI-2, the industry (speci-fically the Electric Power Research Institute in Palo Alto) explored various ways of aiding operator decision making in accident conditions. These in-cluded the following:

(a) The addition of a shift technical adviser to the crew: A suitably qualified individual whose task was to monitor events and advise the shift supervisor regarding the interpretation of data and possible courses of action.

(b) Training improvements: Specifically in the areas of skills, emer-gency procedures, specific plant characteristics, fundamental power plant knowledge and decision skills.

(c) Computerised support systems: These ranged from safety par-ameter display systems (showing trends in important system state vari-ables) to predictive on-line simulation capable of answering 'What if?' questions during the course of an emergency.

Subsequent events have not inspired great confidence in the efficacy of some of these methods. In the Davis-Besse accident (see Chapter 7), for example, both independent safety parameter display systems were out of action before and during the event. According to a U.S. Nuclear Regulatory Commission report (NUREG, 1985), they were inoperable "due to separate but similar problems in the data transmission system between the control room terminals and their respective computer processors." The shift technical adviser was on a 24-hour shift and was asleep in his apartment at the time of the reactor trip. He was summoned to the control room by the shift supervisor, and although he drove there immediately, he arrived some 15 minutes after the trip, by which time the event was essentially over. Thereafter he acted as an administrative assistant.

In 1985 and 1986, two meetings were held in Italy under the auspices of NATO to discuss the issue of providing intelligent decision aids for process operators (Hollnagel, Mancini & Woods, 1986, 1988). A detailed description of the topics covered in these meetings can be found in the published sources. Of more general interest here was the emergence of a debate between two quite opposing schools of thought: those who regarded intelligent decision aids as tools and those who saw them as prostheses. These positions are outlined below.

The optimists believe that the problem of operator error in high-risk installations will ultimately have a technical solution. The same exponential growth in computer technology that made centralised supervisory control possible in the first place can also provide the 'cognitive tools' — felicitous extensions of normal brainpower — that will enable operators to deal successfully with its current problems of complexity and opacity. Such optimists, particularly if they are systems designers, might also wish to claim that, in any case, human involvement in such systems (and hence the attendant risk of dangerous operator errors) will gradually decline as the possible scenarios of failure are better understood and further nonhuman means of coping with them are devised.

A more pessimistic view, and the one espoused here, is that most operator errors arise from a mismatch between the properties of the system as a whole and the characteristics of human information processing. System designers have unwittingly created a work situation in which many of the normally adaptive characteristics of human cognition (its natural heuristics and biases) are transformed into dangerous liabilities. And, the argument continues, since the problem is fundamental to the design of such systems, and since (short of closure) these installations are likely to be with us for many years to come, the only immediate remedy is to provide the human participants with cognitive 'prostheses' (or, in plainer English, 'mental crutches') that will help compensate for some of these artificially-enhanced error tendencies and minimise the exaggerated danger of their consequences.

Let us assume that progress in artificial intelligence will enable a new and powerful set of intelligent decision aids to be developed. For whom should these devices be tailored? In the post-TMI era the focus was upon control room operators; but the more recent developments discussed in Chapter 7 indicate that the operator's mistakes can be traced back to latent decision errors made in the higher echelons of the system long before an accident sequence even began. How far back from the system 'front line' should these aids be deployed? By management? Among regulators? Designers? Governmental decision makers? Then there is the question of dependency. If the decision aid is worth its salt, its users will come to overrely upon it to the neglect of their own unaided diagnostic skills. The history of high-risk technology is littered with instances of accidents being caused by the failure of some safety-enhancing aid combined with operator overdependence, so that alternative sources of evidence are not consulted.

Leaving aside the issue of whether truly intelligent decision support systems are feasible, or even desirable, we must not allow the lure of 'high-tech' prostheses to blind us to two important facts. First, most of the residual human failures that now threaten the safety of high-risk technologies are not amenable to technological 'fixes'; this conclusion applies most especially to latent managerial and organisational deficiencies. Second, there are a number of pressing concerns that can be remedied by simple, well-understood and available measures. An obvious candidate in nuclear power plant operations is the omission of necessary maintenance actions due to memory failure.

5.3. Memory aids for maintenance personnel

As indicated in Chapter 7, the clear conclusion from a number of recent nuclear power plant error surveys (Rasmussen, 1980; INPO, 1984, 1985b) is that maintenance-related omissions constitute a substantial proportion of the human failure root causes in significant event reports. These involved such things as forgetting to set valves in the appropriate position, not removing tools and other objects, and leaving out necessary steps in either preventive or corrective maintenance schedules. This corresponds with the findings obtained from error proneness questionnaires (Reason & Mycielska, 1982; Reason, 1984a) where omitting to carry out planned actions (i.e., failures of prospective memory) comprise one of the most common forms of everyday lapse.

In addition to the general factors that promote absent-minded slips and lapses (the execution of routine tasks while preoccupied or distracted), there are a number of task factors that are likely to increase the probability of making an omission error:

(a) The larger the number of discrete steps in an action sequence, the greater the probability that one or more of them will be omitted.

(b) The greater the informational loading of a particular procedural step, the more likely it is that items within that step will be omitted.

(c) Procedural steps that are not obviously cued by preceding actions or that do not follow in a direct linear sequence from them are likely to be omitted.

(d) When instructions are given verbally and there are more than five simple steps, items in the middle of the list of instructions are more likely to be omitted than either those at the beginning or the end.

(e) When instructions are given in a written form, isolated steps at the end of sequence (e.g., replacing caps or bushes, removing tools, etc.) have a reasonably high probability of being omitted.

(f) Necessary steps in an action sequence are more likely to be omitted during reassembly than during the original disassembly (see Chapter 6).

(g) In a well-practised, highly automatic task, unexpected interruptions are frequently associated with omission errors, either because some unrelated action is unconsciously 'counted in' as part of the task sequence, or because the interruption causes the individual to 'lose his place' on resumption of the task (i.e., he believes that he was further along in the task prior to the interruption than he actually was). Such routinised tasks are also especially prone to premature exits — moving on to the next activity before the previous one is completed, thus omitting some necessary final steps. This is particularly likely to happen when the individual is working under time pressure or when the next job is near at hand.

These observations have a number of practical applications. In the short term, they make it possible to identify in advance those steps in written maintenance procedures that are most likely to be omitted. Consider, for example, the following job description covering valve inspection in preventive maintenance on a compressor (Kelly, 1984): "Check and clean suction and pressure valves. Replace defective valves. Replace packings. Clean valve chambers." The step most likely to be omitted here is the replacement of the packings. Having identified the most probable omissions, it is possible to provide maintenance personnel with a set of procedures, stored in a cheap lap-held computer, that not only give the user step-by-step guidance in what has to be done, but also prompt him to check that easily omitted steps have been completed.

A prototype of such a device, termed a portable interactive maintenance auxiliary (PIMA), has been developed in our laboratory. It is designed to be implemented on an Epson PX-8 lap-held computer or some suitable equivalent and is intended to form part of a maintenance technician's basic equipment in installations such as nuclear power plants where both the informational load (i.e., the amount of technical information necessary to perform a particular maintenance task) and the cost of maintenance-related errors is high. Although PIMA was designed as an external memory aid, its implementation on a powerful but truly portable computer will also allow it to serve surveillance and checking functions in plants possessing computerised maintenance documentation systems (see Kelly, 1984). Moreover, it closes the electronic gap that presently exists within even the most comprehensive of computerised maintenance systems. It provides a fully computerised loop in both the outward (work sheets, technical job information and memory aids) and inward (technical feedback, timesheets, schedule and task checking) directions.

Before concluding this brief discussion of cognitive aids (or prostheses), it would be helpful to remind ourselves of their compensatory functions. The preparation and execution of an action sequence may be divided into three overlapping stages: (a) plan formulation, (b) plan storage and (c) plan execution. Progression through these stages from (a) to (c) is associated with a gradual shift from higher to lower level cognitive processors, from a predominantly attentional (conscious) to a predominantly schematic (automatic) mode of control. Decision aids are designed to minimise failures at the plan formulation stage, while memory aids support performance at the storage and execution stages. The relationship between these cognitive prostheses and their compensatory functions are summarised in Table 8.1.

5.4. Training issues

5.4.1. Procedures or heuristics?

One of the most sustained and coherent programmes of research into training methods in advanced continuous-process industries has been carried out by Keith Duncan and his coworkers, then at the University of Wales Institute of Science and Technology (Duncan & Shepherd, 1975; Duncan & Gray, 1975a, 1975; Shepherd, Marshall, Turner & Duncan, 1977; Duncan, 1987). Their primary concern has been with the training of fault diagnosis. The early studies sought to establish how experienced operators went about diagnosing faults from control panel arrays. The evidence indicated that for the most part they were applying short sequences of heuristics, or diagnostic 'rules of thumb'. Verbal expressions of a few of these often intuitive heuristics are listed below (taken from Duncan, 1987, p. 265).

(a) Scan the panel to locate the general area of failure.

(b) Check all control loops in the affected area. Are there any anomalous valve positions?

(c) A high level in a vessel and a low flow in associated take-off line indicates either a pump failure or a valve that failed in the closed position. If valves OK (see b), then pump failure probable.

Table 8.1. A summary of the compensatory functions of memory and decision aids.

AID TYPE	FUNCTIONS
DECISION AIDS	To compensate for bounded rationality: the fact that attention can only be directed at a very small part of the total problem space at any one time. To direct attention to logically important aspects of the problem space. To correct the tendency to apply familiar but inappropriate solutions. To minimise the influence of availability bias, the tendency to prefer diagnoses and/or strategies that spring readily to mind. To rectify incomplete or incorrect knowledge.
SHARED FUNCTIONS OF DECISION AND MEMORY AIDS	To augment the limited capacity of working memory. This serves two primary functions: (a) as a working database wherein analytical operations can be performed; and (b) as a means of keeping track of progress by relating current data to stored plans in long-term memory.
MEMORY AIDS	To augment prospective memory. That is, to provide an interactive checklist facility to enable the appropriate actions to be performed in the desired sequence at the right time. In short, to prompt the what? and the when? of planned actions. Also to encourage checking that all the necessary actions have been completed before moving on to the next stage.

(d) High temperature and pressure in column head associated with low level in reflux drum indicate overhead condenser failure – provided all pumps and valves are working correctly (see b and c).

(e) If the failure is in the reactor/heat-exchange complex, determine whether it is in the reactor or the heat-exchange system. A failure in the heat-exchange will produce symptoms in Column A but not in B. A failure in the reactor will produce symptoms in both columns.

(f) If the failure is in the feed system, check whether it is in stream X or stream Y. Because of the nature of the control system, a failure in the Y stream will produce associated symptoms in both the X and Y streams. A failure in the X stream will show symptoms in the X stream only.

This group has conducted a number of studies in which novices were trained in the laboratory to diagnose faults from a display panel relating to a fictitious petrochemical plant (to which the above heuristics relate). In one experiment, there were three training conditions: (a) no story, where subjects were not told anything about how the plant worked, (b) a 'theory' condition, where an explanation was given in simple language of the plant's basic workings (i.e., inputs and outputs, the intervening flow paths, the drives, control loops, and so on), and (c) a condition in which diagnostic rules were incorporated. In addition, the subjects were tested on both faults that they had encountered in training (old faults), and ones they had not met before (new faults).

The mean number of correct diagnoses did not differ between the training conditions for the old faults, but there was a marked advantage for the rules condition in the case of new faults. A subsequent study demonstrated that a combination of withholding plant information and diagnostic rules increased the correct diagnosis rate of new faults to a level comparable to that for old faults.

These and other findings from this group have important training implications for installations that rely heavily upon written procedures, often involving elaborate algorithms, to guide operators' diagnoses for fault conditions. These detailed branching structures have, as Duncan (1987, p. 210) points out, the "intrinsic limitation that, by definition, an algorithm will only distinguish the set of conditions which could have been foreseen. If an unforeseen event occurs, the operator is not helped by algorithmic procedures."

Indeed, as the North Anna incident (Pew et al., 1981) showed, operators can on occasions be seriously hampered by the requirement to follow mandatory procedures – in this case, the post-TMI stipulation that the safety injection must be left on for at least 20 minutes after a reactor scram. Fortunately, they decided to disobey the regulation and turned off one of the two emergency cooling pumps for 4 minutes. This incident highlights the dangers of an overly prescriptive approach to abnormal plant states.

5.4.2. Simulator training

Simulators are undoubtedly useful for providing error data and as basic research tools (see Woods, 1984; Norros & Sammatti, 1986). But can they provide operators with generalized recovery skills? Before we can adequately answer this question, we need first to confront two more immediate problems. How do you simulate events that have never happened, but might? Still worse, how can you simulate events that have not been foreseen (see Duncan, 1987)? These problems were touched upon earlier in the context of the 'Catch-22' of human supervisory control (see Chapter 7). One very clear constraint is that any attempts at simulation must recreate the dynamic and interactive nature of an accident sequence. Static simulations cannot capture the problems operators experience in 'tracking' the current plant state (Woods, 1986).

So far we have no satisfactory answer to these questions. But Duncan (1987, p. 266)) was probably correct when he stated that: "[Simulator] training may succeed in providing operators with generalizable diagnostic skill but there are limits to what may be achieved, and post-training probabilities of diagnostic error remain uncomfortably high."

5.4.3. Error management

This is a procedure being developed by Michael Frese and his FAUST (Fehler Analyse zur Untersuchung von Software und Training) group at the University of Munich (Frese, 1987; Frese & Altmann, 1988) from empirical research on errors in human-computer interaction. They note that errors committed in training can have both positive and negative effects. The aim of error management is to promote the positive and to mitigate the negative effects of training errors in a systematic fashion.

The benevolent aspects of training errors derive mostly from the opportunities they provide for further learning about the system. In one training study concerned with word processing, subjects who were denied the opportunity to commit errors performed worse than other groups who were allowed to make errors.

Errors serve different kinds of useful function depending upon the level of performance. At the level of abstract thinking, errors can help the trainee discriminate between those metacognitions that work from those that do not. For example, if a novice thinks of a word-processing system as a typewriter model, the boundaries of this model become apparent when he finds he cannot write over a blank space in the insert mode. Errors also lead to the conscious reappraisal of action patterns that are normally controlled by low-level processors. As such, they delay the premature automatisation of a new skill – so long as adequate feedback is provided. Moreover errors can spur creative problem solutions and new exploratory strategies. Thus, if the trainee has not appreciated the difference between, say, the 'insert mode' and 'overwrite mode' in word processing, then errors resulting from this lack of knowledge can lead him or her to explore these modes spontaneously. Likewise the unintended use of a command can provoke useful curiosity as to what its proper range of functions are.

The negative aspects of training errors have to do, in large part, with the trainee's motivation and self-appraisal. The feedback provided by training errors has two components: informational and affective. If a largely affective interpretation is placed upon the feedback, the trainee may come to regard himself as too incompetent ever to succeed. Errors, particularly mistakes and grave slips (like deleting an important file), can lead to self-blame and additional stress. And even when the motivation to proceed is not seriously impaired, the anxiety provoked by this sense of stupidity can reduce the training to an ordeal. Stress and anxiety increase the cognitive load upon the trainee, which in turn promotes the occurrence of further errors. And, perhaps most importantly, much of the aversiveness of errors in human-computer interactions derives from the fact that slips and mistakes often leave the trainee in a situation where he or she can neither go forward nor backtrack.

These observations, based largely upon attempts to learn word-processing systems, lead to a set of error management principles that are applicable to a wide range of training situations, particularly in more complex systems. They are summarised below:

(a) Training should teach and support an active, exploratory approach. Trainees should be encouraged to develop their own mental models of the system and to use 'risky' strategies to investigate and experiment with still untaught aspects. Proper error management is not possible when training is structured according to programmed learning principles or when the trainee has to follow instructions to the letter.

(b) Error training should form an integral part of the overall training process. This means that the trainee should have the opportunity to both make errors and recover from them. This can include such devices as asking trainees to follow on from mistakes made by others. Error training is less aversive if trainees work in pairs. Clearly, strategies for dealing with errors have to be taught as well as discovered.

(c) Most adults approach training with the belief that errors are undesirable. Moreover, they do not like to be made to feel stupid. To counteract this, it is helpful to present heuristics ('It is good to make mistakes: they help learning', etc.). The goal of such heuristics is to change the attitude of trainees from 'I mustn't make errors' to 'let me see what I can learn from this error'.

(d) Error training should be introduced at the appropriate point. In the beginning, trainees have to struggle consciously with every step; this means that they are working to the limits of their capacity and that error training would be inappropriate at this stage. Some studies (Carroll & Carrithers, 1984; Carroll & Kay, 1985) have demonstrated that denying learners error feedback at this early stage can have beneficial effects. Error training is probably best introduced in the middle phase of the programme. This reduces the initial overload on the complete novice and gives the more advanced trainee the opportunity of exploiting his or her earlier experiences.

If human errors were truly stochastic events, associated with variability in recall, reasoning and the control of movement, then training should act to reduce errors through the structured diminution of this intrinsic variability. However, while it is true that some errors do fall into this category, most errors take systematic forms that are rooted in generally adaptive cognitive processes. Such errors are an intrinsic part of mental functioning and cannot be eliminated by training, no matter how effective or extensive the programme may be. It is now widely held among human reliability specialists that the most productive strategy for dealing with active errors is to focus upon controlling their consequences rather than upon striving for their elimination. Such an approach is discussed below.

5.5. Ecological interface design

This recent development is a product of the extremely influential Risoe National Laboratory in Denmark (Rasmussen & Vicente, 1987; Vicente & Rasmussen, 1987). Its goal is to produce meaningful representations of plant processes that simultaneously support the skill-based, rule-based and knowledge-based levels of operator performance.

In order to identify those areas where design improvements are necessary, Rasmussen and Vicente focus upon four categories of error: (a) errors related to learning and adaptation, (b) interference among competing cognitive control structures, (c) lack of resources and (d) intrinsic human variability. These are also distinguished at the skill-based, rule-based and knowledge-based levels of performance.

Ten guidelines for improved system design are presented. As indicated earlier, the aim of these guidelines is not to remove error, but to increase the system's error tolerance by giving operators more cognitively natural means for limiting their effects upon system performance. The guidelines are summarised below:

(a) Designers should accept that 'experiments' are necessary to optimise the sensorimotor skills of system users. Interface design should aim at making the boundaries of acceptable performance visible to the users while their effects are still observable and reversible.

(b) In general, the above guideline is only possible for direct dynamic interaction at the skill-based level. At the rule-based level, error observability is more difficult to achieve because (i) the effects of an error may be delayed and (ii) they may be rendered invisible by the defence-in-depth philosophy. Thus the designer should provide feedback to support functional understanding and knowledge-based monitoring during rule-based performance. It is also necessary to make visible latent constraints upon action.

(c) In addition, for performance at the rule-based level, a display should represent cues for actions not only as readily interpretable signs, but also indicating the preconditions for their validity. In other words, these signs should also have a symbolic content.

(d) To assist operators in coping with unforeseen situations (by definition at the knowledge-based level), designers should provide them with tools to make experiments and test hypotheses without having to do these things directly upon a high-risk and potentially irreversible plant. The alternative is to make the system states always reversible.

(e) To minimise the likelihood of attentional capture, designers should provide users with overview displays by which 'free-running' skill-based routines can be monitored on the fringes of conciousness.

(f) At the rule-based level, steps should be taken to reduce the possibility of falling into procedural traps (i.e., the activation of 'strong-but-wrong' rules). This can be done by giving integrated patterns as cues for action. These can also provide some degree of symbolic representation necessary for the functional monitoring of performance.

(g) At the knowledge-based level, reduce the chances of interference between possible competing 'mental models' by supporting memory with some externalised schematic of these alternatives.

(h) To aid recovery from errors due to lack of resources, use the available data to present information that is simultaneously suitable for skill-based, rule-based and knowledge-based processing.

(i) Causal reasoning in a complex functional network places excessive demands upon limited working memory resources. Information should be embedded in a structure that can serve as an externalised mental model. This representation should not aim at identifying a specific problem solution, but should aim at indicating an effective strategy (i.e., a category of possible solutions).

(j) Provide the user with external memory aids to support the retention of items, acts and data that are not part of the current operational 'gestalt'.

Guidelines (a) to (d) are directed at errors associated with the learning process. Guidelines (e) to (g) are concerned with mitigating the effects of errors which arise from interference among cognitive control structures. Guidelines (h) and (i) are concerned with compensating for a lack of available cognitive resources. The final guideline seeks to minimise the effects of stochastic errors.

5.6. Self-knowledge about error types and mechanisms

The only satisfactory way to protect aircrew against the effects of in-flight disorientation is to (a) demonstrate directly the varieties of disorientation in both actual and simulated flight, and (b) instruct them as to the ways in which their earthbound senses provide them with erroneous position-and-motion information in three-dimensional flight. Perhaps our understanding of human error mechanisms has now progressed to a point where it may be possible to provide some useful degree of self-knowledge about human error mechanisms to those for whom the consequences of slips, lapses and mistakes are unacceptable. The operators of high-risk technologies are informed about likely system breakdowns and how to deal with them. Why should they not be told something about their own potential for error? They and their colleagues do, after all, constitute the major hazard to such systems. Moreover, the descriptions of human error mechanisms given in this book and elsewhere are couched in broad engineering terms that would not be alien to most operators of high-risk systems.

6. Epilogue

Events drive fashions, particularly in the study of human fallibility. In the 1960s, research involving human error had two quite separate faces. In academic laboratories, experimental psychologists (as they were then called) treated error for the most part as just another performance index. In the applied world, behavioural technologists, called human engineers and ergonomists, strove to make cockpits and control rooms fit for humans to work in. Much of this work involved trying to mitigate the physical and psychological insults created by design engineers for whom the human-machine interface was often an afterthought, an area in which the bare control and display necessities were packed in as and where space could be found for them. And in both the academic and applied camps, the influences of Behaviourism were still very apparent. Their world was a fairly atheoretical place. Techniques were the thing.

The 1970s saw many major changes. Academics (who now preferred to call themselves cognitive rather than experimental psychologists) strayed beyond the laboratory door to study the natural history of everyday errors. They did so primarily to find out more about the covert control processes of human cognition. Since these slips and lapses were collected across a wide range of cognitive activities, it soon became apparent that the limited data-bound theories of experimental psychology were inadequate to explain their evident regularities. Such a diversity of phenomena called for broadly-based framework theories that were more akin to the working approximations of engineering than to the 'binarisms' (see Chapter 2) of natural science. They were greatly helped in these formulations by major developments in AI and cognitive science: for example, the General Problem Solver in 1972 and the rebirth of the schema concept in the mid-1970s (see Chapter 2).

Out in the 'real' world, a microchip revolution was taking place. The consequences for the human components of computerised systems were outlined in Chapter 7. Whereas the physical involvement of the human operator was significantly diminished, the imaginative scope for the design engineer was vastly enlarged. With the advent of soft displays on VDUs, the designer was freed from the physical constraints imposed by fixed display panels and large-scale mimic boards. In theory, at least, most interactions between the operator and the system could be confined to a screen and such input devices as keyboards, joysticks, rollerballs, mice and the like. In effect, the interface designer was provided with a blank sheet. But what should be put there?

Questions such as these, along with regulatory demands to build a safe system from the outset, posed problems that went far beyond the previous concerns of the 1960s ergonomist. Two new breeds emerged: the cognitive ergonomist, someone for whom the major focus of concern was human-computer interaction (or HCI) and the human reliability analyst, whose activities we considered at length earlier in this chapter. In the beginning neither strayed too far from traditional issues. The HCI specialist worried about VDU resolution, screen layout, the use of colour and other formal issues. The HRA specialist dealt at a very surface level with the probabilities of misreadings, omissions and commission errors. Then came Tenerife, Flixborough and Three Mile Island.

For human factors specialists of all kinds, the TMI accident highlighted the distinction between slips and mistakes. In the immediate aftermath, the greatest emphasis was placed upon the diagnostic errors of the TMI-2 operators. These had important implications for both the HCI and the HRA practitioners. To the former, it was clear that these misdiagnoses had been aided and abetted by poor interface design. To the latter, it was clear that current probabilistic techniques were inadequate to capture the likelihood of operators basing their recovery actions upon an incorrect mental model of the plant state. At this point – in the early 1980s – the academics and the practitioners started talking to each other seriously, an interchange greatly facilitated by the existence of a theoretical lingua franca supplied by Jens Rasmussen's skill-rule-knowledge framework.

One of the aims of this book has been to capture something of the excitement of this often stormy debate. The theorists have been enriched by good applied data, and, it is hoped, the practitioners have been helped by an increasingly consensual approach to applied cognitive theorizing. And that would have made a suitably happy ending to this book had not events once again overtaken us. The systems disasters of the mid- to late 1980s, and particularly Chernobyl, make it apparent that a purely cognitive theory concerned with the mental processes of an individual, no matter how widely held, is quite inadequate to explain the actions of the Chernobyl operators. As discussed at length in Chapter 7, these actions originated in organisational failings at all levels of the Soviet nuclear establishment. So to whom can we now turn for help in shaping a new organisational ergonomics? Sociologists? But they are an almost extinct species, at least in Mrs Thatcher's Britain. To parody an old sixties song: Where have all the sociologists gone? Gone for managers every one.

Those concerned with maintaining the safety of complex, high-risk systems face a challenging time ahead. The engineers and technocrats who design and manage these installations have, to some extent, become the victims of their own success. Thanks to the effectiveness of engineered safety measures, complex technologies are now largely proof against single failures, either of humans or components. This is an enormous achievement. Yet it leaves these systems prey to the one hazard for which there is no technological remedy: the insidious concatenation of latent human failures that are an inevitable part of any large organisation.

Future studies of human error will need to encompass organisational as well as individual fallibility. As this book has tried to show, we are beginning to have some understanding of the cognitive bases of human error: but we still know very little about how these individual tendencies interact within complex groupings of people working with high-risk technologies. It is just these social and institutional factors that now pose the greatest threat to our safety. But perhaps it was always so.

Case Study No. 1: Three Mile Island

Chain of events and active errors	Contributing conditions and latent failures
Maintenance crew introduces water into the instrument air system.	Although this error had occurred on two previous occasions, the operating company had not taken steps to prevent its recurrence. *(Management failure)*
Turbine tripped. Feedwater pumps shut down. Emergency feedwater pumps come on automatically, but flow blocked by two closed valves.	The two block valves had been erroneously left in the closed position during maintenance, probably carried out two days prior to the accident sequence. One of the warning lights showing that valves were closed was obscured by a maintenance tag. *(Maintenance failures)*
Rapid rise in core temperature and pressure, causing the reactor to trip. Relief valve (PORV) opens automatically, but then sticks in the open position. The scene is now set for a loss of coolant accident (LOCA) 13 seconds into the emergency.	During an incident at the Davis – Besse plant (another Babcock & Wilcox PWR) in September 1977, the PORV also stuck open. The incident was investigated by Babcock & Wilcox and the U.S. Nuclear Regulatory Commission. However, these analyses were not collated, and the information obtained regarding appropriate operator action was not communicated to the industry at large. *(Regulatory failure)*
Operators fail to recognise that the relief valve is stuck open. Primary cooling system now has hole in it through which radio – active water, under high pressure, pours into the containment area, and thence down into basement.	1. Operators were misled by control panel indications. Following an incident 1 year earlier, an indicator light had been installed. But this merely showed whether or not the valve had been commanded shut: it did not directly reveal valve status. *(Design and management failures)* 2. Operators wrongly assumed that high temperature at the PORV drain pipe was due to a chronically leaking valve. The pipe temp – erature normally registered high. *(Management/ procedural failure)*
Operators failed to diagnose stuck – open PORV for more than 2 hours. The resulting water loss caused significant damage to the reactor.	1. The control panel was poorly designed with hundreds of alarms that were not organised in a logical fashion. Many key indications were sited on the back wall of the control room. More than 100 alarms were activated with no means of suppressing unimportant ones. Several instruments went off – scale, and the computer printer ran more than 2 hours behind events. *(Design and management failures)* 2. Operator training, consisting largely of lectures and work in the reactor simulator, provided an inadequate basis for coping with real emergencies. Little feedback given to students, and training programme was insufficiently evaluated. *(Training and management failures)*
The crew cut back the high – pressure injection (HPI) of the water into the reactor coolant system, thus reducing the net flow rate from around 1000 gallons/min to about 25 gallons/min. This 'throttling' caused serious core damage.	1. Training emphasised the dangers of flooding the core. But this took no account of the possibility of a concurrent LOCA. *(Training and management failures)* 2. Following the 1977 Davis – Besse incident, the Nuclear Regulatory Commission issued a publication that made no mention of the fact that these operators had interrupted the HPI. The incident appeared under the heading of "valve malfunction" not "operator error". *(Regulatory failure)*

Case Study No. 2: Bhopal

Selected latent failures	Origins

1. System errors

Locating a high risk plant close to a densely populated area.
Government/Management

Poor emphasis on system safety. No safety improvements after adverse audits.
Management

No improvement in safety measures, despite six prior accidents.
Government/Management

Storing 10 times more methyl isocyanate (MIC) than was needed daily. Poor evacuation measures.
Management
Government/Management

Safety measures not upgraded when plant switched to large scale storage of MIC.
Management

Heavy reliance on inexperienced operators and supervisors.
Management

Factory inspector's warning on washing MIC lines neglected.
Management

Failure to release telex message on MIC treatment.
Management

2. Operator errors

Reduction in operating and maintenance staff.
Management

Using a nontrained superintendent for the MIC plant.
Management

Repressurising the tank when it failed to get pressurized once.
Management/Operator

Issuing orders for washing when MIC tank failed to repressurise.
Management/Operator

Not operating warning siren until leak became severe.
Management

Switching off siren immediately after starting it.
Management

Failure to recognise that pressure rise was abnormal.
Management/Operator

Failure to use empty MIC tank to release presssure.
Management/Operator

3. Hardware errors

Insufficient scrubber capacity.
Design

Refrigeration plant not operational.
Management/Maintenance

No automatic sensors to warn of temperature increase.
Design/Management

Pressure and temperature indicators did not work.
Management/Maintenance

Insufficient gas masks available.
Management

Flare tower was disconnected.
Management/Maintenance

Vent gas scrubber was in inactive mode.
Management

Iron pipelines were used for transporting MIC.
Management

A manual mechanism for switching off scrubber.
Design/Management

No regular cleaning of pipes and valves.
Maintenance/Management

No online monitor for MIC tanks.
Design

No indicator for monitoring position of valves in control room.
Design

Pressure monitor underreading by 30 Psig.
Design

Case Study No. 3: Challenger

Date	Actions and latent failures
1977	During test firings of solid – rocket booster, Thiokol engineers discover that casing joints expanded (instead of tightening as designed). Thiokol persuades NASA that this is "not desirable but acceptable." It was also discovered that one of the two O – ring joint seals frequently became unseated, thus failing to provide the back – up for which it was designed.
1981	NASA plans two lightweight versions of the boosters in order to increase payload. One is to be of steel, the other made of carbon filament. Hercules submits an improved design for the latter, incorporating a lip at the joint to prevent the O – ring from unseating (termed a "capture feature"). Thiokol continues to use unmodified joints for its steel boosters.
November 1981	Erosion (or "scorching") was noticed on one of the six primary O – rings. This was the same joint that was later involved in the Challenger disaster.
December 1982	As a result, NASA upgrades the criticality ratings on the joints to 1, meaning that the failure of this component could cause loss of both crew and spacecraft.
April 1983	Some NASA engineers seek to adapt the Hercules "capture feature" into the new thinner boosters. The proposal is shelved and the old joints continue to fly.
February 1984	Just prior to the 10th shuttle launch, high – pressure air tests are carried out on the booster joints. On return, an inch – long "scorch" found on one of the primary O – rings. Despite the "critical – 1" rating, Marshall Space Center reports that no remedial action is required. No connection noticed between high – pressure testing and "scorching", although pinholes in the insulating putty were observed.
April 1984	On 11th flight, one of the primary O – rings is found to be breached altogether. This was still regarded as acceptable. No connection made between high – pressure air testing and scorching, even though the latter was found on 10 of the subsequent 14 shuttle flights.
January 1985	Breaches ("blowbys") are found on four of the booster joints. Weather at launch coldest to date: 51 degr F with 53 degr F at the joints themselves. No connection noted.
April 1985	On the 17th shuttle mission, the primary O – ring in the nozzle joint fails to seal. Scorching found all the way round the joint.
July 1985	After another flight with three blowbys, NASA booster project manager places a launch constraint on the entire shuttle system. This means that no launch can take place if there are any worries about a Criticality – 1 item. But waivers may be granted if it is thought that the problem will not occur in flight. Waivers are granted thereafter. Since top NASA management were unaware of the constraint, the waivers are not queried.
July 1985	Marshall and Thiokol engineers order 72 of the new steel casing segments with the capture features.
July 1985	Thiokol engineer writes memo warning of catastrophe if a blowout should occur in a field joint.
August 1985	Marshall and Thiokol engineers meet in Washington to discuss blowbys. Senior NASA manager misses meeting. Subsequently, 43 joint improvements ordered.

Case Study No. 3: Challenger (continued)

Date	Actions and latent failures
December 1985	Director of the solid rocket motor project at Thiokol urges "close out" on the O – ring problem (i.e., it should be ignored) on the grounds that new designs were on their way, and the difficulties were being worked on. But these solutions would not be ready for some time.
January 23 1986	Five days before the accident, the entry "Problem is considered closed" is placed in a NASA document called the Marshall Problem Reports.
January 27 1986	It is thought probable that, on the night before the launch, the temperature would fall into the twenties, some 15 degr F colder than the previous coldest launch a year earlier. (The actual launch temperature was 36 degr F, having risen from 24 degr F.) At this point, Allan McDonald, Thiokol's chief engineer at the Kennedy Space Center (the "close out" man) experiences a change of heart and attempts to stop the launch.
January 28 1986	The Challenger shuttle is launched and explodes seconds after, killing all seven crew members. A blowout occurred on one of the primary booster O – rings.

Case Study No. 4: Chernobyl

Chain of events and active failures	Contributing conditions and latent failures
At 1300 on 25 April 1986, power reduction starts with the intention of achieving test conditions. The tests are to be carried out at 25 per cent full power (in the 700MW range). They are to be conducted in Unit 4, sharing common facilities with Unit 3.	The test was to see whether the "coast – down" capacity of a turbine generator would be sufficient, given an appropriate voltage generator, to power the Emergency Core Cooling System (ECCS) for a few minutes. This would fill the time it took to get the diesel standby generators into operation. A voltage generator had been tested on two previous occasions, but had failed because of rapid voltage fall – off. The goal on this occasion was to carry out repeated testing just prior to the annual maintenance shut – down, scheduled to begin on the following Tuesday. According to Russian sources, the quality of the test plan was "poor and the section on safety measures had been drafted in a purely formal way." In addition, the test plan called for shutting off the ECCS for the entire test period (about 4 hours). Authority to proceed was given to station staff without the formal approval of the Safety Technical Group. In addition, there is some evidence that three other RBMK plants (at Leningrad, Kursk and Smolensk) had refused to carry out these tests on safety grounds. The principal testers were electrical engineers from Moscow. The man in charge, an electrical engineer, "was not a specialist in reactor plants" (Russian report). *(Institutional and managerial errors and violations)*
At 1400, the ECCS is disconnected from the primary circuit.	This was part of the test plan, but it stripped the plant of one of its main defences. *(Managerial failure)*
At 1405, Kiev controller asks Unit 4 to continue supplying grid. The ECCS is not reconnected.	Although this failure to reconnect the ECCS did not contribute directly to the subsequent disaster, it was indicative of a lax attitude on the part of the operators toward the observance of safety procedures. Subsequent 9 hours of operating at around 50 per cent full power increased xenon poisoning, making plant more difficult to control at low power. *(Managerial and design failures)*
0028: Having been released from the grid at 2310, operators continue power reduction. But operator omits entry of "hold power" order; this leads to very low power.	The design of the RBMK reactor renders it liable to positive void coefficient at power settings below 20 per cent full power. After a long struggle, reactor power was stabilised at 7 per cent full power. At this point, the test should have been abandoned in view of the dangerously low power setting. Russian comment: "The staff was insufficiently familiar with the special features of the technological processes in a nuclear reactor." They had also "lost any feeling for the hazards involved." *(Managerial, design and operational failures)*
Operators and engineers continue to improvise in an unfamiliar and increasingly unstable regime to protect test plan. Plant goes super prompt critical. Explosions occur at 0124.	To ensure the continuance of the test, the operators and engineers gradually strip the reactor of its remaining defences. By 0122, the core had only 6 to 8 control rods inserted. An attempt to 'scram' the reactor at 0124 fails. Prompt criticality is now irreversible. *(Managerial, design and operational failures)*

Case Study No. 5: Herald of Free Enterprise

Chain of events and active failures	Contributing conditions and latent failures
Herald is docked at No. 12 berth in Zeebrugge's inner harbour and is loading passengers and vehicles before making the crossing to Dover.	This berth is not capable of loading both car decks (E and G) at the same time, having only a single ramp. Due to high water spring tides, the ramp could not be elevated sufficiently to reach E deck. To achieve this, it was necessary to trim the ship nosedown by filling trim ballast tanks Nos. 14 and 3. Normal practice was to start filling No. 14 tank 2 hours before arrival. *(System failure)*
At 1805 on 6 March 1987, the Herald goes astern from the berth, turns to starboard, and proceeds to sea with both her inner and outer bow doors fully open.	The most immediate cause is that the assistant bosun (whose job it was to close the doors) was asleep in his cabin, having just been relieved from maintenance and cleaning duties. *(Supervisory failure and unsuitable rostering)* The bosun, his immediate superior, was the last man to leave G deck. He noticed that the bow doors were still open, but did not close them, since he did not see that as part of his duties. *(Management failure)*
Chief officer checks that there are no passengers on G deck, and thinks he sees assistant bosun going to close doors (though testimony is confused on this point).	The chief officer, responsible for ensuring door closure, was also required (by company orders) to be on the bridge 15 minutes before sailing time. *(Management failure)* Because of delays at Dover, there was great pressure on crews to sail early. Memo from operations manager: "put pressure on your first officer if you don't think he's moving fast enough...sailing late out of Zeebrugge isn't on. It's 15 minutes early for us." *(Management failure)* Company standing orders (ambiguously worded) appear to call for "negative reporting" only. If not told otherwise, the master should assume that all is well. Chief officer did not make a report, nor did the master ask him for one. *(Management failure)*
On leaving harbour, master increases speed. Water enters open bow doors and floods into G deck. At around 1827, Herald capsizes to port.	Despite repeated requests from the masters to the management, no bow door indicators were available on the bridge, and the master was unaware that he had sailed with bow doors open. Estimated cost of indicators was £400 – 500. *(Management failure)* Ship had chronic list to port. *(Management and technical failure)* Scuppers inadequate to void water from flooded G deck. *(Design and maintenance failure)* Top – heavy design of the Herald and other "ro ro" ships in its class was inherently unsafe. *(Design failure)*

Case Study No.6: King's Cross Underground fire

Chain of events and active failures	Contributing conditions and latent failures
At 1925 on 18 November 1987, discarded smoker's material (probably) sets fire to grease and detritus in right hand running track of escalator 4 (up) Piccadilly Line.	Wooden escalator installed in 1939. Long recognised as being especially fire – prone. Water fog equipment installed in 1948. Could not be used nightly because of rust problems. Smoke detectors not installed: expense not justified. Forty – five per cent of the 400 fires recorded on London Underground over previous 20 years had occurred on MH escalators. Running tracks not regularly cleaned, partly due to organisational changes which blurred maintenance and cleaning responsibilities. Safety specialists scattered over three directorates focused on operational or occupational safety. Passenger safety neglected. Railway Inspectorate took a blinkered view of their role. They did not pursue issues of fire protection. Judged as having "too cosy" a relationship with London Underground. Smoking permitted on London Underground trains and premises. *(Hardware, organisational and regulatory failures)*
At 1930, passenger alerts booking clerk to small fire on escalator 4. Booking clerk rings Relief Station Inspector (RSI), but does not specify precise location of fire.	Inadequate fire and emergency training given to staff. It was accepted by LU that the quality of staff training at its White City training centre had been inadequate. Only 4 of the 21 station staff on duty had had any training in evacuation or fire drills. *(Management failure)*
At 1934, railway police evacuate passengers via Victoria Line escalator. They are unaware of the layout of the station.	No evacuation plan existed for King's Cross underground station. No joint exercises between LU and the emergency services had been conducted. *(Management failure)*
Between 1935 to 1938, RSI enters lower machine room, but fails to detect fire. He enters upper machine room and sees smoke and flames. Fetches fire extinguisher, but cannot get close enough to use it. He is too preoccupied to activate water fog equipment.	Inadequate training. RSI was not regularly based at King's Cross, nor did he have any fire training. He had not so far informed either the station manager (located some distance away due to refurbishment of station) or the line controller of the fire. Trains were still arriving. Location of water fog equipment not widely known. *(Management and communication failures)*
At 1939, police in ticket hall decide to evacuate the area. At 1940, police officer asks for Piccadilly and Victoria Line trains to be ordered not to stop at King's Cross. Trains continue to stop. At 1941, metal gates to ticket hall closed by police officers. At 1942, first fire engines arrive. Two firemen examine fire on escalator.	No established evacuation plan. Locked doors and metal barriers blocked escape routes LU control rooms last modernised in the 1960s. Outdated communications equipment. Headquarters controller had no access to station public address system, which was not used during the emergency. 5 of the 8 TV monitors were either switched off or inoperable. Most cameras were out of service. Trains do not have a public address system. No public telephones at King's Cross tube station. *(Management, hardware, maintenance and communication failures)*
At 1945, flashover occurs. Whole ticket hall engulfed in intense heat and flame. Thirty – one people are killed, many others are seriously injured.	Fires ("smoulderings") regarded as inevitable occurrence on LU. "They are part of the nature of the oldest, most extensive, most complex underground railway in the world. Anyone who believes that it is possible to act as though there are no fires ever is, I fear, misguided" (Dr Ridley, then Chairman of London Underground). *(Management, system and organisational failures)*

References

Abelson, R.P. Script processing in attitude formation and decision making. In J. Carroll & J. Payne (Eds.), *Cognition and Social Behavior*. Hillsdale, N.J.: Erlbaum, 1976.

Adelson, B. Knowledge structures of computer programmers. *Proceedings of the Fourth Annual Meeting of the Cognitive Science Society*, 1981, 4, 243-248.

Adelson, B. When novices surpass experts: The difficulty of a task may increase with expertise. *Journal of Experimental Psychology Learning, Memory and Cognition*, 1984, 10, 483-495.

Alba, J.W., & Hasher, L. Is memory schematic? *Psychological Bulletin*, 1983, 93, 203-231.

Allport, D.A. Patterns and actions: Cognitive mechanisms are content-specific. In G. Claxton (Ed.), *Cognitive Psychology: New Directions*. London: Routledge & Kegan Paul, 1980(a).

Allport, D.A. Attention and performance. In G. Claxton (Ed.), *Cognitive Psychology: New Directions*. London: Routledge & Kegan Paul, 1980(b).

Allport, D.A., Antonis, B., & Reynolds, P. On the division of attention: A disproof of the single channel hypothesis. *Quarterly Journal of Experimental Psychology*, 1972, 24, 225-235.

Allwood, C.M. Error detection processes in statistical problem solving. *Cognitive Science*, 1984, 8, 413-437.

Allwood, C.M., & Montgomery, H. Knowledge and technique in statistical problem solving. *European Journal of Science Education*, 1981, 3, 431-450.

Allwood, C.M., & Montgomery, H. Detection of errors in statistical problem solving. *Scandinavian Journal of Psychology*, 1982, 23, 131-139.

Anderson, J.R. *The Architecture of Cognition*. Cambridge, Mass.: Harvard University Press, 1983.

Arbuckle, T.Y., & Cuddy, L.I. Discrimination of item strength at time of presentation. *Journal of Experimental Psychology*, 1969, 81, 126-131.

Atkinson, R.C., & Juola, J.F. Factors influencing speed and accuracy of word recognition. In S. Kornblum (Ed.), *Attention and Performance (vol. IV)*. New York: Academic Press, 1973.

Atkinson, R.C., & Shiffrin, R.M. Human memory: A proposed system and its control processes. In K. Spence & J. Spence (Eds.), *The Psychology of Learning and Motivation: Advances in Research and Theory (vol. 2)*. New York: Academic Press, 1968.

Baars, B.J. Eliciting predictable speech errors in the laboratory. In V. Fromkin (Ed.), *Errors in Linguistic Performance: Slips of the Tongue, Ear, Pen, and Hand*. New York: Academic Press, 1980.

Baars, B.J. A *Cognitive Theory of Consciousness*. New York: Cambridge University Press, 1988.

Baars, B.J., Motley, M.T., & MacKay, D.G. Output editing for lexical status in artificially elicited slips of the tongue. *Journal of Verbal Learning and Verbal Behavior*, 1975, 14, 382- 391.

Bacon, F. *The New Organon*. F.H. Anderson (Ed.). Indianapolis: Bobbs-Merrill Educational Publishing, 1960. (Originally published in 1620.)

Baddeley, A.D. Short-term memory for word sequences as a function of acoustic, semantic and formal similarity. *Quarterly Journal of Experimental Psychology*, 1966, 18, 362-365.

Baddeley, A.D. Closure and response bias in short-term memory for form. *British Journal of Psychology*, 1968, 59, 139-145.

Baddeley, A.D. *The Psychology of Memory*. New York: Harper & Row, 1976.

Baddeley, A.D., & Hitch, G.J. Working memory. In G.H. Bower (Ed.), *The Psychology of Learning and Motivation (vol.8)*. New York: Academic Press, 1974.

Baddeley, A.D., Thomson, N., & Buchanan, M. Word length and the structure of short-term memory. *Journal of Verbal Learning and Verbal Behavior*, 1975, 14, 575-585.

Baddeley, A.D., & Wilkins, A.J. Taking memory out of the laboratory. In J.Harris & P.Morris (Eds.), *Everyday Memory, Actions and Absent-Mindedness*. London: Academic Press, 1984.

Bagnara, S., Stablum, F., Rizzo, A., Fontana, A., & Ruo, M. Error detection and correction: A study on human-computer interaction in a hot strip mill production planning and control system. In *Preprints of the First European Meeting on Cognitive Science Approaches to Process Control*, Marcoussis, France, October, 1987.

Bainbridge, L. The ironies of automation. In J. Rasmussen, K. Duncan & J. Leplat (Eds.), *New Technology and Human Error*. London: Wiley, 1987.

Baker, S., & Marshall, E. Chernobyl and the role of psychologists: An appeal to Reason. *The Psychologist: Bulletin of the British Psychological Society*, 1988, 3, 107-108.

Bartlett, F.C. *Remembering: A Study in Experimental and Social Psychology*. Cambridge: Cambridge University Press, 1932.

Battig, W.F., & Montague, W.E. Category norms for verbal items in 56 categories: A replication and extension of the Connecticut category norms. *Journal of Experimental Psychology Monograph*, 1969, 80, 1-46.

Bawden, H.H. A study of lapses. *Psychological Review: Monograph Supplements*, 1900, 3, 1-122.

Bell, B.J., & Swain, A.D. *A Procedure for Conducting a Human Reliability Analysis for Nuclear Power Plants*. NUREG/CR-2254. Albuquerque, N.M.: Sandia National Laboratories, 1983.

Bellamy, L.J. *The Safety Management Factor: An Analysis of the Human Error Aspects of the Bhopal Disaster*. London: Technica Ltd., 1985.

Bello, G.C., & Colombari, V. Empirical technique to estimate operator's errors (TESEO). *Reliability Engineering*, 1980, 1, 3.

Bennett, M. *SUBSTITUTOR: A Teaching Program*. University of Edinburgh: Department of Artificial Intelligence, 1976. (Cited by Young & O'Shea, 1981.)

Berkun, M.M. Performance decrement under psychological stress. *Human Factors*, 1964, 6, 21-30.

Beveridge, M. Personal communication, 1987.

Billman, D. *Inductive Learning of Syntactic Categories*. Ph.D. dissertation, University of Michigan, 1983.

Blake, M. Prediction of recognition when recall fails: Exploring the feeling-of-knowing phenomenon. *Journal of Verbal Learning and Verbal Behavior*, 1973, 12, 311-319.

Bobrow, D.G., & Norman, D.A. Some principles of memory schemata. In D. Bobrow & A. Collins (Eds.), *Representation and Understanding: Studies in Cognitive Science*. New York: Academic Press, 1975.

Boden, M. Artificial intelligence. In R. Gregory (Ed.), *The Oxford Companion to the Mind*. Oxford: Oxford University Press, 1987.

Boland, T.B., & Chapman, L.J. Conflicting predictions from Broen's and Chapman's theories of schizophrenic thought disorder. *Journal of Abnormal Psychology*, 1971, 78, 52-58.

Bonaparte, M. (Ed.). *The Origins of Psychoanalysis: Letters to Wilhelm Fliess, Drafts and Notes: 1887-1902*. New York: Basic Books, 1954.

Bousfield, W.A., & Barclay, W.D. The relationship between order and frequency of occurrence of restricted associative responses. *Journal of Experimental Psychology*, 1950, 40, 643-647.

Brehmer, B. Models of diagnostic judgements. In J. Rasmussen, K. Duncan & J. Leplat (Eds.), *New Technology and Human Error*. London: Wiley, 1987.

Brehmer, B., Allard, R., & Lind, M. Fire-fighting: A paradigm for the study of dynamic decision making. Paper presented at the Ninth Research Conference on Subjective Probability, Utility and Decision Making, Groningen, 1983.

Brewer, W.F., & Nakamura, G.V. The nature and function of schemas. In R.S. Wyer & T.K. Srull (Eds.), *Handbook of Social Cognition*. Hillsdale, N.J.: Erlbaum, 1983.

Broadbent, D.E. *Perception and Communication*. London: Pergamon, 1958.

Broadbent, D.E. Word-frequency effect and response bias. *Psychological Review*, 1967, 74, 1-15.

Broadbent, D.E. *Decision and Stress*. London: Academic Press, 1971.

Broadbent, D.E. Task combination and selective intake of information. *Acta Psychologica*, 1982, 50, 252-290.

Broadbent, D.E. The Maltese Cross: A new simplistic model for memory. *The Behavioral and Brain Sciences*, 1984, 7, 55-94.

Broadbent, D.E., Broadbent, M.H.P., & Jones, J.L. Correlates of cognitive failure. *British Journal of Clinical Psychology*, 1986, 25, 285-299.

Broadbent, D.E., Cooper, P.F., FitzGerald, P., & Parkes, K.R. The Cognitive Failures Questionnaire (CFQ) and its correlates. *British Journal Of Clinical Psychology*, 1982, 19, 177-188.

Broen, W.E., & Storms, L.H. Lawful disorganisation: The process underlying a schizophrenic syndrome. *Psychological Review*, 1966, 73, 265-279.

Brown, A.L. Learning and development: The problems of compatibility, access and induction. *Human Development*, 1982, 25, 89-115.

Brown, J.S. & Burton, R.R. Diagnostic models for procedural bugs in basic mathematical skills. *Cognitive Science*, 1978, 2, 155-192.

Brown, J.S., & VanLehn, K. Repair theory: A generative theory of bugs in procedural skills. *Cognitive Science*, 1980, 4, 379-427.

Brune, R.L., Weinstein, M., & Fitzwater, M.E. *Peer Review Study of the Draft Handbook for Human Reliability Analysis with Emphasis on Nuclear Power Plant Applications*, NUREG/CR-1278. Albuquerque, N.M.: Sandia National Laboratories, 1983.

Bruner, J.S., Goodnow, J.J., & Austin, G.A. *A Study of Thinking*. New York: Science Editions, 1956.

Burns, J.T. *The Effect of Errors on Reaction Time in a Serial Reaction Task.* Unpublished Ph..D. thesis, University of Michigan, 1965 (cited by Rabbitt, 1968).

Cantor, N., & Mischel, W. Traits as prototypes: Effects on recognition memory. *Journal of Personality and Social Psychology*, 1977, 35, 38-48.

Card, S.K., Moran, T.P., & Newell, A. *The Psychology of Human-Computer Interaction.* Hillsdale, N.J.: Erlbaum, 1983.

Carpenter, P.A., & Daneman, M. Lexical retrieval and error recovery in reading: A model based on eye fixations. *Journal of Verbal learning and Verbal Behavior*, 1981, 20, 137-160.

Carroll, J.M., & Carrithers, C. Training wheels in a user interface. *Communications of the ACM*, 1984, 27, 800-806.

Carroll, J.M., & Kay, D.S. Prompting, feedback and error correction in the design of a scenario machine. *Proceedings of the CHI '85 Conference on Human Factors in Computing Systems*, San Francisco, 1985.

Catlin, J. On the word-frequency effect. *Psychological Review*, 1969, 76, 504-506.

Champagne, A.B., Klopfer, L.E., & Anderson, J.H. Factors influencing the learning of classical mechanics. *American Journal of Physics*, 1980, 48, 1074-1079.

Chapanis, A. Theory and method for analyzing errors in man-machine systems. *Annals of the New York Academy of Science*, 1951, 51, 1179-1203.

Chapman, L.J., & Chapman, J.P. Genesis of popular but erroneous diagnostic observations. *Journal of Abnormal Psychology*, 1967, 72, 193-194.

Chapman, L.J., & Chapman, J.P. *Disordered Thought in Schizophrenia.* Englewood Cliffs, N.J.: Prentice-Hall, 1973.

Chase, W.C., & Simon, H.A. Perception in chess. *Cognitive Psychology*, 1973, 4, 55-81.

Chi, M., Glaser, R., & Rees, E. Expertise in problem-solving. In *Advances in the Psychology of Human Intelligence (vol.1)*. Hillsdale, N.J.: Erlbaum, 1981.

Colavita, F.B. Human sensory dominance. *Perception & Psychophysics*, 1974, 16, 409-412.

Collier, J.G., & Davies, L.M. *Chernobyl: The Accident at Chernobyl Unit 4 in the Ukraine, April 1986.* Barnwood, Gloucs.: Central Electricity Generating Board, 1986.

Comer, M.K., Seaver, D.A., Stillwell, W.G., & Gaddy, C.D. *Generating Human Reliability Estimates Using Expert Judgment: Paired Comparisons and Direct Numerical Estimation (vol.1).* NUREG/CR-3688. Washington, D.C.: U.S. Nuclear Regulatory Commission, 1984.

Conrad, R. Very brief delays of immediate recall. *Quarterly Journal of Experimental Psychology*, 1960, 12, 45-47.

Conrad, R. Acoustic confusion in immediate memory. *British Journal of Psychology*, 1964, 55, 75-84.

Cooper, H.S.F. Letter from the Space Center. *The New Yorker*, November 10, 1987.

Corcoran, D.W.J. An acoustic factor in letter cancellation. *Nature*, 1966, 210, 658.

Crowder, R.G., & Morton, J. Precategorical acoustic storage (PAS). *Perception and Psychophysics*, 1969, 5, 365-373.

Cyert, R.M., & March, J.G. *A Behavioral Theory of the Firm.* Englewood Cliffs, N.J.: Prentice-Hall, 1963.

Davies, L.M. *The Three Mile Island Incident.* Harwell: Atomic Energy Technical Unit, 1979.

De Keyser, V. Temporal decision making in complex environments. Paper presented at Workshop on New Technology, Distributed Decision Making and Responsibility. Bad Homburg, W.Germany, 5-7 May, 1988.

De Keyser, V., Decortis, F., Housiaux, A., & Van Daele, A. Les communications hommes-machines dans les systemes complexes. *Action Fast.* Bruxelles: Politique et Scientifique, 1987.

De Soto, C.B. The predilection for single orderings. *Journal of Abnormal and Social Psychology*, 1961, 62, 16-23.

Dell, G.S., & Reich, P.A. Toward a unified model of slips of the tongue. In V. Fromkin (Ed), *Errors in Linguistic Performance*. New York: Academic Press, 1980.

Deutsch, J., & Deutsch, D. Attention: Some theoretical considerations. *Psychological Review*, 1963, 70, 80-90.

Dichgans, J., & Brandt, Th. Visual-vestibular interactions. In R. Held, H. Leibowitz & H. Teuber (Eds.), *Handbook of Sensory Physiology, Vol.VIII*. Berlin: Springer-Verlag, 1978.

Dixon, N.F. *On the Psychology of Military Incompetence*. London: Jonathan Cape, 1976.

Doerner, D. Merkmale der kognitiven Struktur guter und schlechter Versuchspersonen beim Umgang mit einem sehr klompexen System. In H. Uerckert & D. Rhenius (Eds.), *Komplexe mensliche Informationsverarbeitung*. Bern: Huber, 1978.

Doerner, D. On the difficulties people have in dealing with complexity. In J. Rasmussen, K. Duncan & J. Leplat (Eds.), *New Technology and Human Errors*. London: Wiley, 1987.

Doerner, D., & Staudel, T. Planen und Entscheiden in sehr komplexen Systemen. In H. Eckensberger (Ed.), *Bericht uber den 31. Kongress der Deutschen Gesellschaft fur Psychologie in Mannheim*. Gottingen: Hogrefe, 1979.

Donnelly, K.E., & Jackson, R.A. *Human Performance Models: Electrical Contact Accident Survey*. Toronto, Canada: Ontario Hydro, 1983.

Duncan, K. Personal communication, 1983.

Duncan, K. Fault diagnosis for advanced continuous process installations. In J. Rasmussen, K. Duncan & J. Leplat (Eds.), *New Technology and Human Error*. London: Wiley, 1987.

Duncan, K.D., & Gray, M.J. An evaluation of a fault finding training course for refinery process operators. *Journal of Occupational Psychology*, 1975, 48, 199-218.

Duncan, K.D., & Shepherd, A. A simulator and training technique for diagnosing plant failures from control panels. *Ergonomics*, 1975, 18, 627-641.

Easterbrook, J.A. The effect of emotion on cue utilization and the organisation of behavior. *Psychological Review*, 1959, 66, 183-200.

Ebbinghaus, H. *Uber das Gedachtnis*. Leipzig: Dunker, 1885.

Edwards, W. Conservatism in human information processing. In B. Kleinmuntz (Ed.), *Formal Representation of Human Judgement*. New York: Wiley, 1968.

Einhorn, H.J., & Hogarth, R.M. Behavioral decision theory: Processes of judgment and choice. *Annual Review of Psychology*, 1981, 32, 53-88.

Ellingstadt, V.S., Hagen, R.E., & Kimball, K.A. *An Investigation of the Acquisition of Driving Skill*. Technical Report No. 11, Vermillon, S. Dakota: Department of Psychology, University of South Dakota, 1970.

Embrey, D.E. *Expert Judgement of Human Reliability*. CSNI Report No.88. Paris: OECD Nuclear Energy Agency, 1985.

Embrey, D.E. *SHERPA: A Systematic Human Error Reduction and Prediction Approach*. Parbold, Lancs.: Human Reliability Associates, 1986.

Embrey, D.E. Human reliability. In R. Anthony (Ed.), *Human Reliability in Nuclear Power*. London: IBC Technical Services, 1987.

Embrey, D.E., Humphreys, P.C., Rosa, E.A., Kirwan, B., & Rea, K. *SLIM-MAUD: An Approach to Assessing Human Error Probabilities Using Structured Expert Judgment*. NUREG/CR-3518. Upton, N.Y.: Brookhaven National Laboratory, 1984.

Embrey, D.E., & Lucas, D.A. Personal communication, 1989.

Evans, J. St. B. T. *Thinking and Reasoning: Psychological Approaches*. London: Routledge & Kegan Paul, 1983.

Fennell, D. *Investigation into the King's Cross Underground Fire*. Department of Transport. London: HMSO, 1988.

Festinger, L. A theory of the social comparison process. *Human Relations*, 1954, 7, 117-140.

Fischhoff, B. Hindsight does not equal foresight: The effect of outcome knowledge on judgement under uncertainty. *Journal of Experimental Psychology: Human Performance & Perception*, 1975, 1, 288-299.

Fischhoff, B. Decision making in complex systems. In E. Hollnagel, G. Mancini, & D. Woods (Eds.), *Intelligent Decision Aids in Process Environments*. Proceedings of NATO Advanced Study Institute, San Miniato, 1986.

Fischhoff, B. Simple behavioral principles in complex system design. Paper presented at the World Bank Workshop on Safety Control and Risk Management, Washington, D.C., October 18-20, 1988.

Fischhoff, B., Slovic, P., & Lichtenstein, S. Fault trees: Sensitivity of estimated failure probabilities to problem representation. *Journal of Experimental Psychology: Human Perception and Performance*, 1978, 4, 330-334.

Fischhoff, B., Lichtenstein, S., Slovic, P., Derby, S.L., & Keeney, R.L. *Acceptable Risk*. New York: Cambridge University Press, 1981.

Fisher, S., & Reason, J.T. *Handbook of Life Stress, Cognition and Health*. Chichester: Wiley, 1988.

Fiske, S.T., & Taylor, S.E. *Social Cognition*. Reading, Mass.: Addison-Wesley, 1984.

Frese, M. A theory of control and complexity: Implications for software design and integration of computer systems into the work place. In M. Frese, E. Ulich & W. Dzida (Eds.), *Psychological Issues of Human Computer Interaction in the Work Place*. Amsterdam: Elsevier, 1987(a).

Frese, M. Human-computer interaction in the office. In C. Cooper & I. Robertson (Eds.), *International Review of Industrial and Organizational Psychology 1987*. London: Wiley, 1987(b).

Frese, M., & Altmann, A. *The Treatment of Errors in Learning and Training*. Unpublished paper. Department of Psychology, University of Munich, 1988.

Freud, S. *Psychopathology of Everyday Life*. London: Ernest Benn, 1914. (Originally published in 1901.)

Freud, S. *Introductory Lectures on Psychoanalysis*. London: George Allen & Unwin, 1922 (trans. Joan Riviere).

Fromkin, V.A. The non-anomalous nature of anomalous utterances. *Language*, 1971, 47, 27-52.

Fromkin, V.A. (Ed.). *Speech Errors as Linguistic Evidence*. The Hague: Mouton, 1973.

Fromkin, V.A. (Ed.). *Errors in Linguistic Performance: Slips of the Tongue, Ear, Pen, and Hand*. New York: Academic Press, 1980.

Garrett, M.F. The analysis of sentence production. In G. Bower (Ed.), *The Psychology of Learning and Motivation (vol.9)*. New York: Academic Press, 1975.

Garrett, M.F. The limits of accommodation: Arguments for independent processing levels in sentence production. In V. Fromkin (Ed.), *Errors in Linguistic Performance*. New York: Academic Press, 1980.

Glucksberg, S., & McCloskey, M. Decisions about ignorance: Knowing what you don't know. *Journal of Experimental Psychology: Human Learning and Memory*, 1981, 7, 311-325.

Goldstein, K. *Aftereffects of Brain Injuries in War*. New York: Grune & Stratton, 1942.

Greenwald, A.G., Pratkanis, A.R., Leippe, M.R., & Baumgardner, M.H. Under what conditions does theory obstruct research progress? *Psychological Review*, 1986, 93, 216-229.

Gregg, V. Word frequency, recognition and recall. In J. Brown (Ed.), *Recall and Recognition*. London: Wiley, 1976.

Grinker, R.R., & Spiegel, J.P. *Men Under Stress*. New York: McGraw-Hill (reprinted from 1945), 1963.

Groenewegen, A.J.M., & Wagenaar, W.A. Diagnosis in everyday situations: Limitations of performance at the knowledge-based level. Unpublished manuscript. Unit of Experimental Psychology, Leiden University, The Netherlands, 1988.

Gruneberg, M.M., & Sykes, R.N. Knowledge and retention: The feeling of knowing and reminiscence. In M. Gruneberg, P. Morris & R. Sykes (Eds.), *Practical Aspects of Memory*. London: Academic Press, 1978.

Habberley, J.S., Shaddick, C.A., & Taylor, D.H. *A Behavioural Study of the Collision Avoidance Task in Bridge Watchkeeping*. Southampton: The College of Maritime Studies, 1986.

Hall, R.E., Fragola, J.R., & Wreathall, J. *Post-Event Human Decision Errors: Operator Action Tree/Time Reliability Correlation*. NUREG/CR-3010. Washington, D.C.: U.S. Nuclear Regulatory Commission, 1982.

Hannaman, G.W., Spurgin, A.J., & Lukic, Y.D. *Human Cognitive Reliability Model for PRA Analysis*. NUS-4531. Palo Alto, Calif.: Electric Power Research Institute 1984.

Harris, J.E. Remembering to do things: A forgotten topic. In J. Harris & P. Morris (Eds.), *Everyday Memory, Actions and Absent-Mindedness*. London: Academic Press, 1984.

Harris, J.E., & Wilkins, A.J. Remembering to do things: A theoretical framework and an illustrative experiment. *Human Learning*, 1982, 1, 123-136.

Hart, H.L.A. *Punishment and Responsibility: Essays in the Philosophy of Law*. Oxford: Clarendon Press, 1968.

Hart, J.T. Memory and the feeling-of-knowing experience. *Journal of Educational Psychology*, 1965, 56, 208-216.

Hasher, L., & Zacks, R.T. Automatic processing of fundamental information: The case for frequency of occurrence. *American Psychologist*, 1984, 39, 1372-1388.

Hastie, R. Schematic principles in human memory. In E.T. Higgins, C.P. Herman, & M.P. Zanna (Eds.), *Social Cognition: The Ontario Symposium (vol.1)*. Hillsdale, N.J.: Erlbaum, 1981.

Hayes, J.R., & Flower, L.S. Identifying the organization of writing processes. In L. Gregg & E. Steinberg (Eds.), *Cognitive Processes in Writing*. Hillsdale, N.J.: Erlbaum, 1980.

Head, H. *Studies in Neurology*. Oxford: Oxford University Press, 1920.

Healy, A.F. Detection errors on the word *the*: Evidence for reading units larger than letters. *Journal of Experimental Psychology: Human Perception and Performance*, 1976, 2, 235-242.

Healy, A.F. Proofreading errors on the word *the*: New evidence on reading units. *Journal of Experimental Psychology: Human Perception and Performance*, 1980, 6, 45-57.

Herrmann, D.J. Know thy memory: The use of questionnaires to assess and study memory. *Psychological Bulletin*, 1982, 92, 434-452.

Hinton, G.E., & Anderson, J.A. (Eds.). *Parallel Models of Associative Memory*. Hillsdale, N.J.: Erlbaum, 1981.

Hintzman, D.L. Repetition and memory. In G. Bower (Ed.), *The Psychology of Learning and Motivation (vol.10)*. New York: Academic Press, 1976.

Hintzman, D.L., & Block, R.A. Repetition and memory: Evidence for a multiple-trace hypothesis. *Journal of Experimental Psychology*, 1971, 88, 297-306.

Hintzman, D.L., Nozawa, G., & Irmscher, M. Frequency as a nonpropositional attribute of memory. *Journal of Verbal Learning and Verbal Behavior*, 1982, 21, 220-229.

Hirst, W., Spelke, E.S., Reaves, C.C., Caharack, G., & Neisser, U. Dividing attention without alternation or automaticity. *Journal of Experimental Psychology: General*, 1980, 109, 98-117.

Hitch, G.J. Developing the concept of working memory. In G. Claxton (Ed.), *Cognitive Psychology: New Directions*. London: Routledge & Kegan Paul, 1980.

Holland, J.H., Holyoak, K.J., Nisbett, R.E., & Thagard, P.R. *Induction: Processes of Inference, Learning and Discovery*. Cambridge, Mass.: MIT Press, 1986.

Hollnagel, E., Mancini, G., & Woods, D. *Intelligent Decision Support in Process Environments*. Heidelberg: Springer-Verlag, 1986.

Hollnagel, E., Mancini, G., & Woods, D. *Cognitive Engineering in Complex Dynamic Worlds*. London: Academic Press, 1988.

Hotopf, W.H.N. Semantic similarity as a factor in whole-word slips of the tongue. In V. Fromkin (Ed.), *Errors in Linguistic Performance*. London: Academic Press, 1980.

Howell, W.C. Representation of frequency in memory. *Psychological Bulletin*, 1973, 80,44-53.

Howes, D.H., & Solomon, R.L. Visual duration threshold as a function of word probability. *Journal of Experimental Psychology*, 1951, 41, 401-410.

Hudson, P.T.W. Personal communication, 1988.

Hull, A., Wilkins, A., & Baddeley, A.D. Cognitive psychology and the wiring of plugs. In M. Gruneberg, P. Morris, & R. Sykes (Eds.), *Practical Aspects of Memory: Current Research and Issues. I: Memory in Everyday Life*. London: Wiley, 1988.

Hunt, R.M., & Rouse, W.B. A fuzzy rule-based model of human problem solving. *IEEE Transactions on Systems, Man and Cybernetics*, 1984, SMC-14, 112-120.

INPO. *An Analysis of Root Causes in 1983 Significant Event Reports*. INPO 84-027. Atlanta, Ga.: Institute of Nuclear Power Operations, 1984.

INPO. *An Analysis of Root Causes in 1983 and 1984 Significant Event Reports*. INPO 85-027. Atlanta, Ga.: Institute of Nuclear Power Operations, 1985(a).

INPO. *A Maintenance Analysis of Safety Significant Events*. Nuclear Utility Management and Human Resources Committee, Maintenance Working Group. Atlanta, Ga.: Institute of Nuclear Power Operations, 1985(b).

Jackson, A.R.G., Madden, V.J., Umbers, I.G., & Williams, J.C. Ergonomics design and operator training as contributors to human reliability. In R. Anthony (Ed.), *Human Reliability in Nuclear Power*. London: IBC Technical Services, 1987.

James, W. *The Principles of Psychology*. New York: Holt, 1890.

James, W. *Talks to Teachers on Psychology: and to Students on Some of Life's Ideals*. London: Longmans, Green & Co., 1908.

Janis, I.L. *Victims of Groupthink*. Boston: Houghton Mifflin, 1972.

Jastrow, J. The lapses of consciousness. *The Popular Science Monthly*, 1905, 67, 481-502.

Johnson-Laird, P.N. Thinking as a skill. In J.Evans (Ed.), *Thinking and Reasoning: Psychological Approaches*. London: Routledge & Kegan Paul, 1983.

Johnson-Laird, P.N., & Wason, P.C. (Eds.). *Thinking: Readings in Cognitive Science*. Cambridge: Cambridge University Press, 1977.

Jordan, N. Allocation of functions between man and machines in automated systems. *Journal of Applied Psychology*, 1963, 47, 161-165.

Jung, C.G. The psychology of dementia praecox. *Nervous and Mental Disease Monographs Series No.3*, 1936. (Originally published in 1906.)

Kahneman, D. *Attention and Effort*. Englewood Cliffs, N.J.: Prentice-Hall, 1973.

Kahneman, D., Slovic, P., & Tversky, A. (Eds.). *Judgment under Uncertainty: Heuristics and Biases*. New York: Cambridge University Press, 1982.

Kahneman, D., & Miller, D.T. Norm theory: Comparing reality to its alternatives. *Psychological Review*, 1986, 93, 136-153.

Kaiser, M., McCloskey, M., & Proffitt, D.R. Development of intuitive theories of motion: Curvilinear motion in the absence of external forces. *Developmental Psychology*, 1986 (cited by Holland et al., 1986).

Karmiloff-Smith, A. Children's problem solving. In J. Lamb & A. Brown (Eds.), *Advances in Developmental Psychology*. Hillsdale, N.J.: Erlbaum, 1984.

Keele, S.W. *Attention and Human Performance*. California: Goodyear, 1973.

Kelly, A. *Maintenance Planning and Control*. London: Butterworths, 1984.

Kemeny, J. *The Need for Change: The Legacy of TMI*. Report of the President's Commission on the Accident at Three Mile Island. New York: Pergamon, 1979.

Kerhli, R.R. The investigative techniques used by the *Challenger* Commission to address information system failures as they relate to the Space Shuttle accident. In J. Wise & A. Debons (Eds.), *Information Systems: Failure Analysis*. Berlin: Springer-Verlag, 1987.

Kerr, B. Processing demands during mental operations. *Memory & Cognition*, 1973, 1, 401-412.

Kimble, G.A., & Perlmuter, L.C. The problem of volition. *Psychological Review*, 1970, 77, 361-368.

King, J.F., Zechmeister, E.B., & Shaughnessy, J.J. Judgments of knowing: The influence of retrieval practice. *American Journal of Psychology*, 1980, 93, 329-343.

Kinsbourne, M. Single-channel theory. In D. Holding (Ed.), *Human Skills*. London: Wiley, 1981.

Kinsbourne, M., & Hicks, R. Functional cerebral space. In J. Requin (Ed.), *Attention and Performance (vol.VII)*. Hillsdale, N.J.: Erlbaum, 1978.

Kirwan, B., 1982. Cited by Williams, 1986.

Kjellen, U. An evaluation of safety information systems of six medium-sized and large firms. *Journal of Occupational Accidents*, 1983, 3, 273-288.

Klatzky, R.L. *Memory and Awareness*. New York: W.H. Freeman, 1984.

Kletz, T.A. *An Engineer's View of Human Error*. Rugby: The Institution of Chemical Engineers, 1985.

Knowles, W.B. Operator loading tasks. *Human Factors*, 1963, 5, 151-161.

Koriat, A., Lichtenstein, S., & Fischhoff, B. Reasons for confidence. *Journal of Experimental Psychology: Human Learning and Memory*, 1980, 6, 107-117.

Langer, E.J. The illusion of control. *Journal of Personality and Social Psychology*, 1975, 7, 185-207.

Lanir, Z. *Fundamental Surprise*. Eugene, Ore.: Decision Research, 1986.

Lashley, K.S. The accuracy of movement in the absence of excitation from the moving organ. *American Journal of Physiology*, 1917, 43, 169.

Lashley, K.S. The problem of serial order in behaviour. In L.A. Jeffress (Ed.), *Cerebral Mechanisms in Behavior: The Hixon Symposium*. New York: Wiley, 1951.

Laver, J. Monitoring systems in the neurolinguistic control of speech production. In V. Fromkin (Ed.), *Errors in Linguistic Performance*. New York: Academic Press, 1980.

Layfield, F. *Report on the Sizewell B Public Inquiry*. London: HMSO, 1987.

Lewis, C. Skill in algebra. In J. Anderson (Ed.), *Cognitive Skills and Their Acquisition*. Hillsdale, N.J.: Erlbaum, 1981.

Lewis, C. Understanding what's happening in system interactions. In D. Norman & S. Draper (Eds.), *User Centered System Design*. Hillsdale, N.J.: Erlbaum, 1986.

Lewis, C., & Norman, D.A. Designing for error. In D. Norman & S. Draper (Eds.), *User Centered System Design*. Hillsdale, N.J.: Erlbaum, 1986.

Lihou, D.A., & Lihou, S.J. *Bhopal: Some Human Factors Considerations*. Birmingham: Lihou Loss Prevention Services, 1985.

Long, J. Reduced efficiency and capacity limitations in multidimensional signal recognition. *Quarterly Journal of Experimental Psychology*, 1975, 27, 599-614.

Luchins, A.S., & Luchins, E.H. New experimental attempts at preventing mechanization in problem solving. *Journal of General Psychology*, 1950, 42, 279-297.

Luria, A.R. *The Working Brain: An Introduction to Neuropsychology*. Harmondsworth: Penguin Books, 1973.

McCloskey, M. Intuitive physics. *Scientific American*, 1983, 24, 122-130.

McCloskey, M., & Kaiser, M. Children's intuitive physics. *The Sciences*, 1984, 24, 40-45.

McClelland, J.L., & Rumelhart, D.E. Distributed memory and the representation of general and specific information. *Journal of Experimental Psychology: General*, 1985, 114, 159-188.

MacKay, D.G. Spoonerisms: The structure of errors in the serial order of speech. *Neuropsychologia*, 1970, 8, 323-350.

Mach, E. *Knowledge and Error*. Dordrecht: Reidel Publishing Company, 1905. (English translation, 1976.)

Mandler, G. *Mind and Emotion*. New York: Wiley, 1975.

Mandler, G. Recognizing: The judgment of previous occurrence. *Psychological Review*, 1980, 87, 252-271.

Mandler, G. *Cognitive Psychology: An Essay in Cognitive Science*. Hillsdale, N.J.: Erlbaum, 1985.

Marcus, A.A., & Fox, I. Lessons learned about communicating safety-related concerns to industry: The Nuclear Regulatory Commission after Three Mile Island. Presented at 1988 Symposium on Science Communication: Environmental and Health Research. Los Angeles, University of Southern California, 15-17 December, 1988

Marsden, P. The actual frequency of encounter of American presidents. Department of Psychology, University of Manchester, 1987.

Marshall, Lord. Foreword. *The Chernobyl Accident and Its Consequences*. United Kingdom Atomic Energy Authority. London: HMSO, 1987.

Marshall, S.L.A. *Men Against Fire*. Gloucester, Mass.: Peter Smith, 1978.

Matlin, M.W., Stang, D.J., Gawron, V.J., Steedman, A., & Derby, P.L. Evaluative meaning as a determinant of spew position. *Journal of General Psychology*, 1979, 100, 3-11.

Megaw, E. Directional errors and their correction in a discrete tracking task. *Ergonomics*, 1972, 15, 633-643.

Meringer, R. *Aus dem Leben der Sprache: Versprechen, Kindersprache, Na-chahmungstrieb*. Berlin: Behrs Verlag, 1908.

Meringer, R., & Mayer, C. *Versprechen und Verlesen: Eine psychologische-linguisticische Studie*. Stuttgart: G.J. Goschen'sche Verlagshandlung, 1895.

Miller, G.A. The magical number seven plus or minus two: Some limits of our capacity for processing information. *Psychological Review*, 1956, 63, 81-97.

Milner, B. Personal communication, 1986.

Minsky, M. A framework for representing knowledge. In P. Winston (Ed.), *The Psychology of Computer Vision*. New York: McGraw-Hill, 1975.

Montmollin, M. *L'Intelligence de la Tache. Elements d'Ergonomie Cognitive*. Paris: Peter Lang, 1984.

Moray, N. *Attention: Selective Processes in Vision and Hearing*. London: Hutchinson, 1969.

Moray, N. Monitoring behavior and supervisory control. In K. Boff, L. Kaufman & J. Thomas (Eds.), *Handbook of Perception and Human Performance (vol.2)*. New York: Wiley, 1986.

Morehouse, W., & Subramaniam, M.A. *The Bhopal Tragedy*. New York: Council on International and Public Affairs, 1986.

Morris, P.A., & Engelken, R.H. Safety experiences in the operation of nuclear power plants. In *International Atomic Energy Agency Principles and Standards*. Vienna: International Atomic Energy Agency, 1973.

Nakatani, L.H. On the evaluation of models for the word-frequency effect. *Psychological Review*, 1973, 80, 195-202.

Navon, D., & Gopher, D. On the economy of the human processing system. *Psychological Review*, 1979, 86, 214-255.

Neisser, U. *Cognitive Psychology*. New York: Appleton-Century-Crofts, 1967.

Neisser, U. *Cognition and Reality: Principles and Implications of Cognitive Psychology*. San Francisco: W.H. Freeman & Co., 1976.

Newbigging, P.L. The perceptual redintegration of frequent and infrequent words. *Canadian Journal of Psychology*, 1961, 15, 123-132.

Newell, A., & Simon, H.A. *Human Problem Solving*. Englewood Cliffs, N.J.: Prentice-Hall, 1972.

Nisbett, R., & Ross, L. *Human Inference: Strategies and Shortcomings of Social Judgment*. Englewood Cliffs, N.J: Prentice-Hall, 1980.

Nooteboom, S.G. The tongue slips into patterns. In Nomen, *Leyden Studies in Linguistics and Phonetics*. The Hague: Mouton, 1969.

Nooteboom, S.G. Speaking and unspeaking: Detection and correction of phonological and lexical errors in spontaneous speech. In V. Fromkin (Ed.), *Errors in Linguistic Performance*. New York: Academic Press, 1980.

Norman, D.A. Toward a theory of memory and attention. *Psychological Review*, 1968, 75, 522-536.

Norman, D.A. *Errors in Human Performance*. Technical Report. La Jolla: University of California, San Diego, Center for Human Information Processing, 1980.

Norman, D.A. Categorization of action slips. *Psychological Review*, 1981, 88, 1-15.

Norman, D.A. Position paper on human error. NATO Advanced Research Workshop on Human Error. Bellagio, Italy, 1983.

Norman, D.A. Working papers on errors and error detection. Unpublished manuscript. University of California, San Diego, Institute for Cognitive Science, 1984.

Norman, D.A. New views of human information processing: implications for intelligent decision support systems. In E. Hollnagel, G. Mancini & D. Woods (Eds.), *Intelligent Decision Aids in Process Environments*. San Miniato: NATO Advanced Study Institute, 1985.

Norman, D.A. Reflections on cognition and parallel distributed processing. In D. Rumelhart & J. McClelland (Eds.), *Parallel Distributed Processing (vol.2)*. Cambridge, Mass.: MIT Press, 1986.

Norman, D.A. *The Psychology of Everyday Things*. New York: Basic Books, 1988.

Norman, D.A., & Bobrow, D.J. On data limited and resource limited processes. *Cognitive Psychology*, 1975, 5, 44-64.

Norman, D.A., & Bobrow, D.J. Descriptions: An intermediate stage in memory retrieval. *Cognitive Psychology*, 1979, 11, 107-123.

Norman, D.A., & Draper, S.W. *User Centered System Design*. Hillsdale, N.J.: Erlbaum, 1986.

Norman, D.A., & Shallice, T. *Attention to Action: Willed and Automatic Control of Behavior*. CHIP 99. University of California, San Diego, La Jolla: Center for Human Information Processing, 1980.

Norros, L., & Sammatti, P. *Nuclear Power Plant Operator Errors during Simulator Training*. Research Report No.446. Espoo, Finland: Technical Research Centre of Finland, 1986.

NUREG. *Loss of Main and Auxiliary Feedwater Event at the Davis-Besse Plant on June 9, 1985*. NUREG-1154. Washington, D.C.: U.S. Nuclear Regulatory Commission, 1985.

Oconee, P.R.A. *A Probabilistic Risk Assessment of Oconee Unit 3*. NSAC/60. Palo Alto, Calif.: Nuclear Safety Analysis Center, Electric Power Research Institute, 1984.

Oldfield, R.C., & Wingfield, A. The time it takes to name an object. *Nature*, 1964, 202, 1031-1032.

Palermo, D.S., & Jenkins, J.J. *Word Association Norms*. Minneapolis: University of Minnesota Press, 1964.

Paul, H. *Prinzipien der Sprachgeschichte*. Halle: Niermeyer, 1880.

Payne, J.W. Contingent decision behavior. *Psychological Bulletin*, 1982, 92, 382-402.

Perrow, C. *Normal Accidents: Living with High-Risk Technologies*. New York: Basic Books, 1984.

Peterson, C.R., & Beach, L.R. Man as an intuitive statistician. *Psychological Bulletin*, 1967, 68, 29-46.

Pew, R.W., Miller, D.C., & Feeher, C.E. *Evaluation of Proposed Control Room Improvements through Analysis of Critical Operator Decisions*. NP-1982, Research Project 891, Cambridge, Mass: Bolt, Beranek & Newman, Inc., 1981.

Phillips, L.D., Humphreys, P., & Embrey, D.E. A socio-technical approach to assessing human reliability. Appendix D. In *Pressurized Thermal Shock Evaluation of the Calvert Cliffs Unit Nuclear Power Plant*. Oak Ridge, Tenn.: Oak Ridge National Laboratory, 1984.

Pickard, Lowe & Garrick, Inc. *Seabrook Station Probabilistic Safety Assessment*. PLG-0300. Newport Beach, CA: Pickard, Lowe & Garrick, 1983.

Pollack, I., Rubinstein, H., & Decker, L. Analysis of incorrect responses to an unknown message set. *Journal of the Acoustical Society of America*, 1960, 32, 454-457.

Posner, M.I., Nissen, M.J., & Klein, R.M. Visual dominance: An information processing account of its origin and significance. *Psychological Review*, 1976, 83, 157-171.

Posner, M.I., & Snyder, C.R.R. Attention and cognitive control. In R. Solso (Ed.), *Information Processing and Cognition: The Loyola Symposium*. Hillsdale, N.J.: Erlbaum, 1975.

Potash, L.M., Stewart, M., Dietz, P.E., Lewis, D.M., & Dougherty, E.M. Experience in integrating the operator contributions in the PRA of actual operating plants. In *Proceedings of the ANS/ENS Topical Meeting on Probabilistic Risk Assessment*, Port Chester, New York. La Grange Park, Ill.: American Nuclear Society, 1981.

Poucet, A. Survey of methods used to assess human reliability in the Human Factors Reliability Benchmark Exercise. *Reliability Engineering and System Safety*, 1988, 22, 257-268.

Rabbitt, P.M.A. Errors and error-correction in choice-response tasks. *Journal of Experimental Psychology*, 1966, 71, 264-272.

Rabbitt, P.M.A. Time to detect errors as a function of factors affecting choice response time. In A. Sanders (Ed.), *Symposium on Attention and Performance*. Amsterdam: North Holland Publishing Company, 1967.

Rabbitt, P.M.A. Three kinds of error-signalling responses in a serial choice task. *Quarterly Journal of Experimental Psychology*, 1968, 20, 179-188.

Rabbitt, P.M.A., & Phillips, S. Error-detection and correction latencies as a function of S-R compatibility. *Quarterly Journal of Experimental Psychology*, 1967, 19, 37-42.

Rabbitt, P.M.A., & Vyas, S.V. An elementary preliminary taxonomy for some errors in laboratory choice RT tasks. *Acta Psychologica*, 1970, 33, 56-76.

Rabbitt, P.M.A., Cumming, G., & Vyas, S.V. Some errors of perceptual analysis in visual search can be detected and corrected. *Quarterly Journal of Experimental Psychology*, 1978, 30, 319-332.

Raskin, A.J. The flow-language for computer programming. *Computers and the Humanities*, 1974, 8, 231-237.

Rasmussen, J. What can be learned from human error reports? In K. Duncan, M. Gruneberg & D. Wallis (Eds.), *Changes in Working Life*. London: Wiley, 1980.

Rasmussen, J. Models of mental strategies in process plant diagnosis. In J. Rasmussen & W. Rouse (Eds.), *Human Detection and Diagnosis of System Failures*. New York: Plenum, 1981.

Rasmussen, J. Human errors: A taxonomy for describing human malfunction in industrial installations. *Journal of Occupational Accidents*, 1982, 4, 311-335.

Rasmussen, J. Skills, rules, knowledge: signals, signs and symbols and other distinctions in human performance models. *IEEE Transactions: Systems, Man & Cybernetics*, 1983, SMC-13, 257-267.

Rasmussen, J. Strategies for state identification and diagnosis. In W. Rouse (Ed.), *Advances in Man-Machine Systems Research (vol.1)*. Greenwich, Conn.: JAI Press, 1984.

Rasmussen, J. *Information Processing and Human-Machine Interaction.* Amsterdam: North-Holland, 1986.

Rasmussen, J. Interdisciplinary workshops to develop a multi-disciplinary research programme based on a holistic system approach to safety and management of risk in large-scale technological operations. Paper commissioned by the World Bank, Washington, D.C., 1988.

Rasmussen, J., & Jensen, A. Mental procedures in real-life tasks: A case study of electronic troubleshooting. *Ergonomics*, 1974, 17, 293-307.

Rasmussen, J., & Pedersen, O.M. Human factors in probabilistic risk analysis and risk management. In *Operational Safety of Nuclear Power Plants (vol.1)*. Vienna: International Atomic Energy Agency, 1984.

Rasmussen, J., & Vicente, K.J. *Cognitive Control of Human Activities: Implications for Ecological Interface Design.* RISO-M-2660. Roskilde, Denmark: Riso National Laboratory, 1987.

Reason, J.T. *Man in Motion.* London: Weidenfeld, 1974.

Reason, J.T. Skill and error in everyday life. In M. Howe (Ed.), *Adult Learning: Psychological Research and Applications.* London: Wiley, 1977.

Reason, J.T. Actions not as planned: The price of automatization. In G. Underwood & R. Stevens (Eds.), *Aspects of Consciousness, Volume I: Psychological Issues.* London: Wiley, 1979.

Reason, J.T. Lapses of attention. In R. Parasuraman & R. Davies (Eds.), *Varieties of Attention.* New York: Academic Press, 1984(a).

Reason, J.T. Absent-mindedness and cognitive control. In J. Harris & P. Morris (Eds.), *Everyday Memory, Actions and Absent- Mindedness.* London: Academic Press, 1984(b).

Reason, J.T. Order of output in category generation. Paper given to the Cognitive Section, British Psychological Society, Oxford, 1984(c).

Reason, J.T. The Chernobyl errors. *Bulletin of the British Psychological Society*, 1987, 40, 201-206.

Reason, J.T. Modelling the basic error tendencies of human operators. *Reliability Engineering and System Safety*, 1988(a), 22, 137-153.

Reason, J.T. Chernobyl: A reply to Baker and Marshall. *The Psychologist: Bulletin of the British Psychological Society*, 1988(b), 7, 255-256.

Reason, J.T. Framework models of human performance and error: A consumer guide. In L. Goodstein, H. Andersen & S. Olsen (Eds.), *Tasks, Errors and Mental Models*. London: Taylor & Francis, 1988(c).

Reason, J.T. Stress and cognitive failure. In S. Fisher & J. Reason (Eds.), *Handbook of Life Stress, Cognition and Health*. Chichester: Wiley, 1988(d).

Reason, J.T., & Brand, J.J. *Motion Sickness*. London: Academic Press, 1975.

Reason, J.T., & Embrey, D.E. *Human Factors Principles Relevant to the Modelling of Human Errors in Abnormal Conditions of Nuclear Power Plants and Major Hazardous Installations*. Parbold, Lancs: Human Reliability Associates, 1985.

Reason, J.T., Horrocks, V., & Bailey, S. Multiple search processes in knowledge retrieval: Similarity-matching, frequency-gambling and inference. Unpublished report. Department of Psychology, University of Manchester, 1986.

Reason, J.T., & Lucas, D.A. Using cognitive diaries to investigate naturally-occurring memory blocks. In J. Harris & P. Morris (Eds.), *Everyday Memory, Actions and Absent-Mindedness*. London: Academic Press, 1984(a).

Reason, J.T., & Lucas, D.A. Absent-mindedness in shops: Its correlates and consequences. *British Journal of Clinical Psychology*, 1984(b), 23, 121-131.

Reason, J.T., & Mackintosh, C. Naming the white of an egg: Evidence for semantic constraints upon phonological priming. Unpublished report. Department of Psychology, University of Manchester, 1986.

Reason, J.T., & Mackintosh, C. Priming verbal errors. Unpublished report. Department of Psychology, University of Manchester, 1986.

Reason, J.T., Manstead, A.S.R., Stradling, S., Baxter, J., Campbell, K., & Huyser, J. *Interim Report on the Investigation of Driver Errors and Violations*. University of Manchester: Department of Psychology, 1988.

Reason, J.T. & Mycielska, K. *Absent-Minded? The Psychology of Mental Lapses and Everyday Errors*. Englewood Cliffs, N.J.: Prentice-Hall, 1982.

Reason, J.T., Wagner, H., & Dewhurst, D. A visually-driven postural aftereffect. *Acta Psychologica*, 1981, 48, 241-251.

Reitman, J.S. Skilled perception in go: Deducing memory structures from inter-response times. *Cognitive Psychology*, 1976, 8, 336-356.

Report of the Presidential Commission on the Space Shuttle Challenger *Accident*. Washington DC: Government Printing Agency, 1986.

Riley, D.A. Memory for form. In L. Postman (Ed.), *Psychology in the Making*. New York: Knopf, 1962.

Rizzo, A., Bagnara, S., & Visciola, M. Human error detection processes. In G. Mancini, D. Woods & E. Hollnagel (Eds.), *Cognitive Engineering in Dynamic Worlds*. Ispra, Italy: CEC Joint Research Centre, 1986.

Rochlin, G.I., La Porte, T.R., & Roberts, K.H. The self-designing high-reliability organization: Aircraft carrier flight operations at sea. *Naval War College Review*, Autumn 1987.

Roediger, H.L., & Crowder, R.G. A serial position effect in the recall of United States presidents. *Bulletin of the Psychonomic Society*, 1976, 8, 275-278.

Rogovin, M. *Report of the President's Commission on the Accident at Three Mile Island*. Washington, D.C.: Government Printing Office, 1979.

Ronan, W.W. *Training for Emergency Procedures in Multi-Engine Aircraft*. AIR-153-53-FR-44. Pittsburgh, Penn.: American Institutes for Research, 1953.

Rouse, W.B. Models of human problem solving: Detection, diagnosis and compensation for system failures. Preprint for *Proceedings of IFAC Conference on Analysis, Design and Evaluation of Man-Machine Systems*. Baden-Baden, FRG., September, 1981.

Rouse, W.B., & Morris, N.M. Conceptual design of a human error tolerant interface for complex engineering systems. In *Proceedings of Second IFAC Conference on Analysis, Design and Evaluation of Man-Machine Systems*, Varese, Italy, 1985.

Roy, E.A. Action and performance. In A. Ellis (Ed.), *Normality and Pathology in Cognitive Functions*. London: Academic Press, 1982.

Rubin, D.C. Associative symmetry, availability and retrieval. *Memory & Cognition*, 1983, 11, 83-92.

Rumelhart, D.E. Notes on a schema for stories. In D. Bobrow & A. Collins (Eds.), *Representation and Understanding: Studies in Cognitive Science*. New York: Academic Press, 1975.

Rumelhart, D.E., & McClelland, J.L. (Eds.). *Parallel Distributed Processing (vols 1 & 2)*. Cambridge, Mass.: MIT Press, 1986.

Rumelhart, D.E., & Ortony, A. The representation of knowledge in memory. In R.C. Anderson, R.J. Shapiro & W.E. Montague (Eds.), *Schooling and the Acquisition of Knowledge*. Hillsdale, N.J.: Erlbaum, 1977.

Savin, H.B. Word frequency effect and errors in the perception of speech. *Journal of the Acoustical Society of America*, 1963, 35, 200-206.

Schank, R.C. *Dynamic Memory: A Theory of Reminding and Learning in Computers and People*. New York: Cambridge University Press, 1982.

Schank, R.C., & Abelson, R. *Scripts, Plans, Goals and Understanding*. Hillsdale, N.J.: Erlbaum, 1977.

Schmidt, R.A. A schema theory of discrete motor skill learning. *Psychological Review*, 1975, 82, 225-260.

Schurman, D.L., & Banks, W.W. *Review of Human Error Assessment Methods and Models*, E.G.&G. Technical Report SCENTPD-84-003, Idaho Falls, Idaho: E.G.&G. Idaho Inc., 1984.

Schweder, R.A. Likeness and likelihood in everyday thought: Magical thinking and everyday judgments about personality. In P. Johnson-Laird & P. Wason (Eds.), *Thinking: Readings in Cognitive Science*. Cambridge: Cambridge University Press, 1977.

Searle, J.R. The intentionality of intention and action. *Cognitive Science*, 1980, 4, 47-70.

Senders, J.W., Moray, N., & Smiley, A. *Modelling Operator Cognitive Interactions in Nuclear Power Plant Safety Evaluation.* Report prepared for the Atomic Energy Control Board, Ottawa, Canada, 1985.

Shaffer, L.H. Intention and performance. *Psychological Review*, 1976, 83, 375-393.

Shaffer, L.H. Multiple attention in continuous verbal tasks. In P. Rabbitt & S. Dornic (Eds.), *Attention and Performance (vol.V)*. London: Academic Press, 1975.

Shallice, T. Failures of supervisory control: Neuropsychological parallels. Proceedings of *Fourth International Conference on Event Perception and Action*, Trieste, August 1986.

Sheen, Mr Justice. MV Herald of Free Enterprise. Report of Court No. 8074 Formal Investigation. London: Department of Transport, 1987.

Shell Safety Committee. *Unsafe Act Auditing.* The Hague: Shell Internationale Petroleum Maatschappij B.V., 1987.

Shepard, R.N. On subjectively optimum selections among multiattribute alternatives. In M. Shelley & G. Bryan (Eds.), *Human Judgements and Optimality.* New York: Wiley, 1964.

Sheridan, T.B., & Hennessy, R.T. (Eds.). *Research and Modeling of Supervisory Control Behavior.* Washington, D.C.: National Academy Press, 1984.

Shiffrin, R.M., & Schneider, W. Controlled and automatic human information processing. II. Perceptual learning, automatic attending, and a general theory. *Psychological Review*, 1977, 84, 155-171.

Siegler, R.S. How knowledge influences learning. *American Scientist*, 1983, 71, 631-638.

Simon, H.A. Rational choice and the structure of the environment. *Psychological Review*, 1956, 63, 129-138.

Simon, H.A. *Models of Man.* New York: Wiley, 1957.

Simon, H.A. *Reason in Human Affairs.* London: Basil Blackwell, 1983.

Slovic, P., & Fischhoff, B. On the psychology of experimental surprises. *Journal of Experimental Psychology: Human Perception and Performance*, 1977, 3, 544-551.

Smith, J.C., & Hogan, B. *Criminal Law*. (Third Edition). London: Butterworths, 1973.

Solomon, R.L., & Postman, L. Frequency of usage as a determinant of recognition thresholds for words. *Journal of Experimental Psychology*, 1952, 43, 195-201.

Spearman, C. *The Nature of Intelligence and the Principles of Cognition*. London: Macmillan, 1923.

Spearman, C. The origin of error. *Journal of General Psychology*, 1928, 1, 29-53.

Spelke, E.S., Hirst, W.C., & Neisser, U. Skills of divided attention. *Cognition*, 1976, 4, 215-230.

Spence, J.T. Contribution of response bias to recognition thresholds. *Journal of Abnormal and Social Psychology*, 1963, 66, 339-344.

Storie, V. *Male and Female Car Drivers: Differences Observed in Accidents*. TRRL Laboratory Report No. 761. Crowthorne: Transport and Road Research Laboratory, 1977.

Sully, J. *Illusions: A Psychological Study*. London: C. Kegan Paul & Co., 1881.

Sussman, G.J. *A Computer Model of Skill Acquisition*. New York: Elsevier, 1975.

Swain, A.D. *A Method for Performing a Human Reliability Analysis*. Monograph SCR-685. Albuquerque, N.M.: Sandia National Laboratories, 1963.

Swain, A.D. *Sandia Human Factors Program for Weapons Development*. SAND 76-0326. Albuquerque, NM: Sandia National Laboratories, 1976.

Swain, A.D., & Guttmann, H.E. *Handbook of Human Reliability Analysis with Emphasis on Nuclear Power Plant Applications*. NUREG/CR 1278. Albuquerque, N.M.: Sandia National Laboratories, 1983.

Swain, A.D., & Weston, L.M. An approach to the diagnosis and misdiagnosis of abnormal conditions in post-accident sequences in complex man-machine systems. In L.Goodstein, H.Andersen & S.Olsen (Eds.), *Tasks, Errors and Mental Models*. London: Taylor & Francis, 1988.

Taylor, S.E., & Crocker, J. Schematic bases of social processing. In E.T. Higgins, C.P. Herman, & M.P. Zanna (Eds.). *Social Cognition: The Ontario Symposium (vol.1)*. Hillsdale, N.J.: Erlbaum, 1981.

Teitelman, W., & Masinter, L. The Interlisp programming environment. *Computer*, 1981, April, 25-33.

Thorndike, E.L. *Animal Intelligence*. New York: Macmillan, 1911.

Timpanaro, S. *The Freudian Slip*. London: NLB, 1976.

Treisman, A. Verbal cues, language and meaning in selective attention. *American Journal of Psychology*, 1964, 77, 206-219.

Treisman, A. Strategies and models of selective attention. *Psychological Review*, 1969, 76, 282-299.

Tuchman, B. *The Guns of August*. London: Four Square Books, 1962.

Tulving, E. *Elements of Episodic Memory*. Oxford: Oxford University Press, 1983.

Turner, B.A. *Man-Made Disaster*. London: Wykeham, 1978.

Tversky, A., & Kahneman, D. Judgment under uncertainty: Heuristics and biases. *Science*, 1974, 185, 1124-1131.

UKAEA. *The Chernobyl Accident and its Consequences*. United Kingdom Atomic Energy Authority. London: H.M.S.O. 1987.

Underwood, E.J., & Schultz, F.W. *Meaningfulness and Verbal Learning*. Philadelphia: Lippincott, 1960.

Union Carbide. *Bhopal Methyl Isocyanate Incident Investigation Team Report*. Danbury, Conn.: Union Carbide Corporation, March 1985.

USSR State Committee on the Utilization of Atomic Energy. *The Accident at the Chernobyl Nuclear Power Plant and Its Consequences*. Information compiled for the IAEA Experts' Meeting, 25-29 August, 1986. Vienna: IAEA, 1986.

Venables, P.H. Performance and level of activation in schizophrenics and normals. *British Journal of Psychology*, 1964, 55, 207-218.

Vicente, K.J., & Rasmussen, J. *A Theoretical Framework for Ecological Interface Design*. Roskilde, Denmark: Riso National Laboratory, 1987.

Von Sybel, A. Uber das Zusammenwirken verscheidener Simesgebiete be Gadachtnisleistungen. *Zeitschrift fur Psychologie*, 1909, 53, 257-360.

Wagenaar, W.A. *The Cause of Impossible Accidents*. The Sixth Duijker Lecture. University of Amsterdam, 1986.

Wagenaar, W.A., & Groeneweg, J. Accidents at sea: Multiple causes and impossible consequences. *International Journal of Man-Machine Studies*, 1987, 27, 587-598.

Wason, P.C., & Johnson-Laird, P.N. *Psychology of Reasoning: Structure and Content*. London: Batsford, 1972.

Watson, J.B. Psychology as the behaviorist views it. *Psychological Review*, 1913, 20, 158-177.

Westrum, R. Organisational and inter-organisational thought. World Bank Workshop on Safety Control and Risk Management, Washington, D.C., 16-18 October, 1988.

Whipple, G.M. Recent literature on the psychology of testimony. *Psychological Bulletin*, 1910, 7, 365-368.

Whipple, G.M. The psychology of testimony. *Psychological Bulletin*, 1911, 8, 307-309.

Whitworth, D.P.D. Application of Operator Error Analysis in the design of Sizewell B. *Reliability Engineering*, 1987, 19, 299-316.

Wickens, C.D. The structure of attentional resources. In R.S. Nickerson (Ed.), *Attention and Performance (vol.VIII)*. Hillsdale, N.J.: Erlbaum, 1980.

Wilkins, A.J., & Baddeley, A.D. Remembering to recall in everyday life: An approach to absent-mindedness. In M. Gruneberg, P. Morris & R. Sykes (Eds.), *Practical Aspects of Memory*. London: Academic Press, 1978.

Williams, J.C. Validation of human reliability assessment techniques. *Reliability Engineering*, 1985, 11, 149-162.

Willner, A. Impairment of knowledge of unusual meanings of familiar words in brain damage and schizophrenia. *Journal of Abnormal Psychology*, 1965, 70, 405-411.

Woodham-Smith, C. *The Reason Why*. London: Constable, 1953.

Woods, D.D. *Operator Decision Behavior during the Steam Generator Tube Rupture at the Ginna Nuclear Power Station*. Research Report 82-1C57-CONRM-R2. Pittsburgh, Penn.: Westinghouse R & D Center, 1982.

Woods, D.D. Some results on operator performance in emergency events. *Institute of Chemical Engineers Symposium Series*, 1984, 90, 21-31.

Woods, D.D. Technology alone is not enough. In R. Anthony (Ed.), *Human Reliability in Nuclear Power*. London: IBC Technical Services, 1987.

Woodworth, R.S. *Experimental Psychology*. New York: Henry Holt and Company. 1938.

Wreathall, J. Human reliability: Fact or fiction? *Proceedings of the ANS/ENS Topical Meeting on PRA*, Lagrange Park, IL: American Nuclear Society, 1981.

Wreathall, J. *Operator Action Trees: An Approach to Quantifying Operator Error Probability During Accident Sequences*. NUS-4159. Gaithersburg, Md: NUS Corporation, 1982.

Wreathall, J. Personal communication, 1989.

Wundt, W. *Grundriss der Psychologie*. Leipzig: Engelmann, 1905.

Young, R.M., & O'Shea, T. Errors in children's subtraction. *Cognitive Science*, 1981, 5, 153-177.

Zechmeister, E.B., & Nyberg, S.E. *Human Memory: An Introduction to Research and Theory*. Monterey, Calif.: Brooks/Cole, 1982.

Zipf, G.K. *Human Behavior and the Principle of Least Effort*. Cambridge, MA: Addison-Wesley, 1949.

Name index

Abelson, R., 35, 66
Adelson, B., 58
Alba, J. W., 129
Allard, R., 16, 91
Allport, D.A., 30
Allwood, C. M., 148, 158, 160, 166, 168
Altmann, A., 244
Anderson, J. A., 46, 47
Anderson, J. H., 82
Anderson, J. R., 44, 45, 59, 75, 77
Antonis, B., 30
Arbuckle, T. Y., 113
Atkinson, R. C., 32, 117
Austin, G. A., 33

Baars, B. J., xv, 15, 16, 47, 156, 159
Bacon, F., 39
Baddeley, A. D., xv, 14, 24, 31, 32, 107, 128, 237
Bagnara, S., 148, 160, 162, 166, 168
Bailey, S., 119
Bainbridge, L., xv, 180, 182
Baker, S., 192
Banks, W. W., 221, 231
Barclay, W. D., 104, 139
Bartlett, F. C., 25, 66, 89, 98, 116, 215
Battig, W. F., 104, 110, 139
Baumgardner, M. H., 89
Bawden, H. H., 13
Baxter, J., xv, 196
Beach, L. R., 37
Bell, B. J., 221
Bellamy, L. J., 192
Bello, G. C., 226
Bennett, M., 83
Berkun, M. M., xii
Beveridge, M., 76
Billman, D., 77
Blake, M., 113
Block, R. A., 124
Bobrow, D. G., 28, 51, 100
Boden, M., 125
Boland, T. B., 108

Bonaparte, M., 22
Bousfield, W. A., 104, 139
Brand, J. J., 150
Brandt, T., 153
Brehmer, B., xiv, 16, 91, 93
Brewer, W. F., 34
Broadbent, D. E., xii, 15, 27, 28, 29, 33, 50, 98, 103, 104
Broadbent, M. H. P., xii
Broen, W. E., 109
Brown, J. S., 83
Brune, R. L., 230
Bruner, J. S., 33, 40, 41, 66
Buchanan, M., 31
Burns, J. T., 154
Burton, R. R., 83

Caharack, G., 30
Campbell, K., xv, 196
Cantor, N., 35
Card, S. K., 48, 50, 97
Carpenter, P. A., 148, 159
Carrithers, C., 246
Carroll, J. M., 246
Catlin, J., 103
Champagne, A. B., 82
Chapanis, A. B., 3
Chapman, J. P., 90, 98, 108
Chapman, L. J., 90, 98, 108
Chase, W. C., 58
Chi, M., 58
Colavita, F. B., 127
Collier, J. G., 54, 83, 192
Colombari, V., 226
Comer, M. K., 223
Conrad, R., 31, 32
Cooper, P. F., xii, 15
Corcoran, D. W. J., 170
Crocker, J., 35
Crowder, R. G., 32, 119, 140
Cuddy, L. I., 113
Cumming, G., 155
Cyert, R. M., 37, 39

291

Name index

Daneman, M., 148, 159
De Keyser, V., xv, 182
De Soto, C. B., 90
Decker, L., 103
Dell, G. S., 106
Derby, P. L., 105
Derby, S. L., 107
Deutsch, D., 27
Deutsch, J., 27
Dewhurst, D., 152, 153
Dichgans, J., 153
Dietz, P. E., 223
Dixon, N. F., 42
Doerner, D., xiv, 16, 92, 94
Donnelly, K. E., 45
Dougherty, E. M., xv, 223
Draper, S. W., 50
Duncan, K., xv, 180, 241, 242, 243, 244

Easterbrook, J. A., 109
Ebbinghaus, H., 31
Edwards, W., 37
Einhorn, H. J., 60
Ellingstadt, V. S., 81
Embrey, D. E., xv, 221, 225, 226, 228, 229
Engelken, R. H., 191
Evans, J. St. B. T., 33, 39, 53, 87

Feeher, C. E., 54, 237
Fennell, D., 194
Festinger, L., 90
Fischhoff, B., xv, 17, 37, 38, 41, 89, 107, 215
Fiske, S. T., 35, 41, 212
FitzGerald, P., xii, 15
Fitzwater, M. E., 230
Flower, L. S., 148, 159
Fontana, A., 149, 160
Fox, I., 214
Fragola, J. R., xv, 224
Frese, M., xv, 244
Freud, S., 11, 14, 22, 105
Fromkin, V. A., 16, 22, 106, 155

Gaddy, C. D., 223
Garrett, M. F., 155
Gawron, V. J., 105
Glaser, R., 58
Glucksberg, S., 113
Goldstein, K., 109

Goodnow, J. J., 33
Gopher, D., 28
Greenwald, A. G., 89
Gregg, V., 104
Grinker, R. R., xii
Groeneweg, J., xiv, 216
Groenewegen, A. J. M., 94
Gruneberg, M. M., 113
Guttmann, H. E., 221, 222, 223

Habberley, J. S., 85, 86
Hagen, R. E., 81
Hall, R. E., 81
Hall, R. E., 224, 225
Hannaman, G. W., 221, 225, 227, 229
Harris, J. E., 73, 107
Hart, H. L. A., 7
Hart, J. T., 113
Hasher, L., 52, 66, 103, 114, 124, 129
Hastie, R., 35
Hayes, J. R., 148, 159
Head, H., 24-5
Healy, A. F., 170, 171
Herrmann, D. J., 14, 15
Hicks, R., 29
Hinton, G. E., 46, 47
Hintzman, D. L., 114, 124
Hirst, W. C., 30
Hitch, G. J., xv, 32, 33, 128
Hogan, B., 7
Hogarth, R. M., 60
Holland, J. H., 74, 75, 77, 78, 82
Hollnagel, E., xv, 238
Holyoak, K. J., 74
Horrocks, V., 119
Hotopf, W. H. N., 101
Housiaux, A., 182
Howell, W. C., 123
Howes, D. H., 103
Hudson, P. T. W., xiv, 205
Hull, A., 237
Humphreys, P.C., 228, 229
Hunt, R. M., 44, 45, 53
Huyser, J., 196

INPO, 184, 186, 187, 188, 239
Irmscher, M., 114, 124

Jackson, A. R. G., 230

Subject index